Measuring and

OPERATIONA

IN FINANCIAL INST

Tools, Techniques, and oth

Measuring and Managing

OPERATIONAL RISKS

IN FINANCIAL INSTITUTIONS

Tools, Techniques, and other Resources

Dr. Christopher Lee Marshall

John Wiley & Sons (Asia) Pte Ltd

Singapore   New York   Chichester
Brisbane   Toronto   Weinheim

Other Wiley Editorial Offices

John Wiley & Sons, Inc., 605 Third Avenue, New York, NY 10158-0012, USA
John Wiley & Sons Ltd, Baffins Lane, Chichester, West Sussex PO19 1UD, England
John Wiley & Sons (Canada) Ltd, 22 Worcester Road, Rexdale, Ontario M9W 1L1,
Canada
John Wiley & Sons Australia Ltd, 33 Park Road (PO Box 1226), Milton, Queensland
4064, Australia
Wiley-VCH, Pappelallee 3, 69469 Weinheim, Germany

Library of Congress Cataloging-in-Publication Data

Marshall, Christopher Lee.
    Measuring and managing operational risks in financial institutions: tools, techniques,
        and other resources/Christopher Lee Marshall.
        p. cm. – (Wiley frontiers in finance)
    Includes bibliographical references and index.
    ISBN 0-471-84595-7 (cased: alk. paper)
    1. Asset-liability management. 2. Financial institutions – Management. 3. Financial
    services industry – Management. 4. Risk management. I. Tiltle. II. Series.

HG1615.25 .M368 2000
332.1'068'1–dc21   00-043850

Typeset in 11 points, Times by Linographic Services Pte Ltd
Printed in Singapore by Fabulous Printers Pte Ltd
10 9 8 7 6 5 4 3 2 1

TABLE OF CONTENTS

Acknowledgments

Writing a book requires more than the efforts of a single author. Inevitably, a host of colleagues, teachers, authors, and friends have contributed to this book in many different ways. Some of the most important individuals I am honor-bound to single out for special acknowledgment include. David Paris—now at Instinet and my former supervisor at Ernst & Young—who shaped directly many of the ideas that have been developed in this book. His willingness and encouragement to innovate has been a major motivator for me, particularly during the early stages of research and development that were the prelude to the writing of this book. Several others from Ernst & Young have also contributed directly and indirectly to the book. Julianne Duncan, a senior manager in Ernst & Young's London office, spent a year in Singapore, working with me to develop and integrate many of the ideas that until then were just theorizing. For her efforts and enthusiasm for the project, I give many thanks.

Many of the ideas described in the book were developed during projects with a variety of industry attachments, at a wide range of financial institutions including UBS Warburg, Andersen Consulting, Royal Sun Alliance, Algorithmics, and JP Morgan. To the individuals involved in these projects, my apologies for not naming you explicitly, I can only give my appreciation and thanks for your warm support.

During most of the writing of this book, I have been a faculty member at the National University of Singapore. Deep thanks must also go to my Dean, Prof. Chua Tat-Seng and Department head, Prof. Wei Kwok Kee, whose forbearance in awarding a research grant to a junior faculty member to take the risky and time-consuming step of writing a practitioner-oriented text is acknowledged and much appreciated. Other staff members at the National University of Singapore also contributed greatly: at the University's Center for Financial Engineering, Profs Lim Kian Guan, Ng Kah Hwa, and Annie Koh gave their time and shared contacts to help make the book a reality. Prof Liu Huan, at the Program for Research in Intelligent Systems, was also very supportive and encouraging. Other staff members at the University, too, were most helpful to me in the inevitably lonely process of writing a book. Tissha Tamm, Stephanie Ng, and Frances Koh worried about all the administrative details, which otherwise would have fallen to me. Also, the staff at John Wiley & Sons (Asia), notably Gael Lee and Nick Wallwork, were most understanding in the face of a first-time author's trials and tribulations. Again to all, I say thanks.

There are three other individuals, in particular, that I must single out with my heartfelt thanks. Vishrut Jain, my research assistant for this project, has always proved himself wise well beyond his years by providing intellectual stimulation and by his willingness to work unreasonably hard. Nancy Marshall, who has performed the Herculean task of editing and coordinating a mass of complex material in a short period of time. To both Vishrut and Nancy, who know the value of their contributions, thank you very much. Finally, the last individual, whose encouragement, faith, and patience in what might sometimes have seemed a lost cause, is my wife, CJ Meadows. Thanks, sweetheart.

Christopher Lee Marshall
Singapore, October 2000.

Preface

COULD ANY OF THESE HAPPEN TO YOU?

Staff in your financial marketing group are accused of selling some complex new products to "unsuitable" clients. Some of the clients bring a class-action litigation suit charging the bank with negligence. Ten percent of balances are affected with 20 percent restitution. The cost: $3 million.

A major earthquake disrupts part of the bank's data center. The cost: a 10 percent reconstruction cost, $200 million in lost assets, and lower client revenues resulting in a 5 percent reduction in income.

A class-action customer suit charged that a firm's security protection was aimed solely at staff and left customers at risk. The cost: $1 million.

Incorrect historical volatilities are accidentally used to price a new series of OTC options. The cost: $20 million.

The head of the bond desk unexpectedly resigns. Her 15 years with the firm have made her indispensable. It will take at least 6 months to find her replacement. The cost: estimated lost revenue of $5 million.

A competitor adopts a critical new data warehousing technology for direct marketing and reduces costs to gain a competitive advantage. The cost: a 50 percent drop in fee revenue is required to remain competitive.

A lower cost producer cherry-picks the bank's lucrative housing loan market. The cost: a 20-basis point fall in interest margin for 3 to 4 years and 40 percent reduced growth for 2 years.

What three things do all these losses have in common? First, all of these actually happened (although fortunately not to the same firm!). Second, they were all completely unexpected. Third—and most importantly—for all of these events, *the risk of loss can be measured and managed systematically.* Some of the losses could have been prevented. Some could have been made less likely through the redesign of processes and systems or the development of new controls. Other risks could have been passed to outside parties by buying insurance, hedging, or outsourcing. Additional capital could have been set aside.

This process of risk identification, measurement, analysis, and remedial action is the subject of this book—the systematic management of losses that can imperil any financial institution. How we manage these potential losses or risks depends on our identifying, understanding, and analyzing the factors that cause the loss and the possible effects that the loss can have. How bad could it get? How likely is it? Answers to these questions will determine both survival and competence in the new competitive financial markets as high capital requirements—the result of unmanaged risks—leaden the firm's ability to remain competitive.

Unfortunately, traditional management approaches to operational risk, such as ad hoc controls or systems patches, do more harm than good by contributing to the complexity that lies at the heart of much operational risk. While the finance sector has led the way in developing sophisticated techniques for measuring market and credit risks, it still can learn much from industries such as nuclear engineering and air traffic control, in which the twin constraints of high safety and expensive maintenance have forced leading-edge solutions for operational risk measurement and dynamic resource allocation. Drawing from reliability engineering, quality management, insurance management, and financial-risk management, this new discipline of operational risk management applies both *quantitative* and *qualitative* techniques to help managers efficiently and effectively deal with the ongoing operational issues they face. This book describes these *systematic* techniques for measuring the operational risks associated with system failure or error, transaction processing or control errors, business interruption, criminal acts, and personnel risks, among others. You cannot manage what you cannot measure. Effective risk assessment always precedes effective management. While measurement can only be a means rather than an end in itself, the strengths and limitations of various techniques must be understood if operational risk management is to enhance, rather than detract from, traditional control and audit systems.

The objective of this book is to develop managers' understanding of the major issues involved in operational risk measurement and management. The book does not specify a single best approach to measuring and managing operational risk exposures. Unlike, say, financial market risks, operational risks are deeply embedded in the contexts of specific businesses, and therefore, simplistic globally prescriptive approaches are inappropriate and potentially damaging. Instead, mangers are encouraged to experiment and develop their own tools and techniques to measure and manage the exposures they face. Consequently, the book takes a contingent view of risk-management tools and techniques, devoting as much time to the circumstances in which a technique is appropriate as to the details of the technique itself.

With these objectives in mind, the book is organized into four major sections, plus two appendices:

Section I: Background. Chapter 1 describes the background to operational risk management, how operations have evolved, and why the markets have become increasingly risk-conscious over time. Chapter 2 explores how practitioners and researchers from a variety of disciplines have developed some basic concepts and techniques for the problem of measuring operational risks. Finally, Chapter 3 provides an overview of different models of operational risks and when they are most appropriate.

Section II: An Operational Risk Management Methodology. Building on Section I, Section II provides a detailed but generic methodology of the entire process of operational risk measurement and analysis. Chapter 4 develops the rationale for operational risk management, while Chapter 5 identifies specific exposures. Chapters 6 and 7 explore the technical issues involved in risk estimation. Finally, Chapter 8 provides guidelines for analyzing the estimated operational risk exposures.

Section III: Risk Management Actions. Section III considers what management can do to prevent, predict, mitigate, and finance the risks uncovered in Section II. In so doing it describes the contingent nature of many commonly, but often inappropriately, used management techniques such as reengineering, insurance, financial hedging, and Total Quality Management (TQM). Understanding the characteristics of operational risks for which these techniques are appropriate (or not) is argued to be the major determinant of successful risk management. Different chapters in Section III cover different aspects of effective operational interventions, such as risk avoidance and factor management (Chapter 9), loss prediction (Chapter 10), loss prevention (Chapter 11), loss control (Chapter 12), loss reduction (Chapter 13), and risk financing (Chapter 14).

Section IV: Operational Risk Management in Practice. This section describes the issues involved in ongoing operational risk management. Chapter 15 looks at risk monitoring and reporting, while Chapter 16 explores the issues involved in risk-based capital allocation and performance measurement.

Appendices: Appendix A contains a glossary of risk types, with myriad examples and suggestions of some general heuristics to help operational risk managers deal with these risks. Appendix B describes some commonly used commercial packages and services for operational risk measurement and management.

In summary, this book emphasizes that the benefits of a firmwide operational risk management program go far beyond keeping out of next week's headlines. Although operational risk management is not a substitute for competent management, trained and motivated personnel, and well-organized controls and procedures, it *can* be a critical tool for directing resources to problem areas through problem prevention, prediction, mitigation, and financing. Indeed, operational risk management should lie at the heart of any firm's core competence, since it enables continuous and ongoing improvements in the *dynamic* allocation of critical resources such as capital, staff, and management attention. In the early 21st century, firms that fail to continuously monitor and systematically adapt their operations face too daunting a challenge.

Section I

BACKGROUND

CHAPTER 1

INTRODUCTION

In a recent survey by PricewaterhouseCoopers and the British Bankers Association (BBA), approximately 70 percent of UK banks considered their operational risks as important as their market or credit risks. Nearly a quarter of these banks had experienced operations-related losses of more than $1.6 million (ISDA/BBA/Robert Morris Associates 1999). Historical loss data from Operational Risk, Inc. (ORI) suggests that the financial-services industry may have lost as much as $200 billion from operational disasters over the past 20 years. ORI's records suggest that in over 50 cases, individual institutions lost more than $500 million each, while in over 30 cases, individual firms lost over $1 billion each.

Why have operational risks become such a concern, and why now? To answer this requires understanding the evolving business and technology context within which operational managers must function, how this context has severely stressed traditional financial-services operations, and why management and regulatory responses have been forced to play catch-up.

1.1 EVOLVING FINANCIAL SERVICES

Financial markets, products, and the technology and techniques used to produce them have undergone a sea change over the past 40 years, and the implications for operations are profound. Changes in markets and products and services (on the demand side) and changes in techniques and technologies (on the supply side), have altered the landscape of operations (Figure 1.1) and fueled the explosive development of operational risk management.

FIGURE 1.1 Drivers of Changing Operations

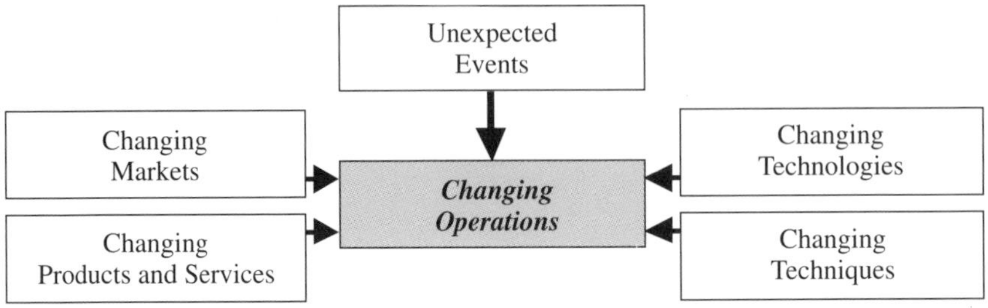

```
                        ┌─────────────────┐
                        │    Unexpected   │
                        │      Events     │
                        └─────────────────┘
                                 │
                                 ▼
┌──────────────────┐    ┌─────────────────┐    ┌──────────────────┐
│    Changing      │    │                 │    │    Changing      │
│    Markets       │───▶│    Changing     │◀───│   Technologies   │
└──────────────────┘    │   Operations    │    └──────────────────┘
┌──────────────────┐    │                 │    ┌──────────────────┐
│    Changing      │───▶│                 │◀───│    Changing      │
│ Products and Services │ └─────────────────┘    │   Techniques     │
└──────────────────┘                            └──────────────────┘
```

Changing Markets

Deregulation, globalization, and disintermediation have changed the definition of the markets and altered the economics of operating within these markets.

Deregulation Deregulation, or more precisely, swings between deregulation and re-regulation, has loosened the ties that bind firms to particular market segments, encouraging consolidation and the development of economies of scale and scope. Consider, for example, the experiences in the United States: the fall of the Bretton Woods agreement fixing exchange rates, the fall of interstate banking laws and interest ceilings, and the growing irrelevance of the Glass-Steagall Act, which in the 1960s and 1970s opened up sleepy US domestic markets to competition from foreign banks and domestic non-bank substitutes. This is not unique to the United States; governments in many countries have placed limits on financial competition and restrictions on expansion across regions or into different business areas. Along with worldwide moves toward deregulation in many areas of competition, these limits are being eroded as firms move toward an integrated "financial supermarket" view of their products and services. A good example of this is the traditional distinction between commercial and investment banks, which in most countries has weakened over the years. Both in Japan (Article 65) and in the United States (Glass-Steagall), such regulations have been undermined and their importance is fading. Other regulatory structures are being repealed as new products, processes, and markets (e.g., swaps market, structured transactions, repurchase (repo) agreements, leveraged buyouts (LBOs), project financing, outsourcing, and shelf registrations) are being created, with success going to new global competitors that face the least onerous regulatory burden. But competition is not only international; it also spans different industries. Traditional competitors in banking and insurance are challenged by commercial corporations, i.e., non-bank financial institutions entering the business. In response, regulation is becoming increasingly cross-country and cross-industry. Developments such as the increasing importance of transnational bodies, e.g., the Bank for International Settlements (BIS) in Basle, the International Monetary Fund (IMF), the World Bank, and the European Central Bank are symptomatic of the change. Even in traditionally isolationist nations such as the United Kingdom and the United States, we have seen the formation of single national regulators such as the Financial Services Authority (FSA) in the United Kingdom and the repeated calls for a merger between the Commodities Futures Trading Commission (CFTC), and the Securities and Exchange Commission (SEC) in the United States.

Globalization With deregulation, many of the barriers to globalization have fallen. Combined with the huge growth of money under management, this has led to investors exploring markets further afield. Seeking wider diversification and higher returns, emerging markets have grown apace, forcing financial-services players to be global in their operations as well as their client base. The implications for operations are immediate: the development of emerging markets has meant that more remote offices are handling more non-standardized local transactions for less-familiar clients. There has been a huge increase in cross-border investments. Custody, depository, and payment services are becoming centralized and globalized. Firms can no longer rely on localized support (specialized by product or geography) for their operations if they wish to provide seamless service. Advances in relational databases and falling communication costs over the past decade have encouraged the development of complex networks that run 24 hours per day, 365 days per year (24/365), and that straddle the world and link otherwise independent systems. With 24/365-global operations, resources can be allocated quickly and flexibly to managing risks and other problem areas.

Box 1.1: The Risks of Global Operations

As operations become more global and run 24/365, operational risk management becomes more concerned with questions of ensuring internal control of diverse distributed operational and front-office staff. Operational risks tend to increase with distance from the head office. This is particularly true of emerging markets. Operational risks also tend to increase with distance from the source of the risk. For example, in an increasingly global and real-time trading environment, there is no longer time for offline back-office processing. Instead, processing follows the sun: New York trades are settled within Japan's trading day, Japan trades begin during London daylight hours, and so on. The danger of this is that operational problems are often passed around the world without anyone necessarily taking ownership of them until it is too late and the problem has grown out of control. Inevitably, this distances risk control from risk initiation, with the danger that something may fall through the cracks.

Disintermediation   Part and parcel of globalization has been the tendency toward disintermediation as many financial claims (such as loans and securities) begin to bypass banks and are bought and sold by end users electronically with minimal transaction costs. Nor will high-margin transactions necessarily save service providers if customers begin to react to the excess complexity and risks of many of their offerings. This is especially critical for investment banks; however, all financial services are moving toward flexible customer-centered processes and greater market segmentation. Given the decreasing set-up and transaction costs fueled by breakthroughs enabled by information technology (IT) such as Enterprise Resource Planning (ERP) and the World Wide Web (WWW), the trends toward disintermediation and the resulting emphasis on customer-focused strategies seem set to continue.

Changing Products and Services

Product and service offerings have also seen tremendous innovation. The first fillip to new products and services followed deregulation in the 1970s, which brought greater competition and an increase in market volatility—and a desperate need to manage these risks, differentiate products and services, and provide risk protection to customers. With their high margins, new products are particularly attractive to competitors and so quickly become commoditized. This is especially so with the case of derivatives in the past 20 years, during which once-exotic over-the-counter (OTC) products became exchange-traded vanilla ones, fueling an ever-increasing cycle of product innovation.

Box 1.2: The Risk of Complex Operations

More complex products and services lead to greater operational risk. Of course, complexity is not just a function of the product—it also depends on the sophistication of the user. The rise of consumerism means that financial-services firms are being held liable for the operational knowledge of the customer, as well as for the short-comings in the product offering. Operational risk is therefore not just internal; it can result from any component of the value chain.

Changes in scale have marched hand in hand with changes in scope in financial services. Take just one example from trading: the average number of shares traded each day at the New York Stock Exchange grew from 11 million in 1970 to 670 million in 1998. Similar stories of volume growth can be told in a variety of financial-services segments. But it is not just a general increase in the level of volumes that has made operations more difficult. Unexpected increases in transaction volumes have often been accompanied by market volatility, which also tends to cause increases in operational losses as operations staff and systems are stressed beyond their capacity.

Box 1.3: Volatility and Operational Risks

Increased transaction volumes and increased volatility of these volumes lead to greater operational risks. It follows that under-standing the patterns in volume (and other external risk factors) and their effects on operations is the essence of effective operational resource allocation.

Changing Technologies

Advances in IT are stoking many of the changes in all financial firms: a transistor that once cost $5, today costs less than a staple. The cost of storing one megabyte of data in 1965 was about $100,000. Now it is $20; in 10 years' time, it may cost less than a dollar. In 1975, it cost $10,000 to send one megabyte of data from New York to Tokyo. Now it costs about $5. Within 10 years, it may cost a cent. The cost of a processor to handle one million instructions per second has declined from about $1 million in 1965 to about $1.50 today. In another 10 years, it may cost a few cents. (All figures have been adjusted for inflation) (Guldimann, 1996).

Progress in IT is geometric because each advance feeds on the others as improvements in processing speeds are helped by better data communications and greater storage. In turn, newly developed operating systems and application software demand greater improvements in hardware, and so the cycle continues, with no sign of abating. Theoretically, this enables the financial services to operate on a much more complex level than before. New technology also offers new ways to market and distribute financial services using targeted mailing and a wider variety of delivery channels including telephone-, ATM-, and Internet-based services.

Consider the case of the Internet. In less than a decade, the Web has gone from a research tool to one that is dramatically changing organizations and the industries in which they operate. Business-to-consumer (B2C) and business-to-business (B2B) electronic-banking services, and products, including electronic money, promise significant new opportunities for financial services as potential customers become and connected comfortable with Internet-based transactions. The massive dealing rooms found in most banks and securities houses are threatened with extinction as more of their lower margin businesses can be performed more cheaply on the Web. Electronic sales and marketing channels allow banks to expand their markets for traditional deposit-taking and credit-extension activities, offer new products and services, or strengthen their competitive position in existing service offerings. At the same time, there are risks for banks engaging in electronic-banking and electronic-money activities.

Box 1.4: Importance of Credit Risks

As businesses go online to service their customers, operational risk managers will spend more of their time helping to manage reputational risk and legal risks, as the barriers to customer defection decrease and as it becomes more difficult to evaluate one's customers. Managing the indirect effects of operations such as these will become a crucial role of operations. This is especially important for diversified international banks.

But hardware advances have not been accompanied by similar developments in software. Software still needs to be developed by people, and despite some advances in software engineering (such as CASE, software metrics, and structured methodologies) it is still essentially a slow, error-prone process. Virtually all IT systems are delivered late and at about 50 percent over the budget. In fact, 10 percent of all large systems are not completed at all (Jones, 1994).

Box 1.5: Importance of Project Risks

As hardware becomes less critical as a determinant of operational risk, and software development projects take an increasing share of the IT budget, operational risk management will focus more on project risk management.

The cost and performance of existing legacy systems also act as brakes on new development. Nowhere is this more apparent than in back-office operations where systems from different generations co-exist in a troubled synthesis. Monolithic mainframe systems with centralized batch data-entry processes from the 1970s are still used to support general ledger accounting and statement reporting, particularly in more transactional-intensive operations. Middle-office support technologies from the 1980s, such as PCs, spreadsheets, and databases, are still accessible on local area networks (LANs). Slowly, 1990s client–server technology has tried to integrate mainframes, minicomputers, and PCs into wide area networks (WANs) and LANs. Client–server architectures do not just integrate hardware, they also allow dedicated software applications for specific users with shared data.

Box 1.6:   Change in a World of Legacy Systems

As legacy systems become more complex, incremental change becomes more difficult and operational risk management focuses on contingency planning rather than problem solving. For example, in 1999, the most pressing operational risk area for many firms was Y2K. This was a result of earlier limitations on available memory and, more recently, careless programming, and could cause program failures due to date-related issues. Unfortunately, most Y2K risks were external to the firm, caused by other organizations' failure to handle Y2K problems. Y2K is not without precedent. Earlier the same year, the pegging of European Monetary Union (EMU) currencies to the Euro led to a huge number of transactions being rebooked/amended by banks and their counterparties simultaneously during a single weekend. Conversion to the Euro went smoothly because most banks had developed well-orchestrated contingency plans. Unlike most operational risks, however, Y2K and the introduction of the Euro are one-off events and will not be repeated; while their timing is known, the impact is not. This very uncertainty of impact is leading firms to adopt contingency planning as a means to manage their risks.

Changing Techniques

Another source of innovation in the financial marketplace has come from academics. Few industries have adopted theoretical advances from academia with as much gusto as the financial-services industry.

Take just one example: *portfolio theory* and, to a lesser extent, the *efficient-markets hypothesis* have changed the way the securities and insurance industries perceive risk and return. Portfolio theory holds that firms do not gain returns for carrying risks that can readily be diversified. This can be done by holding a large number of assets and by actively measuring asset correlations to ensure that positive returns on one asset tend to offset negative returns on another. The practical implications are twofold. First, more assets and better data about correlations mean less risk without decreasing returns. Second, formal centralized quantitative risk management groups have come to prominence to oversee financial risks. This has meant a move from a single-product/single-location basis toward a single-portfolio view of operations and an integrative view toward trading systems and databases. As many commercial and retail operations become commoditized, and investment and trading portfolios become more important for bottom-line profits, financial risk management (essentially an outgrowth of portfolio theory) has also become increasingly mission critical. For traders and portfolio managers, financial risk management has gone beyond mere support, becoming the basis of a profit center where they help their clients move closer to their desired risk return profiles by offloading unwanted risks or acquiring the risks that suit them. Much of the drive toward operational risk measurement and risk-based capital allocation and performance measurement is the result of the success of financial risk management.

Box 1.7:   Rise of Analytics

Managers will increasingly try to quantify their operational risks as risk measurement techniques from the finance and insurance industries are applied more widely. Many of the firms that pioneered the development of financial risk measurement, such as Algorithmics, Union Bank of Switzerland (UBS), and Deutsche Bank, are also at the forefront of developing tools for operational risk management.

Unexpected Events

It is a truism in finance that one should never discount the unexpected. In the past 30 years, many of the old certainties that locked suppliers and users of capital into a rigid matrix have disappeared. Some of this is the result of a general increase in market volatility, but much of it is a consequence of unexpected geopolitical events that have fundamentally changed the operating landscape for business in many parts of the world. From the OPEC oil embargo and concerns about inflation in the 1970s to Black Monday in 1987, protests in Tiananmen Square, and the fall of the Soviet Union in the late 1980s, the best analysts of the day would have discounted all these events as extremely unlikely only a few years earlier. The 1990s did not see any let-up. Indeed, without the stabilizing influence of the Cold War, event risks seem more prevalent than ever, with the 1990s witnessing a major stock-market crash almost every other year. But the events relevant to operations are not just market crashes. Natural disasters, from fires to floods and earthquakes to hurricanes, have the potential to devastate banks with poorly formulated contingency plans, as do human-created shocks ranging from terrorist attacks to fraud and government-imposed currency controls.

Box 1.8: Expect the Unexpected

For operations managers, managing event risks through contingency planning and crisis management is becoming at least as important as managing ongoing factor-based risks.

Changing Operations

Operations has long been viewed a cost center, with the implication that efficiency is the primary measure of effective operations. A drive toward greater efficiency has certainly been the mantra behind much change in operations during the past few decades. Initially, back-office operations were largely clerical and administrative, with large amounts of paper processing. From the 1960s through to the early 1980s, operations were almost entirely clerical and frequently manual. Securities firms' back offices, for instance, would manually enter trade tickets, confirm the trade, reconcile the trade against the trader's blotter, and produce daily reports. Huge increases in volumes in the 1960s led to the introduction of mainframe technology that automated and speeded up the existing manual processes. The mainframe systems were well suited to the daily batch-based processing cycles of deal exchange, trade processing, and payment settlement. With the 1970s and 1980s, the race was on to find more efficiencies in processing, with machines replacing clerks but without drastically changing the nature of the task performed. The huge mainframe systems took no account of the subtle value added by the staff—the systems meant greater processing speed and fewer simple human errors.

With the drive toward greater operational efficiency, the trend toward automation hardly diminished in the 1990s. For instance, technology has destroyed traditional open-outcry trading in most non-US equity and derivatives markets. The slow integration of human operations knowledge into databases and programs has made the systems more complex and less amenable to change or understanding once the initial developer has left the organization. With the wave of mergers and acquisitions (M&A) and internal restructuring in financial services during the past decade, previously independent systems have had to be integrated, adding further to the complexity of operations. Sometimes so many different specialists (such as managers, model builders, programmers, analysts, and database staff) are involved in system development that no one understands the system as a whole. This problem is particularly acute in valuation and risk management systems, which by their nature are firmwide and generally centralized. Obviously, as the complexity and scale of information systems for valuation and trade processing begin to defy the ability of individuals to understand them, the likelihood and impact of systems failures increase.

Box 1.9: The Dangers of Automation and Integration

Carelessly applied automation and integration of systems can actually increase operational risk by decreasing the firm's ability to handle change. For example, while automation decreases the likelihood of simple human errors, it actually increases the likelihood of major losses that otherwise would have been caught by a human operator. Removal of organizational slack removes a buffer that shields end users and customers from operational problems. This is partly why human error is increasingly cited as the source of most operational failures. However, this is often just an excuse for poor management and badly designed systems and processes that remove checks and controls in an effort to improve efficiency by lowering costs.

In the past decade, the marketplace has bifurcated more clearly. There are firms that do not consider operations an important part of their core competence and there are those that do.

For firms with differentiated product strategies, operational transaction processing is often secondary to their competitive advantage, and consequently, ripe for partnering and outsourcing. Outsourcing of management information systems (MIS) has been particularly important, with many investment banks, pension funds, credit-card companies, and asset managers announcing major outsourcing contracts. Although outsourcing does not remove the importance of operational risk management, it changes its focus from an operational risk to a financial and legal one. Currently, however, the inefficiency of the market for operational risks means that firms must be able to evaluate the risks of their internal operations for themselves if they are to obtain a favorable deal from external outsourcers, insurers, or systems vendors.

Box 1.10: All Risks Must Be Priced

Without an assessment of the operational risk of a business or product, firms may find that they are subsidizing their customers and other business partners by not accounting for the true cost of the risk.

Very different issues face organizations with operations as a core competence—typically high-volume transaction-processing firms such as insurance companies, retail banks, clearinghouses, custodians, exchanges, brokerages, and other operational services. Many have been consolidated into much larger businesses to obtain greater economies of scale. Others, particularly retail firms, have slowly come to realize that their competitive advantage lies not in the storing, safeguarding, verifying, reporting, and transferring of transactions but rather in the information that was typically embedded within these steps. Decision support and analytical systems grew out of this maelstrom of operational data coming out of the transaction pipeline. Data mining and analysis for improved customer segmentation has become crucial for the success of retail banks and insurance companies alike. So too has the cross-selling of an integrated set of service offerings, although for most firms, organizational and technological problems still prevent this from happening.

Box 1.11: More Than Just Efficient Operations

As operational systems become critical sources of management and customer-related information, operational risk managers become less focused on managing the efficiency of ongoing operations and more concerned with business growth by ensuring the accuracy of operational data, process reporting, and follow-on analysis.

In the next decade, a strategic concern for low-cost and differentiated providers alike will be the Web. The Web promises to revolutionize the economics of operations and also the marketing and sales of financial services. For example, transactions over the Internet are routinely priced much lower than standard brokerage fees. The question remains whether the scale-based cost economies of external operations providers plus the low cost of Web-based communications can overcome the traditional vertical integration of operations.

At stake is the structural integrity of the organization; many argue that service providers are already leaving their traditional organizational structures behind and evolving into a 24-hour virtual global network of temporary service providers, with technology providing the glue that keeps the network together. Whatever the competitive future, neither differentiated nor low-cost service providers will be inclined to shoulder inefficient and risk capital-intensive operations.

Further Reading: Financial Innovation

See Merton Miller's classic article on the financial innovations over the past 25 years (Miller, 1992), Finnerty (1992), and Chapter 1 of Smith (1990) for insights into past innovations in financial markets; look at Sanford (1993) for some suggestions about its future. Crane (1995) examines the entire financial industry as a system and argues that while specific institutions may change radically, the underlying functions provided by financial services are stable and will continue to be needed.

FIGURE 1.2 Summary of Financial Innovations

	1970s	1980s	1990s	2000+
Markets	Rise of institutional investors—Global, more sophisticated clients and competitors, 24-hour operations, Rise of emerging markets			
	End of high fixed commission Breakdown of Bretton Woods system of fixed exchange rates Change in Federal Reserve's open-market policy Double-digit inflation	Collapse of commercial real-estate markets US deregulation (fall of Glass-Steagall and McFadden Acts) 24-hour trading LBOs[1] and M&A[2] Latin American loans Savings & loans crisis London Big Bang	Bank consolidation Disintermediation of financial services Free-trade area Corporate downsizing Low interest rate Greater cross-border risk	European integration Increased insurance and banking competition
Products and Services	Increasingly complex products with reduced time-to-market, Declining margins on vanilla transactions, Declining revenues from commissions, Blurring of traditional markets, Product-to-client service orientation			
	Growth of Euro markets Credit card Exchange-traded futures and option Floating-rate loans, bond futures Discount brokerage NOW accounts Automated teller machines (ATMs) Money-market fund, adjustable-rate mortgage Cash-management accounts	CHIPS[3] 24-hour securities trading Universal/variable life insurance Asset-based financing, growth of derivatives, caps, floors, and collars, FRAs,[4] option on fixed-income securities Commodity option Swaps and OTC, exchange derivatives Index derivatives, EFT,[5] repo market, CD[6] market, floating-rate note, CMOs,[7] junk bond, zeros Wrap account Portfolio insurance, index arbitrage, Euro markets	RiskMetrics[TM] Project financing Catastrophe options Decline of branch banking Rise of telephone, WWW-banking Asset securitization VaR[8] Power derivatives Global futures trading Collateral trading	Electronic commerce Real-time settlement Digital money "Particle finance"

1 LBOs — Leveraged buyouts
2 M&A — Mergers and acquisitions
3 CHIPS — Clearing House Interbank Payment System
4 FRAs — Forward Rate Agreement
5 EFT — Electronic Funds Transfer
6 CD — Certificate of Deposit

7 CMOs — Collaterized Mortgage Obligations
8 VaR — Value at Risk
9 RDMS — Relational Data Management Systems
10 LTCM — Long Term Capital Management
11 GSTP — Global Straight Through Processing

FIGURE 1.2 (cont'd)

	1970s	1980s	1990s	2000+
		Integrated coverage of more risks		
Techniques	Portfolio theory Agency theory Theory of options pricing Credit risk management	Applied options pricing Market risk management Program trading	Exotic option Integrated financial risk management Risk-based capital allocation	Operational risk management Virtual organization
		Faster processing, Communications, More Powerful Memories: Any thing, any time, any place ...		
Technologies	Mainframe/mini Flat file database Handheld calculator	PC, spreadsheet RDMS[9] Internet Telecommunications Exchange order system Fax machine	Distributed network (WANs and LANs) Data warehousing The Web Rise of screen-based trading	Electronic personal assistant, rise of telecommuting
		Greater interconnectedness/Systemic effects and greater volatility		
Unexpected Events	OPEC oil embargo US inflation	Black Monday (Oct 1987) Fall of Drexel Fall of Soviet Union Tiananmen Square protests	Market crashes in 1990 (Nikkei), 1992 (ECU), 1994 (Mexico), 1998 (Russia), 1998 (Southeast Asia), 1999 (Brazil) Chicago flood; Hurricanes Hugo and Mitch; earthquakes in Japan, Turkey, and Greece	

1 LBOs — Leveraged buyouts
2 M&A — Mergers and acquisitions
3 CHIPS — Clearing House Interbank Payment System
4 FRAs — Forward Rate Agreement
5 EFT — Electronic Funds Transfer
6 CD — Certificate of Deposit

7 CMOs — Collaterized Mortgage Obligations
8 VaR — Value at Risk
9 RDMS — Relational Data Management Systems
10 LTCM — Long Term Capital Management
11 GSTP — Global Straight Through Processing

FIGURE 1.2 (cont'd)

	1970s	1980s	1990s	2000+
			Greater Interconnectedness/Systemic Effects and Greater Volatility	
Unexpected Events			Bombings in New York and London Barings failure; major losses at hedge funds, including failure of LTCM[10] Y2K, Euro integration Global warming	T+1 settlement Real-time trade matching Dematerialization Cross-border GSTP[11] Intelligent trading agents
Operations	One product processed at one location Clerical and largely manual	Process reengineering, standardization	Straight-through processing Global support for business by global centers of excellence More cross-border transactions Dematerialization/immobilization of securities Reduced time to settlement	

1 LBOs — Leveraged buyouts
2 M&A — Mergers and acquisitions
3 CHIPS — Clearing House Interbank Payment System
4 FRAs — Forward Rate Agreement
5 EFT — Electronic Funds Transfer
6 CD — Certificate of Deposit

7 CMOs — Collaterized Mortgage Obligations
8 VaR — Value at Risk
9 RDMS — Relational Data Management Systems
10 LTCM — Long Term Capital Management
11 GSTP — Global Straight Through Processing

1.2 THE OPERATIONS CHALLENGE

With revolutions taking place in the financial-services markets, products, and technologies, the industry's back-office operations have been challenged to adapt. But what exactly are operations? In this book, because of our multi-industry perspective covering a number of business areas (banking, trading, insurance, and advisory services), we necessarily take a broad view of operations. While the precise nature of operations varies according to different service areas, most face the same challenge of implementing and supporting an efficient process of transaction execution, entry, confirmation, reconciliation, payment, and accounting. Operations managers also face the same basic objectives, namely:

- Efficiency: To make the service delivery process consisting of marketing, sales, transactions processing, settlement, and accounting as efficient as possible.

- Change management: To manage and facilitate flexible and cost-effective change to improve the service delivery process.

- Internal control: To act as an independent control on the actions of the service initiators (the front office) and on various aspects of the operations process.

Inevitably, these three objectives conflict: an overemphasis on efficiency removes operations' responsiveness to change, as can an overzealous concern for maintaining internal control. The choice of operational objective depends on the strategy of the business unit. These three objectives relate directly to business value drivers such as capital expenditure, growth in operating assets, operating margins, cost-income ratios, and, as we shall see, the risk adjusted cost of capital. Indeed, the linkages between operational processes and these measures of business performance are the subject of much of this book, and yet it is surprising that the importance of operations is only now being fully appreciated.

TABLE **1.1** Comparison of Operational Objectives

Operational Objectives	Typical Planning Horizon	Business Objectives	Business Value Drivers
Efficiency	Short term	Minimize expected costs Lower headcount Increase automation	Cost-income ratios Operating margins
Flexibility and change management	Medium term	Decrease turnover Less reworking Managed growth	Capital expenditures Growth in operating assets
Internal control	Long term	No surprises Asset protection Efficient use of capital	Cost of capital Shareholder value added Risk adjusted performance measures
Opportunism	Medium term	Maximize upside Building a reputation More differentiated services	Cross-selling opportunities Customer retention

Efficiency

Obviously, efficiency is a prerequisite for operational excellence in mature businesses. Inefficient operations can ruin competitive positions, or even lead to class action suits and regulatory penalties. Efficiency focuses on expected costs and revenues over some time period, and can only be increased by decreasing inputs or increasing process outputs. Since back-office operations are typically evaluated as a cost center with a short time horizon, reducing the short-term expected cost of process inputs is viewed as the easiest way to increase efficiency. For financial-services firms, this largely means keeping the permanent headcount as low as possible. This is in keeping with the current trends of downsizing, outsourcing, mergers, and consolidation within the financial industry. When a merger occurs, a 10–20 percent reduction in combined staffing is common. Cost-reduction exercises, as well as efforts to improve productivity, often reduce staff size by 5–8 percent. With cost reduction, a heavy additional burden is placed on remaining staff, which, in many cases, is reflected in the reduction of the quality of service provided and an increase in the unexpected losses of the process. This makes skilled back-office staff even more eager to migrate to the front office and hampers the recruitment of competent employees to replace them. Some of this burden is alleviated at a low cost by the heavy use that operations makes of temporary and contract staff. Unfortunately, inexperienced staffing is another important risk factor that leads to unexpected errors. To some extent, operations managers can alleviate such errors by improved staff allocation, ongoing inspection and checking, as well as improved personnel selection and training.

Alternatively, managers can increase efficiency by redesigning the operational tasks and the operational processes used to perform them. Techniques as diverse as reengineering, activity-based costing, security dematerialization, electronic dissemination and storage of investor information, and improved electronic data interchange (EDI) links have been used to identify and remove specific activities that lead to costs without adding value. Process change through increased automation and straight-through processing decreases expected costs by limiting fallible and expensive human interventions, and streamlines the fissures between subprocesses (particularly between the front and back offices) where errors often develop. Also, the work itself can be redesigned by standardizing transactions, resources, and processes, and allocating costly resources to problems on a just-in-time basis. Increasing efficiency is also being forced by the steady compression of settlement cycles.

A strict focus on efficiency implies that control systems and risk management will only be developed for the more-frequent events likely to occur during the budgetary period or planning horizon, for example, fewer duplicated transactions, fewer failed transactions, and fewer late settlements. It also means a shorter settlement time and more efficient use of collateral, reduced settlement risks, and therefore, lower capital requirements. Less frequent events will be handled on an *ad hoc* or fire-fighting basis. In short, managing for efficiency means minimizing slack, preventing the most frequent losses, and limiting risk management to loss provisioning, crisis management, and occasional contingency planning for the less frequent losses. A focus on efficiency has some negative side effects: over-automating a process can decrease staff morale and increase the impact of less frequent events. Too tightly integrated a process can make it unresponsive to change. The challenge is to take automated approaches and apply them to more customized transactions, such as over-the-counter (OTC) derivatives. Just-in-time management, although cost effective in the short term, can rebound in the wake of unexpected events.

Flexibility and Change Management

While a product-based efficiency perspective makes sense for mature products in stable environments, the 1990s have demanded a more flexible response to rapid change. Under intense competition from non-banks, banks and other financial institutions have had to redesign their internal operations with an eye toward greater customer responsiveness or risk losing their most lucrative business areas to lower-cost competitors. The increased importance of more complex high-margin, high-value-added services in differentiated markets makes a liability of the narrowly defined operational efficiency. The rise of the WWW has exacerbated this.

An overemphasis on transactional efficiency can actually increase operational risks if it limits the firm's flexibility to deal with the unexpected. There are several aspects to this. First is the potential for transaction risk—the risk to earnings or capital arising from problems with service or product delivery. This risk is a function of internal controls, information systems, employee integrity, and operating processes. Transaction risk exists in all products and services, and arises daily in all financial institutions as transactions are processed.

The easiest, although most expensive, approach to handling transaction risks is by providing some organizational slack. This may come in the form of buffers between different processes or in redundancies between different staff functions, systems, and processes. However, when the present competitive climate demands that operational support be 24/365, excessive slack is almost impossible to justify to efficiency-minded operations managers.

An alternative to introducing slack is developing tight control of resource quality and process reliability in every stage of service delivery. Total Quality Management (TQM) techniques are useful for ensuring resource quality. It is especially important in retail and other people-intensive operations, where customer service is strongly linked with staff skills and motivation. Ongoing process reliability can also be obtained in the short term by frequently monitoring diagnostic controls that give rapid feedback about process performance relative to a benchmark.

In the longer term, major innovative projects also pose problems to operations managers. For these, strategic business planning and project risk management can be helpful. For example, a well-organized budgeting process and consistent follow-up of any operating variances to budget can limit unexpected losses. Scenario analysis can be used to force managers to consider the operational impacts of extreme business scenarios.

External change can be also managed at the business level. For example, a firm's responsiveness to volume fluctuations can be decreased by lowering its operating leverage—the ratio of its fixed to total assets. A firm's sensitivity to market factors can be changed by financial hedging or corporate diversification. Other financing strategies such as leasing, securitization, and insurance can also be used to limit the problems associated with uncontrolled, externally induced change.

Internal Control

Internal control aims to safeguard the firm's assets from external and internal threats. Internally, the risk comes from breakdowns in internal controls and corporate governance that can lead to financial losses through error, fraud, or failure to perform in a timely manner. Such breakdowns can also cause the interests of the bank to be compromised in some other way; for example, by its dealers, lending officers, or other staff exceeding their authority or conducting business in an unethical or risky manner. Managing this risk requires both the prevention and mitigation of extreme events—catastrophes such as fraud and insider trading that could bring the firm down. For internal events, control focuses on effective compliance, well-designed limits and sanctions, and frequent internal and external audit.

Externally, market crises, natural disasters, and political shifts pose similar threats. For example, fueled by deregulation and globalization, the sudden growth in scale and scope in the 1980s and the 1990s led to a series of market- and credit-related financial crises, which in turn resulted in an increased emphasis on internal control. Poorly controlled growth in lending also led to crises in the United States, Sweden, Spain, Japan, and New Zealand.

External events, whether natural disasters (such as major fires, floods, and earthquakes) or caused by humankind (such as wars, power outages, or attacks by a pressure group), are usually uncontrollable, and therefore, can only be managed through loss mitigation. This can be done using a variety of methods such as conventional insurance contracts, facilities management, public relations, contingency planning, and crisis management.

Opportunism

Operations managers are just starting to see that an assessment of operational risks can leverage a firm's resources to take better advantage of business opportunities. For instance, banks, whose calling officers are familiar with risk management, are more likely to provide better advisory services to clients, thus differentiating themselves from their competitors and producing a more profitable business. A reputation for reliable operations might be a key aspect of a firm's marketing strategies. Risk aware operations affect the likelihood of customer defections and a better assessment of the risks associated with different customers, making the firm's customers cheaper to service and more willing to purchase higher value services. Custodians are a good example of this, providing not only services to support institutional investors settlement and valuation, but also their accounting, collateral management, and regulatory reporting requirements.

1.3 WHAT IS OPERATIONAL RISK?

Definitions

Risk can be broadly defined as the potential for events or ongoing trends to cause future losses or fluctuations in future income. The risks faced by most financial-services institutions are typically broken down into *market, credit, strategic,* and *operational risks.*

Market risks are those fluctuations in net income or portfolio value resulting from changes in particular market risk factors. Techniques such as asset–liability management (for long-duration, interest-rate-sensitive portfolios) and financial risk management (for short-term market portfolios) can be used to measure and design strategies to hedge market risk (for a discussion, see Smithson and Smith, 1990). Credit risks are fluctuations in net income or net asset values that result from a particular type of external event—the default of a counterparty, supplier, or borrower. Credit risk management has evolved from simple credit scoring of individual borrowers to sophisticated aggregate models of borrowers' default probabilities and the extent of asset recovery (for further information, see Caouette, Altman, and Narayanan, 1998). Strategic risks are those long-term environmental changes that can affect how a business adds value to its stakeholders. Strategic risk management is inherently more open-ended and builds on the tools and frameworks used by strategic planners (such as scenario analysis).

Of the four types of risks that firms face and allocate capital toward, the management of operational risk is the least advanced, and yet in a sense demands the most general approach. And, as we shall see, it suggests a potential framework in which to integrate all the other exposures. To a large extent, operational risk provides a useful banner behind which managers can communicate and enforce a more consistent and inclusive perspective toward all risks throughout the organization. Just as managers, salespeople, and traders initiate transactions that cause market and credit risks for the firm, operations managers take actions that produce operational risks. But operations are not the only source of operational risks. Intuitively, operational risk is the potential for *any* disruption in the firm's operational processes. The disruption may come from one-off events, ranging from rogue trading and accounting mistakes to terrorist activities and landmark legal settlement, and from improper sales practices and systems failures to sabotage, regulatory violations, and acts of God. The very diversity of events that lead to operational risk makes precise definitions elusive. Questions of definition become questions of categorization with two extremes of thought. The "narrow" view of operational risk holds that these risks result from operational failures within the back office or operations area of the firm. The other extreme, the "wide" view of operational risk, suggests it is a quantitative residual, i.e., the variance in net earnings not explained by financial risks such as market and credit risks. While easy to understand and act upon, the more narrow view is extremely limiting because it fails to capture so many risks that lie at the interface of operations and other business areas, e.g., reputational, legal, or facilities risks. In contrast, the more inclusive definition is popular and has the advantage of separating risks that are relatively easy to measure from those that are not. The problem with this view is that it is too broad and too negative. One can only use this definition to measure operational risks for capital-allocation purposes— it is almost impossible to use it to manage operations because it lacks specificity; one commentator compared it to defining a dog as something that is not a cat.

Most regulators have adopted definitions that lie somewhere between these extreme views, focusing on the risk of failures in technology, controls, and staff. For example, the Board of Governors of the Federal

Reserve System Trading Activities Manual defines operational and systems risks as: the "risk of human error or fraud, or that systems will fail to adequately record, monitor and account for transactions or positions." This is similar to the influential definition of the Basle committee *1994 Risk Management Guidelines* (Vol. 16) for OTC derivatives, which adopted a definition that has been used by a number of banks. It holds that operational risk is: "Risk that deficiencies in information systems or internal controls will result in unexpected loss. This risk is associated with human error, systems failures, and inadequate procedures and controls." The Office of the Comptroller of the Currency (1989) described operational risk as including system failure, system disruption, and system compromises.

This book argues for a more inclusive definition than that of the regulators. Operational processes are more than controls, information systems, and operating staff. A more reasonable definition of operational risk is provided by Laycock (1998), who suggests that: "operational risk is the potential for adverse fluctuations in the profit and loss statement or the cash flow of the firm due to effects that are attributable to customers, inadequately defined controls, system or control failures, and unmanageable events." Equally acceptable is the process-centric focus of Bankers Trust, which suggests that operational risks "relate to all phases of the business process, from origination through to execution and delivery, spanning the front, middle and back office(s)" (Hoffman, 1996).

Examples

Examples are perhaps as a more effective means of identifying operational risks. Research by Operational Risk, Inc. suggests that since 1980, financial institutions have lost more than $200 billion due to operational risks. Table 1.2 shows some of the most well-known examples of operational risks during the past two decades. A more complete set of examples can be found in Appendix A, which describes many operational failures, their impact, and how they might have been avoided.

Tᴀʙʟᴇ **1.2** Examples of Operational Risks

Institution	Activity	Year	Loss $ million*
Daiwa Bank, New York	Unauthorized bond trading caused by poor management controls	1984–95	1,100
Sumitomo Corp, London	Unauthorized copper trading, fraud, and forgery	1986–96	1,700
UK life-insurance industry	Pensions mis-selling and non-compliance	1988–94	18,000
Standard Chartered, India	Irregularities on Bombay Stock Exchange	1992	400
Credit Lyonnais	Poor lending control	1980s, 1990s	29,000
US banks, corporations, retailers	Check fraud	1993	12,000
London Stock Exchange and members	TAURUS system cancellation	1993	700
Kidder Peabody	Bond trading, lack of internal controls	1994	200
Proctor & Gamble	Lack of management understanding	1994	157
Morgan Grenfell	Misrepresentation	1990s	640
Orange County	Bond trading, lack of management oversight	1994	1,700
Barings, Singapore	Inadequate control of futures trading – in particular poor segregation of duties	1995	1,600
Deutsche Bank (Morgan Grenfell), London	Investment outside authority	1996	600
eBay	Internet auction house, technology failure	1999	5,000 wiped off market value

*Approximate US$ cost as cited on at least one occasion in the press

Box 1.12: General Resources on Operational Risk

The first book on the general topic of operational risk in financial institutions was by Arthur Andersen and Risk Publications (1998). *Risk Magazine* (Risk Publications) has regular features and special issues on operational risk management. Another useful resource also produced by Risk Publications (www.riskpublications.com) is the monthly newsletter *Operational Risk*. Insurance and management consulting firms such as Tillinghast-Towers Perrin, Arthur Andersen, PricewaterhouseCoopers, and Ernst & Young regularly produce reports on this topic, as do a number of financial-services research groups such as Tower Group and Meridien Research. A small number of operational risk management consulting groups are in existence, such as NetRisk, ORI, and RiskMatters (Appendix B), that either focus on collecting operational loss data, developing tools, or implementing risk methodologies. With a more academic perspective, the UK-based Centre for Operational Risk Research and Education was formed in 1999 with the goal of encouraging research into operational risk management. Financial risk management system vendors, such as Infinity and Algorithmics are also involved in developing operational risk management solutions. Other useful resources for operational risk managers are found in specific operational areas. For instance, Chapter 17 of Klein (1996) provides one of the earliest discussions on operational risk in the context of securities operations. In industry areas such as banking, operating risks are described by Mayland (1993), in computing systems (Ardis, 1987), and in software projects (Jones, 1994). A general overview of business risks is provided by Nader (1998). Several books discuss operational risk management as an extension of financial risk management including Klein (1996), or as an extension of internal control and audit (Risk, 1998).

1.4 WHAT IS OPERATIONAL RISK MANAGEMENT?

Activities

Operational risk management comprises a host of activities:

- Identifying the risk: What can go wrong?

- Measuring the risk: Approximately how critical is a particular risk?

- Preventing operational losses, e.g., standardized deal documentation.

- Mitigating the loss impact after it has occurred by reducing the firm's sensitivity to the event, e.g., disaster contingency planning.

- Predicting operational losses, e.g., projecting the potential legal risks and market cannibalization associated with a new product or service.

- Transferring the risk to external parties presumably better able to handle the risk, e.g., insurance, hedging, surety.

- Changing the form of the risk to another type of risk and dealing with that risk, e.g., transforming market risk into credit risk by using OTC products, transforming credit risk into operational risk by the use of margin or collateral.

- Allocating capital to cover operational risks.

Disciplines

Many of these activities are common to a wide range of staff functions in a number of different industries. Each discipline, co-opting the term risk management, imbues it with its unique set of techniques and concepts. But some things are shared across all approaches. Risk management always involves the *systematic* and *continuing* process of exposure identification, risk measurement, analysis, control, prevention, reduction and assessment, and financing. Operational risk management is no exception. Given an inclusive definition of operational risk, operational risk management also helps to integrate financial and non-financial risks, traditional financial risk management with insurance and legal liability, and the management of one-off loss events with that of continuous systemic risks. It should also structure an effective management response to different risks. In Section III, we will discuss these responses, which range from reengineering to reinsurance, performance measurement to outsourcing, and loss prevention to contingency planning. It is a huge area, but one with many interactions across different subdisciplines, and hence, desperate for an integrated approach.

For example, some of the most important disciplines that underlie effective operational risk management are presented in Figure 1.3.

FIGURE 1.3 Operational Risk Management and Related Disciplines

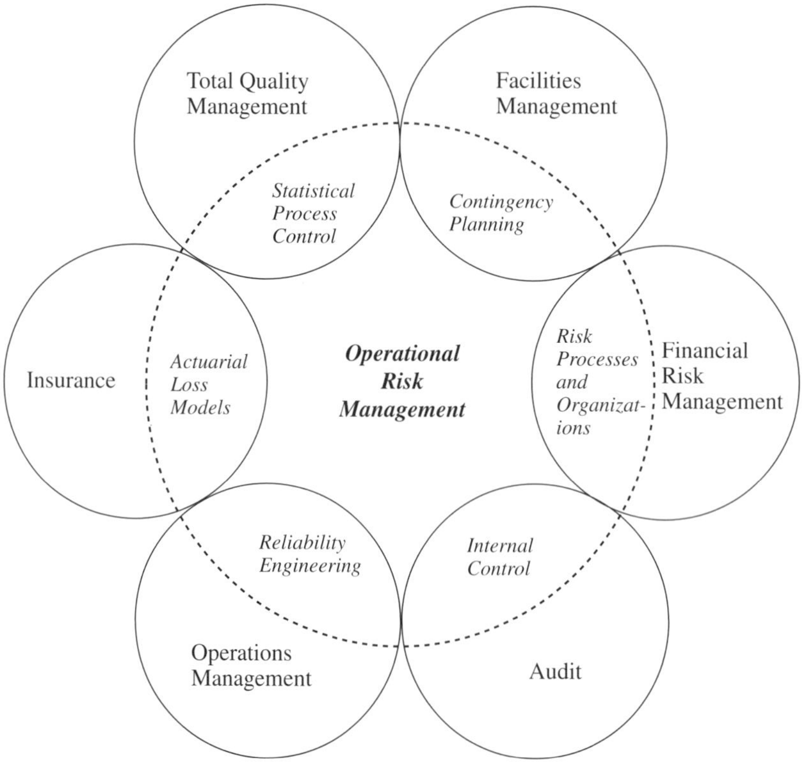

Financial Risk Management   Financial risk managers have developed well-defined risk processes and organizational structures to measure, analyze, and manage financial risks within businesses (see Subsection 14.6 for further details). There are several reasons for this. First, financial assets have well-defined mark-to-market values. Second, financial institutions can estimate the risks of these assets. Third, financial instruments such as swaps, options, and futures are widely available to offset these risks. The spur toward quantifying market and credit risks has naturally led to an interest in applying similar techniques to operational risk management. Some specific techniques such as stress testing and value at risk (VaR) have found application in operational risk management. But the most important has been the adoption of an integrated set of risk processes and an organizational structure to handle operational risks. Most financial-modeling techniques are not easily applicable, however: the lack of reliable data, the uniqueness of exposures to particular firms, and the absence of "hedging" vehicles all make it difficult to transfer financial risk management techniques to the problem of operational risk management.

Total Quality Management   Quality management involves changing the risk profile of processes and resources by improving its input and output availability, quality, relevance, and attractiveness. Unlike operational risk management, which has the clear goal of aggregate risk assessment, TQM techniques, such as Motorola's Six Sigma process, are really smorgasbords of different techniques combining inspection, statistical quality control, quality assurance, and strategic quality management (see Subsection 9.2 for further information). Many of these techniques, although not yet widely used in financial services, have tremendous potential provided they are applied appropriately and consistently. For example, inspection emphasizes product or service uniformity—particularly important for distributed retail-banking operations. Statistical quality control evaluates process outputs using statistical sampling techniques (For an example, see the discussion on control charts—Subsection 15.4). Quality assurance tries to build quality into operational processes through better design. Finally, quality management also has a strategic aspect; strategic quality management evaluates the firm's competitive position with respect to the various dimensions of its product and service quality, e.g., product-based, user-based, manufacturing-based, and value-based aspects of quality.

Insurance   Insurance can be used to transfer some (but not all) operational risk from the insured (the firm being insured) to the insurer. A typical insurance contract requires the insurer to provide funds to pay for specified losses in exchange for a premium from the purchaser at inception. Insurers then reduce their risk by diversification using a pool of non-correlated exposures. This has the effect of decreasing the standard deviation (unexpected losses) associated with the individual claims, and in theory, has no effect on the expected losses. However, insurance does not cover all forms of operational loss, and even if a loss is covered, insurance pricing often includes a high margin. Not surprisingly, insurance companies have leveraged their huge volumes of payout data to develop some of the most sophisticated actuarial models of operational loss (see Chapters 2, 3, 6, and 7 for further information).

Audit and Internal Control   Accounting control systems are designed to ensure that the operations of the business are in accordance with the strategic plans and policies developed by senior management. Diagnostic controls and a series of limits and sanctions are used to ensure operations are kept in check. Internal and external audit focus on confirming the existence of the assets and liabilities for which the firm is responsible (and accountable). To do this, they traditionally use a series of interviews and checklists to confirm operational integrity (see Chapter 12 for a discussion). Operational risk management uses similar qualitative techniques but goes beyond them to quantification and ongoing resource allocation based on the resulting estimates of risk.

Operations Management and Reliability Engineering   Reliability engineering is a body of statistical and analytical techniques concerned with the reliable, safe, and efficient operation of engineering systems. The focus of reliability engineering is the maintenance of system function and the reduction of operational uncertainty by making sure that realistic operating specifications are set for process outputs and then ensuring that those specifications are met. Operational risk management tools derived from reliability engineering have been used in a variety of safety-conscious areas such as nuclear plant safety, aircraft maintenance, and medical informatics.

However, the same discipline of systematically gathering, categorizing, analyzing, and prioritizing data as used in engineering disciplines can help in developing rigorous operational risk management methodologies (see Chapter 11 for more details). Techniques such as redundancy, preventative maintenance and replacement, Pareto analysis, Failure Modes and Effects Analysis (FMEA), hazard analysis, Markov chains, fault trees, and event trees have revolutionized the design of fault-tolerant systems. For the most part, however, these techniques have yet to be widely applied outside industrial engineering applications.

There are several reasons for this. For one, reliability engineering approaches tend to be very data-intensive and focus on the evolving reliability of complex multicomponent hardware systems for which destructive and accelerated testing techniques can be used. By contrast, the organizational systems that comprise ongoing operations are data-poor and involve people. This makes gathering data and predicting the systems' failure patterns much more challenging than for hardware systems. Another difference between operational risk management and reliability engineering is their focus. Whereas engineers focus on reliability (the likelihood of the system functioning correctly), operations managers are more concerned with the financial impacts of any downtime and try to estimate the range of potential costs that could be incurred during the next time period.

Facilities Management and Contingency Planning Some risks can never be entirely removed. Contingency planners seek to anticipate the nightmare scenarios posing major threats to the firm's fixed assets and ongoing operations. The heart of contingency planning has two elements—providing back-up resources (people, facilities, and capital) and applying them quickly to bring business operations back online (Levitt, 1997). For example, as a result of a well-thought-out contingency plan, Fuji Capital Markets' office was able to recover two days after the World Trade Center—the location of its office—was bombed. Closely related to contingency planning are scenario analysis, crisis management, and, in particular, reputation management, which describe appropriate management responses after a crisis has begun. All of these techniques are only relevant for the very infrequent, high-impact events, in contrast with operational risk management, which generally focuses on the more frequent, lower impact events (discussed in detail in Chapter 13).

1.5 WHY IS OPERATIONAL RISK MANAGEMENT IMPORTANT?

There are several common justifications for firms to manage their operational risks. They include:

Regulatory Pressures

Regulators are proposing that increasing amounts of capital be set aside for operational risks. Having an operational risk management program in place can help quantify these risks. Operational risk managers can then work with regulatory bodies to confirm compliance and help convince them of the quality of a bank's risk management, thereby helping to free up expensive risk capital.

Mergers and Acquisitions

The increase in M&A activity, both friendly and hostile, has forced industry-wide consolidation and led to a plethora of operational risks caused by the need for post-merger integration.

Integrating Best Practices

Operational risk managers can take the lead in integrating and disseminating best risk practices over a wide range of functions such as compliance, insurance, risk management, operations, and facilities management. In particular, this means standardizing management responses to common risks rather than relying on the *ad hoc* approaches of particular staff functions or business units.

Aggregating Risks

Operational risk programs can aggregate risks across a number of business lines to obtain a bird's-eye view of firmwide risks. This helps identify natural hedges and direct management attention to firmwide exposures and away from expensive piecemeal risk management through locally developed control systems.

New Products and Services

Senior management as well as front-office sales, marketing, and trading may not fully understand the hidden risks involved in many of their new products and services, e.g., liquidity risks, model risks, and credit exposures. Operational risk managers should actively investigate new product and service proposals for hidden risks. They should also lead the development of management and control solutions/policies to minimize unnecessary risk.

Resource Allocation

Performance measurement and resource allocation assume measures that incorporate all the risks associated with that business or activity.

Measures of operational risk help avoid problems of moral hazard whereby the risks are passed from one business area to another.

1.6   REGULATORY AND INDUSTRY INITIATIVES

Much of the impetus for operational risk management has come from regulators and industry-wide groups. Qualitative and quantitative standards have been proposed and, in some cases, widely adopted. Consider the qualitative standards first—these define good practices in the field of operations or specify general guidelines for assessing process and control quality.

Qualitative Standards

Three types of qualitative guidelines are particularly relevant to operations managers:

- Industry guidelines for good operations practices

- Guidelines for internal control

- Process and resource quality guidelines

Industry Guidelines for Good Operations Practice   In 1993, one of the most important industry groups—the Group of Thirty, an elite group of global investment banks—issued a highly influential report (G30, 1993) outlining 20 recommendations for good practice for derivatives dealers and end users. Although its focus was derivatives, its conclusions have set the tone for securities dealing and processing as a whole. The report argued that the scale, leverage, and complexity of derivatives trading make effective market, credit, and operational risk management a necessity. In particular, it made a strong case for precisely defined risk management policies covering the scope and authorization of trading, acceptable control, product valuation and risk management approaches, and the critical importance of adequate disclosure and active senior management involvement.

Many of the guidelines in this G30 report have become *de facto* industry standards. The separation of front-office from back-office operations, independent risk management reporting to senior management, periodic and effective audits, quality information systems (IS), and risk integration across the firm have become accepted as essential practices for dealers and users of marketable securities alike.

On the operational side, one of the major challenges noted by the G30 report was dealers' reliance on a variety of information systems across a number of different business lines for valuation, deal processing, settlement and accounting, and risk management. Vertical and horizontal operational integration of these systems pose a major challenge for dealers. The lack of integration tends to encourage reconciliation errors and settlement fails. Not too long after the landmark G30 report, the public-sector response to the same report noted that:

"The limitations of a firm's MIS are directly related to the effectiveness of risk management. Because the development and ongoing modification of MIS are very costly and take time, the limitations of these systems may prove a significant constraint on the ability of firms to rapidly implement some of the valuable recommendations in the G30 report."

Industry groups increasingly began to appreciate the importance of operations and the risks to the business if they were poorly managed. A focused discussion on current practices in operational risk management had to wait for a later consultative document (1998) from the BIS. This resulted from a working group of the Basle Committee on Banking Supervision, which interviewed 30 major banks to discover their approaches to operational risk management. Perhaps the paper's most important contribution was its emphasis of operational risk management as a means to develop management incentives to heighten awareness of the importance of risk. Most banks, the report noted, have risk profiling systems for major operational risk factors and events such as volume, turnover, settlement fails, delays, errors, and confirmation aging. Although many of the respondent banks were quickly moving in the direction of more formal approaches, few had formal integrated systems for measuring operational risks. The report also suggested that most operational losses were also due to breakdowns in internal controls and corporate governance. Other aspects of operational risk cited by the report include major failures of information technology systems or events such as fires or other disasters. The challenge, noted the BIS report, was the integration of these disparate factors into a coherent picture of the operational risks of a business, in much the same way VaR is used to measure risks in a market portfolio. The report also described a number of techniques for managing operational risk, including internal controls and external and internal insurance. Most of the banks responding to the BIS survey suggested that operational risk management was not yet sufficiently developed for regulators to advocate a single approach to quantifying operational risks.

Guidelines for Internal Control Following several high-profile scandals in the early 1990s involving the failure of corporate governance, internal control has become an important concern for regulators. At financial institutions in particular, failures in internal control played an important role in the scandals at DG Bank, Kidder Peabody, Bank of Tokyo-Mitsubishi, and IBJ, to name a few. Commissions on corporate governance and the need for improved internal controls have issued reports in the United States (COSO, 1992), Canada (CoCo, 1995), and the United Kingdom (Cadbury, 1992). One such report was issued by the Committee of Sponsoring Organizations (COSO) of the Treadway Commission (COSO, 1992). It focused on internal control and went beyond financial service needs, emphasizing that organizations with quality internal control must incorporate the following elements:

- Process-based risk assessment: A set of techniques to identify, measure, analyze, and manage the risks related to various activities.

- Sound control environment: The culture, values, and resources available within an organization must be risk aware.

- Robust control activities: Carrying out policies and procedures to secure management objectives.

- Effective information and communication: Systems to capture and exchange the information required for effective operations.

- Ongoing monitoring: The means to monitor operations to enable flexibility and responsiveness to changing conditions.

One of the common themes of many of the recent pronouncements on internal control is that instead of internal control being considered an end in itself, internal control has as its principal aim the management of risks. This suggests that with a rigorous corporate risk management system, an effective internal control system should follow. Unlike the quality management perspective (see later in this section), internal control is viewed as a core corporate process rather than some external "best practice" that has to be adhered to. What remains unclear from the current work on internal control practices is how internal control relates to business strategy and the management of upside risk.

Process and Resource Quality Guidelines   With the radical wave of restructuring, reengineering, reverse reengineering, downsizing, and so on, there has been an increasing global emphasis on quality management. Traditionally the domain of manufacturing companies, TQM has become a competitive issue for many service organizations, particularly retail banks and insurance companies. TQM may be defined in a generic sense to refer to the considerable amount of philosophies, concepts, methods, and tools used globally to manage quality. One of its leading advocates, the International Standards Organization (ISO), has defined it as a "management approach of an organization centered on quality, based on the participation of all its members and aiming at long-term success through customer satisfaction, and benefits to all members of the organization and to society" (Juran, 1999). International quality metrics such as the Malcolm Baldrige National Quality Award, the Deming Prize, and the ISO 9000 standards provide checklist-based frameworks to certify the quality of organizational processes and resources. The Baldrige award confirms organizational quality in a variety of forms, such as leadership, strategic planning, customer satisfaction, reporting, human resources (HR), process management, and good business results. The Deming Application Prize is similar, although it has a stronger emphasis on the use of statistical methods. The ISO 9000 standards exist principally to facilitate international trade and provide quality management guidance for a number of generic product categories: hardware, software, processed materials, and services. The standards require quality features that *should be* present in the management system, but do not dictate their implementation. The ISO requirements can be briefly summarized as a control loop of effective goal-setting and resource allocation, implementation, maintenance and record keeping, performance assessment, and learning.

Quantitative Guidelines

As the 1998 BIS report suggested, quantitative approaches to measure operational risk are nowhere near so advanced as qualitative guidelines for its management. Nor are quantitative measures for operational risks as advanced as those for market and credit risk. Yet it is precisely the drive toward regulatory capital requirements based on assessments of banks' market and credit exposures that is prompting many operational risk assessments.

Regulatory Capital Requirements   Financial regulators are concerned about risks to the general public and to investors, especially systemic risks—the risk of major losses in the financial system resulting from numerous potentially unstable interrelationships between different financial-services providers (particularly banks). While regulators' worst fears have yet to be realized, recent scandals such as those at Herstatt, BCCI, Drexel, US S&Ls, Barings, Metallgesellschaft, UK Pension Funds, and LTCM have tested regulators' confidence in their oversight capabilities. While industry regulators have traditionally focused on checklist-based audits and measuring certain key ratios (such as banks' liquidity ratio of short-term assets to liabilities and interest margin), they increasingly look to limit institutional guarantees and accurately estimate capital adequacy measures as a proxy for institutional solvency. The required level of risk capital is determined by the nature of the catastrophic risks associated with the various assets, liabilities, and operations of the institution and the acceptable probability of insolvency.

Box 1.13: Morale Hazard

There are unintended consequences associated with the imposition of risk reducing regulatory guidelines. Limiting systemic risks by using risk-based capital requirements often conflicts with the demand for competition. *Morale hazard* may occur, in which the risk incurred by banks is mitigated by government without any negative consequences for the banks themselves. For instance, the structure of guarantee funds such as the US Federal Deposit Insurance System can encourage banks to take additional risks because their depositors are guaranteed to get much of their funds back in the event of a default. Banks take on more risks with this protection than they would otherwise. In fact, *any* rule that limits the impact of a risk, such as deposit insurance, may also encourage further risk taking.

Regulatory risk capital requirements, although far from optimal, have dramatically changed the nature of banking services. The realization that capital is a scarce resource, fueled by the use of techniques such as shareholder value added (SVA), has translated the intangible problem of additional risk taking by banks into a tangible problem of additional risk capital. Regulatory capital requirements also offer a broad-brush approach to economic capital allocation in which the level of capital (equity, retained earnings, and some forms of long-term debt) depends on the level of risk that the bank has—specifically, a measure of the risk that the bank will become insolvent. Without capital, losses other than those expected would cause a bank to fail. Additional capital covers unexpected losses and also, in extreme cases, catastrophic losses up to some threshold—the firm's likelihood of default (which varies from less than one percent p.a. for investment grade to much more for speculative grades). Additional capital is also expensive and places a limit on the risk taking appetite of the firm, which prevents the firm from conducting certain types of business. Given the constraint of a minimum capital level firms can adapt by raising new capital (retained earnings, new equity), liquidating assets, or reducing risk.

Not surprisingly, risk-based capital requirements have encouraged the development of risk management efforts for market, credit, and operational risks. This is despite the fact that regulators are more concerned with infrequent catastrophic losses than with ongoing operational losses, the primary concern of most operations managers. Risk-based capital requirements were first implemented for credit risk (1988) and then extended to cover market risk (1993) and, at a later time, may also be extended to cover operational risks. The 1988 Basle Accord estimates the risk capital required to cover commercial banks' credit risk and decrees the minimum required capital (the Cooke Ratio) to be a fixed percentage (8 percent) of the firms' assets weighted according to the degree of risks associated with them. These weights depend on the credit quality of the borrowers and start from zero for commitments with public counterparties, to 20 percent for banks in OECD countries, 50 percent for mortgage-backed loans, and up to 100 percent for private businesses. Controversially, the Cooke Ratio does not incorporate diversification effects across loan issues, countries, and industries, nor does it account for netting only for gross exposures (a major issue for swap portfolios). The 1988 Basle Accord also sets limits on what it calls "excessive risk taking." These risks result from positions backed by more than 10 percent of the bank's capital. These positions must be reported to regulators directly. Positions that utilize more than 25 percent of the firm's risk capital are prohibited entirely.

But perhaps the biggest limitation of the Cooke Ratio was its failure to incorporate market risk. This was rectified in 1993 when the so-called standard model proposal (implemented in 1997) outlined its more sophisticated rules for market risk. The standard model estimates a separate VaR for trading portfolios' individual exposures to interest rate, forex-rate risk, equity-rate risk, and commodity risks. The total portfolio VaR is the sum of these individual risk estimates. The precise calculations vary according to the type of risk.

For interest-rate risk, for example, the model defines a series of tenors, each with its own duration (or sensitivity) measure, to which positions are mapped according to their maturity. The sum of these duration-weighted positions provides a measure of the interest-rate risk of the portfolio. While netting of positions is allowed within a tenor, it is not allowed across different tenors. For forex and equities, the capital charge is essentially a fixed percentage of the position (8 percent). For commodities, the charge is higher (15 percent). Higher capital charges are also levied for specific risks—the proportion of price fluctuations not generated by market movements.

Box 1.14: Value at Risk

VaR is widely used as measure of a portfolio's market risk, although strictly speaking, it can be applied to any risk exposure. Simply stated, it is the expected maximum loss of some portfolio during some time period at some predefined level of confidence. Increasingly, VaR has been applied to the aggregate level of all the firm's exposures, in order incorporate several factors affecting the value of the firm into a single number. Moreover, it focuses on a major concern of senior managers—the potential for significant loss in a firm's portfolio of assets. Closely related to VaR is the concept of earnings at risk (EaR)—the expected maximum fall in earnings over a given period. Unlike VaR, EaR considers extreme fluctuations in earnings rather than value, but the two concepts are approximately related by

$$\text{Value at Risk} = \frac{\text{Earnings at Risk}}{\text{Risk-free rate}}$$

provided we assume exposures remain constant over time. Both EaR and VaR have a range of possible uses:

- To estimate the firm's capital at risk—the amount of capital put aside to cover potential future losses.

- To estimate risk adjusted performance—techniques such as RAROC use VaR as a denominator with which to normalize performance.

- To estimate market risks and set trading limits.

Several parameters define the concept of VaR. First is the time period. In general, this should reflect the liquidation period of the asset with fluctuating values. The time horizon used for VaR should reflect the time period required to control or change asset positions. Liquid market securities will have a very short time horizon. Illiquid operational assets have a time horizon equal to the control horizon, typically a year. Another important parameter is the degree of confidence that the loss will not be exceeded more than some chosen percentage of time. For instance, for market risk, this might be 95 percent; for catastrophic risks, we might use 99 percent or more. The higher the confidence chosen, the less frequently will larger losses be seen and therefore, the greater the estimation error. The most contentious assumption in using VaR is the choice of distribution assumed to represent the future unrealized losses. This may be based on analytical distributions, such as normal or log normal, or on historical distributions over some time period. Real market return data is only partially matched by parametric distributions, particularly at the extreme where empirically observed fat tails make it very difficult to accurately estimate extreme losses using VaR. The use of historical distributions is more robust but makes the heroic assumption that the recent past is a good indicator of the near future. Related to the choice of return distribution is the use of correlations between return factors. Estimating correlations accurately is difficult, and correlations tend to break down in abnormal situations—precisely those circumstances for which VaR is needed.

For further information on VaR, Jorion (1997) provides a good overview of the use of VaR for market risk calculations. Kevin Dowd (1998) goes into even further detail.

This approach to market risk is clearly more sophisticated than that for credit risk, but it still has major limitations. It does not, for example, incorporate diversification effects across different risks. In 1995, the standard model was revised to allow banks to use their own internal models of risk and, subject to external validation, use them to estimate their risk-based capital requirement (currently, internal models are allowed only for market risks). Internal models, unlike the standard model, do allow consideration of some correlation effects across asset classes in estimating VaR. However, additional capital penalties are charged if the bank's internal model fails to sufficiently capture historical market risks. Capital charges for the bank's balance-sheet credit risk are then added to the charge for the trading portfolio's market risk to provide a total capital requirement.

In June 1999, the Basle Committee on Banking Supervision published proposals for changing the 1988 Basle Accord. The changes proposed include a more sensitively calibrated risk weighting system incorporating a greater use of external rating agencies for different claims. However, at a subsequent conference of industry professionals, academicians, and regulators in June 1999 (as reported in *The Economist),* the general agreement was that the Basle approach was fundamentally flawed. Participants suggested an increased role for the markets to enhance regulation. Two methods were suggested. First, minimize the role of deposit insurance, and second, issue subordinated debt to reflect the market's assessment of the risks the bank is undertaking. Part of the reason for practitioners' misgivings is regulatory capital guidelines treat hard-to-measure risks such as operational risk, interest-rate risks in the banking book, and reputational risk only in terms of the arbitrary multiple (of the aggregate market and credit risk) used to estimate the capital requirement. Some different approaches to risk-based capital requirements have been proposed—the so-called precommitment model (Kupiec, 1995) argues that banks should precommit to a particular maximum loss over a forthcoming period. This loss would then be the capital charge for the period; exceeding the limit would bring about regulatory penalties or higher capital charges in the future. Closely related to the BIS 1993 market risk proposal is the EU's Capital Adequacy Directive (Littlejohn, 1995), which outlines the capital requirements for European Union securities houses.

Non-bank financial intermediaries also encounter capital requirements. Although pension funds have no risk capital requirement (to cover their unexpected losses), they must hold capital sufficient to cover defined benefit pension payments. In Europe and the United States, insurance companies must also comply with capital requirements to cover the credit risks associated with their assets (usually bonds and mortgages) and the actuarially fair value of their future insurance cash flows. Securities firms carry securities as both assets and liabilities, and are bound by risk-based capital restrictions to cover them. In addition, securities firms' trading books are covered by rules similar to those faced by banks.

Further Reading: Risk-based Capital Allocation

See Chapter 16 for more information. Chris Matten (1998) provides an excellent overview of the issues involved in risk-based capital allocation for banks. The BIS (1995) report outlines the internal model approach for market risk estimation. This and other BIS reports can be accessed at www.bis.org. Paul Kupiec (1995) compares the effectiveness of risk-based capital measures and argues strongly for the precommitment approach.

CHAPTER 2

BASIC CONCEPTS

Before launching into a methodology to identify, measure, analyze, and report operational risks, some basic concepts need to be made explicit. These concepts, which are not unique to operational risk management, are drawn from a number of different disciplines, such as accounting, financial risk management, actuarial sciences, and reliability engineering. These concepts contribute to a shared language with which to analyze and communicate risks, as well as provide the theoretical basis for understanding the methodology that follows.

2.1 THE DIMENSIONS OF RISK

The world we live in is changing. Unfortunately, we often do not know how many of these changes will affect us. When we use the word "risk," it captures both the effects of change and our inability to predict that change. It follows that as our knowledge and understanding of the impacts and causes of change increase, the risks that we face decrease. But no amount of knowledge will remove all risks. Some risks are inherent to business. Careful selection of the risks to be exposed to lies at the heart of a firm's core competence. Acceptance of these core risks as a necessary part of being in business is an important preamble to managing risk. Risk management rarely means risk elimination.

Defining Risk

For such a fundamental concept, risk has a wide range of definitions. When we rank the possible outcomes of change (e.g., a business unit's profit and loss along an axis), several natural definitions of risk begin to emerge (Figure 2.1).

FIGURE 2.1 Possible Distribution of Profit and Loss of a Business

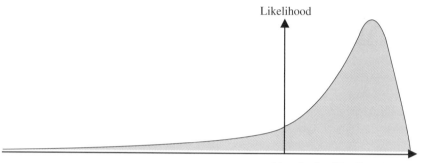

Risk as Mean Outcome Actuaries denote the risk of an event to be the expected outcome. In operations, this is typically a loss. Of course, the mean outcome tells us little about the range of potential outcomes—something that risk managers and planners with growth and capital allocation objectives are instinctively concerned about (although, as we shall see, this is not necessarily an issue with investors who can hold diversified portfolios).

Risk as Variance in Outcome A common definition holds that risk refers to the statistical *variance* or *standard deviation* of outcomes, typically profit and loss (P&L) or losses. Risk management, in this case, means reducing the variance between expectations and the potential outcome. Line management and financial risk management often focus on this loss variance because of its importance in facilitating planning and growth. Many statistical control and TQM approaches also use transaction and process variance as a proxy for process, transaction quality, and reliability.

Risk as Catastrophic Downside A more defensive view of risk holds it to be a hazard to the firm and looks to minimize major negative impact events such as loss from client default, fraud, or natural or human disaster. Insurance, contingency planning, internal control, compliance, and internal audit traditionally focus on potential worst-case loss scenarios. A downside risk perspective is most useful when a very conservative approach is required or when institutional decision-makers are constrained by a fiduciary responsibility that imposes high standards of care. For example, regulators concerned about catastrophic losses prescribe the amount of capital to set aside to cover insolvency risk. This usually calls for estimating some extreme percentile of the loss distribution, say 99 percent (a level of loss exceeded only once in every 100 occasions). It is also the justification for much of the recent work on the concepts of VaR and Extreme Value Theory.

Risk as Upside Opportunity Often neglected is the view of risk as opportunity. Managing upside risk means evaluating the opportunities in taking risk. Business is inherently risky; success comes to those who take risks that work out. Managers generally spend too much time worrying about downside risk and not enough time worrying about risk as opportunity. Expectations should be used to guide opportunistic risk taking. For instance, a bearish view on a long bond portfolio might not be consistent with an existing portfolio. In this case, increasing the position may actually decrease the variance relative to expectations. In the same way, the risk of operational processes should incorporate expectations of future learning and improvements in technology. It follows that medium- and long-term forecasting is an important part of this forward-looking perspective of risk as upside. Opportunistic risk taking must be driven by these presumably informed expectations. Provided such expectations are in place, risk management can become proactive and aggressive rather than passive and reactive.

Risk and Uncertainty It is important to distinguish between *risk* and *uncertainty*. Risk applies to outcomes that, while not certain, have probabilities that can be estimated by experience or statistical data. Uncertainty is present when the outcome cannot be predicted even in a probabilistic sense. In practice, uncertainty is always present and any analysis should test its risk assumptions (e.g., theoretical distributions) by sensitivity analysis, i.e., using alternate assumptions and assessing the impact of the change.

No single definition of risk is perfect. All of these definitions capture some aspects of risk, but ignore others. No number can ever capture a distribution of all the possible outcomes. In practice, risk is best evaluated on all of these dimensions (which is one reason that techniques such as Monte Carlo simulation, with the ability to capture distributions, are so appropriate).

2.2 WHY MANAGE RISK?

Risk tends to reduce business value and individual welfare by limiting management's ability to achieve its objectives. Risk management tries to limit this reduction, thereby increasing business value. We have seen that operations has four core objectives—efficiency, change management, internal control, and opportunistic risk taking. Operational risk management must be organized to facilitate all of these objectives (Table 2.1).

TABLE 2.1 Integration of Operational Objectives

Operational Objectives	Business Objectives	Risk Components	Rationale
Efficiency	Cost reduction	Expected losses	Lower costs Lower taxes Lower insurance costs
Change management	Growth	Unexpected losses	Ease of planning Less use of external financing
Internal control	Efficient use of capital	Catastrophic losses	Decreased likelihood of financial distress Greater use of debt financing with associated tax shields Satisfying regulatory requirements
Opportunism	Revenues increase	Upside potential	Typically strategic options such as those provided by infrastructure investments

Managing Expected, Unexpected, and Catastrophic Losses

Managing expected losses is the easiest to justify since these directly affect P&L and, when discounted, the value of the firm to shareholders. More subtle is the management of variance, or unexpected losses. Usually, most cultures, professions, and individuals are naturally averse to outcome variance. But financial institutions are ambivalent. On the one hand, these firms are in the business of taking on and managing risks. It is only through such risks that firms can obtain their required returns. On the other hand, as we shall see, there are good reasons for a firm's stakeholders (although not necessarily its shareholders) to fear variance in outcomes.

For private or closely held businesses, management of variance is easily justified by owners because a large portion of their wealth is likely to be invested in the business. But for public corporations, the story is more complex because the corporations's shareholder-owners can hold diversified portfolios that remove much of the non-systematic risks faced by firms. Portfolio diversification by shareholders and firm risk management are naturally such close substitutes that it makes sense to ask which has the lower cost of risk. The marginal cost of diversification through the stock market is very low compared with risk management. So, the extent to which we should involve ourselves in risk management diminishes with the ability of shareholders to reduce risk on their own through portfolio diversification. Nonetheless, risk management of both those risks that managers can control (through prevention and mitigation) and those that they cannot control directly (only through risk transfer and financing) can still add value to shareholders. For controllable risks, risk management is assumed to be a competitive necessity—a firm that does not manage preventable and mitigable losses is more likely to go out of business than one that does. There are several reasons for public corporations to manage the uncontrollable portion of their unexpected losses:

- Business planning of financing and investments is made easier without fears of uncontrollable risks.

- For firms facing convex tax schedules (i.e., an increasing marginal rate of taxation), minimizing variance in the firm's pretax income decreases tax payments.

- Risk management may reduce the expected costs of financing losses because trips to the external markets are generally very expensive relative to the use of internal funds. For example, external funding (debt or equity) involves large legal fees, regulatory costs for filing, and the possibility of an undervalued offering. Risk management helps managers limit expensive forays to the capital markets by better aligning investment sources of internal capital with projected uses of capital.

- Risk management might change the level of systematic risk by positioning the firm's risk profile to be more in keeping with investor demands. This can be done using derivatives or by changing markets, products, and service offerings. While this should be appropriately priced by the market, there may be fashions or fads for particular investor niches.

- Risk management reduces the likelihood of financial distress. Catastrophic losses threaten the firm with bankruptcy, which would involve legal expenses and other costs associated with reorganizing or liquidating the business.

- Risk management allows the increased use of debt financing. Debt creates interest tax shields, i.e., the interest payments on debt usually are deductible when calculating taxable income. In contrast, firms cannot deduct dividends from their taxable income. Without risk management, debt financing is limited because it increases the possibility that the firm could experience financial distress. This can also be used to justify managing catastrophic losses.

- Regulators may require certain levels of risk management through their mandate of particular risk-based capital levels. As already explained, this too can be used to justify managing catastrophic losses.

Managing Upside

Risk management, through better analysis of business opportunities or through portfolio diversification, allows financial-services firms to take on opportunities that other firms cannot. Operational risk management can also have revenue implications because many customers will be drawn to the superior operational reputation that results from the systematic development of an operational core competence. This, in turn, may lead to a competitive advantage.

Risk Management and Discount Rates

Risk management, ostensibly focused on variance of cash flows, finds its greatest use in increasing expected cash flows rather than reducing the discount rate for those cash flows. In general, risk management has a limited effect on the rate used to discount future cash flows. To understand this, recall that theoretically at least, the discount rate reflects only those risks that are systematic or non-diversifiable.

Within this category of non-diversifiable risks, losses are either controllable or uncontrollable. If losses cannot be controlled internally, the risks can be transferred externally—one of the two techniques typically used to manage uncontrollable risks. However, risk transfer can nearly always be replicated by investors directly, e.g., by investing in a portfolio of insurance firms bearing that risk. This suggests that risk transfer of uncontrollable risks has little or no effect on the discount rate.

In contrast, most (but not all) controllable losses affected by loss prevention and loss mitigation activities are firm-specific and therefore not correlated with other firms' losses. These firm-specific losses can in theory be diversified away by shareholders; therefore, loss control activities too should have limited effects on a firm's cost of capital. To conclude, the only operational risks that have an effect on the discount rate are those for partially controllable risks for which the only other management strategy is decreased business levels or business exit.

While the academic debate continues as to the rationale of risk management, its use is increasing dramatically. Operational risk management applies the perspectives of financial risk management to operations and makes a strong call to integrate the techniques of financial risk management if only to take advantage of netting opportunities and systematic resource allocation based on risk adjusted performance measurement both ex post and ex ante.

The Costs of Risk Management

Risk management is not without its costs. The danger of operational risk management (and risk management in general) is what is not measured might be assumed not to exist. An overemphasis on the quantitative measurement of operational risks may be very dangerous to firms without good staff or well-designed processes because it may lull them into a false sense of security and lead to unnecessary risk taking (the problem of morale hazard). Ultimately, the main defense against operational risks must be staff who are knowledgeable about the risks and the good processes and systems that embody that knowledge. But operational risk management is precisely the means to make staff knowledgeable.

Box 2.1: Why Do Firms Manage Risk?

The rationale for risk management hinges on the famous Modigliani-Miller Hypothesis, which states that in a world with no taxes and no transaction costs, only the firm's investment decisions affect firm value. This means that financing decisions such as risk management do not affect the value of the firm and are therefore irrelevant to shareholders. Therefore, the justifications for risk management must lie in the inefficiencies that befall firms operating in the real world. For a more detailed discussion on this, see Brealey and Myers' classic text (1981) on corporate finance. For a more focused justification of risk management, see Froot (1993).

2.3 LOSS EVENTS

Unlike market risk management, in which the risks largely result from continuous changes in market prices and rates (risk factors), operations management is often about preventing, controlling, and mitigating loss events. But just what is a loss event? What is the relation between loss events and risk? An event is an occurrence or happening (in our case, ordinarily, but not necessarily, a loss). Events usually involve a subject and an active verb (e.g., counterparty defaults, incorrect counterparty entered, and fax machine fails). Examples of loss events may range from the trivial, such as backlogged confirmations resulting from a misfiled transaction, to the more contentious, such as the resignation of a head trader or the default of a counterparty. Events need to be well-defined; we should be clear whether the event has occurred or not, although we may not know this until after some of the impact of the event has been realized. For instance, a trade that is not confirmed within three days would be an event, so too would be an incorrect currency recorded for a deal, but slow confirmations are not.

A moment's thought reveals that there are a large number of events that could potentially affect a business. No analysis could ever consider all of them. Event models invariably assume the Pareto Principle, which holds that most of the risk comes from a very small number of events. This is especially likely to be true for mature operations, in which the more critical risks will have been designed out over time.

Box 2.2: The Pareto Principle and the Danger of Unk-Unks

Vilfredo Pareto (1848–1923), an Italian economist, argued that approximately 80 percent of the wealth of a society will always be held by approximately 20 percent of the population. A similar principle can be applied to risk and cost analysis. Consider risks first. The Pareto Principle suggests that 80 percent of the risk comes from 20 percent of the identified loss events. On the cost side, handling the 20 percent of all transactions that are exceptions in any process will require 80 percent of the total process cost. Even for complex processes, the bulk of the costs will come from a handful of possible loss events, perhaps 10–20. The Pareto Principle implies that decreasing loss events by just 5 percent can decrease costs by as much as 20 percent. It also implies that having hundreds of potential loss events is just too complex and ends up being a distraction. *Pareto diagrams* can help us focus on the subset of the identified events that cause the bulk of the risk. An over-reliance on the Pareto Principle has its own dangers, however. So-called *Unk-Unks*, short for unknown unknowns, are events that have not even been considered as a possibility and yet have the potential to invalidate any analysis by occurring, with some devastating impact on the firm.

Aspects of Event Risk

A loss event has several important aspects that should affect how operations managers try to deal with them. These include:

- The likelihood of the event occurring in a particular time period.

- The impact on the firm should the event occur.

- Event criticality—an approximate measure of the event's risk.

- The time structure of the event—precisely how the event unfolds over time.

- Event uncertainty—how well can we predict the various aspects of the event's risk.

Consider each of these in turn.

Likelihood of Future Events   The likelihood, or probability, of an event occurring in the future is very difficult to estimate through either subjective or objective methods. Not only is the future unknowable ex ante, but humans have systematic biases that impede accurate estimations of event likelihood, even when data are present (typically in the form of historical event frequencies). For instance, managers tend to bias their probability estimates according to how easily they can remember an incidence of the event (*availability bias*—Subsection 6.6). This may be a reasonable heuristic if the respondent is the person responsible for dealing with the event and has been with the firm for a long time. But ask a confirmations clerk about the frequency of systems failure and you will receive a very different response from that offered by legal staff who have just completed a client litigation procedure following lost client records. It follows that one way to limit the effect of biases in risk estimation is to make sure that the right people are asked the right questions about risk. As we shall see, the structure of processes and the events and factors that affect them provide important guidelines for structuring the information-gathering process.

The most commonly used proxy for the likelihood of a frequent event is the number of occurrences of the event during some time period—its frequency. In this case:

$$\text{Event likelihood in a future period} = \frac{\text{No. of event occurrences during representative historical time period}}{\text{Length of the historical time period}}$$

This assumes that the future will be like the past—quite reasonable with static processes and systems, but much less so if the process is changing dramatically or new products are being introduced. Organizations, systems, and people, and therefore risks too, change over time. This also assumes that the event is equally likely to occur during the different (but same length) chronological time periods. This may be valid. Sometimes errors are more likely to occur at particular times of the day, week, month, or year. Dig a little deeper and event occurrences can often be redefined in terms of operational time, rather than just chronological time. This can be used to incorporate those causal factors that drive most of the events, such as holidays, staff numbers, trading days, opening hours, machine cycles, transactions, volumes, or batch runs.

For less-frequent events, historical frequencies are less helpful and we must rely on very different approaches, which are either purely subjective (such as scenario analysis) or imply the likelihood based upon our knowledge of the causal relations between events (for example, using fault trees or belief networks).

Box 2.3: Stochastic Models of Loss Events

Operational managers want to know aggregate statistics about the total number of events and the total losses during a particular time period rather than the precise impact and timing of a particular event. To answer questions like this, statisticians and actuaries have developed stochastic *counting models* that tell us the distribution of the cumulative number of events (N) occurring in time period (t). The most commonly used counting model is a *Homogeneous Poisson Process (HPP)*. An event follows an HPP if the times between events are independent and exponentially distributed with a constant failure rate λ. For an HPP, the number of events occurring within any time interval is Poisson distributed with mean λ times the length of the interval. *Renewal processes* are generalizations of the HPP, with arbitrary although independent distributions for the times between events. *Non-homogeneous Poisson Processes* differ from HPP only in that the failure rates vary over time (for this reason they are used with product populations; see the later discussion on Weibull distributions and bathtub curves). Notice that these models make important assumptions about the time it takes to repair the system following a loss event and the stability of the organizational system. In particular, they assume that no major structural changes occur that would alter the likelihood of events or their impacts (i.e., a constant failure rate). For less frequent, high-impact losses, these may not be reasonable assumptions.

For a detailed discussion on counting processes, see Hoyland and Rausand (1994).

Impacts of Events   As well as an event's likelihood, we are concerned with the event's *impact*. Operational loss events may have three general types of financial impact on the firm—their direct, indirect, and opportunity costs.

- Direct costs: Events can cause direct financial losses—either through a reduction in income or a loss in value of the firm's assets and liabilities.

    The impact of specific loss events on income is the marginal costs of handling the event, as well as any fixed costs allocated to the event. Marginal costs are usually quite small in the case of more-frequent events for which staff and systems are already in place (essentially, these costs would have been incurred anyway, irrespective of whether the event occurred or not). For example, settlement failures require additional overtime to handle, or fire damage causes some noninsured expenses. If the event can be prevented over the planning horizon, the "fixed costs" of handling the event, such as budgeted staffing and selling, general, and administrative (SG&A) expenses, should also be allocated to the income losses caused by the event.

    Alternatively, events can directly cause one-time damage to assets (either in terms of the asset's valuation, book or market value, or replacement or firm-specific value) or bring about liability claims and defense costs. In general, the firm-specific costs or, most frequently, the replacement costs are the most appropriate measures of the event's impact. The cost of final products or services that are affected should be valued in terms of their fully allocated unit costs. Impacts should be stated in terms of common units of consequence (perhaps US dollars, or non-currency units such as staff-hours).

- Indirect costs: Events may cause indirect losses as a result of damage to the firm's reputation or downstream effects on other loss events or functions of the firm; for instance, the possibility of counterparty withdrawal following repeated late execution of transactions, regulatory penalties, or staff errors resulting from additional overtime worked. Large indirect losses usually suggest the occurrence of other intervening events that should be investigated in their own right. For example, huge indirect losses associated with settlement failures might suggest investigating client withdrawal in more detail. When possible, it makes sense to strip out indirect losses from an event's direct and opportunity costs, and then use those indirect losses to build a causal analysis of the links between different loss events. Major indirect losses should be a spur to further investigation of other events. Indirect costs are often much greater than direct costs, e.g., in the recent bombing of the World Trade Center in New York, the property loss in a bank's computer center was a mere $100,000, whereas the indirect costs (excluding business interruption) were more than $700,000. One of the most important indirect losses is the result of a loss of reputation. Reputational risk is the risk of significant negative public opinion that results in a critical loss of funding or customers, and can arise in response to actions a bank or insurance company itself takes, or in response to actions of third parties. When made public, direct losses from any operational event can lead to even greater indirect losses if they damage the firm's reputation and, thus, hurt the willingness of creditors (decreased credit lines, higher cost of funding), customers (lower sales), and suppliers (undesirable terms) to deal with the firm. The same event may also lead to greatly increased advertising costs to remedy a well-publicized operational failure. For example, in 1994, a group of Russian computer hackers made $10 million of illegal transfers out of Citibank. All but $400,000 was ultimately recovered, but the indirect losses were much greater than these direct losses. Twenty of its top customers moved their business to other banks, claiming the need for more stringent security. Academic studies of reputation losses (as expressed in the stock price) following a major business catastrophes tend to suggest that almost immediately there is a sharp initial fall of 8 percent in the share price followed by high volatility and a slow recovery in a few months.

- Opportunity costs: These are the maximum potential earnings foregone because of the occurrence of the loss event. They represent a sacrifice on the part of the firm. Opportunity costs include those resources (financial, physical, and human) used to deal with these events that would otherwise have been available for profit opportunities. These can be estimated in terms of the disruption caused to the usual revenue streams generated from the resource (assuming, of course, the status quo is a reasonable benchmark).

Box 2.4: Example — Impact of Late Settlement

What is the impact of a late settlement loss event? Late settlements may lead to counterparty withdrawals, late penalties, regulatory penalties, staff overtime, and staff opportunity costs. Of these, staff-related costs are the only direct costs associated with late settlement. If counterparty withdrawals can be caused by events other than late settlements, it may make sense to have counterparty withdrawals as a separate event with its own direct costs. In that case, including the indirect costs of counterparty withdrawal in late settlement costs would be double-counting.

The impact of loss events should also be estimated net of everything that currently mitigates the risk if that mitigating factor (say, an experienced manager or an effective control system) is not made explicit. For instance, a loss event such as an office fire should be covered by insurance for the replacement value of the asset. The impact of the loss event is therefore net of the presumed insurance payout following the event. The following checklist can be used to verify that all the possible impacts of a particular event have been considered (Table 2.2).

Criticality The simplest measure of an event's risk is its criticality— the product of the likelihood of the event's occurrence in a particular time period and its impact on the firm should the event occur in that time period:

$$\text{Event criticality} = \text{Event likelihood} \times \text{Event impact}$$

The most critical events are those that occur frequently with high impact. Plotting the position of events on the frequency and impact axes can be revealing (Figure 2.2):

TABLE 2.2 Direct, Indirect, and Opportunity Costs

Types of cost		Definition	Examples
Direct Costs	Loss of income	Marginal costs incurred directly as a result of an event occurring	Unbudgeted staff cost for investigation and mitigation, e.g., overtime
			Irrecoverable errors Regulatory penalties
		Fixed costs allocated to the event	Budgeted staffing costs SG&A expenses
	Loss of value	Decrease in the value of assets and increase in the value of liabilities	Physical damage Loss of records Stolen assets Asset loss/write-offs Loss of principal Market exposure
Indirect Costs	*Direct costs of other events caused or made more likely by the event occurring*	Loss of income	Interest costs Legal and litigation costs Increased insurance costs Counterparty/client withdrawal Additional operating costs
		Loss of value	Key staff loss Market share loss
	Other indirect costs		Increased cost of capital Loss of normal cash flow Loss of reputation
Opportunity Costs	*Loss of income Loss of value*		Foregone business opportunities Foregone resources Foregone processes

For further discussion on how to measure event impact, see Subsection 6.5.

FIGURE 2.2 Likelihood versus Impact

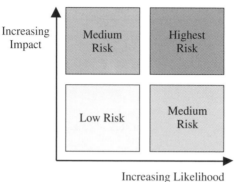

Fortunately, in general, the greater the event's impact, the lower its likelihood, and vice versa. Few events fall in the highest risk category (high frequency and high impact) simply because firms move away from taking on such risks in their operations either by changing business processes or by exiting the industry. It is the two medium risk quadrants that take up most management attention. Events with high likelihood but low impact occupy the attention of efficiency-oriented operations managers. In contrast, events that are less likely but have high impact— such as fraud, counterparty withdrawals, and major systems failures—are the greater source of insolvency risk and are the focus of most efforts to allocate risk capital to cover operational exposures. High-likelihood, low-impact shocks are less a source of insolvency exposure to banks because organizations have the experience and the incentive to price high-frequency shocks properly and to make adequate provisions to serve as a buffer against the losses.

The location of a loss event in Figure 2.2 has other important implications. It means, for instance, that for high-probability events, likelihood reduction—rather than impact reduction—should be the focus of risk management efforts. Similarly, for infrequent but devastating events, risk is most efficiently removed by mitigating the impact rather than reducing still further the likelihood of the event. We will explore the management implications of these ideas in Section III.

FIGURE 2.3 Likelihood versus Impact—Implications

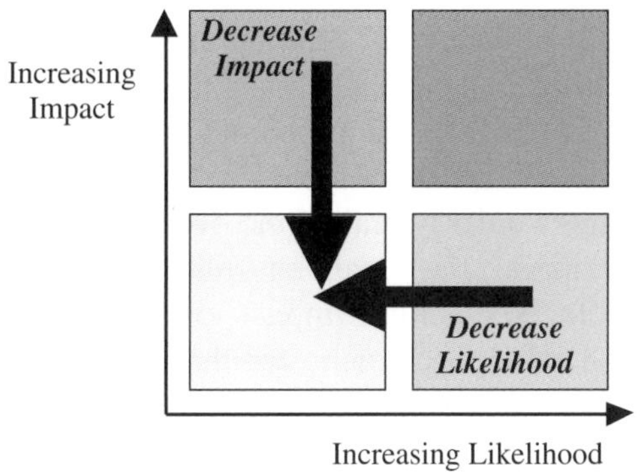

Increasing Impact

Decrease Impact

Decrease Likelihood

Increasing Likelihood

Event Structure For some complex events (sometimes called *incidents*) involving extensive opportunities for human mismanagement, it can be helpful to analyze the detailed structure of the event—precisely how the event unfolds over time. Diagrams such as Figure 2.4 can be used to formalize existing incident reports or case studies of high-impact events to reveal important lessons for managers dealing with similar events in future.

FIGURE 2.4 Analysis of Loss Event Structure

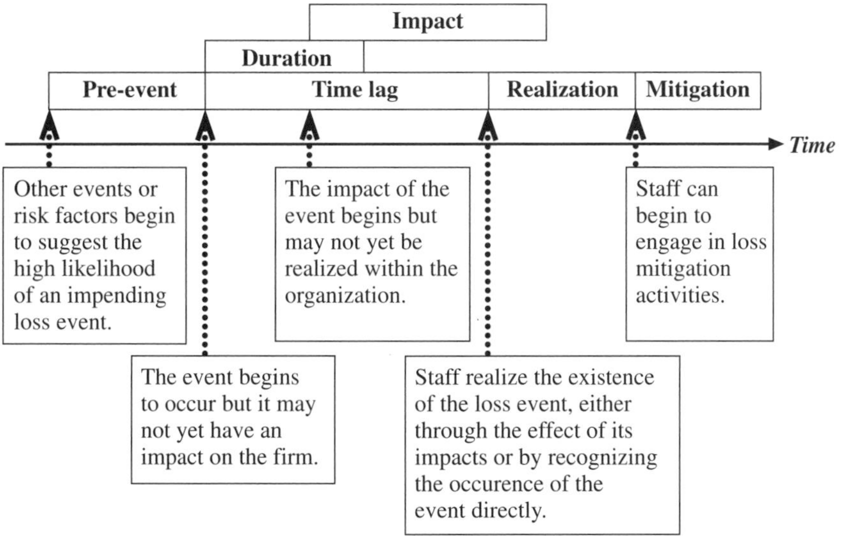

Impact		
Duration		
Pre-event	Time lag	Realization	Mitigation

Time

Other events or risk factors begin to suggest the high likelihood of an impending loss event.

The impact of the event begins but may not yet be realized within the organization.

Staff can begin to engage in loss mitigation activities.

The event begins to occur but it may not yet have an impact on the firm.

Staff realize the existence of the loss event, either through the effect of its impacts or by recognizing the occurence of the event directly.

Making the event structure explicit helps us answer certain key questions for managers. Is it critical to: Predict the event? Minimize the length of the impact of the event? Shorten the time it takes to realize that the event has occurred? Or perhaps lessen the time by which we bring a mitigation strategy to bear on the problem? Different events will require different focus. Some will require advance warnings of events, some will require that managers quickly realize the event has occurred, and others will necessitate bringing the repair and mitigation processes online as quickly as possible. Many high-impact events have a long time lag, which can be especially problematic for those events with impacts that increase the longer they remain undiscovered. A good example of one of these snowballing events would be fraud, which tends to spiral out of control as one fraud is covered up by another and so on. Subsection 8.4 explores these issues in greater detail.

Box 2.5: Example — Daiwa Securities

As a US bond trader at Daiwa Securities in New York, Toshihide Iguchi created a loss of $1 billion by switching funds out of clients' custody accounts. As head of Daiwa's New York bond trading, Iguchi made his first loss back in 1983 and proceeded to cover up his losses by taking on greater bets on the market. He did this by selling securities without clients' authorization and hiding the corresponding trade confirmations. Remarkably, he did this for *nearly 10 years.*

High interest rates, indicating a high time-value of money, are also a source of snowballing losses. Another typical example of such an event might be a model error; its effect might take months to be detected, but it could be producing cumulative losses from mispricing throughout that period. Loss events with a long time-lag usually require an additional external trigger event to make the losses apparent—perhaps an external audit, a recession, or a sudden upward or downward market move.

The time period during which the loss event occurs can also be relevant. The duration and intensity of the event can make significant differences, particularly for power-related events, which are a major cause of systems-related failures. For example, a power overvoltage or undervoltage of 10 percent would have no effect on electronic typewriters but could be devastating to desktop computers. A three-second break in voice transmissions might be annoying, but a loss of communication for a fraction of a second can result in corrupt data transmission. Similarly, a 50 percent drop in the power supply lasting 20 microseconds may have little effect, but a 20 percent drop in power for a half-hour can be devastating. In contrast, a split-second interruption or a lightening surge to the power supply can be lethal to computers or set off a fire alarm.

Uncertainty   The probability distributions of both frequency and impacts, and therefore of risk, are known only imprecisely. In other words, they are subject to uncertainty beyond any objective risks. For more frequent events, we can generally produce more accurate risk estimates. For instance, we have a good idea how often a confirmation failure will occur (a few times in a day) or what the loss will be in the event of fire damaging a particular building (perhaps a few million dollars). Less frequent events are much more insidious; by definition, these are events for which firms have little or no experience (for example, a terrorist attack). Our only guides in this case are external data and the fallible experience of experts close to the problem. Even here, there are ways to use the formal probabilistic framework to guide decision-making and actions in a systematic manner. One way to handle uncertainty uses sensitivity analysis, and should be used with any risk estimate. It asks the question: What would be the effect on our decision-making if we have made major errors in our distributional assumptions?

However, a lack of certainty does not make the effort of operational risk management irrelevant. *Prioritization,* not precision, is the objective, particularly for efficiency-minded operations managers. In almost every case, ballpark estimates of likelihood and impact can be produced. The difference between a likelihood of 1E-3 (on event that occurs once in 1,000 opportunities) and 1E-1 (an event that occurs once in 10 opportunities) is profound and an important one to capture. Will the impact be a million dollars or a few hundred? As we will show, estimates can always be produced, and even when this is difficult—for instance, for the impact of infrequent events—a range of possible outcomes can be suggested.

Box 2.6: Integrating Imprecise Estimates of Events' Likelihood and Impact

A firm may produce the following estimates of risk for some certain well-defined loss events.

Table 2.3 Frequency and Impact Data of Various Operational Events

	Frequency/Day			Impact/Occurrence		
	Minimum	Likely	Maximum	Minimum	Likely	Maximum
Trade-entry error	35	60	90	10	50	10,000
Missing trades	1	5	10	15	100	20,000
Unfunded position	0.01	0.04	0.17	500	12,000	2,000,000
Incorrect payment	0.03	0.12	0.37	500	10,000	150,000
Minor fraud	0.004	0.012	0.04	0	10,000	100,000
Major fraud	0.0004	0.001	0.004	100,000	1,000,000	10,000,000
Major fire	0.00008	0.0004	0.0008	2,000,000	3,000,000	12,000,000

One relatively simple way to organize a number of these events uses the following likelihood/impact table. As we shall see later, assuming shape (e.g., triangular) distributions for these events provides a quick and actionable basis for operational risk assessment and analysis.

FIGURE **2.5** Multiple Loss Events

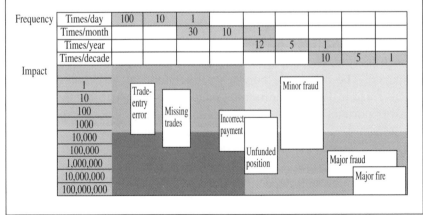

2.4   RISK FACTORS

Not all risks are the result of discrete operational loss events. Unlike loss events, continuous risk factors have a long history of use in safety analysis (where they are called hazards), in finance (where market factors are extensively used for pricing and estimating portfolio risks), and in sales (where factors are used to predict volumes and capacity requirements). To specify a risk factor requires three basic elements, namely:

• The factor's *probability distribution* during a defined time period.

• The factor's *direct impacts* on the target variables such as cash flows, net income, or asset values.

• The factor's *indirect impacts* on the frequency or mean impact of loss events during some time period.

Probability Distribution

Risk factors with values that change over time can be said to follow a *stochastic process*. These are usually either discrete time or continuous time processes; a discrete time process only allows the variable to change at specific fixed points in time, whereas a continuous time process can change at any time. For most risk factors, the simpler discrete models are sufficient; however, for rapidly changing factors with good data, continuous processes provide a better model. For instance, while inventory changes are best understood as a discrete process, market prices are often modeled as a continuous stochastic process. Subsection 7.1 discusses some of the models used to simulate, predict, and control the evolution of risk factors over time. These include simple models based on trend analysis and exponential smoothing techniques used to identify general trends (such as linear trends or seasonality) in risk factors. Alternatively, more sophisticated Box-Jenkins (ARIMA) models, GARCH, or neural network modeling techniques can be used to understand the time series structure if both sufficient and reliable data is available.

Direct Impact

Risk factors can have direct impacts on a firm's cash flow, net income, and, ultimately, value. The most important risk factors are usually external to the firm and therefore cannot be managed by internal risk prevention or mitigation. However, if the firm has operational flexibility, it can change its business exposures (say by adjusting its production to reflect changes in demand) and reduce its sensitivity to the external risk factor. More commonly, financial risk management and insurance are used to mitigate risk factors' direct impacts. These direct impacts affect the value of the firm through the income statement or the balance sheet. For example, external risk factors—such as the market prices of the firm's product and service outputs, the cost of its inputs, or the costs of processing—directly affect P&L. Business strategy models, such as Michael Porter's often-used Five Forces Model (Porter, 1980), suggest a whole array of would-be risk factors that can affect P&L. The more easily quantified include interest rates, which affect a bank's revenues through the net duration of the assets and liabilities by altering the terms of credit or by changing the customers' demand for the firm's products. The general level of the economy, as measured by a broad market equity index, may also be a determinant of demand and therefore company profits, particularly in consumer markets. Competitive risk factors (typically measured by indexes of selected competitor equities) also may determine the intensity of competition and, therefore, the profitability of a business. On the balance sheet, for example, lending and deposits are affected by interest rates; market portfolios (both on and off the balance sheet) are affected by various market rates' risk factors (Box 2.7).

Box 2.7: Factor Models Such As CAPM and APT

A large part of the theory of investment finance is based on developing models of direct risk factors. The Capital Asset Pricing Model (CAPM), for instance, suggests that shareholders' market returns depend only on the sensitivity (or beta) to a value-weighted market index. Arbitrage pricing models use techniques such as multiple regression, factor models, principal components analysis, and other data-mining techniques to incorporate additional factors such as the commodity prices, and market and macroeconomic indicators. Consider, for instance, the following analysis of the drivers of returns at Shell Transport drawn from 1987–1996 (Bickerstaffe, 1998).

TABLE **2.4:** Risk Factors at Shell

Capital Asset Pricing Model (One-factor CAPM)		Arbitrage Pricing Theory Model (Multifactor APT)	
Unexplained event and factor risk	45%	Unexplained event and factor risk	39%
Market risk	55%	Exchange rate	1%
		Industrial production	1%
		Inflation	2%
		Term structure	5%
		Oil	6%
		Market risk	46%
Total	**100%**		**100%**

If we assume that the residual unexplained variance is a measure of the business' operational risk, then factor models of return due to the direct impacts of risk factors can always be used independently of any further analysis as guides to the operational risk in any publicly traded business unit. Although a useful first step in any analysis, and essential for a systematic model of the discount factors used in pricing internal projects, these high-level factor models suffer from an important limitation—they provide no guidance to operational managers. See Chapter 3 for more details.

Indirect Impact

Risk factors may also indirectly affect other risk factors or loss events. For example, an increase in the risk factor "staff turnover" may drive the incidence of fraud; falls in political risk indices may increase the possibility of expropriation (i.e., the seizure of assets by foreign governments); or the level of environmental litigation paid out in the industry may be an indicator of a firm's legal liabilities. Using risk factors as drivers of event frequency, the event's mean impact during a time period, and, therefore, aggregate event losses helps focus attention on shared risks that otherwise would be ignored. Factors' indirect impacts are just a one example of possible dependencies between risk factors and loss events and are discussed in more detail in subsections 2.8 and 7.4.

Other Issues

To understand risk factors and prevent developing a model with too many factors, there are several important points that analysts should keep in mind:

- Changes in factors must directly make a significant difference to the cash flows, P&L, and asset and liability values, or indirectly affect the aggregate impact of loss events. If the factor is unlikely to change during the decision horizon, there is no need to explicitly model the factor.

- Risk factors differ from loss events because risk factors represent ongoing states or conditions.

- Factors may be intrinsic to particular products or processes, or extrinsic to the firm as part of its broader competitive environment.

- Factors should never be entirely under the control of business managers, i.e., there is a random component of the factor. Although there are many levers that managers can pull that influence cash flows, P&L, asset and liability values, and loss events (see Section III, in particular Chapter 9), these are not so much risk factors as decision variables. Management levers are usually relatively stable over time and, as a result, are best modeled as what-if scenarios rather than ongoing risk factors. The key issues are choice of decision variable and whether managers are willing to allocate further resources to changing this variable. Examples of these levers include the quality levels of key organizational resources such as staff, systems, policies, and procedures.

To summarize, understanding and making explicit the direct and indirect impacts of risk factors is important because they more or less correspond to a range of operational objectives and techniques.

TABLE 2.5 External and Internal Risk Factors

	Different Effects		
	External	**External/Internal**	**Internal**
Impacts	Direct impacts on P&L and asset values		Indirect impacts (by increasing the likelihood of loss events)
Ease of change	Changeable only in the long term		Changeable in the short term
Stakeholder focus	Investor focus	Senior managers' focus	Operational managers' focus
Strategic objectives	Capital management	Growth	Efficiency
Typical targets	Sensitivity to the risk factor	Variance of the risk factor	Level of risk factor
Techniques	Risk transfer Risk mitigation	Risk control	Loss prevention
Examples	Output and input prices Market levels Interest rates Commodity rates	Revenues Scale Volumes Complexity Change Complacency	Staffing levels Amount of overtime Number of temporary staff Training levels Quality of staff Quality of other resources Quality of processes

2.5 AGGREGATE, EXPECTED, AND UNEXPECTED LOSSES

The Basle Committee's *1994 Risk Management Guidelines* (Vol. 16) adopted a definition that has been used by a number of banks, which holds that operational risk is: "risk that deficiencies in information systems or internal controls will result in *unexpected* loss." The distinction between expected and unexpected losses is important, and we will consider it in more detail in this subsection.

Aggregate Loss

If the data are available, they are often useful to decompose this distribution of aggregate losses into separate distributions of event frequencies and event impacts. There are several reasons to do this. First, it is generally easier to estimate frequency distributions and impact distributions separately. Second, actuaries have a great deal of experience in the appropriate models to use for event frequencies. These have been validated with extensive, usually insurance-based, loss data. Finally, separating the frequency analysis from that of impact makes it easier to evaluate the many control interventions that tend to either reduce frequency or decrease impact, but less often, both.

Given a distribution of the frequencies ($\tilde{N}$) and impacts ($\tilde{I}$), the aggregate or cumulative loss (L) at time t is:

$$L(t) = \sum_{i=1}^{\tilde{N}_{(t)}} \tilde{I}_i$$

where i = a paticular event occurrence.

In this case, $L(t)$ is said to follow a *compound process*. Actuarial studies provide extensive literature on the distribution of the aggregate loss amount (see Rolski et al., Chapter 4 for a review). While different events have different characteristic distributions for the aggregate loss in some time period, most tend to look something like the following sharply skewed distribution, with very limited potential upside and many low-impact losses, but with the small possibility of a few very large losses (Figure 2.6).

FIGURE 2.6 A Typical Aggregate Loss Distribution

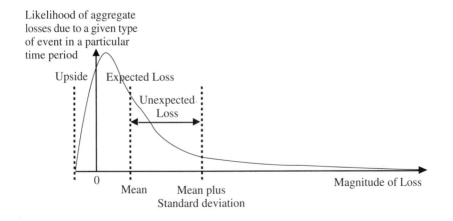

If we make some strong assumptions about the distributions of impacts and the frequencies, we can make some quantitative statements about the aggregate loss (see the sections on Expected Loss and Unexpected Loss). For some special cases of compound processes, we can even estimate the aggregate distribution function of cash flows in the period. In general, however, these do not produce closed-form formulas for the distribution, and the mathematics is complex and therefore difficult to justify, particularly given the paucity of data in most operational risk applications. In this book, we have focused on conceptually simpler simulation models to estimate the aggregate loss distribution (see Chapter 8).

Expected Loss

This is the mean loss resulting from a particular loss event that a firm anticipates for the next time period. Expected losses are the mean of the aggregate loss distribution for the event. For very infrequent events, i.e., those that are extremely unlikely to occur more than once in a given time period, expected losses are:

$$\text{Expected loss} = \sum_{\text{event i}} \text{Loss}_i \times \text{Likelihood of Loss}_i$$

For more frequent events, expected losses $E(L)$ depend on the form of the probability distribution $p(L)$ for the event frequencies and impacts; and in the continuous limit can be written as:

$$E(L) = \int_{-\infty}^{\infty} L\, p(L)\, dL$$

However, some general results have been found e.g., if the number of event occurrences in a time period and the individual event impacts are independent and identically distributed random variables, then it can be proven (a statistical result known as Wald's Equation—see Rolski, page 101 for a proof) that the mean of the aggregate loss is the product of the mean frequency $E(N)$ and the mean impact $E(I)$:

$$E(L) = E(N)\, E(I)$$

This essentially states that the event's criticality is a good measure of the event's expected loss. For example, if N has a Poisson distribution, in which case $E(N) = \lambda t$, and $Var(N) = \lambda t$, then the expected loss is:

$$E(L) = \lambda t\, E(I)$$

The assumptions of Wald's Equation often do not hold. Some errors, particularly fraud, "save up" their impact over time, which means that if the event is not caught early, the impact is likely to increase over time. Hence, event frequencies may be negatively correlated with event impacts. Also, different events' frequencies may be correlated with each other because of common risk factors or similar causal drivers, again invalidating the result.

Box 2.8: Provisioning Expected Losses

By definition, management expects these losses to occur and accepts them as a part of being in business. For instance, it expects a certain amount of money will be lost from failed settlements, bad loans, or failed confirmations within a particular time period. These losses should be explicitly budgeted for and formal loss provisions constructed. Consequently, expected losses are covered by the firm's ongoing revenues and theoretically, should not require additional risk management. Of course, the use of formal provisions to cover expected losses assumes that the firm has data from which to estimate the expected losses. In other words, for very infrequent events such as natural disasters or major frauds, no formal loss provisions are likely to have been set up because the firm has no evidence of the need. (See Subsection 16.1 for a further discussion).

Unexpected Loss

Expected losses tell us little about the range of possible losses or the *unexpected loss*. This range is often measured by the standard deviation of the distribution (sometimes a multiple of standard deviation is used and, assuming a particular distribution, converted into an estimate of

VaR). For infrequent events, we can use the following formula to estimate the unexpected loss over a number of possible outcomes *(i)*:

$$\begin{matrix} \text{Unexpected} \\ \text{loss} \end{matrix} = \sqrt{\sum_{\text{event i}} \text{Likelihood of Loss}_i \times (\text{Loss}_i - \text{Expected Loss})^2}$$

or its continuous equivalent:

$$\text{Unexpected loss} = \sqrt{\int_{-\infty}^{\infty} [L - E(L)]^2 p(L)dL}$$

As with expected losses, if we assume the number of occurrences (N) of the event in a time period, and the individual event impacts (I) are independent and identically distributed random variables, and the appropriate moments exist, then:

$$\text{Unexpected loss} = \sqrt{\sigma^2[N](E[I])^2 + E[N]\sigma^2[I]}$$

This is just another application of Wald's Equation.

For example, if N has a Poisson distribution, in which case $E[N] = \lambda t$ and $\sigma^2[N] = \lambda t$, then:

$$\text{Unexpected loss} = \sqrt{\lambda t (E[I]^2 + \sigma^2[I]}$$

For more general compound processes, there is no such closed-form solution for unexpected losses, and so we must rely on Monte Carlo simulation techniques to capture the complexity of real-world losses. Nonetheless, Wald's Equation implies some useful rules of thumb:

• The greater the expected loss, the greater the unexpected losses.

• Higher frequency events have higher (although marginally decreasing) unexpected losses.

Box 2.9: Example — Calculating Expected and Unexpected Losses

In a retail bank, amended transactions can be a significant cause of operational losses. Let's assume that the following weekly losses related to amended transactions have occurred during the last year.

FIGURE 2.7 Weekly Losses Due to Amended Transactions

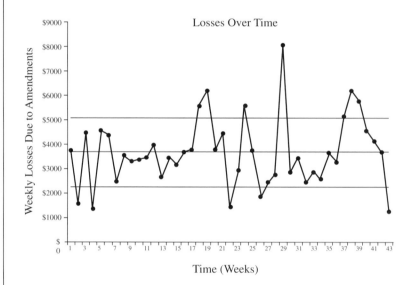

From the losses over time, we can produce the frequency distribution of the weekly amend-related losses (see Chapter 7 for further information). The moments of the sample distribution produce the expected weekly losses of $3,800 and unexpected weekly losses of $1,300.

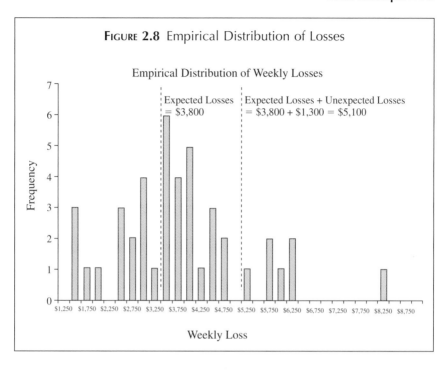

FIGURE 2.8 Empirical Distribution of Losses

2.6 CATASTROPHIC LOSSES

The real nightmares facing bank directors and senior executives are not the expected or unexpected losses for which risk management (in all its forms) provides some level of protection. Like regulators, senior managers face their biggest concerns from catastrophic losses that threaten the viability of the company. These typically involve rogue trading, insider fraud, bad lending, poorly understood derivatives, poorly rolled out new products, inadequate controls in emerging markets, counterparty failures, natural disasters, or snowballing reputational losses. Catastrophic losses imperil the business: 40 percent of organizations that suffer a major disaster go out of business within one year. Forty-three percent of organizations that suffer a major disaster never reopen, and a further 29 percent go under within two years.

Box 2.10: Banking Banana Skins

Research by the London Centre for the Study of Financial Innovation in 1997 asked banking practitioners to rank the key "banking banana skins." This was their top 10:

1. Poor management
2. EMU-related turbulence
3. Rogue traders
4. Excessive competition
5. Bad lending
6. Derivatives
7. Fraud
8. Emerging markets
9. New products
10. Technology "snafus"

The Tails of the Aggregate Loss Distribution

Although the frequency of catastrophic events is low, their impact can be devastating. For catastrophic losses, managers have to look beyond the body of the outcome distribution and toward the tail of the distribution. This usually means at least 99 percent of the possible outcomes (three standard deviations of a normal distribution).

FIGURE 2.9 Catastrophic Loss

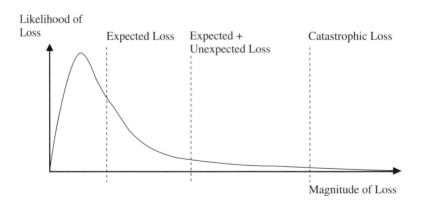

Box 2.11: The True Meaning of Catastrophic Losses

The precise percentile chosen for measures of catastrophic loss depends on the importance of the loss. It is worth remembering that getting it right 99.9 percent of the time sounds acceptable, but would lead to:

- 1 hour of unsafe drinking water per month

- 2 unsafe landings at O'Hare airport every day

- 16,000 pieces of lost mail

- 20,000 incorrect drug prescriptions each year

- 50 newborn babies dropped at birth each day

- 22,000 checks deducted from the wrong account each hour

- 32,000 skipped heartbeats each year

Measuring Catastrophic Risk

Quantitative techniques such as VaR and Extreme Value Theory (EVT), and qualitative techniques such as stress testing and scenario analysis have been used to measure catastrophic risks. The maximum probable loss, or VaR (see Box 1.14 in Subsection 1.6), is often used to estimate the catastrophic losses. VaR is defined as the amount or loss that is expected, not to be exceeded in more than some large percentage (say, 95 percent or 99 percent) of the time. Parametric VaR models can then estimate extreme percentiles assuming a specific distribution (usually normal) and given specific moments of that distribution (usually the standard deviation). Problematic even for market risk, parametric VaR is particularly questionable for operational risks because of its very non-normal probability distributions. Simulation-based VaR models make no such distributional assumptions. They simulate and rank-order the possible losses and count the loss associated with the worst five percent or one percent of outcomes.

Quantitative measures of catastrophic risk are based on extreme percentiles of return. Unfortunately, at these extremes we have very few observations with which to accurately estimate these distributions. Extreme value approaches leverage existing data to fit the extreme tails rather than the body of the distribution.

Box 2.12: Extreme Value Theory

Rather than model the general distribution of losses, EVT tries to fit the distribution of *maximum* losses in some time period. EVT is appropriate for catastrophic, high-impact, low-frequency tail events, when the maximum is likely to be much larger than most of the other observations. In this case, the loss distributions will be extremely skewed and poorly fitted by most parametric distributions.

The Extreme Value Theorem argues that subject to a number of conditions, the distribution of extreme values x converges asymptotically independent of the underlying parent distribution to:

$$H_{\xi,\mu,\sigma}(x) = \exp(-[1 + \xi(x - \mu)/\sigma]^{-1/\xi}) \text{ if } \xi \neq 0$$

$$H_{\xi,\mu,\sigma}(x) = \exp(-e^{(x - \mu)/\sigma}) \text{ otherwise}$$

The *generalized extreme value distribution* combines three commonly used distributions—Frechet, Gumbel, and Weibull—into a single distribution. If $\xi > 0$, this results in the Frechet distribution. If $\xi < 0$ we have the Weibull, and if $\xi \to 0$, we have the Gumbel distribution (see Chapter 7 for further discussion of these distributions). μ and σ are the usual mean and standard deviation of the distribution while ξ—the tail index—is a measure of the heaviness of tails. Estimating the parameters of these distributions proceeds as follows:

Let X_1, X_2, X_3,...X_n be the losses associated with a particular business area or process. $X_{1,n}$ denotes the maximum loss, $X_{2,n}$ the second largest, and so on. EVT aims to estimate a distribution for the maximum, $y = X_{1,n}$. The tail index is usually estimated using the Hill estimator—the difference between the kth largest observation and the average of the k largest observations.

$$\xi_{n,k} = \frac{1}{k}\sum_{j=1}^{k}\log_e X_{j,n} - \log_e X_{k,n}$$

where $X_{j,n}$ is the largest observation in a block j of n observations
k is the tail threshold.

Given an estimate of ξ, we can produce an estimate of the value associated with any percentile, for instance, by extrapolating an in-sample percentile $X_{k,n}$ using the formula:

$$[(n(1 - p)/(k - 1)]^{-\xi}X_{k,n}$$

Alternatively, using the estimates of the parameters we produce:

$$x_p = \hat{\mu} - \frac{\hat{\sigma}}{\hat{\xi}}[1 - (-\log_e p)^{-\hat{\xi}}]$$

One challenge of EVT is its complexity, which makes the approach opaque to end-users of the results. It is also difficult to produce good estimates of the reliability of the model in certain circumstances. For further information, see Cruz (1998), McNeil (1998), Embrechts (1997), and Dowd (1998).

The lack of data regarding infrequent events makes fitting any quantitative model to the extreme reaches of the distribution very difficult. Instead, many businesses focus on qualitative techniques such as scenario analysis and stress testing to test the implications of massive failure (see Chapter 3).

Inevitably, either external industry data or subjective expert opinions must be leveraged (see Chapter 6) because no individual firm will have objective experience of many catastrophic losses. Of course, these have their own dangers. External data might not be relevant to the idiosyncratic circumstances of a particular set of operations. There may also be some biases in external data; for instance, some major losses may not be made public, leading to data censorship. Subjective opinion is also rife with a number of individual and group-related biases.

Managing Catastrophic Risks

One obvious protection against catastrophic losses is the firm's capital. Without a capital buffer, losses, other than those expected, would cause a bank to fail. Additional capital covers unexpected losses and also, in extreme cases, catastrophic losses up to some threshold. The final protection against disaster is provided by its debt holders and its deposit holders. Consequently, the firm's credit rating offers an approximate measure of the default rate and therefore the capital that should be made available to cover catastrophic losses.

Figure 2.10 Managing Catastrophic Loss

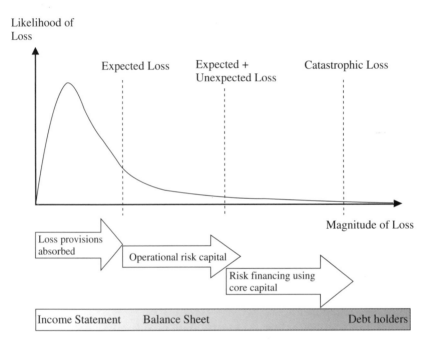

Box 2.13: Example — Lloyds of London

Lloyds is an association of more than 7,000 insurance underwriters specializing in a wide range of insurance offerings such as marine, motor, and civil aviation. On June 25, 1992, Lloyds faced a loss of $3.82 million on policies written in 1989. This followed a loss of $944.8 million in 1988. There were several major disasters in 1988 such as the Exxon oil spill, Hurricane Hugo, and the San Francisco earthquake, but most argue that Lloyds' problems were the result of inadequate provisions and insufficient risk capital to cover these potentially catastrophic losses.

Given the expense of risk capital, other types of risk financing techniques can be used to limit catastrophic losses (see Chapter 14). At the micro level of specific losses, insurance, collateral, third-party guarantees, covenants, asset securitization, and direct loan sales provide some protection from catastrophic losses. At the aggregate level of the firm, one can use external insurance, captive insurance, catastrophe options, and credit and liquidity lines to keep the firm afloat should the nightmare become real. Because most catastrophic losses also have an operational element, contingency planning and public relations can play a vital role in keeping the firm viable in the crucial few days after a catastrophic loss.

Box 2.14: Financial Proxies for Operational Risk

Sometimes it is possible to use the financial markets to provide proxies for the valuation of specific assets with identifiable cash flow. Forward markets and options provide pricing for many elements of financial risk. There is also a growing number of hybrid securities and bonds such as catastrophe bonds, Y2K bonds and options, and energy futures that may soon be used to produce a market-derived price for operational risk. Alternatively, subordinated debt can also be used as a proxy for the level of a firm's operational risk.

2.7 EVENT/FACTOR CONTROLLABILITY

Loss events and risk factors vary according to the degree to which they can be controlled by a particular business unit. *Controllability* denotes the ability of a particular organizational unit to prevent (i.e., decrease the frequency) or mitigate the loss (i.e., decrease the impact) associated with the specific event or factor during a given time period. Of course, just because a risk can be controlled does not mean that it is cost-effective to do so. Almost all risks are controllable over a sufficiently long period, and therefore a controllable risk implicitly assumes a particular time period during which risk prevention or mitigation can take effect. This period is usually the budget period or short-term planning horizon of the firm.

A lack of control over a particular factor or event implies nothing about our ability to transfer or finance the risk associated with the factor or event. Risk transfer and risk financing do not change the event or risk factor, rather they transfer or offset the risks to limit the effect of the event or factor on the organization.

When we say a risk factor or event is controllable, it can help to estimate the extent to which it can be controlled and precisely who in the organization can control it. An assessment of an event's degree of controllability can either be a ranking or a measure of the extent to which the aggregate expected or unexpected loss can be removed. Notice too that the business area able to control the risk is rarely the same area affected by the event.

FIGURE 2.11 Event Controls and Impact

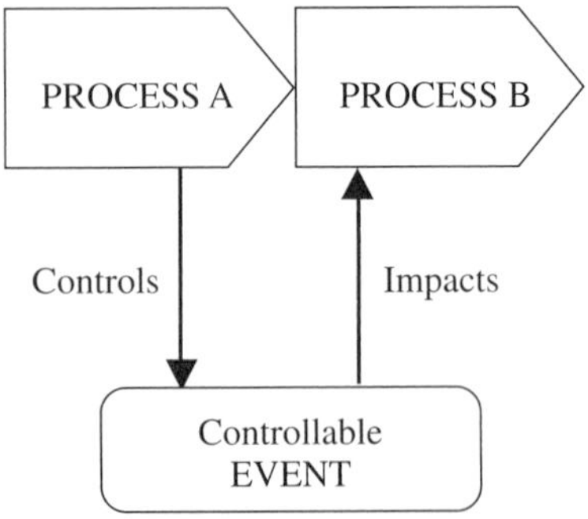

Moral hazard can be a major problem whenever the controller of the risk does not bear the impact associated with the risk and therefore fails to take necessary actions to control it. Risks are moved around the firm both horizontally and vertically. Risk in one business area is frequently passed horizontally to another; for instance, customer risks may be passed on to back-office operations but are largely under the control of sales and marketing. Risk is moved around vertically too. Often a risk factor cannot be controlled at one level of the firm but it can be controlled at a higher level. For instance, regulatory risks may be inevitable should a firm choose to enter a heavily regulated business such as retail banking, but the firm's managers (theoretically at least) could choose to take the firm out of that business. By contrast, some low-level operational risks can only be controlled by frontline staff despite the dictums of senior management.

To prevent moral hazard within the organization, it is helpful to explicitly tag events according to the locus of control and the business resources or processes in which the events' impacts are realized. Separating events, factors, and hence risks into controllable and uncontrollable categories also helps ensure that the unit most able to control the risk takes responsibility for it either in the form of allocated risk capital or reporting responsibility. As we shall see in Section III, the distinction between controllable and uncontrollable risks also determines the range of prevention and repair responses available to the firm.

Controllable Events

Controllable events usually involve a problem with internal processes or resources. Managing controllable events usually requires focusing on decreasing the event frequency rather than mitigating event impacts. For controllable events, priority should be given to redesign and ongoing maintenance of the system to improve flexibility and responsiveness to failure rather than simply to fix things when they are broken. Risk transfer is rarely viable for managing controllable risks because of the implicit morale hazard—the danger that having transferred the risk, the managers who control the risk are then tempted to limit their risk prevention and mitigation activities.

Uncontrollable Events

These are usually external to the processes and resources that make up the organization. Examples include acts of God, political turmoil, market and financial risks, or power outages. By definition, uncontrollable events cannot be controlled by any business unit through loss prevention or mitigation. However, these events can be managed by:

- Risk financing: E.g., accepting the risk of the event and putting aside extra capital to cover the risk.

- Risk transfer: Passing the risk to an external party that is better able to handle the risk through hedging or insurance.

- Business exit: Limiting the risky activities or, in the extreme case, leaving the business that gives rise to the risk.

Risk financing is appropriate when the firm has some special knowledge about the risk that outside parties do not have. If there is a party outside the firm that has a competitive advantage in managing the risk, the firm should try to transfer the risk to that party. If the risk is unacceptable and risk transfer is not a viable alternative, then the firm has no choice but to exit the business that leads to the risk.

Partially Controllable Events

Of course, events are rarely completely controllable or completely uncontrollable. Much more common is that they lie on a continuum between these two extremes. Some factors/events are only controllable over years rather than months. These "influenceable" or partially controllable events or factors are partially under business control and often result from previous decisions (such as long-term or fixed-cost expenditures or the existing product line). Examples of partially controllable risk factors and events include the complexity of developing the product or service (including retail operations), infrastructure development, existing operation size, constraints imposed by the financial product life cycle, research and development (R&D) investments, level of automated processing, or related internal loss events such as key personnel risk or fraud. What many partially controllable risks have in common is that they result from management's limited flexibility to respond to changing environmental conditions. In particular, while firms may not be able to prevent the loss event from occurring, they may be able to limit the firm's sensitivity to that event. For instance, for some very large European universal banks, changes in industry regulatory requirements such as BIS and European Capital Adequacy Directive (ECAD) are influenceable because the banks can take action to decrease the probability (e.g., through regulatory lobbying) or the impact of the event (e.g., by making sure systems are changeable), but the event itself is largely outside management's control. Alternatively, management may be able to limit the indirect impacts of events through contingency planning and reputation management.

The Need to Understand Control

Responsibility should be to always focus on control—where the risks can be controlled is where the responsibility should lie. Although not all risks can be controlled, someone must take responsibility for managing every risk, whether controllable or uncontrollable, internal or external. Identifying the controlling agents for particular risks helps allocate the responsibilities for those events. If the risks cannot be controlled, then either the risk is diversifiable or it is not. If diversifiable (e.g., insurable risks), then the risk should be accepted as part of the staff function responsible for transferring the risk to some external party. If it is not diversifiable, the risk must be accepted as part of doing business and therefore passed to shareholders. Agreement on the responsibility for events helps price the risks and direct organizational resources to better manage them. Making an explicit mapping of loss events' and risk factors' controls and impacts also lifts the problem to a higher management level where it can be dealt with more rationally and therefore more effectively.

TABLE 2.6 Examples of Controllable, Uncontrollable, and Partially Controllable Risk Factors and Loss Events

Controllable	Partial	Uncontrollable
Product development	Operating leverage	Market volatility
Processing speed	Loss of key staff	Economic performance
Number and variety of distribution channels	Product complexity Infrastructure	Competitive position Regulation
Volume and diversity of business	development Operation size	Customer demand Natural disasters
Risk policies	Level of	Power outages
Process errors	automated processing	
Quality of customer service		

Box 2.15: Diversification and Controllability

Another lens with which to evaluate uncontrollable risks is the extent to which shareholders can diversify away the risk by holding a broad portfolio of securities. This suggests that uncontrollable risks subdivide further into *diversifiable* and *non-diversifiable* risks. One commonly used pricing model, the Capital Asset Pricing Model (CAPM), suggests that investors do not obtain any added value from firms managing diversifiable risks because these can usually be managed more cheaply by the shareholders themselves. From the manager's perspective, however, diversifiable risks can be managed by risk financing and risk transfer, whereas non-diversifiable risks can only be managed by leaving the business. Again, from the manager's perspective, responsibility for uncontrollable diversifiable risks should be allocated to the appropriate staff function (usually risk management or treasury). In contrast, uncontrollable non-diversifiable risks should solely be the responsibility of senior managers whose beta-weighted performance is evaluated by stockholders in terms of renewed contracts, stock options, etc. After all, senior executives willingly take on uncontrollable non-diversifiable risks to create competitive advantage and increase returns to their stakeholders.

2.8   DEPENDENCIES BETWEEN RISK FACTORS AND EVENTS

We have already seen the importance of analyzing the indirect impacts of loss events and risk factors, which may be other events and risk factors. We will now formalize this by analyzing the dependencies between different risk factors and events.

Independence

The easiest way to handle dependencies between different risk factors and events is simply to ignore them and assume risk factors and events are independent. This massively simplifies our analysis of aggregate risks. Expected losses of different events, for instance, then add linearly:

$$E(L_1 + L_2) = E(L_1) + E(L_2)$$

The assumption of independence is appropriate if the data suggests no correlation, and operations managers cannot make a strong case for a logical link between the risk factors and events. If we go further and make the additional, rather heroic, assumption that aggregate losses are normally distributed or exist in large enough samples such that no single loss has a major effect, then the unexpected loss of a number of events is just the square root of the sum of the squares of the events' unexpected losses, i.e.,

$$\sigma^2[L_1 + L_2] = \sigma^2[L_1] + \sigma^2[L_2]$$

Dependencies

In practice, dependencies between risk factors and events abound. Errors tend to lead to other errors; for instance, data-feed errors can lead to market exposure, hedging errors, settlement errors, and reporting errors. Error rates are also correlated with staff turnover as well as staff experience and capacity. Some problems are more common in certain circumstances, such as particular offices, particular staff members, particular types of transactions, or high-volume periods. Mathematically, this means that events and risk factors may be *interdependent*. Dependencies are usually revealed in four ways:

- Dependencies between different risk factors, e.g., correlation between market risk factors.

- Dependencies between event frequency in a time period and the mean level of a risk factor in the same time period, e.g., between errors and extent of overtime, staff turnover and bonus levels.

- Dependencies between the mean impact per event in a time period and the mean level of a risk factor in the same time period, e.g., insurance payouts for flood damage and rainfall levels.

- Dependencies involving causal relations between different events, e.g., a corrupted database may cause lost customer records, which in turn may lead to lost sales opportunities.

FIGURE 2.12 Causation and Correlation-based Dependencies

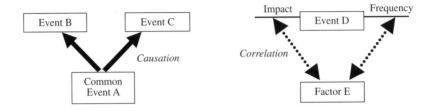

Generally, however, any event attribute (impact, frequency, times to occurrence, time lag) may be dependent on another attribute of an event or a risk factor. Risk factors and events can quickly form a complex hierarchy of dependencies made up of their many indirect impacts.

FIGURE 2.13 Hierarchy of Dependencies

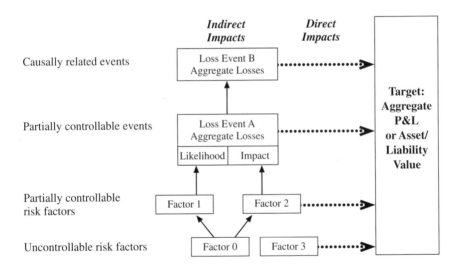

When Dependencies Are Needed

Analyzing dependencies is useful in several circumstances. These include:

- When there is some significant event or risk factor that is dependent on another risk factor that is easier to estimate, usually because better quality data is available for the second factor. Given the dependency and the independent factor or event, we can estimate the dependent event/factor.

- When the dependent factor or event is not as easily controlled as the independent factor or event. In this case, understanding the dependency reveals the implications of any risk management intervention.

- When we wish to allocate the risks associated with the dependent event to different business units. The dependency can help in structuring the transfer pricing of risks to different business units.

- When managers wish to manage the causes of specific events rather than just their symptoms. In this case, dependency models (particularly causal models) help managers rapidly determine the likely causes of an event and what preventative actions to take.

- When managers are concerned about overhedging. Dependency models can reveal natural hedges, e.g., a recession may decrease the demand for particular products but it may also decrease the costs of funding and other basic input costs.

- When dependent risk factors are very likely to change over the decision horizon.

Dangers of Dependencies

There is always the danger of developing an expensive and overly complex dependency model that actually obscures analysis and management decision-making. A dependency must be justified by data or by prior logic. Without this, models will be difficult to explain and justify to end-users in the various business areas. In all cases, incorporating the dependency must make a significant difference to the analysis. An easy way to check this is to at first assume an extreme simplistic relation to test the magnitude of the dependency's effect. If insignificant, the dependency should be removed.

Box 2.16 Dependencies, Interactive Complexity, and Tight Coupling

A landmark study on the nature of systems failure by Charles Perrow (1984) argued that understanding dependencies provides the only way to develop fault-tolerant organizations. Perrow held that there are two aspects of dependencies that cause major unexpected accidents inside organizations.

- Interactive complexity: This describes the difficulty that managers and operators have in understanding the complex dependencies implicit in the feedback loops, contingent decisions, and non-linear interactions between the different business areas that make up the business process. These interactions may confuse managers and operators trying to fix the problem. The classic example in financial services would be certain structured securities and derivatives, the complexity and high degree of leverage of which has been at the heart of several derivatives debacles such as those at Paine Webber and Orange County.

- Tight coupling: This prevents rapid recovery from problems because of the absence of slack between different elements of the system. Slack might be internal (staff, systems availability following business reengineering) or external (just-in-time delivery or liquid markets are more tightly coupled because of their low liquidation horizon).

One way to deal with both tight coupling and interactive complexity is by building causal models of how events and factors drive potential losses. Making the model explicit and accessible addresses the problem of complexity, while identifying the trade-off between expected and unexpected operational losses is critical in justifying the need for tightly coupled systems and processes.

Consider in more detail the two main forms of dependencies: statistical and causal-based dependencies.

Statistical Dependencies

Interdependencies between loss events and risk factors can be understood *statistically* in terms of correlation between events (or more precisely, the events' impacts or frequencies), or *causally* as a logical model describing relations between events. Statistical dependencies may be as simple as an estimated correlation (for subsequent use in Monte Carlo simulation), a linear regression model, or a more general mathematical function (usually with a stochastic component). Correlation describes the degree to which one variable is related to another and comes in two forms. The most commonly used form of correlation is Pearson's correlation coefficient as used in linear regressions and is a measure of the quality of a linear fit between the two variables. It is given by:

$$\rho = \sqrt{1 - \frac{\sum_{i=1}^{n}(y_i - \hat{y}_i)^2}{\sum_{i=1}^{n}(y_i - \bar{y}_i)^2}}$$

where $\hat{y}_i$ is the calculated least squares regression values for y at each x_i.

Bear in mind when using Pearson's correlation that linear regression models assume the dependent variable is normally distributed with a variance that is the same for all values of the independent variable.

In contrast, the other commonly used form of correlation— Spearman's rank correlation coefficient—makes no such assumptions. It is defined by:

$$\rho = 1 - \frac{6\sum_{i}(x_i - y_i)^2}{n(n^2 - 1)}$$

where x_i and y_i are the ranks of the *i*th pair of X and Y variables.

As we shall see, Spearman's rank-order correlation offers a quick and easy way to incorporate the dependencies between non-normally distributed risk factors and loss events into a simulation.

Both Pearson's and Spearman's correlations lie between −1 and +1, with either extreme denoting a negative or positive relation between the variables, respectively.

Box 2.17: Correlations of Booking Errors and Product Volumes

Typically, greater volumes lead to greater errors in data entry. For example, the following data shows the volumes and the number of forex booking errors in 10-minute intervals throughout the day, averaged over two months. Spearman's and Pearson's correlations were calculated to be 0.835 and 0.796, respectively. A linear regression was performed to find the relationship between the booking errors and product volumes.

FIGURE 2.14 Booking Errors and Product Volumes — Linear Regression

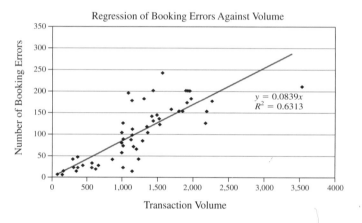

The regression suggests that about 8 percent of transactions have problems, and that to a first approximation, a 10 percent increase in volumes leads to a 10 percent increase in booking errors. However, the preponderance of data points above the regression line for higher volumes also suggests there may be non-linear relations (perhaps a regression against volumes-squared is needed). The R-squared for the linear regression is the percentage of variance explained. Simply put, this means that 63 percent of the losses from booking errors are directly attributable to increases in volumes.

There are number of more complex techniques that can be used to produce a stochastic model of the dependence between risk factors and the dependent loss events (or other potential risk factors).

Box 2.18: Envelope Dependency Model of Booking Errors and Product Volumes

One of the simplest and most robust dependency techniques is the envelope method. This uses shape distributions (uniform, triangular, general) based on boundary lines that capture all the available data (see Vose, 1996, for further examples). It involves building upper and lower boundary lines (usually set informally by viewing the data) and then setting the parameters of the conditional dependent distribution to equal the corresponding point on the boundary lines.

For instance, in our previous example, we might assume volume is independent and normally distributed whereas booking error has a triangular distribution that is conditional on the volume. More precisely, the minimum and maximum of the triangular distribution are defined by the lower and upper boundary lines respectively. The mode level is set to the level of the straight line regression through the data.

FIGURE 2.15 Booking Errors and Product Volumes — Envelope Model

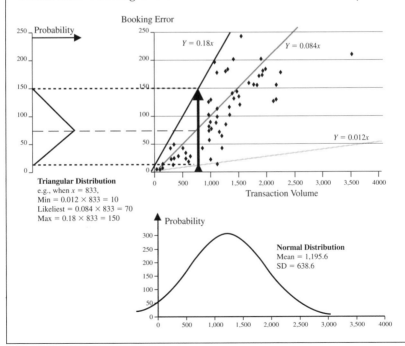

More sophisticated *covariate* models, as they are called, make some parameter (typically the mean or standard deviation) of the dependent variable's (usually the time between events rather than event frequency) distribution a function of a linear combination of independent variables. Unfortunately, although more complex models have been used to good effect in analyzing the reliability of hardware components, for which techniques such as accelerated testing can produce vast quantities of data, covariate models are harder to communicate and, therefore, justify in the data-poor environment of operational management. For further information on covariate models, refer to Meeker (1998) Chapter 17 and Klugman (1998).

Causal Dependencies

Events are often causally dependent on other events—the domino effect. For example, flooding in a basement damages records stored there. This affects the information and makes it inaccessible. The users of the information are not able to access it and, as a result, may lose some clients. Following the flood, a road crew may repair a road and damage some telephone cabling. This, in turn, interrupts telephone service and makes accounts payable unable to do its job. As a result, some key supplier may be forced into financial difficulties. An interruption in the power supply caused by an explosion at a transformer station may shut down computers in a service center with the result of lost customers and, therefore, lost revenues. Tools such as fault trees and event trees (Figures 2.16 and 2.17) can be used to capture these causal structures. But any causal model makes many assumptions, most notably that all the causal relations are captured. Causal relations are often not obvious. For instance, power surges can also corrupt data, disrupt communications, and there is even some evidence of a link between major surges and leukemia and other diseases.

Box 2.19: Causal Structure of Late Settlements

Late settlements are usually held to be the responsibility of the settlements area. But how much real control do settlements have over the losses due to late settlement? Let's assume that the losses due to reconciliation problems in a particular business area depend on

---

problems such as telecommunications failure in settlement systems, late confirmations, or staff negligence. The rest of the risk is the result of unknown factors for which (together with staff error) the settlements area takes responsibility. But the reality is more complex than this. Back in the confirmations department, late confirmations are not entirely its responsibility. Some are the result of booking errors made by traders, mistakes by counterparties, and systems errors—all outside the responsibility of confirmations. Booking errors may be the result of business risk factors outside the control of traders and their clerks, such as the complexity of the product or product volume targets set by business planning and therefore allocated to all business areas. Fault trees are particularly effective in describing these causal relationships. A real-world example of a loss causal structure is shown in Figure 2.16.

FIGURE 2.16 Causal Structure of Late Settlement Losses

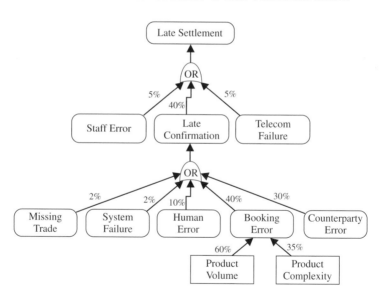

The percentages reflect the extent to which the child event is likely to be the cause of the dependent or parent event. *OR* nodes suggest that the same parent event can be caused by multiple-child events.

Analyzing these causal relationships between events helps managers focus on the underlying causes rather than the symptoms. Loss events frequently do not have a single cause—they usually result from a conjunction of different events. Causal analysis allows resources to be allocated to the causes rather than to where the loss is realized, thus avoiding managers' temptation to go no further than the smoking gun. This is particularly true of recent "lending crises," "hedge fund crashes," or "derivatives debacles"; mindlessly applied labels like this often hide the true causes of losses. Not understanding the causal structure always increases the tendency to reduce or mitigate the impacts rather than prevent the loss.

FIGURE 2.17 Causal Analysis and Risk Management

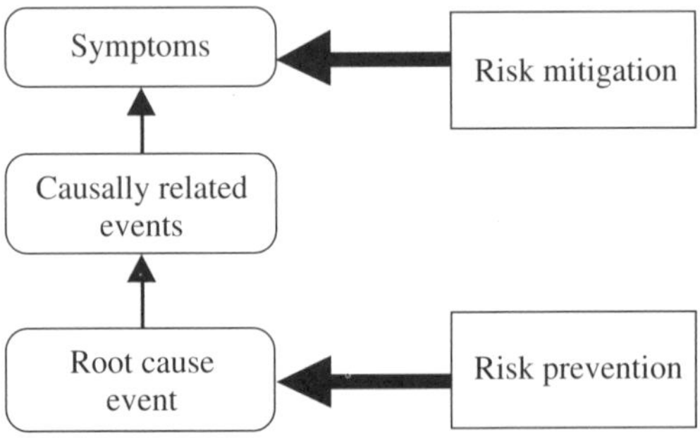

Managing losses through contingency planning, insurance, etc., is often an admission of ignorance of the ultimate causal drivers of the loss. Effective loss prevention requires understanding the causal model that drives events and not just the symptoms. For instance, a large number of manual reconciliations does not mean more resources should be thrown at getting the reconciliations done faster, but rather asking why these workarounds are needed in the first place. Rather than improving mechanisms for bad debt recovery, it is better to develop tools to predict credit risk, and so on. Causal models can also be used to inform or validate existing control structures and transfer pricing. After all, different business areas are usually responsible for different loss events—but if events are driven by other events or factors controlled by other business areas, how can the first business area be held responsible?

Causal Dependencies and Operational Competence

Despite the inevitably imprecise nature of our understanding of the factors that drive process and resource risks, causal information is still extremely valuable to capture. Firefighting after a loss event is usually an intensely personal experience involving intuition and instinct, and one that is soon forgotten. Building causal models helps managers transfer knowledge of how to deal with problem events rapidly before they get out of control. Making managers' knowledge about the true causes more explicit and objective helps leverage each individual's experience for the benefit of the entire organization and helps guide more appropriate responses to the problem in future. While formal event analysis can be too time-consuming and cumbersome to perform on a firmwide basis for a large number of possible events, it can be particularly effective in directing management actions in emergencies for selected high risk processes and resources. Some companies go further and recognize this causal event information for what it is—a shared organizational memory of how to deal with operational risk. For example, Syncrude, a major Canadian oil company, places employees' responses to questions about potential loss events on their ID tags for rapid access when loss events occur (EIU, 1995).

In this way, operational risk measurement becomes of real value not just to resource allocation but also in developing a shared knowledge base of the causal drivers of losses. Making explicit the events that drive process and resource risks is a major benefit of any operational risk management program. It lies at the heart of understanding and developing many financial firms' operational competencies.

CHAPTER 3

MODELS OF OPERATIONAL RISK

Operational risk measurement techniques come in two basic varieties: bottom-up or top-down. Top-down approaches take aggregate targets, such as net income or net asset value, to analyze the operational risk factors and loss events that cause fluctuations in the target. Bottom-up approaches disaggregate the targets into many subtargets and evaluate the impact that factors and events have on these subtargets. The results are then integrated to produce aggregate effects. In general, top-down approaches have the benefit of being inexpensive and easy to do, while bottom-up models can be more accurate and relevant to the needs of operational managers.

3.1 TOP-DOWN RISK MODELS

Top-down models focus on aggregate measures of an organization's performance and seek to develop a model of the factors and events that cause changes in that performance. It usually involves the following steps:

1. Identify target variable.

2. Identify major external (and sometimes internal) factors and events that influence the target variable.

3. Develop a model of the dependencies between the target and the risk factors and events. (This is most commonly a linear regression model between the dependent target variable and the independent risk factors.)

4. Calculate operational risk as the variance in the target that is

unexplained by the external factors or as the variance that is explained by some operational factor.

The major benefits of top-down approaches are their simplicity and low resource requirements. This transparency may be critical for firmwide applications such as capital allocation when a more accurate bottom-up model may be politically impractical because of a lack of buy-in from various stakeholders.

Top-down models have their limitations. They are, in general, less relevant for operations managers because the source of the operational loss is not made explicit and is therefore not actionable. They also provide only very approximate solutions and should really be seen as a first cut for more sophisticated bottom-up techniques such as asset-based and causal models. Top-down models that estimate operational risk as a residual are always backward looking; it is difficult to extrapolate the results to the next period. However, if internal factors are used to explain operational risks, as in expense models, then a top-down model can be used proactively to project the level of operational risk over the next period.

There are a variety of top-down approaches. Several top-down models, e.g., stock models, income models, and expense models, vary in terms of their choice of performance target. Others make no attempt to link random factors to targets and instead focus on general symptoms (e.g., risk profiling) or potential scenarios (e.g., scenario models).

Stock Factor Models

If the business is publicly traded, analysts can use the current market value of equity as a performance target. This approach is much like that used to estimate a stock's "beta" and requires estimating the sensitivity of the stock's rate of return to different factor returns.

For example, we could use a simple linear regression to explain stock returns:

$$r_t = a + b_1\left(\frac{\Delta P_t^1}{P_t^1}\right) + b_2\left(\frac{\Delta P_t^2}{P_t^2}\right) + b_3\left(\frac{\Delta P_t^3}{P_t^3}\right) + \dots \varepsilon_t$$

where r_t is the rate of return on the firm's equity

$\Delta P_t^i / P_t^i$ is the ith factor return.

the estimates of b_i give the sensitivity of changes in the factor.

Therefore, knowing the risk factors that drive the security price tells us the likely impact of market movements on net earnings, and any discrepancies from this are assumed to result from operational risk. Operational risk can thus be approximated by the level of the total variance that is not explained by the model:

$$(1-R^2)\sigma^2_{return}$$

Like all top-down models, stock-based approaches can be modeled quickly and inexpensively. In addition, the process is transparent and requires few assumptions about accounting conventions (unlike income- or expense-based models). They are particularly useful in the case of conglomerates with a number of publicly traded business units. For further reference, see Smith and Smithson (1990).

FIGURE 3.1 Stock Return Models

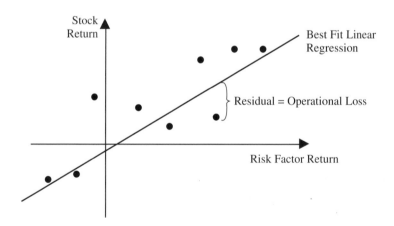

Income-based Models

If management's focus is relatively short-term and immediate income statement protection is paramount, and if historical earnings are available, then income-based models are an inexpensive and effective way to measure operational risk. Income-based models of operational risks, sometimes called EaR, analyze historical income or losses in terms of specific underlying risk factors.

These risk factors are external to the firm and include historical market, industry, or credit factors. As with stock-based models, operational risk is assessed as a quantitative residual after these external factors have been removed from the historical earning fluctuations. More accurate (and more complex) income-based models can be developed by integrating separate factor models for revenues (prices and volumes) and external factor-related costs. The historical residual between the predicted pretax income and the actual income is assumed to be the operational risk. Of course, building this hierarchy of factor models requires substantial data and assumes extensive modeling skills on the part of the analyst. One of the difficulties with income-based models is the absence of many years of relevant historical data. Hence, income-based models typically use monthly earnings or loss information, and from this infer the volatility of annualized earnings or losses by assuming that earnings or losses follow a Wiener Process (the so-called $\sqrt{t}$ rule).

Assuming that historical data are available, income-based models are quick to construct and easily comparable. They incorporate diversification across business areas and as a result are easily used for capital allocation. By focusing on net income, income-based models ignore those operational factors and events that affect long-term assets and liabilities on the balance sheet. They also tend to be less relevant for operational managers because the source of the operational loss is not made explicit.

EaR models such as this are described in detail in Matten (1996).

Expense-based Models

These are probably the simplest approach to operational risk identification, measurement, and analysis. Expense-based models associate operational risk with fluctuations in historical expenses. This involves gathering historical expense data, adjusting the data to reflect any structural changes in the organization, and then estimating unexpected losses as the volatility of the adjusted expenses. Expense volatility refers to the operational errors, fines, and losses that a business may incur during its operations. These are generally posted to the P&L accounts in the general ledger. Expenses can be scaled according to some constant basis (e.g., assets, volumes, staff levels) to incorporate the effect of any organization-wide event that significantly changes the level of expenses. Examples of these events include M&A or major changes in staffing, systems, or businesses. Alternatively, this can be done more formally using time-series models that strip out the effect of the exogenous event on the expenses (see Makridakis, 1998).

The primary benefits of expense-based models are their simplicity and low cost. Unfortunately, focusing on expenses only captures part of the risks—it ignores the non-expense risks such as reputational risks, opportunity costs, or those losses that decrease revenues. It also penalizes risk management and the development of expensive controls. Neither does it motivate behaviors to manage risk more effectively. It is also inappropriate for capital allocation.

Operating Leverage Models

Variable costs (such as most operating expenses) increase approximately in synchrony with revenues and therefore do not contribute much to net income volatility. *Operating leverage risk* is the risk of a less-than-perfect match between revenue fluctuations and expense fluctuations, and depends on the size of the asset base (fixed costs) relative to operating expense (variable costs). Proxies for operating leverage are usually simple functions of the fixed assets and the operating expenses. For example, one bank estimated its operating leverage risk to be 10 percent multiplied by the fixed asset size plus 25 percent multiplied by three months of operating expenses. Another bank calculated its operating leverage risk as $2\frac{1}{2}$ times the monthly fixed expenses for each line of business. Operating leverage risk is an important component of operational risk but it does not include many other aspects of operational risk such as the risk that losses will be sustained due to failure of internal controls, information systems, or human factors.

Scenario Analysis

Scenario analysis provides a qualitative technique for better understanding the impact associated with major operational and business events, and for developing contingency plans to respond to them. Scenario analysis is top-down, strategic, and externally focused rather than bottom-up, operational, and inward-looking. It builds a number of scenarios—essentially stories describing a particular combination of events that occur in an envisioned future state of the world. These events are, by definition, abnormal, infrequent, potentially catastrophic, and therefore often without extensive statistically relevant data. Many scenarios describe external shocks such as massive credit and market losses. Some scenarios, however, focus on internal operations such as a critical systems failure, major regulatory changes, loss of key people, or class legal actions. It also pays to at least consider major disaster scenarios that have happened to other firms and develop preventive measures and contingency plans as appropriate. Other examples of scenarios are constrained only by the imagination of the staff involved but might include the following:

- A new settlement system has been implemented at the bank and it cannot be reconciled with the original system. As a result, payments cannot be made and trades cannot be booked.

- A large corporate client sues the investment firm because it does not disclose all the necessary risks associated with a particular transaction in the prospectus.

- A significant political event occurs in a country in which the business has a large investment.

- A firm's top five credit exposures are hit by market movements of 15 percent.

- An employee embezzles funds for a year before being caught.

- Subdued economic conditions in the region cause less lending volumes, 50 percent below current growth expectations.

- Retail staff mount a union strike.

- A disgruntled employee sabotages the computer systems, undermining the bank's reputation.

- Government increases the corporate tax rate by 20 percent.

- A significant political group makes unfounded attacks on the firm.

- There is inadequate due diligence of the firm's public issue prospectus.

- Non-reconciliation between general ledger and back-office systems leads to incorrect published results.

Most scenarios are effective because they structure the likely implications of unexpected shocks. Their infrequency means these events can rarely be captured statistically. It follows that scenario analysis is appropriate for analyzing important infrequent events and catastrophic losses that are generally (but not always) driven by external events. Of course, the price paid for the flexibility of scenario analysis is its subjectivity. First, it is subjective because the choice of scenarios to consider is arbitrary, developed on the basis of either the individual's idiosyncratic historical experiences or his/her subjective assessment of the risk factors affecting the firm's environment. Second, the analysis is subjective because it lacks an explicit model of the sensitivities of the firm's assets to guide the financial impact of different scenarios. Third, strictly speaking, scenario analysis tells us nothing about the risks because it gives us no idea of the likelihood of the scenario. Despite this subjectivity, scenario analysis adds value by helping managers question their assumptions, better understand the firm's sensitivities to catastrophic loss, and develop contingency plans to mitigate them.

For most users of scenario analysis, the goal is not prediction but prescription. Managers use the scenarios as a learning exercise to deal with uncertain future states. Scenario analysis leads us to rethink the assumptions behind existing business practices and suggest other approaches that may become essential in the future. Scenario analysis is useful when there is extreme uncertainty and ambiguity. If the business is evolving rapidly or is very complex with many different interrelated causal forces, scenario analysis may be the only viable approach.

Readers interested in further exploring scenario analysis may find the following thought-provoking books of value: *The Art of the Long View* by Schwartz and *Scenarios: The Art of Strategic Conversation* by van der Heijden.

Risk Profiling Models

These focus on tracking a handful of risk indicators that reflect process or system health. No attempt is made to link these risk factors to any target variable. Typical indicators include trade volume, mishandling errors or losses, the number of exception reports or "no deals" outstanding, staff turnover rate, and percentage of staff vacancies. Other measurements include:

* Number of incident reports
* Number of repeat violations
* Amount of overtime worked in a business area

- Ratio of contractors to staff
- Supervisory ratio
- Pass–fail rate in staff licensing exam
- Downtime
- Number of limit violations
- Number of temporary procedures
- Number of process "fails"
- Number of personnel errors
- Average years of staff experience
- Backlog levels
- Backlog of change requests

Provided that consistent measures are used, profiling models are good for analyzing the evolution of operational risks over time, thus focusing operations managers' attention to problems before they get out of hand. They are particularly effective when used with a structured hierarchy of indicators such as Balanced Scorecard (Kaplan, 1996) or statistical quality control tools such as control charts (see Chapter 15 or Montgomery, 1997). The downside of profiling is that the absence of a link between a target variable and the risk indicators makes factors arbitrary. It also makes managers focus too much on the symptoms rather than the causes of operational problems.

3.2   BOTTOM-UP RISK MODELS

The rise of quantitative techniques in banking and risk management, managers' increasing familiarity with simulation-based techniques, and the development of historical loss databases have made bottom-up models more widely used. These models begin with the basic elements of operations, such as assets and liabilities or processes and resources, and in a bottom-up fashion describe how potential changes to these elements could affect targets such as mark-to-market asset values and net income. These potential changes are modeled as either risk factors or specific loss events.

Designing a quantitative bottom-up model involves several steps:

1. Identify target variable. Typically this will be P&L, costs, or perhaps net asset value.

2. Identify a critical set of processes and resources (in the case of an operational risk analysis) or a key set of assets and liabilities (in the case of a purely financial risk analysis). Model developers should recall the Pareto Principle—most of the risks are found in a small number of assets and liabilities or processes and resources.

3. Map these processes and resources to a combination of risk factors and loss events for which we have gathered historical data (that we believe to be relevant for the future) or for which we have strong expectations as to possible future scenarios.

4. Simulate the potential changes in risk factors and events over the time horizon, taking into account any dependencies (usually correlations) between risk factors and events. This can be done analytically, assuming particular parametric distributions for factors and events, or by using Monte Carlo simulation methods.

5. Infer from the mapping and the simulated change the effect on the relevant target variables such as interest margin, net income, or net asset value.

When are Bottom-up Models Used?

The target audience of bottom-up models is wider than that of top-down models and includes middle managers, operational managers, internal planning, and resource allocation rather than just high-level strategic planning or capital allocation. Asset-based models are also appropriate to business units seeking to protect their balance sheets. Bottom-up models are general in that they can be integrated with other models used for operational management. Asset-based models are often more accurate than other models (such as income-based models) but require more time and resources to develop. They require detailed data about specific losses that can affect the assets and liabilities in the organization. Without this data, subjective assessments must be used, which seriously limit the validity of the approach. Asset-based models also rely heavily on the Pareto Principle. It follows that analysis should focus on the most critical assets and liabilities.

To better understand the bottom-up approach, it helps to consider some common examples:

- Asset–liability management
- Market factor models
- Actuarial-loss models
- Causal models
- Operational variances
- Stress tests
- Operational checklists

Asset–liability Management

Traditional asset–liability management (ALM) looks at projected future earnings in a number of financial (usually interest-rate) scenarios. ALM approaches range from simple interest-rate gaps in different time periods, through more sophisticated duration and convexity models, to complex Monte Carlo simulations of the balance sheet. In all of these cases, ALM aggregates the interest-rate sensitivities of specific assets and liabilities to infer net profits (in particular, the interest margin component) in a wide range of interest-rate scenarios. ALM approaches are most appropriate for those assets that are not marked to market, i.e., booked at historical costs $+/-$ accruals, for which market factor models (see next section) are inappropriate. One of the difficulties of ALM models is the long time horizon typically used (usually when the transactions mature)—it is very difficult to simulate or develop market-rate scenarios over such long time periods. ALM models used for balance sheet simulation are also very sensitive to the precise accounting principles used. For further information on ALM models, see Subsection 14.2 or refer to Bessis (1998).

Market Factor Models

For marketable assets (e.g., trading portfolios) affected largely by continuous market risk factors, parametric models based on an assumed factor distribution can be used. J.P. Morgan's RiskMetrics™ model of VaR (Guldimann, 1995) is a good example of this approach. Knowing the distributions of factor returns for a short time horizon (usually days), the mapping between assets and risk factors, and the initial value of the asset allows us to estimate the distribution of asset values in the forthcoming time period. In the case of J.P. Morgan's RiskMetrics™, the factors are assumed to be normally distributed, which allows us to completely specify the distributions in terms of the factors' means (assumed zero) and the covariance matrix. Most factor models also assume a linear mapping; this is usually a reasonable assumption except, for example, in the case of non-linear positions (e.g., options portfolios). Given the return distribution (and thereby the distribution of potential asset values), the portfolio VaR is taken as just a percentile. If the assumption of normality is not made, factor models resort to simulation approaches to infer the effect of factor changes on asset values.

With the trend away from accounting-based valuation conventions and toward market-based valuation, has come a move toward market factor models and away from ALM techniques. Even those assets and liabilities without a ready market price can be marked to a valuation model, further extending the universe of assets to which market factor models can be applied. Market factor models have the benefits of being relatively transparent and forward-looking and avoid the idiosyncrasies of accounting amortization and depreciation schedules. On the other hand, market prices are very volatile and the resultant fluctuations in asset values can be hard to intuitively understand. Firms often find market targets make sense for the shorter term whereas ALM measures are more operationally useful for the long term. For further information on market factor models, see Jorion (1997) or the RiskMetrics™ Technical document (Guldimann, 1995).

Actuarial Loss Models

Actuarial models are used to estimate the random incidence of claims (loss events, in our terminology) when an insured party suffers damages that are partially covered by an insurance contract. Each event may cause a payment (in our terminology, the impact of the event) to be made to the policy holder as a result. Insurance actuaries model events' frequencies and impacts in much the same way as described in this book and similarly use analytical or simulation techniques to estimate the aggregate cash flow. Actuarial risk models have long been used by insurance companies to assess the effect of policy changes, marketing practices, and concentration changes on the payout of insurance claims and receipt of premiums. Unlike operational risk managers, actuaries have no shortage of data to fit their models. However, insurance companies have less short-term control over their insurance payouts than operational managers have over their operations. This makes insurers' historical experience more valuable in estimating the future loss profile. For further information about the use of loss models in insurance, see Klugman, Panjer, and Willmot (1998).

Causal Models

Causal models combine data about historical losses with subjective causal relations to produce estimates of conditional probabilities of one loss event given that another has already occurred. This is most useful for small but complex and risky systems that can be broken down into a number of simpler subsystems. Causal models focus on helping users understand how failures propagate in the system as a whole and indicate causes, rather than symptoms, that require dynamic attention as the system begins to fail. While very suitable for operations managers, causal modeling is complex—almost impossible—to do on a large scale and less relevant for aggregate resource allocation. Formal causal models (such as fault trees, event trees, and event simulation) generally demand a great deal of data about the sources of failure in systems. More informal causal models (such as belief networks, affinity and interrelationship diagramming, cognitive maps, wishbone diagrams, and root-cause analysis) are inherently much less demanding, but also less precise and operationally useful.

Box 3.1:   An Informal Causal Model of Market Contagion

For example, the BIS, when reviewing the turmoil that hit global markets in the second half of 1998, developed its own causal model of how initial market shocks caused massive volatility, higher credit risks, and a drying up of liquidity.

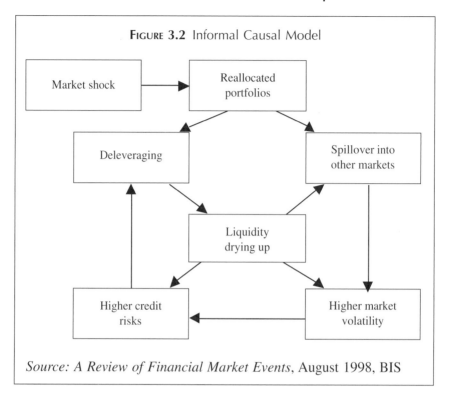

FIGURE 3.2 Informal Causal Model

Source: A Review of Financial Market Events, August 1998, BIS

See Subsection 7.4 for more information about causal models and their use in operational risk assessment.

Operational Variances

Management accountants have long used standard costs as a predetermined cost of some activity based on current and projected costs. These standards are set at the beginning of the period and used to benchmark subsequent activities. One measure of operational risk is then the difference between the actual cost and the standard cost—known as the accounting or operational variance (not to be confused with statistical variance). Sometimes this difference is standardized by dividing it by the standard cost. Variance analyses help control costs and highlight problem areas by focusing management attention on exceptional variances. Furthermore, variances can be separated into volume and unit cost components, allowing accountants to distinguish between the effect of volume changes and the effect of changes in the unit cost per transaction.

Stress Tests

Stress tests are quantitative and shock the system to discover the impacts of the stresses. Key risk factors (such as price, volume, supplier price, resource availability, and quality level) are "stressed" or given values beyond their "normal" operating ranges to reveal deficiencies in processes and systems that might lead to unexpected errors. These tests point the way to redesigning systems internally or updating the embedded controls. Like scenario analysis, stress tests estimate events' impact and not their frequencies and, therefore, only capture a single dimension of the risk. Stress tests also usually ignore the relationship between different stress factors—this would be captured by correlations (if data were available) or more likely through informal scenario analysis. Despite these simplifications, stress testing can be a powerful diagnostic tool for operational risk management. We can stress information and communication systems using mock data to discover their deficiencies. For example, Y2K problems in a settlement system can be studied by feeding a day's worth of mock transactions dated after 2000 (after of course taking the system offline). We might estimate the impact of a tenfold increase in volume or estimate the downstream implications of a jump in the number of processing errors.

Like scenario analysis, stress tests have many strengths. They are easy to set up—one only needs to give extreme inputs and analyze the results. They force time bombs to the surface where they can be handled offline. They reveal the inherent structural limitations of a given system— operating parameters can be set more realistically or the system redesigned. They also can be used by audit and internal control to evaluate existing controls, for example, by forcing abnormal transactions.

However, the very simplicity of stress testing can be deceptive. The choice of factors to stress, systems to focus on, and linkages between risk factors and impacts can all be subjective and uncertain. It can quickly become an *ad hoc* process if strict criteria are not determined for selecting the systems and variables to stress. The range of potential stresses that can be considered make the technique potentially highly time-consuming and a source of data overload for managers. It can be disruptive, especially if real-time systems need to be stressed. Stress tests are usually simplistic and do not consider the effects of combinations and relationships between variables (or they are assumed constant).

Much that has been written on the use of stress testing for financial portfolios is relevant to this discussion. For further information, see for example, Chapter 2 of Alexander (1998).

Operational Checklists

Checklists and other control self-assessment (CSA) tools are qualitative techniques for transferring good operational practices from one place to another. They can also be used to assess the current state of operational practices within an organization and suggest remedial actions (see Subsection 1.6 for a discussion of their importance). Checklists provide managers with a series of canned questions to discover what can go wrong, where this can happen, its importance, and what can be done about it. Checklists are best administered through structured interviews; while they can be self-administered, this approach is increasingly out of favor in the wake of the self-assessments at banks that suffered major frauds.

Risk measurement using checklists is purely a subjective assessment by the interviewee(s). Many operational checklists focus on the limitations of available control systems, assuming that major loss events are driven by the failure of internal control. In particular, checklists direct managers' attention to four aspects of operational risk:

- Existence of controls

- Magnitude of the exposure

- Potential (assuming perfect compliance by staff) of the control to prevent the event from occurring or from having an impact

- Extent to which staff comply with the practices required by the control

Checklist-based audits usually rank assessments on these four dimensions using scales as presented in Table 3.1.

TABLE **3.1** Checklist of Risk Likelihood and Impact

Likelihood		Impact
Potential	*Compliance*	
5: Eliminates the risk if followed	5: 100%	6: Financial impact on objectives and financial targets
4: 80% elimination	4: 80%	5: Loss of asset or an increase in liability
3: 60% elimination	3: 60%	4: Loss of reputation
2: 40% elimination	2: 40%	3: Loss or exaggeration of P&L
1: 20% elimination	1: 20%	2: Distortion of balance sheet
0: No effect	0: None	1: No impact on balance sheet or income statement

Breaking potential and compliance apart lets auditors direct their attention to improving compliance or improving control systems. The compliance or risk ranking will then be compared with some standard (internal or external) or target and, based on the difference, appropriate actions proposed. The mapping of controls to risks is often represented in a matrix with controls or risk management alternatives against exposures, the logic being that a control can affect multiple exposures.

Risk assessment in particular tends to require input from several interviewees. Their risk rankings can be aggregated according to a weighted sum, with each weight reflecting the respondent's level of experience. Alternatively, with pair-wise comparison of risks (frequency, impacts, or compliance), the consistency of individual rankings can be used as a weight for cross-interviewee resolution. Given rankings or subjective levels that reflect consensus of the risks, we can map specific risk rankings to known frequencies/impacts/compliance levels and scale the rest of the rankings to a quantitative (usually logarithmic) scale. Using aggregated risk assessments, we can produce a matrix of operational risks similar to that found in evaluating bond credit ratings.

Of course, subjective checklists cannot be used without independent verification of the some of the issues they bring up. Standard auditing techniques for gathering evidence can then be used to confirm the checklists' implications. Analysis, benchmarking, and reporting then complete the cycle.

TABLE 3.2 Operational Risk Matrix

Business Units	A	B	C
Technology	High	Low	High
Processing	Medium	Low	Low
Compliance	High	High	Low
Staffing	High	Low	High
Legal	Low	Low	Low
Communications	Low	High	Low
Fraud	Medium	Medium	High
Control	High	Low	High

Checklist tools are very simple to use, easy to understand, and relatively inexpensive to implement. Although most often used by auditors or external consultants, internal operational and facilities managers can use checklists as the basis of periodic scorecards (Kaplan, 1996) for both quantitative and qualitative data about operations, especially when it is integrated with a system of key performance or risk indicators (risk factors in the terminology of this book). Many banks and fund managers use checklists on an intranet to support risk management for distributed business processes. Subjective rankings can also be used as the basis of an informal capital allocation program for operational risk. Checklists are also particularly useful when expertise exists externally but cannot be quantified and is too expensive to bring internally on an ongoing basis. It follows that checklists are tailormade for novel situations or when internal expertise is not available. Control situations involving new staff members, new business areas, new transactions, and new systems for which historical experience is not available internally, but to which external experience can be usefully applied, are good candidates for checklists.

Checklists are also suitable for project risk assessment, when the lack of data and the uniqueness of the project make more quantitative approaches too cumbersome. An example of this is seen in software project management, which often involves an initial risk assessment. New project checklists will not focus on existing controls (there might not be any and those in place might be unsuitable). Instead, they look at the attributes of the project (such as newness of the technology, level of internal competence, experience of doing similar projects, resources, and time line). See Subsection 10.4 for a discussion on project risk management.

Checklist-based models are also used to implement TQM principles under ISO, British, or other standards, many of which are being increasingly applied to financial institutions. Although most auditors' use of checklists is strictly bottom-up, regulators have developed a number of top-down checklists to evaluate bank performance and the quality of their assets and liabilities. Examples of these include the US Federal Deposit Insurance Corporation's (FDIC's) CAMEL and the Uniform Bank Performance Rating Systems. Several consulting firms offer checklist-based approaches for banks to evaluate their operational risks (see Appendix B).

The major issue with checklists or CSA tools is their tendency to cover the need for major changes. It is simply too easy for staff to cover up problems rather than face them directly.

For further information on operational checklists, see Chapter 3 of Chambers (1997), which provides a series of checklist examples of control audits to estimate the operational risk of a system.

3.3 SELECTING A RISK MODEL

As we have seen, a variety of models can be used to estimate operational risk. These are not mutually exclusive. In many cases, they can be integrated. Their use and focus varies with managers' operational objectives.

Different risk modeling techniques should be seen as complementary rather than as substitutes for one another. As Table 3.3 shows, no single model provides a panacea for all the risks facing operations managers in financial businesses. As systems and data have become more widely available, and managers become more familiar with different techniques, some trends have become evident. In particular, a 1999 survey by PricewaterhouseCoopers (Operational Risk Management – The Next Frontier) suggests a slow progression from the reliance on skilled audit staff, through simple top-down subjective models (such as simple checklists, income- and expense-based models, and cost variances) and toward more proactive, quantitative, bottom-up models (such as income modeling, causal, and asset-based models).

TABLE 3.3 Comparison of Different Risk Models

Type of Model	Objectives	Strengths	Limitations
		Top-down Models	
Stock factor	Capital allocation	Uses publicly available data. Inexpensive. Makes few assumptions.	Inaccurate and not operationally focused.
Income-based	Growth and capital allocation	Focuses on income-statement management. Makes few assumptions.	Requires historical earnings data. Not particularly useful to operations managers.
Expense-based	Efficiency	Focuses on cost management. Simple, inexpensive to implement.	Inaccurate and ignores non-expense items. Penalizes against risk management activities.
Operating-leverage	Growth and efficiency	Simple, inexpensive to implement.	Ignores many non-revenue-related operational risks.
Scenario analysis	Growth	Focuses on long-term strategy involving great uncertainty or ambiguity. Theoretically, simple to perform.	Highly subjective and potentially time-consuming.
Risk profiling	Efficiency and internal control/ capital management	Easy to understand. Operationally relevant.	Difficult to relate to any important business targets. May be arbitrary.

TABLE 3.3 Comparison of Different Risk Models (cont'd)

Type of Model	Objectives	Strengths	Limitations
		Bottom-up Models	
Asset–liability	Capital management	Focuses on balance-sheet protection. Relatively accurate. Long-term focus.	Complex and requires lots of data.
Market factor	Capital management	Focuses on market risk management. Relatively accurate. Short-term focus.	Requires lots of data, in particular, information on expected returns and covariances.
Actuarial loss	Efficiency and internal control/ capital management	Accurate for frequent loss events. Relevant to operations managers.	Requires lots of data; in particular, event frequencies and impacts.
Causal	Internal control	Highly relevant to operations managers.	Needs a well-defined system in which consequences predictably follow from antecedents. Typically useful for hardware-related systems. Can be extremely complex.
Operational variance	Efficiency and internal control	Simple, relevant to operations managers.	Purely cost-based. Highly sensitive to budget estimates.
Stress test	Internal control/ capital management	Simple to understand, easy to set up, and can reveal structural limitations of systems.	Ignores dependencies between risk factors. Arbitrary in its choice of risk factors, levels, processes, etc.
Operational checklist	Efficiency and internal control	Captures current practices against a standardized benchmark. Highly relevant to operations managers.	Subjective, dependent on choice of benchmark. Too easy to cover up problems.

FIGURE 3.3 Operational risk Measurement

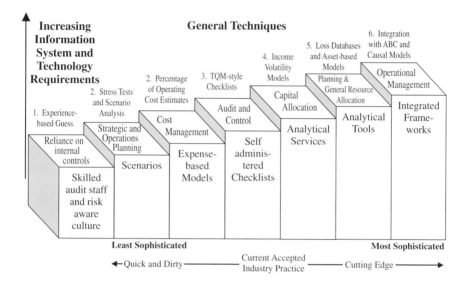

Later sections will consider a number of different techniques and propose a hybrid approach that combines the best of multiple methods. For instance, it incorporates:

- Factor models (as used in income-based models)

- Loss events (as used in asset-based models)

- Actuarial techniques (as used in insurance actuarial models)

- Causally related events (as used in causal models)

Rather than be purely prescriptive, Section II shows the different tools and techniques that can be useful for estimating and analyzing operational risks. The book goes further, explaining the circumstances in which these tools and techniques are most appropriate so that managers and risk analysts can tailor the different approaches to suit their own specific organizational and business circumstances.

Section II

AN OPERATIONAL RISK MANAGEMENT METHODOLGY

A Systematic Risk Management Process: In Subsection 1.4, we defined operational risk management as a *process* of *systematic analysis* of critical processes and resources and the loss events and risk factors that may affect those processes and resources. Risk management is not just a set of techniques, reports, or databases. Like quality management, the output of the analysis is only a part of the value created by operational risk management. It is a process that inculcates a sensitivity to risk and its drivers throughout all the organization—not just in the risk management function, but in the business lines as well.

Operational risk management is systematic in analyzing the underlying causes of expected and unexpected losses and in evaluating the rationale for risk prevention, mitigation, transfer, and financing. It is an attempt to avoid developing controls and risk management practices in an *ad hoc* fashion, which only results in wasted resources, unnecessary exposures, and greater complexity—leading to even further risks. It is an assessment of both the firm's current operational exposures and its future exposures. Banks may employ such a process when committing to new operations and as they evaluate existing commitments to these activities.

But what is the process of operational risk management? Like most models of quality and risk management, the process of operational risk management involves the following basic steps (Table II.1):

TABLE II.1 The Operational Risk Management Process

Steps	1. Define scope and objectives	2. Identify critical risks	3. Estimate risks	4. Analyze	5. Implement management actions	6. Monitor and report
Relevant chapters	Chapter 4	Chapter 5	Chapters 6–7	Chapter 8	Chapters 9–14	Chapter 15
Issues	Project management Defining an agenda Organization Targets Risk policies	Benchmarking Process and resource risks Risk factors Loss events Categorization	Risk data Measurement techniques Historical data Subjective assessment Loss distributions Dependency models Building an operational risk database	Risk aggregation Simulation models Risk management alternatives Analyzing events, factors, processes, and resources Evaluating alternatives	Risk avoidance Factor management Loss prediction Loss prevention Loss control Loss reduction Contingency management Risk financing	Learning and response loops Effective reporting Different risk reports Model evaluation and update
Deliverables	Project structure and scope Operational strategy Risk organization Risk targets Formal and informal policies Change control	Event, factor, and risk definitions Key processes Key resources Key risks	Event frequencies and impacts Expected, unexpected, and catastrophic losses Dependencies	Loss origination Loss responsibility Aggregated risk estimates Risk management alternatives	Specific guidelines for actions Flexible response to operational problems Proactive operational management	Systems and controls Risk breakdown by: process, resource, event/factor, business, expected vs unexpected losses
Involvement	Senior management		Operational risk management			Line management

These steps and their ramifications will occupy much of the rest of the book, but the major issues are briefly summarized below:

Define Scope and Objectives (Chapter 4). First, senior management, in consultation with the board of directors, must clearly define the objectives of and scope for the firm's operational risk management program. The operational objectives of efficiency, change management, capital management, and growth depend on the broader business strategy, which is likely to vary from one business unit to another. Operational objectives should also build on a candid assessment of an appropriate baseline representing internal or external best practices and should be followed by a series of intermediate targets designed to take operations to that benchmark. These targets must be clearly communicated throughout operations to indoctrinate personnel as to the importance of managing operational risk and to guarantee line managers' support and commitment to the project. In addition to the basic mandate to measure, analyze, and manage operational risks, risk managers should take the lead in extending the benchmark into an operational risk management policy. Banks increase their ability to control and manage the various risks inherent in any activity when policies and procedures are set out in written documentation and made available to all relevant staff. Given the risk management objectives, management must establish a risk organization and provide it with adequate resources and authority. Operational risk managers should also encourage adequate reserve funding for specific risks, communicate firmwide best practices, implement audit trails, initiate motivational programs, and reward risk aware performance.

Identify Critical Risks (Chapter 5). With support from senior management, staff must identify critical processes, resources, and loss events. Operational risk management often founders by trying to be too inclusive, so its focus should be strictly in line with the precise objectives set by senior management.

Estimate Risks (Chapters 6 and 7). Using data from a variety of sources (interviews, surveys, and historical data), the major drivers of operational risks in the most critical processes and resources must be estimated. Risk management should form a reasonable and defensible judgment of the magnitude of any risk with respect to both the impact it could have on the bank (including the maximum potential impact) and the probability that such an event will occur. If risks cannot be quantified, management may still identify how potential risks can arise and the steps it has taken to deal with and limit those risks. Risk estimation should also incorporate any important dependencies between different risks.

Analyze Risks (Chapter 8). In the risk analysis stage, the aggregate effect of losses (particularly operational events) should be estimated. Alternative management interventions need to be evaluated so as to deal with these events and factors either individually or on a business-wide basis.

Implement Management Actions (Section III, Chapters 9–14). This covers a wide range of activities to reduce ongoing process and resource risks. For instance, risk management typically begins by deciding whether to accept or avoid certain risks, and by managing the key risk factors that affect a company's P&L. It also might involve developing a capability to predict or prevent future losses before they arise, or better controlling losses by preventing the growth of their impact over time, or reducing the impact of the events after the event has occurred. Finally, management may decide the risks are inherent to their business and therefore requires some form of risk financing to mitigate or offset the effect of potential losses.

Monitor and Report (Chapter 15). Risks should be continuously monitored, and periodic reporting loops should bring management together to reassess the overall need for and performance of operational risk management. Ongoing monitoring is a particularly important aspect of any risk management process because the nature of the activities is likely to change rapidly due to product and market innovations and the reliance of some products on open networks such as the Internet.

CHAPTER 4

DEVELOPING OBJECTIVES FOR RISK MANAGEMENT

4.1 PROJECT MANAGEMENT

Developing enterprise-wide operational risk management can be daunting. Operational risk analysis requires the support of a multitude of business areas, all with very different agendas. It also requires the management of a host of data sources, analysis techniques, and management options. No surprise then that operational risk management projects must be carefully controlled to keep them down to a reasonable scope. The challenge is to ensure that risk analysis is done in a rigorous manner and that the risk management activities themselves provide added value rather than contribute to the general "noise" surrounding management activities. Meeting this challenge requires that would-be operational risk management groups address the following issues:

Understand the Firm's Broader Risk Management Agenda

The most important determinant of a successful operational risk management project is a precise statement of management's objectives with respect to risk. We must be able to answer some difficult questions: What is the board's appetite for risk? How much can the firm afford to sustain if a given problem materializes? How does this appetite for risk fit with the firm's broader strategy? What is the role of the board? Subsection 4.2 elaborates on these issues.

Develop the Business Case for Operational Risk Management

How would this project add value to the organization? Senior management must be completely convinced of the viability and usefulness of the project. If not, any risk management project is unlikely to succeed. Subsection 1.5 discusses some of the typical justifications of operational risk management. It follows that a major part of any operational risk management typically begins with a comprehensive education and training program. Staff need to understand the reality behind the models and risk analysis. This is particularly important if operational risk is used as a basis for capital allocation.

Define the Project Scope

A well-defined project scope is key to success in operational risk. A complete quantitative simulation from scratch is unrealistic. But focusing on smaller and simpler objectives, such as improving work-flow quality, changing the risk culture, or providing early warning bells for deterioration of control systems, would be easier and more manageable. The choice of project scope should reflect a host of issues, such as the source of management support, the business areas at greatest risk, and the availability of data and other resources. Subsection 4.3 discusses this in more detail. The scope will also typically vary by the type of organization. For small, particularly privately held businesses, it is generally not worth their effort to estimate the probability distribution of every possible loss. Instead, small firms should focus purely on catastrophic losses—these being most critical as they may not have large capital buffers or lines of credit to cover the losses. This information would then be fed into the decision-making on capital allocation rather than more efficient operational management. For larger firms, the value of information gathered from statistical analysis is very likely to exceed the cost of undertaking the analysis (the cost of data collection, analysis, and interpretation). In general, subjective estimation will be cheaper than historical analysis, and so again will be more cost-effective for smaller operations with limited risk exposures.

Have Clearly Defined Targets and Objectives

Do not perform any risk analysis without a clear target that is in line with senior management objectives. The choice of strategy will strongly determine the choice of the operational risk modeling approach. For example, firms focusing on asset-based targets will use asset-based models; if income statement protection is a priority, then an income-based model should be used. Subsection 4.4 elaborates this in more detail.

Although it is important to view operational risk systems and tools as an ongoing process rather than a one-time initiative, we must also estimate how quickly operational risk management objectives can be achieved. Furthermore, at every stage of the risk management process, there should be deliverables of immediate value to operational and business managers. Support from, and access to, business managers will be almost impossible if early benefits are not produced.

Define the Project Organization

What are the resources required to do the project, and over what time scale? Inadequate resources are a surefire way to hamstring any operational risk management pilot program. So too is poor organization of the available resources. Roles and responsibilities of everyone involved in the risk management program need to be well-defined to ensure coordinated communication within the risk group and outside to senior, business, and line managers. Subsection 4.5 develops these issues further.

Develop Formal and Informal Policies

Operational risk management presupposes the existence of relatively well-trained and motivated staff and well-designed processes. The main defense against infrequent catastrophic losses must be staff who are knowledgeable about the risks and systems, and formal and informal policies that embody that knowledge. Such policies and guidelines provide a consistent internal benchmark against which measurement and analysis can proceed. This is also a good way to get line managers involved from the outset. Managers must understand the benefits of the project, and a formal policy document should reassure them that operational risk management leverages internal expertise from operations, rather than imposing some external (and potentially irrelevant) standard from the outside. Subsection 4.6 elaborates these issues further. Another aspect of effective risk policy formulation is documentation of the risk management process itself. At every stage of risk measurement, analysis and action need to be documented in the form of operational audit trails. The goal is to develop documentation of sufficient quality to enable audit teams to review the rationale and allow subsequent assessment teams to repeat and improve on the efforts. Such documentation is also important if major risk mitigation and prevention efforts are under way—we need to see how effective the new programs are in relation to initial expectations.

4.2 DEFINING THE FIRM'S RISK MANAGEMENT AGENDA

The agenda for risk management must be clearly defined. An organization's risk management objectives depend on the appetite of the different stakeholders for different types of risk exposure. Foremost among these stakeholders are the shareholders and their representatives—the board of directors. Directors have a fiduciary responsibility to understand the exposures (both diversifiable and non-diversifiable) that the firm takes on behalf of the shareholders, and to confirm that these risks are being managed appropriately. The days of directors' rubber-stamping the decisions of senior management are disappearing in many parts of the world as shareholders become more active in demanding that their voices be heard. Firms are susceptible to takeovers (friendly or otherwise), and major shareholders can sue directors and managers for breach of their fiduciary responsibility. It follows that directors will often tend to base their risk appetite on the prescribed norms for the industry or their own perceived peer group.

The firm's appetite for risk must be set from the top of the organization, and widely and consistently disseminated to operational and business lines. Risk management is too important to be delegated to technical specialists in finance or operations without adequate board and senior management oversight. Without the backing and direction of the board and senior management, risk management is doomed to failure.

Box 4.1: Whose Agenda?

Board members' and senior management's appetite for risk management may differ from that of shareholders. As was suggested in Subsection 2.2, value maximization does not necessarily imply risk management. Unlike shareholders, managers and directors typically hold undiversified portfolios and therefore are prone to the businesses' otherwise diversifiable risks. On the one hand, directors' fiduciary responsibility is a major incentive for directors and senior managers to insist on a "no surprises" strategy for both financial and operational risks. On the other hand, acceptance of the inevitability of some surprises is part and parcel of maximizing shareholder value.

It follows that overzealous shareholder litigation can be value-destroying rather than value-enhancing. To some extent, this can be mitigated (at a cost of the premium) by the use of Directors' and Officers' insurance.

A business unit's appetite for risk depends on its senior managers' perception of the nature of its business. As a general rule, firms should keep their exposure to those risks aligned with the firm's strategy and its core competence. Business areas that are already seen by senior management as reliable performers, so-called cash cows, should focus on minimizing expected costs so that their competitive position is not damaged. Business units with a high potential will look to manage their growth trajectory—this means focusing on unexpected losses that might derail that growth. Troubled business units could be looking for turnaround or exit strategies and safeguarding investors' capital might be the priority. A related proxy for management's risk appetite is their time horizon. This determines whether the firm focuses on cash flow, income statement, or balance-sheet protection. In more volatile industries, a short-term focus will demand management of the income statement and cash flows rather than the balance sheet.

TABLE 4.1 Business Strategy and Risk

Strategic objectives	Efficiency	Growth	Capital management
Type of business unit	Cash cow: Steady earnings potential	Star: High earnings potential with high volatility	Troubled performer: Uncertain earnings with high volatility
Targets	Cash flow and income statements	Balance sheet, reputation	Use of capital
Time horizon	Short-term focus	Long term	Long term
Willingness to take on additional risk for higher returns	Low	Medium	High
Critical dimensions of risk	Expected losses	Unexpected losses	Catastrophic losses

Rather than infer the firm's risk appetite from its business strategy, we can look at the market's perception of the business. The qualitative features that investors look for in a firm's stock price are an important function of investor relations and owe more to an understanding of the firm's position in the investment market than necessarily to rational analysis of the firm's future prospects. A proxy for investors' preferences is the firm's beta—a measure of the firm's sensitivity to the market and thus a measure of existing investors' willingness to take on non-diversifiable risks. If an APT-like factor model is used to price securities in the same industry, beta can be determined for a variety of important industry-specific risks. Another proxy for a firm's risk appetite is its target credit rating. This determines the probability of default and is largely driven by the firm's capital structure. Borrowing increases shareholders' leverage and the risk that shareholders must take; specifically, the risk that after interest payments, there will not be sufficient funds available to pay dividends or reimburse shareholders in the event of liquidation.

4.3 DEFINING THE PROJECT SCOPE

Several heuristics should guide risk managers in defining the scope of their operational risk management activities.

Start Small

Focus on the most critical processes, the most critical resources, and the most risky events. At all times, remember the Pareto Principle (see Subsection 2.3)—most (about 80 percent) of risk comes from a small number (about 20 percent) of loss events. Focus on what counts. Even for complex processes, the bulk of losses will come from a handful of possible loss events, perhaps 10–20 percent. Having hundreds of potential loss events is just too complex and ends up being a distraction.

Start Where You Gather Resources

Operational risk management requires significant resources to be effective. Begin the project where resources are available. These may be a budget, available staff, data, systems, or a combination of these. If resources come from selected operations managers, work with them to prove the concept and then roll out to other businesses. If support comes from strategic planning or research, roll out by risk category may be appropriate. If support is from financial risk management or insurance, then the roll out should be an extension of these staff functions. The goal is to develop a firm's first steps in operational risk management in a few selected business units or locations with friendly and supportive operations managers. It is, therefore, essential that these line managers understand the project's objectives, and how it will affect their daily business. A general understanding of the tools and the techniques is also needed if line managers are to trust the results.

Focus on Areas That Are Not Partially Covered by Other Control or Audit Activities

Excessive overlap with other areas, particularly audit, insurance, and financial risk management will result in potential battles over turf and a reluctance of business areas to work with the operational risk group. Avoid this by co-opting any potential opposition. Operational risk management is not a cure-all. It is a way of integrating existing risk practices, and not a replacement for them.

Simultaneously Go Bottom Up and Top Down

A purely top-down approach (for examples, see Subsection 3.1) is problematic, because the data on which the analysis depends is typically to be found within the business lines. Furthermore, the results of any analysis need to be implemented typically within the business lines themselves and therefore their enthusiastic support is essential. In contrast, a purely bottom-up approach (for examples, see Subsection 3.2), is difficult for three reasons:

- The need for senior management support
- The critical importance of economic risk capital as the driver for many operational risk projects
- The inherent difficulties associated with operational risk management data

The most effective means of overcoming these obstacles is to simultaneously adopt a top-down approach (for capital and the allocation of other resources) and a bottom-up approach (to get operational managers involved).

Be Opportunistic

Another critical success factor is a detailed project plan that is both strict enough to gauge progress and flexible enough to take advantage of data and access opportunities. Remember that access to many managers may be difficult and sporadic. Anticipate this by planning ahead and preparing all your questions and issues for discussion. Furthermore, make sure that the project makes for frequent deliverables that have immediate value. This is not as difficult as it might seem. For example, an operational risk management project with the general goal of developing risk capital measures, might build loss logs useful for internal audit, control charts for operational managers, or fault trees for training purposes.

4.4   DEVELOPING RISK MANAGEMENT TARGETS

Financial Targets

Knowing the directors' risk management agenda and general scope of the risk management project, senior managers should develop high-level financial and operational risk targets for different business units. These targets should be tightly coupled with the strategic objectives of each individual business rather than be imposed in an *ad hoc* fashion. Typically, financial targets come first. For instance, for business units with steady earnings potential, so-called cash cows, financial targets will focus on optimizing operating cash flow and minimizing variation on the income statement. Business units involving greater operational risks will require more balance-sheet protection and more careful management of scarce risk capital.

Operational Targets

Operational targets must be made consistently with these financial targets. Balance-sheet protection, for example, implies targeting *VaR* and the estimation of unexpected and catastrophic losses, while income-statement management will focus on EaR and, in particular, the expected and unexpected component of the risk. Furthermore, this determines whether managers should focus on events that are relatively frequent with low impacts or those that are much less frequent but with very large impacts. This makes a huge difference in choosing data-gathering and measurement techniques. A focus on frequent low-impact events is most appropriate if the project is being implemented within a relatively low-level business unit with strategic objectives of greater efficiency and cost control. In contrast, a focus on infrequent major contingencies is more appropriate if the firm has a capital management agenda and is looking to risk-based capital allocation for operational risk. If most of the major contingencies are independent of internal operations, then it is wise to separate the two analyses because trying to force-fit these very different types of events into a single system can confuse and limit the effectiveness of either approach.

These are summarized in Table 4.2.

TABLE 4.2 Business Strategy, and Operational and Financial Targets

Strategic objectives	Efficiency	Growth	Capital management
Type of business unit	Cash cow: Steady	Star: High earnings potential with high volatility	Troubled performer: Uncertain earnings potential with high volatility
Financial targets	Cash flow and income statements, EaR	Balance sheet, reputation	Use of capital, VaR
Operational targets	Developing a risk aware culture Risk analysis Risk-based performance measurement		
	Continuous operational process improvement	Change control Limits	Limits, Contingency planning
Dimensions of risk	Expected losses	Unexpected losses	Catastrophic losses
Risk focus	Frequent events with low impact	Project risks	Infrequent events with high impact

We will develop some of these operational targets in more detail in the rest of this subsection.

General Operational Targets

Some high-level organizational initiatives can be very effective in the longer term, no matter what the type of risk or the organizational level at which it is managed. These would include operational targets for:

- Risk awareness: Convince staff at all levels of the need for a risk aware perspective and how to enact such a perspective. All managers must understand the different types of risks initiated in their area and what they can do about them.

- Proactive risk analysis: Risks should be understood and a systematic approach to identifying, measuring, and managing them developed.

- Risk-based performance measurement: Used at lower levels for resource allocation and developing incentives.

Increasing Risk Awareness Any operational risk management program must actively sell the case for a risk aware operational culture to the business areas. Operational risk management should be seen as a helpmate rather than a big brother. While making the process as transparent and as unobtrusive as possible will go far in fostering acceptance of the importance of operational risk management and translating the high-level risk targets into actionable business ones, additional measures are required. These include training and education to increase the level of understanding of the operational risks at all stages of the operational process. Staff should know why their existing practices need to be changed. This is especially important for operational risk managers whose approval is essential to any product or process change. Particularly at the early stages, risk assessment may require extensive self-assessment of exposures by business units themselves. Thus, it is imperative that managers be educated in general terms about the techniques of risk analysis and the limitations of more informal and subjective risk assessment approaches. They should also be schooled in the need to take any risk management actions contingent on the *type* of risk exposure, rather than making knee-jerk responses based on managerial familiarity or accessibility. Doing this requires managers to understand how operational risk management can prevent, mitigate, and predict the risks that affect their operations. Risk education and communication are particularly essential in risk-based performance measurements since a confusion of ends will only lead to internal game-playing and frustration about implementing just another control system.

Proactive Data-gathering and Risk Analysis   Analysis should begin with data-gathering (rather than complex model-building) and developing short-term deliverables of immediate value to line operations whose support is so crucial to the long-term success of the program. Several intermediate targets can be used for further analysis:

•   Name and precisely define the major loss events: Staff then have a common language in which to discuss and analyze operational problems more easily.

•   Develop an event log: Begin the task of obtaining historical data.

•   Statistical dependency models such as event and fault trees: What causes specific events and what are their implications?

•   Statistical dependency models: What is the impact of changes in resource allocation on specific losses?

•   Simulation: Perform risk-based resource allocation and scenario analysis.

Risk Adjusted Performance   Risk adjusted measures of profitability such as Return on risk adjusted capital/Risk adjusted return on capital (RORAC/RAROC) let firms assess the desirability of risk management efforts in specific business areas (see Subsection 16.3). At lower levels of the organization, it must identify particular risk targets that feed into the higher level risk adjusted performance measures. The choice of target business variables depends on the risk and the importance of the business area to group P&L. For example, Commercial banking operations focus on interest margin, whereas an investment bank may focus on net present value (NPV) of a market portfolio. Another important issue is the extent to which overhead operating costs are variable—this would suggest the importance of operational risk targets relative to financial and credit risk targets. For many banks, much of the variance in net income is the result of variance in the interest margin, and so at first glance might not suggest the need for operational risk management. However, this ignores the fact that many operational risks are controllable, in marked contrast to largely uncontrollable market risks. Assuming a focus on income-statement protection, you can identify targets by isolating the sources of the greatest variance in the net income. This can be done formally using linear regression models (assuming the data are available) or informally using simple risk profiling models.

Specific Operational Targets

Some risk targets are less general and more appropriate for particular types of risk exposures:

- Operational efficiency improvements: Setting the baseline for risk assessment

- Change control process: Evaluating the risks of changes and disseminating information about the changes

- Limit management: Defining aggregate exposures that potentially threaten the survival of the firm

All of these elements are needed since they are mutually reinforcing in the development of an operational risk management competence.

Improvements in Operational Efficiency Operational risk measurement provides general approaches for more economically efficient resource (not just capital) allocation. Business area managers should be encouraged to view operational risk management as a means to escape the *ad hoc* and political approaches that has managers in different business units compete more fiercely with each other than they do with their external competitors. Operational risk techniques such as dependency models offer managers a way to leverage internal knowledge about what can go wrong in their operations, why that can happen, what the possible impacts are, and what can be done about it. Developing common definitions of loss events and risk factors is an important first step in helping staff discuss internal problems and develop common approaches for dealing with them. Building a standard set of processes and resource descriptions leverages best practices in one part of the organization to standard practices within the entire organization. This is the shared memory of the firm regarding best practices in operational risk management and is discussed in more detail in the next section. Developing a loss log helps identify major problem areas for subsequent analysis and direct rapid contingent responses for emergency situations.

Implement the Change Control Process One of the most cost-effective operational risk management interventions is the development of a systematic process of change control. The risks of major business, system, and product changes are supervised by a change management committee comprising the relevant business area heads and staff functions. This should be supported by a dedicated staff function, either in the operational risk group or internal control, that rapidly disseminates notice of changes to all who may be affected. Firmwide intranets are increasingly being used to do this, given the difficulty of predicting some of the downstream impacts of changes.

Develop Operational Limits Limits are the guidelines put in place to monitor, constrain, and avoid risk exposures (see also the subsection on Boundary Systems). Limits have traditionally been used in a market risk setting where the range of risks and the variety of organizational units over which these risks can be incurred mean that limit structures can range from the simple aggregate level to complex hierarchies. Operational risk limits are much simpler because of the less-dynamic nature of and the paucity of accurate data for operational exposures. Nonetheless, operational limits have an important role. They set the maximum risk levels that a firm is willing to tolerate. Limits constrain staff from risk taking beyond some threshold without prior approval from their superiors. Exceeding these risk limits should only be allowed with formal approval from more senior managers as well as risk managers (and ultimately the board itself).

Limits can be most simply defined in terms of an aggregate exposure in a specific time period under the control of a specific area or in terms of the individual or marginal risk of the additional transaction being considered. The former allows individuals more freedom to manage the risk themselves while increasing the potential for human error, fraud, and transaction concealment. The latter may allow decentralized management of the risk by business managers.

Limits should also have associated well-defined actions to be taken by operations or risk managers—plans for what happens if the limits are exceeded—that vary from the mundane (a check with the supervisor) to exception reporting to extreme sanctions (such as firing the responsible staff member or criminal prosecution). An action-tracking mechanism should be in place to make sure that actions provoked by limit excesses are taken quickly to prevent problems getting out of hand. Without well-defined actions that are consistently followed, limits have no meaning and just contribute to confusion. Limits must be consistently applied; exceptions undermine the usefulness of limit-setting when staff realize that the system can be circumvented. For instance, a successful business unit must follow the defined limits just as much as a less-successful unit.

Limits may be based on the level of risk factors or the number of loss events during a time period. Examples include the daily loss level; limits on total purchases of each type of financial instrument, on the total investment in any single issuer, or on the total purchases of any single issue; market concentrations; or perhaps the dollar value (NPV or nominal value) of those transactions. Techniques such as *control charts* and *probability charts* utilize *statistical quality control* approaches to develop limits that define whether an operational process is in control.

Limits usually reflect consistent extremes of a probability distribution and prompt warnings for either increased management attention or immediate action. In market risk management, limits are based on a direct measure of the risk associated with the position—either the net exposure of the trader's portfolio or the marginal risk exposure of an additional trade. VaR measures can be used for limits as can stress levels, which look at the effect of extreme shifts.

Limits should also reflect the extent to which a business unit has control over the risk during the prescribed time horizon. It is important to specify the time horizon explicitly; increase the time horizon sufficiently and almost all risks are controllable. Less-controllable risks are usually managed at the aggregate firm level through risk financing techniques such as insurance or hedging. A manager's limits should focus on those risks that he or she can control.

4.5 RISK MANAGEMENT ORGANIZATION

Given the risk agenda set by the firm's senior management, directors, and shareholders, every financial-services organization must answer the following:

- Who should initiate risks?
- Who should manage the risks?
- What are the roles and responsibilities of risk managers?

Who Should Initiate Risks?

Front-office functions of financial institutions such as sales, marketing, retail, and trading make business decisions that lead to operational risks downstream, in back-office and middle-office operations. The front-office authority to commit the institution to decisions that lead to operational risks needs to be well-defined (usually by level or position within the firm) and clearly communicated throughout both the front and the back offices of the business.

Box 4.2: Apparent Authority

Management should recognize that the legal notion of "apparent authority" may bind the organization to decisions to which unauthorized individuals have committed. Similarly, counterparties or clients should realize the potential for transactions to be *ultra vires*. The most famous example of this was the recent decision of the Hammersmith and Fulham councils in the UK to renege on their swap agreements with several investment houses. This followed a House of Lords decision that the councils were not legally authorized to agree to the transactions.

Risk authorization is usually organized according to its extent of risk. As operational risks increase, authorization is passed up the hierarchy. Ideally, a formal system of approvals must be followed before committing the firm to risky decisions, and should include time limits on obtaining such approval. This is especially important when the risks are unfamiliar or fall between organizational units. Thus, firms should develop clear policies on infrequent, off-hour, or off-site operational activities, and carefully assess the legal risks involved. It is also essential that as new businesses, markets, products, and operations are changed or developed, the risks inherent in these activities are identified and assessed, and the board and senior management are kept informed of these changes.

Who Should Manage the Risks?

Every risk should have an owner—someone who is responsible for accepting, preventing, mitigating, transferring, or managing the contingencies associated with that risk. The risk owner must be authorized to take action and have the power to demand reduction in levels of operational risks incurred by those authorized to initiate the risks. Ownership for loss events and risk factors related to risk exposures needs to be assigned to specific knowledgeable individuals according to the similarity of mechanisms for dealing with them, rather than necessarily by their source or business area.

For many operational risks, the owner should be the operational risk management group. However, the choice of the risk owner depends on the business focus and the nature of the business exposure. When the focus is one of internal control, operational risk management will work more closely with senior management and corporate staff to produce a centralized solution. When efficiency is the major objective, business coordination and the need to share knowledge among risk managers and business lines require a decentralized approach of allocating risk ownership to the operational and business lines.

FIGURE 4.1 Risk Management Efficiency and Internal Control

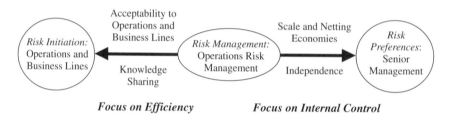

Deciding the owner of the risk is a compromise between two conflicting principles. First, responsibility should generally reside with those in the best position to manage it (usually the initiator of the risk—for example, account managers or trade desk managers). Second, the manager of the risk should maintain some independence from the authorized initiator of the risk (in other words, there should be segregation of duties). Those who initiate the risks should differ from those who are responsible for the risks.

Box 4.3:   Segregation of Duties in Front and Back Offices

Front and back offices are separated organizationally to maintain segregation of duties. Consider that there are at least five steps in purchasing or issuing a financial instrument:

1. Decide what to purchase or issue.

2. Place the order with a transacting bank or brokerage firm.

3. Verify a confirmation slip from the bank or brokerage firm.

4. Approve the transfer of funds to pay for the financial instrument (or approve receipt of funds).

5. Account for the transaction.

In some companies, five different people do the five separate tasks. In others, one person does more than one task. In general, the more tasks done by one individual, the greater the potential efficiencies but the greater the opportunity for errors and dishonesty, for example the rogue trading scandals at Barings and Daiwa. When a large amount is at stake, internal control and asset protection become a greater priority and efficiency a lesser one.

This compromise also depends on the nature of the risk. With financial risk management, the answer seems straightforward; the existence of reasonable data on correlative effects across different portfolios argues strongly for a centralized portfolio perspective. For operational risk management, the call is harder to make. A decentralized approach places operational risk control close to the source of the risks. Centralized approaches, however, have the ear of senior management and provide the opportunity for incorporating correlation or portfolio effects, as well as a level of independence not found within the business line. For example, centralized treasury, audit, or corporate financial risk management may be well-positioned to also handle both credit and market risk measurement and aggregation, and to take advantages of the economies of scale associated with risk management (such as sharing best practices or developing an integrated process and framework). In general, however, operational risks should not be managed under the financial risk group. It is important to recognize operational risk management and award it as an entity separate from market and credit risk to define and allocate risk capital required to be set aside; unlike market and credit risk, operational risks have a very low correlation with either of the other two risks commonly faced by financial institutions.

The incentives for these risk managers must be aligned with those of the firm's appetite for risk to ensure that only the appropriate risks are managed, and only to the required extent. This responsibility should be formally signed off periodically by the risk manager concerned and made explicit and widely communicated to other risk management staff so that the boundaries of risks are well-defined. Clarity of risk ownership is crucial: one of the conclusions of the Bank of England report following the Barings Bank collapse was the need for clarity of responsibility, particularly when firms have a matrix operating structure (BoE, 1995). Both the ownership and the authorization of risks should be periodically re-evaluated to reflect changes in the magnitude and controllability of the risk. As magnitude increases, authorization and ownership should rise up the hierarchy. As the controllability changes, the management techniques used may change and, therefore, the business owners also may change.

What Are the Roles and Responsibilities of Risk Managers?

The operational risk management group needs to do the following:

- Perform data-gathering, measurement, and risk analysis of operational risks.

- Liaise with a variety of internal and external parties on the firm's risk management practices, for example, line managers, senior managers, regulators, and audit (internal and external).

- Provide advice on policy and leadership on issues related to risk management, for example, contingency planning, re-putation management, reengineering, HR, training, etc.

- Liaise with financial risk management and insurance to provide risk transfer for residual risks.

- Provide training and a justification for operational risk management.

- Develop risk practices, standards, technologies, and policies.

- Participate in supporting the management of high risk strategic projects, products, or markets.

A dedicated operational risk control group could be formed just below corporate management and staffed with middle managers having line-management experience and familiarity with risk management techniques as well as their respective specialties (such as audit, insurance, and legal). This central group focuses on the risk management approaches to operational risk, but implementation is performed by business units, office operational managers, or asset specialists. For example, the organizational structure in Figure 4.2 is typical of that employed by financial groups with an enterprise-wide risk management focus.

FIGURE **4.2** Typical Risk Management Organization

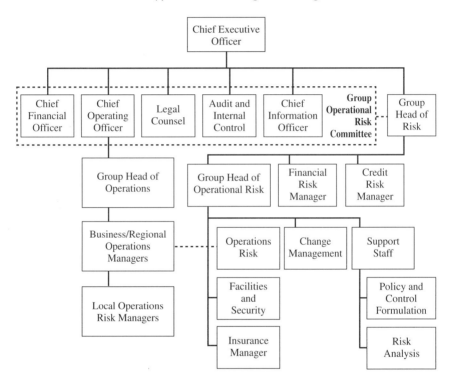

A dozen staff members is probably sufficient within the core operational risk group. A major constraint on operational risk centralization is the availability of staff. Staff members require not only knowledge of analytical risk management techniques, but they also must also have access to a wide range of operational knowledge, often in diverse geographic locations.

There are several roles within this prototypical operational risk management group.

Many institutions, such as UBS, Republic Bank, and Bankers Trust, have established formal operational *risk management committees* that oversee all aspects of operational risk authorization and ownership. Such committees should meet regularly (usually monthly) depending on the rate of change of operations within the firm. Its composition should reflect areas of highest operational risk. Reporting to the committee, the senior manager responsible for firmwide operational risk must have clearly defined powers that are documented and made explicit throughout the organization. The role of the committee is to evaluate risk issues of escalating importance, direct action and general policy, and recommend changes to internal control.

The *group head of risk* is responsible for strategic risk exposures and managing the escalating risk, financial, or operational exposures. He or she may also take the lead in inculcating a risk aware culture—perhaps by developing risk-based performance measurements or risk aligned incentives programs, or by changing the organizational culture regarding risks. This person may also represent the firm to regulators and clients concerned about the firm's exposures.

The *operational risk manager* liaises with senior management, strategic planning, corporate finance, internal audit, and other risk management functions such as credit and market risks. This may be done either directly or through a risk committee that meets periodically. Responsibility, authority, accountability, and funding must flow directly from the chief executive officer (CEO) to those charged with risk control for it to succeed. Effective operational risk management groups must report to a senior level of management.

Other members within the group include *risk analysts* who provide analytical and technical support for risk measurement, analysis, and *policy analysts* who update internal best practices and policies databases. *Facilities managers and security personnel* manage the potential threats to the firm's fixed assets.

Operations risk management forms liaisons with local operations and business lines. The focus for operations risk management is several-fold:

- Define best practices in the field of operations.

- Help line and operations staff optimize processes and resources.

- Document base-level processes and the operational risk database.

- Generate an operational risk management plan.

While general categories of risk may be managed by middle managers using risk transfer or major system loss prevention or mitigation programs, line and support areas have to be responsible for managing most of the events and risk factors that lead to operational risks. They also produce most of the data for operational risk measurement. For example, in one Australian bank, the probability distributions for various loss events and risk factors are defined by the centralized group, but the parameters of those distributions are determined by the local managers. To make the relationship between regional operations and centralized operations risks more effective, an operations risk officer can be designated within the local office. Although not necessarily a full-time position, this person would have a dotted-line relationship with the centralized operations risk group. The strength of the links between regional and centralized operations risks is critical to the effectiveness of the entire risk management program. Having such a decentralized approach often swaps the underlying risks for the difficulties of managing the local risk managers. Consequently, decentralized approaches demand more formalized reporting and routine procedures.

Change control is responsible for managing, disseminating, and collating information on change requests to products, systems, and businesses. In some firms, there may be a change-control committee to which this staff member has a dotted-line relationship. The change-control committee approves the changes whereas the change-control staff informs the rest of the organization about these changes and works with operational risk management on the potential risk related implications.

4.6 RISK POLICIES AND PRACTICES

Risk Policies

The firm's risk policies codify both the firm's appetite for risk, as well as its major operational processes, limits, risk-based performance targets, and procedures for managing the risk. They must incorporate general principles as well as specific action guidelines. They need to be formal and written down with the backing and endorsement of senior management and the board. Policies are usually developed by the chief operating officer (COO), the chief financial officer (CFO), and the treasurer in conjunction with the various operating lines. Formal policies are particularly important in the case of firms with high staff turnover because they operate as a collective memory about risks within the firm and how to deal with them. The policies should clearly and unambiguously address the following:

- The goals of risk management: Which risks are transferred; the criteria for prevention, mitigation, and prediction efforts.

- Approved risk management strategies: For a given exposure, define what risk management actions are appropriate (see the later section on risk management actions).

- The criteria with which these strategies are evaluated: How to choose among the different feasible risk management actions.

- The specific individuals authorized to engage in these risk management strategies (insurance buying, derivatives, audit).

- Defined reporting and authorization structures for managing these individuals.

- Delimited role of the board and senior management, particularly in corporate treasury.

- Established risk limits and targets.

- Established procedures for measuring and monitoring risks.

Operational risk managers should understand that policy documents are as much for external review as internal. Risk policies are important from a compliance perspective because regulators often use the risk documentation as an indicator of the quality of internal risk management practices. Periodic review of policies and procedures by internal and external audit helps ensure completeness of risk measures, consistency of application, and proper accounting under generally accepted accounting principles (GAAP). External consultants also make use of procedures described in the policy document to validate the risk measurement approach and implementation.

Informal Risk Management Guidelines

Real-world risk management can never be completely codified or captured in formal rules described in any policy document. This is not to say that policies should not be well-documented, but rather that the firm's ultimate defense for loss prevention always lies in the attitude and resourcefulness of its staff. With this in mind, here are some useful guidelines for risk managers with which to inculcate their staff (Table 4.3).

TABLE 4.3 Informal Risk Management Guidelines

Guideline	Rationale
Understand your profits	Large profits you don't understand are more dangerous than large losses you do. Focus on quality of earnings, not their magnitudes.
Learn to avoid but do not learn to blame	Everyone finds it easy to blame and harder to compliment. Proactive operational risk management will not occur if management'sactions after losses are sackings and reprimands. Instead, staff will learn to cover up mistakes, letting them grow further into potential devastating losses. It is much better to encourage staff to reveal their mistakes early so they can be rectified. Superior performance is the result of experience. Unfortunately, experience is often the result of mistakes.
Do not think "Not my problem"	Functional organizations are notorious for developing a silo mentality about their problems. Staff often only take responsibility for problems that fall squarely into their narrow discipline or area of responsibility. As we have seen, operational problems involve sequences of events being mismanaged because they don't fall into any particular person's area of responsibility. To some extent, an effective system of risk transfer within the organization will help rectify this, but no formal system will succeed without the flexible support of staff in these areas.
Beware of "out of sight, out of mind"	Operational risk increases with distance from the head office.
Disclose the risks	There should be incentives in place to make staff disclose risks rather than hide them. In practice, there is often a strong temptation to keep risks hidden.
Keep holidays holy!	People who don't take holidays may be trying to avoid revealing some unpleasant truth. Vacation policies should be developed to ensure that every one does someone else's work for part of every year.
Pay peanuts, get monkeys	Risk management requires the investment of resources. Risk managers need to know as much as traders if they are to police them.
Risk policy vs risk control	Risk policy sets up a framework for effective risk management; risk control ensures that it is followed.
Little problems are a harbinger of big problems	Manage the problems before they grow. Problems tend to snowball. Reconcile quickly. Emphasize the prompt solution of problems.
Track the cash	Don't emphasize accounting entries. Focus on the cash.
Risk financing	Purchase insurance to cover any loss that might seriously affect operations. This typically means, for example, keeping uninsured or unhedged losses below a specific percentage of revenues.

CHAPTER 5

IDENTIFYING THE RISKS

5.1 BENCHMARKING INTERNAL PROCESSES AND RESOURCES

Need for a Benchmark

Risk identification should always proceed from a benchmark. The benchmark should be either a description of the current state of the firm's operations or a description of the target best practices. Without a benchmark, risk management runs the danger of institutionalizing current practice, which may be dangerous if current practice is a poor standard. The benefits of a set of formal descriptions of the firm's core process are enormous and not restricted to risk management. Benchmarking can:

Improve the firm's understanding of how its own processes work Process benchmarks help firms understand their own processes better. Making formal process descriptions widely accessible to new staff members will bring them up to speed faster and encourage identification with the process and the quality of its results. An expanded view of the process structure also helps managers and back-office staff understand their broader roles and interdependencies with other parts of the business. In practice, processes will be complex vertical and horizontal combinations of subprocesses. Process maps of these combinations explain just how their actions affect others and where the true source of many day-to-day problems actually lies.

Improve efficiency through reengineering and process redesign Process mapping is a preamble to process reengineering. Process mapping can be used to develop an understanding of which activities add value by increasing returns or decreasing risks and which do not.

Help understand risk transfer within the organization and help design risk pricing strategies Risks tend to be transferred downstream from one part of the process to another. Process mapping can be used to allocate risks back to the initiator or the manager of the risk. For example, if a customer database is not properly maintained, payment instructions will be in error and there will be an increased risk of customer dissatisfaction and loss. Who is responsible for the risk? Database management or customer support (or even both)? In multiproduct companies, different business areas and business processes will often unknowingly cross-subsidize each other, either directly in terms of costs or indirectly by passing the operational risks of one business to another. For example, brokerage clients may be given cheap custodian services or securities investors may get free analyst reports. Process maps, in conjunction with process risk estimates, reveal the extent of these cross-subsidies.

Help dictate a systematic approach to contingency planning through resource and process mapping Without it, the process is highly susceptible to the loss of key personnel or other critical resources. A lack of documentation dramatically increases the risk that the process will not be able to function. The basic objective of disaster planning is to enable each process to continue or be restarted if interrupted. In analyzing each process, it is important to focus on the *function* of the process. The function might be order entry, payroll, accounts payable, receivables, invoicing, advisory services, quality assurance, training, tax accounting, or any of a hundred others. Each of these processes varies in terms of its criticality to the short-term survival of the firm as a whole. With catastrophe planning, the most important objective is to resume overall organizational functioning as quickly as possible. To do this means focusing attention on those processes that cannot be postponed if the organization is to survive. For example, while payroll may need to be done within a week, promotions and advertising might be postponed for several weeks before they become critical. The levels to which processes can be postponed may also vary by business volume, day of the week, or season of the year. Processes should be identified as those critical elements without which the organization cannot function on an as-intended basis during a medium term. Therefore, individual processes need to be analyzed separately because the organization's survival as a whole depends on the proper functioning of each of these processes. Note that whether the process is internal or external to the firm is *not* critical. The failure of a major contractor (such as a systems vendor, telecoms provider, utility, or even the post office) may be just as devastating as the failure of an internal process. Finally, we must ask: After being knocked out, how long would the process take to return to normal functioning and how long can the firm as a whole survive without that process? Planning would then focus on providing an alternative site for the discrepancy between process downtime and assessing the criticality of the process for the firm as a whole.

Benchmarking Steps

Benchmarking involves several steps:

1. Process and resource identification
2. Process description and analysis
3. Process evaluation

Identifying Critical Processes and Resources This requires going down the management chain to senior department heads responsible for critical business processes and resources. During these preliminary meetings with senior managers, core process and resources for each strategic business unit (SBU) or profit center must be identified. Processes need not match SBU, profit, or cost center, but linkages between these should be captured. High-level processes can be broken down into a number of generic subprocesses such as sales and marketing, deal commitment, confirmations, settlement and maintenance, and accounting, as well as support processes including legal, systems, audit, risk management, and reconciliation. Typically, such processes cross operating lines between front, back, and middle offices and will affect firmwide financial results. A process can be thought of as a measurable interconnected group of activities that can flow across departments. Michael Porter, in his influential book, *Competitive Advantage* (1985), argues that components of the value chain or process should be segregated if:

- Different elements represent a large proportion of operating costs or of the total risks of the entire process
- The cost behavior of the various components differs
- The components are performed differently by competitors
- The activities afford the opportunity for differentiation

Another important issue in describing processes is the extent to which the process is changing over the decision horizon. Preliminary identification and description should always focus on those processes and resources whose attributes are relatively static.

Describing Critical Processes and Resources Once the core processes and resources have been identified, risk management staff should compile answers to the following questions for each process or resource:

- What is the role of the process within the organization?
- Is the process critical to the survival of the organization? How long a downtime in the process could the business tolerate?
- What is the relationship of this process to other organizational processes?
- What are the physical resources normally used by the process? What are the minimum requirements of each? Are any of these resources shared with other processes?
- Which staff are engaged with the process? What general skills do these staff have?
- What long-term information and data (records, files, etc.) are essential to the functioning of the process? Where are these information resources maintained and stored?
- What would be the impact on the process if these information resources were unavailable?
- What information resources are transferred to other processes as part of service delivery?

- How sensitive are other processes to the absence of the information transfer?

- What computing and communications resources are required to gather, process, store, and transfer this information?

Many of these questions seek to identify the resources (such as capital, information, data, equipment, furnishings, power, personnel, and communications) required for each process. Resources are anything that, when incorporated into the firm's process structure, yields economic benefits. The term *resource* is used rather than assets because of the importance of non-balance-sheet resources for many processes. These intangible resources—such as management attention or the skills and knowledge of the work force—are important factors that determine the effectiveness of many real-world processes.

Answering these questions will require in-depth interviews with the relevant middle managers responsible for those processes and resources. The purpose here is to identify the interfaces between processes and resources—the source of many critical loss events. The result of these interviews is a *process analysis* of the organization—an overview of the firm's core processes and the resources they consume.

A major issue in describing processes is the appropriate level of detail to include. The goal should be to reveal just the amount of detail appropriate for a particular user seeking to understand the process. Process maps should be detailed enough to identify the processes that add value and those that do not. It is not necessary to cover each and every organizational process and resource. In practice, the level of detail also depends on the degree of risk in the area, and for this reason process benchmarking will be performed iteratively in conjunction with risk assessment. What is required is to *focus on those processes and resources that,* a priori, *appear to be driving much of the variance in target variables such as net earnings or stock value.* It follows that the operational risk methodology makes the important empirically confirmed assumption (the Pareto Principle) that most (80–90 percent) enterprise risks result from only a few processes or resources, and a relatively small set of possible loss events. More levels of detail in process maps hide information from staff members and discourage them from learning about issues outside their own particular area. This can be rectified by putting process maps on an intranet system and allowing users to expand process areas to the required level of detail. For risk management uses, it is rare that more than two or three levels of detail will be required. Another major issue in developing process maps is the representation. Standard flow chart symbols such as those in Figure 5.1 can be used.

FIGURE **5.1** Common Process Mapping Symbols

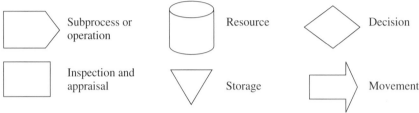

	Subprocess or operation		Resource		Decision
	Inspection and appraisal		Storage		Movement

Box 5.1:   Market Risk Management Process

A high-level description of the risk management process in a large trading operation might look similar to this:

FIGURE **5.2** Market Risk Management Process

Market Feeds — Market Risk Management — Collateral and Risk Reports

Trading Books — Credit Risk Management

Sales — Trade Execution — Trade Entry — Confirms — Settlement — Accounting — General Ledger

Counter-parties — Delivery and Payment — Depot Statements

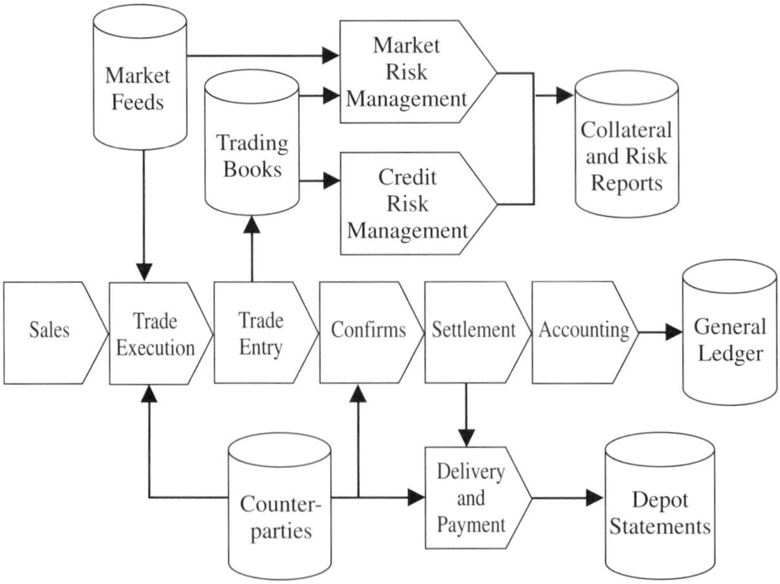

Evaluating Processes

Once processes and resources have been identified and described, they should be evaluated against specific benchmarks. Benchmarks should be chosen according to the firm's strategic objectives for the business. A mature operational group may happily take internal practices as a stable benchmark, but this is unlikely to be useful for a turnaround situation. Benchmarking that involves comparisons with the best direct competitor would then be appropriate. Benchmarking can also be internal, involving comparisons of similar operations within the same organization. Sometimes functional benchmarking is used, which compares a firm's processes with similar process methodologies. Sources of information for benchmarking include the Internet, in-house publications, universities, customer feedback, and trade associations.

5.2   IDENTIFYING PROCESS AND RESOURCE RISKS

Following identification and description of the critical operational processes and resources, we must discover the risks that can affect process performance and resource utilization. Producing this breakdown of risk factors and loss events by process and resource requires interviews with line managers and senior supervisors who have the experience of what can go wrong in a process. A good start is to ask which factors outside of their control affect the outputs of the process; this helps put managers at ease in what can be a stressful interview. Managers generally do not like to admit that things can go wrong and that sometimes the source of the problems can be in their own department. An initial focus on loss events originating in another part of the organization, or even completely outside the control of the firm, can warm up managers' acceptance of the potential for risks. It is important to find out in which business unit the manager believes the loss event *does* originate and then cross-check this against the beliefs of managers in that business unit. Disagreements are inevitable and are an important side-effect of the entire operational risk management effort. They suggest confusion about responsibilities, controls, and even how the process works—all of which need to cleared up if a real operational disaster is to be averted. Also be aware of possible manager complacency—a "no problem here" attitude can hide potential disasters.

During open-ended unstructured interviews, managers, taking into account the firm's overall experience, should be prompted for their risk priorities and exposures, as well as industry/competitive trends. This contextual information frames subsequent risk analysis. It suggests what is important and what is not. Prioritizing directs attention to risk management. It needs to be made clear to all concerned that no attempt to capture all the organization's risks will ever be complete. What will work, however, is a *focused* search for the *critical* risk factors and loss events associated with *core* processes and resources. This is important because operational risk measurement is *not* an enterprise modeling technique—only *critical* areas with highest risk should be examined. This prioritization can be directed in several ways:

- By analyzing external historical losses
- By analyzing internal historical losses
- By using strategic frameworks
- By following industry best practices

In practice, several of these approaches should be used to triangulate the major exposures faced by the firm's operations.

External Historical Losses

Research into other firms' experiences with similar processes can shed light on the potential loss events (particularly catastrophic losses) that could impact the process, but because of the infrequency of these events, managers may not have any experience with them. Again, an attitude of "not at this company" needs to be examined with healthy skepticism.

Box 5.2: Could This Happen Here?

Historical losses such as those shown here prompt the inevitable question: Could this happen here? To be effective, this line of questioning requires that a centralized risk management group take the lead in forcing managers to resist the temptation to assume that internal processes/resources are innately superior.

TABLE 5.1 Recent Operational Losses

Risk category		Firm	Event	Impact
Operational Risk	Asset				
	Tangible	McDonald & Co	Water main breakage	Loss of billing records and stocks
	Intangible	Salomon Bros	Failure to report trading "irregularities"	$1 billion, reputation plus legal
		Security Pacific	Fraudulent transfer of money	$10 million
	Loss of HR investments	Major finance company	Kidnapping of key executive	$5 million+
	Human resources			
	Errors and unauthorized activity	Barings	Rogue trading	$1.3 billion and bankruptcy
		Daiwa	Fraud	$1.1 billion
		Equity Funding	Executive/employee fraud	Several hundred million dollars
	Technology			
	Production	Major finance company	Network failure	$10 million
		DBS	IT interface error with public system	
	Information	Major finance company	Software logic bomb	$50 million
		Major finance company	Six-hour mainframe failure	$15 million
		Kidder Peabody	Model arbitrage	$1 billion+
	Project/ coordination	Major finance company	IT systems scrapped	$10 million+ write-off and $15 million revision
		Metalgesellschaft	Basis risk and not tied to corporate strategy	$1.3 billion

TABLE 5.1 Recent Operational Losses (cont'd)

Risk category		Firm	Event	Impacts
Supplier Risk	Item availability	Major finance company	Power supply failure	$15 million
	Contract availability	Major finance company	Drop in credit usage	$100 million
Customer Risk	Terms/quality	Barclays Bank	Operational credit risk	$4.1 billion
		BankAmerica	Credit risk	$1.4 billion
	Exit	Citibank	Hackers	20 top customers and $400,000
Competi-tor Risk	Entry/exit	Major finance company	Risk of entrant capturing three percent of market	$500 million
Stakeholder Risk	Legal constituents	Merrill Lynch	Negligence	$2 million
	Customers	Prudential	Failure to warn investors of risk	Several hundred million dollars
	Employees	Major finance company	Class-action anti-discrimination suit	$20 million
	Competitors and suppliers	Potentially all	IT "downstream liability"	Millions of dollars
	Investors and Creditors	Major finance company	Executive corruption	$400 million
	Government	Major finance company	Regulatory non-compliance	$100 million+
		Major finance company	Incorrect interpretation of tax legislation	$10 million

TABLE 5.1 Recent Operational Losses (cont'd)

Risk category		Firm	Event	Impacts
Compet-itor Risk				
Entry/exit		Major finance company	Risk of entrant capturing three percent of market	$500 million
External				
Economic Financial	Production factors	Major finance company	Change in money supply terms	$50 million
	Market	Quantum Fund	Loss on foreign investments	$2 billion
		Orange County	Derivatives losses (funded by bonds)	$1.6 billion and bankruptcy
	Liquidity	LTCM	Illiquid position	$4 billion
Regulatory		Major finance company	Change in legislation/regulatory requirements	$10 million
Acts of God		Credit Lyonnaise	Earthquake	$100 million

Internal Historical Losses

If historical earnings, loss, or risk factor data are available, then the most effective way to identify risk areas is by qualitative analysis of *internal historical losses* through case studies. Any large variances in P&L and earnings should be analyzed for their potential operational causes. Also, don't neglect positive as well as negative shocks to earnings—large profits that you do not understand are often more dangerous than the large losses you do.

Strategic Risk Frameworks

Management frameworks can also be used to direct this search for major risks. One such framework, which builds on Michael Porter's famous Five Forces Model (Porter, 1980) is shown in Figure 5.3, and covers as many possible critical risk areas as possible. Frameworks act as checklists to jog a manager's mind into considering risks that, while potentially infrequent, may be devastating. Remember that our goal here is complete risk coverage of all the major risk areas rather than specific analysis of any one risk. Senior management will be quickly discouraged if we drill down too quickly in our analysis.

FIGURE 5.3 A Framework for Identifying Operational Risks

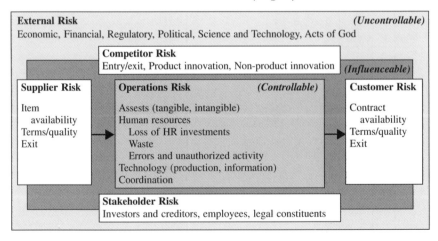

An important facet of risk that this framework makes clear is that whereas market and credit risks are largely uncontrollable, many operational risks are controllable and therefore *must* be managed if the firm is not to find itself at a competitive disadvantage. Broad strategic frameworks such as this provoke creative thought and suggest ways in which operational risk can be the spur for an operational core competence.

Industry Practices

Qualitative evaluation of the risks faced by a business can also be based on the *benchmarking of risk practices* relative to the leaders within the same industry. Commercial banks will focus on lending and deposits. Investment banks focus on market transactions. Universal banks combine market portfolios with banking portfolios. The risk priorities and the techniques used will reflect this.

TABLE 5.2 Assets and Risk Management Techniques

Business area	Assets	Equity and liabilities	Risk management technique
Treasury and banking transactions	Cash	Short-term debt	Cash management, process reengineering, TQM
Financial intermediation	Lending	Deposits	Asset–liability management— interest-rate risks Credit management— credit risks
Market transactions	Financial assets and liabilities		Portfolio management— market risk
Off-balance-sheet items	Contingent claims received	Contingent claims given	Derivatives management, financial risk management, real options
Long-term assets and liabilities	Fixed assets	Long-term debt Equity	Operational risk management, ALM, insurance, facilities management

5.3 IDENTIFYING RISK FACTORS

There are several rules of thumb to be kept in mind when identifying the risk factors that affect particular processes and resources:

- **Keep it simple:** One can very quickly develop a complex model comprising just internal and external risk factors and the dependencies between them. This is invariably a mistake. The secret to making risk factors work is not to have too many of them. Two to four internal risk factors and two or three external risk factors are more than sufficient for most businesses. In any case, just a few of the most critical (that is, explanatory) risk factors should be used at any given level of analysis. Too many risk factors and the whole model becomes unmanageable and hard to interpret by managers.

- **Risk factors should be significant:** The risk factor should have a significant effect, that is, a large proportion of the variance in the output of the organization under study should depend on the risk factor. This means that only a small number of risk factors need to be used. Pareto's Principle generally holds, whereby most of the risk is the result of only a small number of risk factors. No more than two or three risk factors are usually required for a given process or resource.

- **Risk factors should have a random component:** Factors should never entirely be under the control of business managers, that is, there is a random component of the factor. Risk factors should not be confused with management-decision variables. The latter are levers that managers can pull that influence cash flows, P&L, asset and liability values, and other loss events (see Subsection 8.3). Examples of these levers include the quality levels of key organizational resources such as staff, systems, policies, and procedures.

- **Start with external factors:** There are two types of risk factors. External risk factors are usually price-related with (generally) direct impacts that are assumed to drive fluctuations in the firm's revenues or asset values. Internal risk factors have indirect effects on P&L or asset values by changing the losses associated with particular events. Given a particular level of the analysis, a small number of actionable external risk factors should first be used to gain an approximate measure of the aggregate factors affecting the process's output.

- **Factors should affect outputs:** External risk factors should relate directly to the outputs of that organizational unit (which depend on the chosen level of analysis) and not just to the inputs or to some intermediate output of the unit.

- **Factors depend on the level of analysis:** The choice of risk factor depends on the level at which the analysis is being performed. For instance, at the level of the firm's net incomes, we might use the S&P 500, interest rates, and commodity prices as our risk factors. Within an operating unit, we might use revenues; for service areas, the number of customers, etc. In general, risk factors are most useful at the aggregate level of the firm rather than any particular business or operations area. There are several reasons for this. First, it is easier to measure the direct impacts of risk factors at a more aggregated level. Second, the higher the level of the business, the more the target variables are immunized from the idiosyncratic risks that affect lower levels.

- **Use actionable risk factors:** Make sure you can do something about the risk factor. Either you can control the level of the risk factor (through prevention or mitigation) or relatively cheaply hedge the risk factor with some other offsetting exposure (for instance, using insurance or forward contracts).

- **Use justifiable risk factors:** There should be a logical link explaining why the risk factor has the effect that you claim; this is important because without it, senior management will not find the analysis credible.

- **Risk factors should have reliable and timely data:** Ideally, timely and accurate data should be available for the risk factor. Risk factors should be measurable without too much lag between the level of the factor and its measurement. In practice, proxy measures for the risk factors, often called *key risk indicators* (KRIs), are used. But a note of caution. Risk indicators are merely easily measurable historical proxies for risks, while risk factors are the actual drivers of the risks.

- **Risk factors should be relatively independent of one another:** Strong correlations between risk factors suggest that the same underlying risk factor is being measured, and also extensively complicates the analysis.

- **Risk factors should be ongoing:** Risk factors' distributions should be stable over time. This is likely to be the case for processes with large volumes of transactions at different stages of the process at any instant. It is not so appropriate when the decision-making period is short and involves processes with large lumpy transactions such as a new product development or time-consuming batch operations. In such cases, the risks (factors and loss events) may depend on the stage the transaction is in within the process. It is also inappropriate for project management in which the risks may vary dramatically during different stages of the project. In this case, project risk techniques such as discrete event simulation, Critical Path Method *(CPM)*, Program Evaluation and Review Technique *(PERT)*, or *Markov* models can be used to help managers understand the time sensitivity of the process risks. In general however, complex dynamic models are usually unnecessary because risks can be modeled much more simply as the result of a dependency on some single time-varying risk factor (the most common example being volume).

The precise choice of risk factors depends on the particular business unit, and analysts should be careful to avoid any preconceived notions of where operational risks lie. Backward-looking analysis of historical internal and external losses combined with interviews with experienced line managers will suggest factors that may drive losses in a particular process area. In some cases, more forward-looking techniques can be used. *Designed experiments* can systematically identify which risk factors are most important on the output of the process. Such experiments can be used, for example, to infer how changes in the levels of staffing in different parts of the organization affect errors, or how changes in staff incentives affect performance levels.

The following risk factors are widespread and deserve more detailed comment here:

- Operating leverage

- Scale and volume

- Interest rates

- Complexity

- Time effects

- Change

- Management complacency

Operational Leverage

Most fixed-asset-intensive businesses are susceptible to the *operational-leverage* risk factor. Operational leverage describes the ability of a business to cover its fixed costs. Operational leverage risk is the risk of a less-than-perfect match between revenue fluctuations, and expense fluctuations and depends on the size of the asset base (fixed costs) relative to operating expense (variable costs). Proxies for operational leverage are usually simple functions of the fixed assets and the operating expenses. For example, the operational leverage risk might be 10 percent of the fixed asset size plus 25 percent of the last three months of operational expense. Another bank calculates its operational leverage risk as $2\frac{1}{2}$ times the monthly fixed expenses for each line of business.

Scale and volume

In addition to their direct impact on revenues, the volume and scale of transactions have an indirect impact on costs (particularly in the short-term). Furthermore, unexpected operational losses also increase with the number and the size of individual transactions. For example, the number of reworked transactions in one securities firm was closely related to the total volume of transactions, as shown in the example illustrated in Figure 5.4.

FIGURE 5.4: Average Volume and Reworked Transactions by Input Time

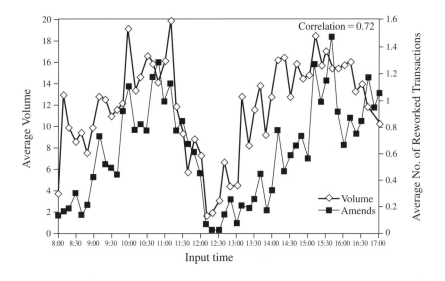

At the firm level, the simplest KRI proxy for these scale and volume risk factors is business revenue. Revenue is perhaps the most familiar and the easiest risk driver to use because many aggregate event costs fall naturally into two categories: variable (increasing with the numbers of transactions and, therefore, revenues), or fixed (independent of revenues). It sometimes helps to distinguish the pricing element of revenues (which may be outside the control of managers due to competitive pressures) from the volume (which is partially under the control of marketing and sales). It follows that volumes are much more effective as risk factors at the operational levels. KRIs for volume risk factors include the number of customers serviced by a sales person, the transaction volume per trader, or perhaps the number of a particular type of transaction done. Even more useful than absolute volumes, particularly over the short term and as a driver of unexpected human errors, is the level of undercapacity; that is, the difference between the volumes and the ability of the unit to handle those volumes. Proxies for undercapacity might be the number of temporary staff or the amount of overtime worked.

Interest Rates

Interest rates have both a direct and an indirect impact. They can directly affect asset values through changes in the values of fixed-income portfolios, or affect revenues through changes in prices or the demand for services. Interest rates can also indirectly change the impact of some events, particularly those with a long repair and recovery period for which the total interest costs may be significant. The level of overnight interest rates may also be important when assessing compensation payments made to counterparties because of delayed transactions or services. The precise KRI proxy chosen for the interest-rate risk factor depends on the nature of the effect; for instance, the short-term repo rate may be used to estimate indirect impacts or a five-year spot rate for the direct impacts.

Complexity

Although most short-term fluctuations in costs are driven by volume-based risk factors, longer term cost fluctuations are driven by product and service complexity and diversity. Complexity has two aspects. First, complexity that is intrinsic to the structure of the business or product itself will result in more unexpected losses. For instance, if a process has many steps, many calculations, many decisions, or many subsystems, it will be more complex and tend to have a wider range of performance levels (unexpected losses). Other proxies for intrinsic complexity include the margin on the product, the number of distribution channels, the number of services offered, the number of products, and the quality of the service.

The second aspect of complexity is extrinsic—it depends on the subjective experiences of the organizations managing the products or businesses. For example, the level of training of internal staff or the number of temporary staff may be good proxies for extrinsic complexity. Extrinsic capacity also occurs because products and businesses are at different stages of their product life cycle; however, the organization's experience and familiarity with the product or business likely depend on this life cycle. Such learning effects are really limitations of the human and organizational systems supporting those products and businesses. This is why newly developed instruments such as structured products are more likely to have booking errors than spot forex. Tools such as *experience curves* and *learning curves* can be used to estimate the variance in performance and how this variance will evolve over time.

Box 5.3: Risk Factors in a Payments Process

The following risk factors are believed to be important in a particular payments process.

TABLE 5.3 Risk Factors in a Payments Process

Risk factor	Factor description	Logical link	Proxy
Product volumes	Number of transactions of a particular product type per unit time	Assuming a constant probability of a loss per transaction, with a larger number of transactions we should find an increased amount of loss	Monthly volume
Product complexity	Usually subjective—how complex the product appears to the staff processing the transaction, or the user of the final result	As transactions become more complex to handle, the likelihood of an error increases	Number of cash flows, size of non-linear effects (e.g., gamma for derivatives)
Interest rates	Short-term repo rate	As short-term rates rise, so too do the penalties for late performance	Overnight rate

---

Time Effects

Another important risk factor is time. Seasonality and day-of-the-week effects drive many losses. Time-related effects can be analyzed in their own terms using time-series analysis, or you may begin a search for more "fundamental" underlying risk factors, which may themselves be seasonal. If possible, try to break through a time-based trend to the underlying risk driver. For example, an apparently seasonal effect in losses might really be the result of the high level of temporary staff at particular times of the year. Operational losses may peak on Mondays and Fridays because of high volumes on those days rather than because of it being Monday or Friday, *per se*. Of course, the question is when to stop digging for ultimate causes; however, a risk factor that is controllable and, therefore, actionable is always preferred to chronological time, which is not.

Change

New technology, new systems, new products, new businesses, and new organizational structures impinge on operations and lead to unexpected operational losses. Change management staff should develop statistics and measures for the levels of product, service, organizational, and system changes in different business units. KRI proxies for change include the rate of new product launches, organizational changes, new systems, levels of customers, and staff turnover.

Management Complacency

This seems to be a defining cause of two very different types of loss events. First, at the senior management level, complacency is a major driver of strategic and operational high-impact events ranging from the loss of market share, and hostile takeovers, to employee fraud, counterparty fraud, unauthorized trading, counterparty defections, and payment settlement failures. Second, at an operational level, complacency can also result in very high frequency events going unnoticed by managers because they seem part of the scenery (the so-called *threshold biases*—see Subsection 6.6). Complacency is also tied to business conditions. Problems tend to be stored up in prosperous times due to complacency, only to strike when the bad times come, exacerbating an otherwise manageable situation. Ironically, risk management itself can lead to management complacency because the assumption that risks are under control can therefore increase risk taking in the hope of obtaining greater returns (*morale hazard*). The importance of complacency as a risk factor notwithstanding, the difficulty is in measuring it, thus making it generally impractical as a driver of the firm's risk profile.

Other Risk Factors

Some other risk factors affecting different aspects of financial institutions' operations are listed in Table 5.4.

TABLE 5.4 Risk Factors and Business Areas

Business area	Critical risk factors
Forex operations	Market risk exposure, credit risk exposure (mainly OTC derivatives)
Commercial banks	Credit risk exposure, interest-rate risk exposure
Retail banking	Credit risk exposure, interest-rate risk exposure
Private banking/ asset management	Exposures to change in financial markets (revenues partly driven by portfolio value)
	Exposure to financial market sentiment (greater portfolio activity in bull markets generates more fee income)
	Credit risk exposure (loans to private clients)
Investor relations	State of the market, number of investors
Planning	Market volatility, number of customers and competitors
Sales and marketing	Market volatility, customer demand, staff morale, number of customers and competitors
Underwriting	Market volatility, customer demand, number of customers and competitors
Lending	Interest rate volatility, customer demand, competitor behavior
Deposit-taking	Interest rate volatility, customer demand, competitor behavior
Trade finance	Economic performance, interest-rate volatility, customer demand, competitor behavior
Corporate finance	Economic performance, interest-rate and exchange-rate volatility, customer demand, competitor behavior
Payments transmission	Investment of technology, volume of business, quality of service
Card services	Use of technology, volume of business, quality of service
Financial accounting	Volume and diversity of business
Claims	Volume of business, quality of service
Premium accounting	Volume of business, customer demand, quality of service
Treasury management	Market volatility, corporate strategy
Dealing	Market volatility, customer behavior
New product development	Market volatility, competitor actions, corporate strategy
Compliance	Volume and diversity of business and regulation

5.4   IDENTIFYING LOSS EVENTS

Following the identification of the general risk factors that affect business performance, analysts should turn their attention to specific events. Event identification is an iterative process of *brainstorming*, *defining*, and *screening* the events that may damage a resource or degrade process output through increased costs, decreased quality, decreased throughput and availability, and higher obsolescence.

Brainstorming Potential Events

Event identification should begin with an open-ended exploration of the potential events that could affect a particular process or the business as a whole. This leverages a variety of information sources, such as internal and external surveys, line managers, business-level managers, internal and external loss logs, and internal and external audits. For a given level of analysis, investigators should ask:

- What specific unexpected events could affect the process?

- What direct impacts would these events have on this process? On other processes?

- What impacts would these events have on critical resources used by the process?

- How long would the process take to recover from the event? How does this compare with the business's tolerance for process downtime? Which of these impacts and consequences would affect the recovery time of the process?

- What are the long-term consequences of these events on the firm as a whole?

Box 5.4: Events and Information Flows

Many loss events are caused by delay, failure, or inaccuracies in various information flows. It follows that a useful strategy for identifying operational loss events is therefore to map out information flows between key parties in your business process. For example, the following information flows might occur between investment managers and their brokers/dealers, the delay of any one of which could presage problems later on.

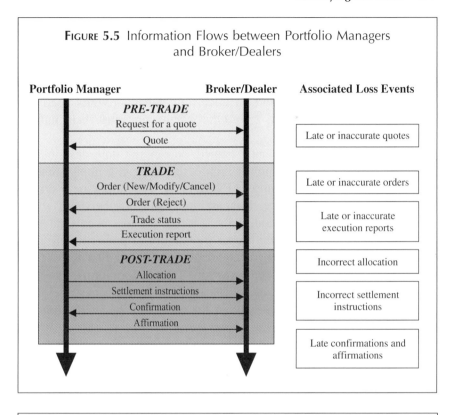

FIGURE 5.5 Information Flows between Portfolio Managers and Broker/Dealers

---

Box 5.5:   Contingency Analysis and Event Identification

Understanding the events that would prevent a critical process from functioning lies at the heart of contingency planning (see Subsection 13.3). Typically, operational scenarios assume that some critical internal resource is either severely degraded or completely unavailable for some period because of some internally or externally derived shock. For instance, a flu epidemic might knock out half the back-office staff, or flooding might take out a communications link. Exploring the impact of these events in advance when mitigating resources (for example, insurance, redundant systems) can be easily put in place, can make the difference between business survival and disaster.

Defining Events

Every event should be well-defined, easily understood, and clearly communicated. For any event, we should always know after a reasonably short time whether or not it has occurred. Events are assumed to occur with a random frequency and an uncertain impact. Events need not be independent of risk factors or of other events, nor must their impacts be always negative.

Events should be consistently named. Names not only describe the event, say PWR_FAIL for a power failure, they may also imply some of the event structure, for example, PWR_FAIL_NY might be a power failure in the New York office. This additional structure only adds value if the event is significantly modified as a result. For instance, if the New York office has a significantly higher probability of power failure than the Cleveland office, then using an aggregate event definition across both offices may ignore important information. Tighter definitions, although more informative, demand more data (which is often unavailable), and generally increase the complexity of the modeling by increasing the number of events.

One of the most immediate deliverables from any operational risk project should be a dictionary of events, precisely defined, so that everyone within the organization can understand an event's meaning. Simple but surprisingly important, this dictionary of events can be used as a stand-alone tool for training, control, and operational management, or it can form the basis of the more structured event database that describes the available resources and management responses for dealing with the event (see Subsection 7.5).

Box 5.6: Event Dictionary for a Settlement Process

The following loss events were found to be worrisome in one particular securities settlement process (Tables 5.5).

Tᴀʙʟᴇ **5.5** Settlement Events

Loss event	Description
Unconfirmed_Deal	Deals that are not confirmed within one week
Misplaced_Deal	Deal documentation has been misplaced or associated with a different deal
Inacc_Confirm	A confirmation with more than one significant error is sent out
Late_Confirm	Confirmations are not sent out within three days
Pwr_Fail	Power failure
Nost_Break	Nostro Break
Unauth_Deal	Internal staff has engaged an unauthorized transaction
Reg_Err	Transaction processed not in accordance with regulatory guidelines
Doc_Err	Inaccurate or incomplete documentation
Comms_Fail	Major communications failure (>1-hour outage)
Cntpy_Wdrl	A counterparty withdraws as a result of our having processing problems
Settle_Err	Incorrect settlement of transactions
Late_Deliv	Untimely physical deliveries
Sec_Deficit	Required securities unavailable when needed
Cntpy_Err	Settlement error at counterparty
Duplicated_Deal	Deal duplicated; entered more than once in trading blotter
Limit_Cntrl_Bkdn	Limits exceeded without being caught by internal control systems
New_Cntpy	Engage with a new counterparty for which we have no information
New_Pdct	New product introduced requiring structural database changes

Screening Events

Following the exploration and definition stages, a large number of events and risk factors may be discovered. To simplify subsequent data-gathering and risk analysis, it is important to screen the events. This should reflect the objectives of the analysis; for instance, capital management and asset protection would imply focusing on low-frequency, high-impact events whereas operational efficiency concerns would target high-frequency, low-impact events. In general, however, events should be included if an approximate qualitative assessment of the event's worst-case likelihood and impacts suggests they are critical or if these events are believed to have significant dependencies with other critical events.

5.5   CATEGORIZING EVENTS AND RISK FACTORS

Once events are identified, they need to be categorized. Risk analysis is based on comparing risks across various meaningful categories. Slicing and dicing the risks can only be performed if the events and risk factors have been appropriately categorized. It follows that there is no perfect set of risk categories—it depends on the objectives of the analysis. Here are just some of the ways to categorize events and risk factors:

- According to where the impact of the event or factor is realized (for example SBU, process, function, resource, geography, market, product, customer)

- According to the source of the event or factor (for example SBU, process, function, resource, geography, market, product, customer)

- According to where the impact of the event or factor is controlled (for example SBU, process, function, resource, geography, market, product, customer)

- According to the resources used to manage the risk (for example, insurance, hedging)

- According to industry or regulatory conventions

To expedite reporting and decision-making, it is generally wise to gather information on multiple risk categories during event identification; that way, you won't have to collect such data later on.

Consider the advantages of the various commonly used risk categorizations.

By Location of Impact

This describes where the impact of an event or risk factor is realized—which business or process owner pays the price of the event. The same event often impacts multiple processes and resources, and so the impact may not map to just one process. This is often a reason as to why no one business area takes responsibility for the event and, consequently, nothing gets done about it.

FIGURE **5.6** Events and the Processes They Impact

Box 5.7: Categorizing Events by the Location of Their Impacts

All event categorizations can be represented as a matrix with processes (or SBUs, geographic areas) along the left and loss events or factors along the top. Returning to our earlier example of a settlements process, we might use a matrix like the one in Table 5.6 to capture the extent to which event cash flows are realized in different subprocesses.

TABLE 5.6 Processes and Event Impacts

Process or resource	Fraction of realized losses by event									
	Late settlement	Systems failure	Telecoms error	Staff error	Late confirmation	Booking error	Counterparty error	Product complexity	Product volumes	Interest rates
(Un)Controllable/ Influenceable	C	I	I	C	C	I	U	I	I	U
Settlement process	50%	0	0	10%	40%	0	0	0	0	0
Info. systems	0	80%	0	30%	0	10%	10%	0	0	0
Telecom	10%	0	100%	0	0	0	10%	0	0	0
Trading	0	0	0	20%	0	80%	70%	10%	20%	70%
Confirmations	40%	20%	0	40%	60%	10%	10%	20%	50%	0
Sales and marketing	0	0	0	0	0	0	0	70%	30%	30%
Sum	100%	100%	100%	100%	100%	100%	100%	100%	100%	100%

In this example, different business areas are described as processes, but the same approach could be used for a vertical slice of the business as for a horizontal one. This would allow us to allocate risks initiated through senior management decision-making to junior staff.

By the Source of the Risk

In Subsection 2.7, we noted the distinction between the owner of the risk—either where the risk is initiated or where the risk is managed—and the impact of the risk. For instance, marketing and sales may be responsible for the development and sales of some complex product, but the resulting operational risks are realized in the operations group. It is there that additional staff specialists will be needed to process the documentation and legal risks associated with the product.

FIGURE 5.7 Events, Their Upstream Sources, and
Their Downstream Impacts

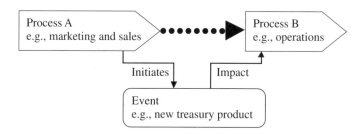

By Control Responsibility

Events or risk factors, if controllable, are always controllable by some organizational function or combination of functions working together. Sometimes the areathat is able to control a factor or loss event is also the area that is impacted by the factor or event. More often, control is shared between the upstream authorized source or initiator of the risk (they can always choose not to do the activity that gives rise to the risk) and the organizational unit responsible for managing the risk. For example, a trader initiates a risk by proprietary trading; the back and middle offices manage the risk through limits, reconciliation, and risk control.

FIGURE 5.8 Event Initiation, Impacts, and Controls

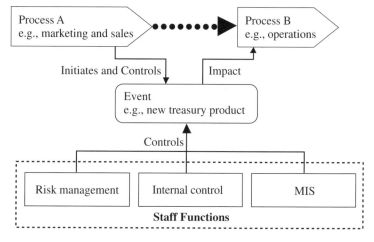

Recall the meaning of the word "control." Control denotes the business area's ability to prevent or mitigate the loss associated with the specific event. In the case of a fraudulent employee, for instance, the control might be shared between the HR staff who hired the employee and the internal controls area whose procedures and systems failed to anticipate the fraud event. The closer it is to the originating causes, in general, the more viable loss prevention activities become compared with loss mitigation. Categorization by risk controller is necessary if risk transfer pricing is to be performed within the organization. The locus of control, rather than where the events are realized, should determine internal risk transfer and risk-based resource allocation. Because risks may be borne by parts of the organization other than those able to control the risk, moral hazard can be a major problem, whereby the controller of the risk does not bear the costs associated with the risk and therefore fails to take necessary actions to control it. Knowing which events map to specific processes and resources that can control them tells us which areas should be held responsible for these events. Even for uncontrollable events in which no business area holds direct control of the event, we can allocate the events to some corporate group responsible for risk financing such as financial risk management or insurance management.

Box 5.8: Control Matrix in a Settlement Process

The control matrix for our example settlements process might look something like this (Table 5.7).

TABLE 5.7 Processes and the Locus of Control

Process or resource	Fraction of realized losses by event									
	Late settlement	Systems failure	Telecoms error	Staff error	Late confirmation	Booking error	Counterparty error	Product complexity	Product volumes	Interest rates
(Un)Controllable/ Influenceable	C	I	I	C	C	I	U	I	I	U
Settlement process	50%	0	0	10%	30%	0	0	0	0	0
Info. systems	0	80%	0	10%	0	10%	10%	0	0	0
Telecoms	10%	0	70%	0	0	0	10%	0	0	0
Trading	0	0	0	10%	0	40%	10%	10%	20%	0
Confirmations	40%	10%	0	20%	60%	10%	10%	0	0	0
Sales and marketing	0	0	0	0	0	10%	0	70%	30%	0
External	0	10%	30%	50%	10%	30%	60%	20%	50%	100%
Sum	100%	100%	100%	100%	100%	100%	100%	100%	100%	100%

By Cost Account

Expenses and write-offs will often be posted to a loss account within the general ledger. This will reflect accounting conventions rather than any economic reality but may still be useful in developing *pro forma* estimates of cost items in the income statement. It is also appropriate for use with expense-based models (see Subsection 3.1).

By Asset or Liability

Loss events can be thought of as perpetuities, that is, bonds with a stream of expected cash flow extending indefinitely into the future. In Subsection 8.1, we estimate the NPV of a loss event, either within a given reporting period (for EaR estimation), or for all future periods (for VaR estimation). In this way the loss event can be viewed as a liability associated with particular operational assets.

By Convention

Risk categorization may also reflect regulatory or internal conventions. Despite their many differences reflecting their different agendas, risk categorizations share a similar structure as that in Table 5.8.

TABLE 5.8 A Typology of Risks

Business event risks	Shift in credit rating Reputation risk Taxation risk Legal risk	
	Disaster risk	Natural disaster War Collapse of markets
	Regulatory risk	Capital requirement breach Regulatory changes
Operations risks	HR risk	Employee turnover Key personnel risk Fraud risk Error Rogue trading Money laundering Confidentiality breach
	Technology risk	Programming error Model risk Mark-to-market error Management information IT systems outage Telecommunications failure Contingency planning
	Relationship risk	Contractual disagreement Dissatisfaction Default
	Facilities risk	Safety Security Operating costs Fire/flood
	Transaction risk	Execution error Product complexity Booking error Settlement error Commodity delivery risk

CHAPTER 6

ESTIMATING POTENTIAL LOSSES — DATA

Once the loss events have been identified, mapped to the processes, and categorized, we must estimate their frequency and impact to evaluate their risks. But first some words of warning.

6.1 THE CHALLENGES OF OPERATIONAL RISK DATA AND MEASUREMENT

There are several challenges unique to operational risk analysis. The process of estimating a wide range of different risks, their impact, and their frequency is not an easy task nor an unimportant one. The process can be tedious and error-prone. Loss data may be unavailable, difficult to apply, or politically sensitive. Some have discounted operational risk management purely on these grounds (see Ong's critique at the end of Andersen, 1998 or Jones, 1995). While operational risk management can be highly effective for prioritization and resource allocation, it is true that these limitations can quickly derail any risk management effort unless they are well-managed. Understanding the problems is the first step. The following issues must be faced head-on:

Losses Are Politically Sensitive

Loss data is inherently sensitive, and data-gathering may become a political process if high-level authorization is not driving it. A related issue is the tendency toward secrecy. Firms are unwilling to reveal information about losses, partly because of political issues and partly because of a lack of awareness as to the potential benefits of such data.

Lack of Data for Infrequent Events

For rare events with potentially devastating impact, there is little data on which to base estimates of impact or frequency. In practice, very infrequent events can rarely be estimated with an accuracy closer than an order of magnitude. For instance, a tidal wave may have last occurred in 1950, 1877, and 1600. What is the frequency of such events? One in 50? One in 100? One in 150? One solution to the problem of infrequent events is to look at the experience of many firms in the same business. In an ideal world, industry-wide studies based on a range of similar operational tasks, processes, and resources would produce standards conducive to risk assessment benchmarking. Several industry consortia have been formed to develop shared databases of operational losses (Appendix B).

Applicability of External Data

Even is external data is available, there may be legitimate concerns about the ability to generalize data to other processes, other resources, other tasks, or other businesses in slightly different environments. External loss data may ignore the unique context of this particular firm. This said, external data is more often disregarded, not because of its irrelevance but because of its perceived irrelevance. This is the so-called *Lake Woebegone* effect, where every firm believes itself "above average" and, therefore, industry data is perceived as less relevant than it ought to be.

Integrating Internal and External Data

Internal and external data sets capture different risk characteristics of the losses. While there is a question mark over the applicability of external data, most observers agree that the best results are obtained by integrating the use of both. Integration procedures can range from the simple—for instance, weighted averages of observations or interpolation between the two data sets—to the more complex, using techniques such as *Extreme Value Theory* and *Maximum Likelihood Estimation*.

Integrating Different Modeling Approaches

Bottom-up approaches to operational risk management often fail because there are insufficient data and resources to maintain the resulting database (see Subsection 3.2). This is exacerbated when organizational structures evolve rapidly. By contrast, top-down approaches can be too vague about what operations managers should actually do to solve specific problems (see Subsection 3.1). Combinations of bottom-up and top-down approaches seem to be most effective (Hoffman, 1998). But how can this be done? As discussed in Subsection 3.3, top-down approaches offer quick but non-actionable approaches to risk assessment that can be used as pilot estimates of critical risk areas within the firm and also to validate more complex, bottom-up asset-based approaches.

Modeling Human Errors

Human behavior is particularly difficult to capture in any model. This is unfortunate because even if human actions are not the *direct* cause of many events, their failure to remedy situations is a cause of most losses. Some of these mistakes are physiological: for instance, those related to the stress, time of day, or seasonal effects. The probability of an error, in a particular transaction, tends to increase on opening, after lunch, and on Friday afternoons! Other mistakes result from motivational problems. Staff get bored if there are not sufficient "events" to keep them occupied. Cognitive factors, another source of mistakes, result from the inability of people to respond to complex events in real time. Researchers of human factors engineering (see Subsection 11.5) have discovered much about the factors that cause learning and burnout. Stress, matching of the system's capabilities to the demands of the task, and personal factors are all important drivers of individual errors.

Human Behavior Is Reflexive

Unlike hardware, software, or many organizational processes, individual human behavior is *reflexive* in that it reacts and changes in response to any effort to change it. This leads to time-varying risks that are hard to measure. For example, internal and external audits cause staff to change their behaviors, perhaps leading to increased vigilance (and lower event frequencies) in the periods immediately before and after audits. Any control system is actually an intervention into an organizational system that will naturally try to minimize the disruptive impact of this intrusion. One of the most important and potentially insidious reflexive effects is that of morale hazard, where staff use the existence of risk management and control systems to justify even greater risk taking.

Risks Change

Risk analysis is an ongoing activity. Risks change. People and systems learn and improve. But they also forget and degrade. At the individual level, age, experience, and work load affect the variance in performance over time (see Subsection 11.5). The development of an organizational memory allows firms to transcend individual learning and aging. In most organizational environments, learning occurs following the experience of a wide range of situations, customers, products, and transactions. Organizational learning means that the risks are dynamically evolving rather than static. Some events that were uncontrollable become controllable. Learning leads to an evolution of risk prevention, mitigation, and transfer activities. This obviously affects risk exposures and changes the firm's future learning experiences with these exposures. Although models have been developed to incorporate learning and scale effects, in general, learning as a process is hard to quantify. For instance, control systems tend to be developed in a knee-jerk response to major loss events, and this may have unexpected dysfunctional side effects, for example, high cost, complexity, and staff alienation.

Just as learning is a feature of both organizations and individuals, so too is forgetting and burnout. Sometimes they are borne of slow reductions in capabilities (as in physical aging), but more often burnout is the result of complacency and a reluctance to question the rationale for previous decisions. *Burnout models* are particularly important with physical systems such as electronic components, for which *reliability engineering* techniques (see Subsection 7.3) have focused on non-constant failure processes with failure rates (the time-dependent frequency) that increase (burnout) or decrease over time (learning or burn-in).

6.2   OVERCOMING THE CHALLENGES

The biggest challenge for any operational risk management effort is overcoming these data problems. The following guidelines can help:

Acknowledge the Problem of Operational Risk Data

Don't try to hide anything. This is always the first step because it focuses attention on developing robust measurement procedures. Expect that other managers (particularly those without the necessary training) will feel uneasy about accepting heroic assumptions based on limited data. Acknowledge the uncertainty over estimates, explicitly or with sensitivity analyses, but do them anyway. Justify and communicate widely the approach taken to deal with the data problems.

Focus on Understanding

For many events, the objective is not accuracy, but rather the understanding of and informed debate on possible outcomes, followed by agreement and consistent action on how the firm may marshal resources to handle these outcomes. Measurement of operational risks is merely a means to focus analysis and is not an end in itself; while many operational risks cannot be easily measured, they *can always* be understood. *Understanding* risks, rather than *measuring* risks, is the prerequisite for effective operational risk management.

Avoid Subjective Measures

Although some analysts believe the difficulty of quantification means that purely subjective risk levels (such as low, medium, or high risk levels) should be used, relying on these purely subjective assessments thwarts risk aggregation and the assessment of any dependencies between risks. Subjective measures also only allow for comparison of risks by the same subject. Lacking a more formal ranking, one manager's high risk is another's medium or low risk. Vague feelings or impressions about measurement can never be a substitute for formal quantifyication, and surprisingly often we can develop formal measures for many of the operational risks faced by a firm. The act of trying to quantify the exposure also forces the analyst to better understand the exposure, rather than accepting a vague, purely subjective assessment.

Focus on the Critical Risks

The choice of risks depends on the objective of the analysis, which should be precisely defined by management. The objectives of business growth, efficiency, and capital management imply a focus on very different types of risk and sets of events and risk factors. Given these objectives, meaningful risk calculations can be produced using small samples because most of the contributions to these risks come from a few critical loss events and risk factors. This means we do not have to model every possible event and risk factor to produce a useful model. Models will never be complete, and the more complete models tend to be more complex, and harder to understand and be accepted by management.

Box 6.1:   Pareto Analysis

Pareto analysis is an important tool for focusing on the key drivers of risk. Pareto charts are rank-order frequency distributions. They can be based in terms of the frequency or the cost of the event, or in terms of the risk criticality (impact multiplied by frequency). For example, consider the Pareto chart, in Figure 6.1, of the causes of a particular high-impact event.

FIGURE **6.1:** Pareto Analysis of the Causes of a No-Deal Event

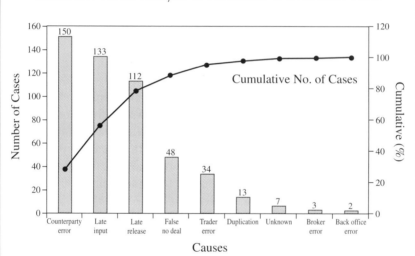

Pareto charts emphasize risk priorities. In Figure 6.1 we see that about 80 percent of the causes of high-impact events are the result of three more frequent events. Knowing this directs our attention to the underlying causes rather than wasting resources on less-critical events and risk factors. Pareto charts can be broken down further into subcategories such as event type or source.

6.3   GENERAL MEASUREMENT TECHNIQUES

There are three basic techniques used to gather the frequency and severity estimates for loss events and the factors that lead to them. These techniques—historical analysis, subjective risk assessment, and implied risk estimation based on dependencies—all have their own limitations and therefore should be used in concert to counter these limitations (see Table 6.1).

TABLE 6.1 Risk Measurement Techniques: Strengths and Limitations

Technique		Strengths	Limitations
Historical analysis (Subsections 6.4 and 6.5)	Based on internal loss data	Captures idiosyncratic features of firm's own controllable risks Appropriate for mature processes and business areas that are unique to the firm Potentially more accurate	Backward looking Limited tail risks. Availability of data Data-gathering is time-consuming Requires internal data management and analytical expertise
	Based on external loss data	Biased toward major uncontrollable or influenceable losses Provides a larger sample to capture catastrophic losses (tail risks) Inexpensive Appropriate for mature processes and business areas generic to many businesses	Backward looking May not be a representative sample (different context) Data-gathering is more expensive Availability of data
Subjective risk assessment (Subsection 6.6)		Gets business managers involved Leverages a broad range of expertise and experience May be useful for estimating tail risks May be forward looking Good at focusing on the interfaces between processes where many losses originate Identifies risk factors or loss events controlled or realized within the respondent's area	Subject to individual and group cognitive biases such as availability and threshold biases, group-think Difficulties in selecting appropriate individuals/ groups Estimates may be inconsistent
Implied from causal or statistical models (Subsection 7.4)		Appropriate for frequencies of statistically or causally dependent but relatively rare events for which other approaches are inappropriate	Only as good as the model developed Needs statistical or causal structure of implied event; used for frequencies rather than impact estimation
Combination		Combines strengths of all the above	Integration is difficult and can lead to a lack of transparency for end users

6.4 HISTORICAL DATA — FREQUENCIES

Although frequency distributions can be estimated subjectively or inferred using dependencies in general, these approaches should be used only if historical data is unavailable or it is not a realistic guide to the likelihood of future events. For firms with stable processes that face controllable loss events, historical analysis using internal loss data offers the most objective estimate of the frequency of loss events they face. Unfortunately, while internal sources are cheaper and generally more relevant, particularly for controllable events and risk factors, they are often neither of the same quality nor cover the same range of possible outcomes as can be obtained from external sources. For instance, internal data (one hopes) does not have a range of disastrous tail events that give rise to catastrophic losses. Nonetheless, internal data sources should be the start of any loss frequency analysis, particularly for the more-frequent events.

Box 6.2:   The Basic Assumption of Historical Analysis

The critical assumption underlying all historical analyses is that the causal structure driving the events does not change appreciably over the time horizon. This would not hold if, for instance, a major operating process were re-engineered and old loss events ceased to be relevant and new ones became more so. This does not mean that the internal or external risk factors need to remain constant; in most cases, we can strip out the effect of the risk factors (such as volume) from the historical losses by modeling dependencies to produce a scale-invariant measure of risk. If the causal structure changes frequently (for instance, every time a shock occurs), then the events no longer generate useful evidence regarding future likelihoods. The causal structure is particularly likely to change if there has been a massive catastrophic loss because it is precisely these losses that tend to force new controls and new organizational structures to prevent such a loss from recurring. If the shock occurs many times while the event structure remains stable, then the probabilities may be estimated with confidence. This would be the case for analyzing the number of defaults on a portfolio of car loans or credit-card receivables—in both cases, we can assume that the underlying causal

---

structure remains stable despite the occurrence of these loss events. Asset-based models usually assume an equilibrium model that does not capture the dynamics of particular loss events, only the random variation of the events' frequencies and losses; for instance, using Poisson distributions to model event frequencies. Event-based simulation or reliability engineering models, by contrast, explicitly attempt to model the evolving dynamics of the causal structure and their implications for risks.

Event/Incident Reports

Much internal experience of risks is derived from firms' event/incident reports. These are short and usually unstructured, and are produced by a staff managers answer some of the following questions about an unexpected event with a significant negative impact:

- What really happened?
- Why did it happen?
- What was the (direct and indirect) damage or consequence?
- What was different or unusual about this event?
- What additional controls might have prevented this?
- Did staff know what they were supposed to do?
- Did staff do what they were supposed to do?
- Did any event or action occur that might have made it better or worse?
- Has this happened before?
- What was done before to fix it, if anything?
- Who reported this event/incident?
- What are the organizational or policy implications of the event?

Event reports are qualitatively useful for determining the dependencies and nature of infrequent events, and can have important ramifications for internal control and contingency planning. However, event reports have their limitations. First, event reports are usually not performed consistently. Managers tend to demand reports only when there is a significant loss. Event reports are not defined purely by their timing or the magnitude of the loss; unexpected events that lead to increases in cash flow are just as important to analyze as events that cause additional expenses. An event report's lack of consistency makes it difficult to estimate frequencies. Many event reports fail to define precisely the loss events they describe, with events, their causes, and their symptoms often being ill-defined and ambiguous. Incident reports often have the goal of allocating blame rather than building the operational capability to deal with the problem. For this reason, political factors will tend to blur any attribution and confuse the causes and dependencies affecting the event.

Internal Loss Logs

One step removed from event reports are internal loss logs. These tend to focus on more-frequent operational events and aim to improve operational efficiency rather than mitigate risk. The frequency of logged events necessitates using a small number of key event descriptors, usually selected from a pull-down menu of alternatives. Fields in the loss log typically include:

- Event identification code
- Time stamp—when the event occurred (not necessarily when it was reported)
- Magnitude of direct loss—usually the cost of resources committed to handling the event
- Current status—what is being done to handle the event
- Source of the event

Ideally, the operations- or risk management group should develop its own internal loss logs, describing categorized loss events that are time-stamped both as they occur and as they are dealt with. The choice of events that are logged should partly be determined by the extent of the loss, but also by the ability to measure the loss associated with the event, and whether the event may cause other major loss events. In general, loss logs should try to include near misses as well as actual incidents that cause losses, as these provide important information on system capabilities. While loss logs are a major improvement over event incident reports for operational risk assessment, to be effective they must contain measures (such as input-data validation, and automatic time-stamping) to ensure data quality. First and foremost is the need for accurate event time stamps. Often, events are not correctly time-stamped. Events for which the time is not exactly known are called censored data; a wide range of statistical tools exist for dealing with censored data and producing bounds on the actual event times (see Meeker, 1998 and Ansell, 1994). Like event reports, loss logs may suffer from a lack of adequate event definitions or end-user uncertainty about these definitions. Often, the largest source of losses is the event category called UNKNOWN, a surefire indication that more effort must be devoted to data entry and cause analysis. Loss logs often do not provide data-entry checking or automatic validation before the data is added. This can lead to massive outliers that corrupt subsequent analyses. Elementary validation and data analysis can be performed automatically during data collection. Developing users' understanding of the need for the loss log and the motivation to maintain and use it, is also a key safeguard to data quality.

Box 6.3: Example — Loss Events in a Settlement Process

The following loss events were found to be worrisome in a particular settlements process.

TABLE 6.2 Actual Settlement-Process Loss Log

GMT		EVENT	TYPE	DURATION	$ Loss	Aging	CNTRLR	Comments
Jan 1	2000	SGP110	Unconfirmed_Deal	NA	NA	34 hours	C-SGP-3	No response from counterparty
Jan 1	2000	SGP111	Unconfirmed_Deal	.1	$183	COMPLETE	C-SGP-3	
Jan 1	2000	SGP112	Unconfirmed_Deal	.2	$183	COMPLETE	C-SGP-2	
Jan 1	2000	SGP113	Inacc_Confirm	.1	$0	COMPLETE	C-SGP-2	
Jan 1	2000	SGP114	Unconfirmed_Deal	.1	$183	COMPLETE	C-SGP-4	
Jan 1	2000	LDN115	Misplaced_Deal	.3	$3,782	COMPLETE	C-LDN-4	Called in NY staff specialist
Jan 1	2000	LDN116	Inacc_Confirm	NA	NA	10 hours	C-LDN-9	
Jan 2	2000	LDN117	Inacc_Confirm	NA	NA	7 hours	C-LDN-3	
Jan 2	2000	NYC118	Unconfirmed_Deal	.1	$0	COMPLETE	C-NYC-2	
Jan 2	2000	NYC119	Inacc_Confirm	NA	NA	2 hours	C-NYC-9	

Internal loss event logs are natural candidates for Web-based intranet applications, allowing users from all over the business to enter losses and access up-to-date information about risks, loss events, and how others have dealt with the losses. Transaction processing systems may also automatically generate exception reports that produce loss log records. The current event log should provide access to the current status of ongoing events such as outstanding failed transactions and aging incomplete transactions. Users should then be able to view these loss events by age, potential loss, source, owner, and location. End users should also be supported by online documentation of the loss log. To facilitate complete event logs, data-warehousing techniques can be used to shield users from underlying transaction databases.

FIGURE 6.2 Loss Logs and Supporting Data Flow

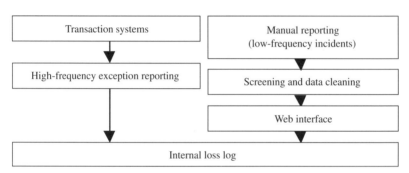

Box 6.4: Adjusting Historical Losses to Reflect Major Structural Changes

Over a long-enough time period, the scope and scale of operations are very likely to have changed. These structural changes can affect dramatically many of the loss events' frequencies and at the same time severely limit the immediate applicability of available data. This does not necessarily imply that the old data are irrelevant. Most parametric distributions used for frequency and impacts are so-called scale family distributions. This means that we can rescale the distribution to reflect some scale parameter. A parametric family of distributions is called a scale family if, for any random variable X, the random variable $Y = cX$ is also a member of the family. Weibull, Pareto, exponential, log normal, normal, and beta are all scale families (see Chapter 7). Using scale parameters to model structural changes such as those caused by major volume changes, reorganizations and acquisitions can dramatically extend the amount of available data.

Change Logs

Unlike the internal event log, the change log is forward-looking and captures scheduled future events that are likely to cause loss events. Typical changes include systems changes, new businesses, new product and new market introductions, new offices, and changes in organizational structures. Sudden unexpected increases in loss events resulting from business changes can be avoided if a system to capture these changes is in place and used. Again, it is necessary that the change log be widely accessible online and that operations managers be encouraged to proactively check the log to forestall loss events. Change logs may also actively signal the advent of changes to managers who might be affected.

Other Internal Data Sources

If a formal loss log has not been instituted, other internal historical data sources may be needed to bolster internal experience. These include:

- Audit reports
- Reengineering and information systems projects
- Middle management reports
- Expert opinions
- Contingency plans
- Business plans
- Operations plans

Traditional control databases such as the general-ledger system, the cost-accounting system, and the budgeting and forecasting systems can also be mined for loss-frequency information. The accounting department often has loss accounts that, following some restatement, can map to many event categories. The transaction processing systems, accounting applications (payroll, fixed assets), customer databases, risk management systems, and trading books may also provide useful frequency data. In addition, the HR department can often produce information on the risk of staff turnover in a trading area. The compliance department can describe the frequency of limit-breaking or authorization failures. The research department can suggest the frequency of model failures. The information system department or data centers can produce information on the frequency of hardware, software, or data errors. Facilities management may have data for the probability of line equipment failure. These estimates may not be completely accurate, but this is hardly the point; the issue is consistency in measuring risks that were previously unknown and therefore unmanaged. These internal data sources are easily accessible and often have hard-won face validity in the eyes of managers.

External Historical Data Sources

These can also be used, especially for the uncontrollable and less-frequent, higher-impact (usually) external events and risk factors. In such cases, external data may capture the tails of the risk distribution or be more reliable for evaluating catastrophic losses, and therefore useful, for example, to estimate the level of economic risk capital. PricewaterhouseCoopers, NetRisk, the Global Association of Risk Professionals and the British Bankers Association have developed databases of public bank losses (Appendix B). So too, more narrowly defined commercial databases of credit losses, claims losses, and even court decisions are also available. The major limitation of external data is that it may be unique to specific circumstances of an outside organization—circumstances that are not found in the particular case of this firm. In any case, external data provides a valuable benchmark or sanity check against internal risk estimates. For many particularly common risks (such as software and facilities risks), trade-association data are available for the likelihood of major errors. Trade information may also be used to estimate the likelihood of benchmark losses relative to revenue of firms within a similar market or industry. For some insurable events, actuarial data from insurance companies can often be used. Some survey evidence exists on the magnitude of the cost of pure risks, such as asset risks for large corporations. For a good example of this, see the annual report, *Cost of Risk Survey,* Risk and Insurance Management Society, New York, NY. In this report, corporate respondents give estimates of the amounts spent on property liability insurance, the level of uninsured losses, and risk management programs. These are not specific to any one company and therefore may ignore certain hard-to-quantify elements of the cost of risk. Other external frequency data sources include research services such as Lexis/Nexis, EDGAR regulatory filings, newspapers and magazines, insurance industry reports, consulting reports, Internet searches, and official government reports. Often, rather than provide frequency or impact data directly, external sources may be used to provide useful proxies. One example of this should be familiar to risk managers, as credit ratings, for instance, can be used to assess the likelihood of counterparty default.

TABLE 6.3 External Event Proxies for Default Frequency

Rating	Default likelihood distribution		Maximum (%)	Minimum (%)
	Mean (%)	Standard deviation (%)		
AAA	0.0	0.0	0.0	0.0
AA	0.0	0.1	0.3	0.0
A	0.1	0.1	0.3	0.0
Baa	0.5	0.4	1.3	0.0
Ba	4.4	3.0	10.5	0.5
B	14.8	5.3	22.2	3.0

Source: Moody's Investors Service
Note: Corporate bond default rates 1973–94: Two-year cumulative rates

Looking at similar competitors on a case-by-case basis can also be helpful. As part of their market intelligence, some larger firms may find it valuable to develop *external loss logs* that track major external losses in a number of strategic areas. Loss information can often be found in public corporations' financial reports. The footnotes can provide information about loss reserves (particularly bad debt). External event logs have a similar structure to internal event logs, but they should be managed centrally rather than at the level of the business units or through an intranet application. External event logs will tend to be more case-based rather than record-based because of the unavailability of detailed data about the event and generally should capture the major loss events that affect a well-defined group of similar-sized competitors. External data would focus on catastrophic losses that have been made public. These would range from instances of fraud, major litigation, or regulatory penalties affecting competitors, to embarrassing systems failures that have made the headlines. In each case, analysts should go beyond the obvious symptoms of the failure to examine the underlying causes. The external event logs may then be used for competitive strategy; for example, to take advantage of a competitor's sudden weakness in a particular market segment, or to produce estimates of the impact and frequency of potential catastrophic losses in the industry. In some cases, external event logs can use simulated events based on aggregate industry losses (for example, using actuarial data) to help focus attention to the risks faced in the industry.

Integrate Multiple Data Sources

In general, one should triangulate the likelihood data from any single source with that from other sources. This validates the data, benchmarks internal perceptions with external reality, and leverages the strengths of the different techniques for data-gathering.

6.5   HISTORICAL DATA — IMPACTS

Difficulties of Measuring the Impact

Measuring the impact of loss events presents some unique difficulties. In particular:

Absence of Market Values   There is no liquid market for many of the firm's assets in the operational value chain, and yet we must esti-mate potential losses. In theory, these should be based on reasonable replacement value rather than accounting or book value (which tend to reflect accounting conventions about depreciation and amortization rather than economic value). In practice, the absence of alternatives to general-ledger and other accounting data may force us to use accounting values.

Potentially Wide Range of Impacts   Some events have a wide range of possible impacts. For example, an extra zero in a settlement instruction could lead to payment to a counterparty of $10 million rather than $1 million. The wide range of impacts is often the result of poorly designed data-entry screens, compounded by inadequate control systems. It is one reason as to why analysis should not be based purely on risk criticality measures, which by their very nature focus on expected losses rather than the potential for unexpected losses.

Reputational Effects Reliability of operations is a major reason behind customers and counterparties continuing to deal with a firm. A failure or degradation in these operations tends to make existing customers and counterparties defect, resulting in an economic loss to the firm. Reputational effects are particularly important for larger, more well-known retail banks in competitive markets whose customers can easily transact elsewhere.

Indirect reputational impacts should also include the effects on potential customers, as well as on actual customers. For the firm's potential customers, estimating the negative publicity value of loss events is more difficult, but it can be done by looking at event studies where the impact on the firm's stock price following various well-defined loss events (such as major operational failure and fraud) are analyzed.

Unfortunately, both direct and indirect effects are rarely priced. One reason for this is the complex causation of customer defection. Existing clients do not leave after a single loss event (say delayed service or trading at inferior terms); it is only after repeated problems with the service they receive that customers disavow any relationship-specific investments and take their business elsewhere. In many situations, the problem of reputational effects on existing clients can be solved by using another event—counterparty withdrawal, which occurs with some frequency and can impact if a (usually large) number of service failure events (for example, late settlement and misplaced order) occur. Client retention should be made a priority at most banks. Yet remarkably few even know the value of a specific client. The value of clients, and therefore the impact of the loss event caused by their defection, can be determined as the extrapolated set of cash flows associated with each client, basically an annuity—extrapolated either from experience with that client or similar clients. The likelihood of client defection can also be inferred from historical experience with similar clients. For instance, a risk factor that affects the likelihood of client defection is the extent of our experience with the client; new clients are even more sensitive to reputational effects because they face fewer sunk costs. Exit investigations following major client/counterparty losses should be conducted to determine the loss events and risk factors that caused the loss of this resource.

Opportunity Costs   Another reason for the difficulty of estimating impacts is the calculation of opportunity costs. These costs are the revenues foregone because of the loss event, and they are often ignored. The bulk of the losses associated with events that impair transactions processing through downtime, such as power failures and key personnel losses, are the opportunity costs of lost business rather than direct or indirect costs. The opportunity costs of operational loss events can be estimated by assuming that future revenues would be similar to past revenues during the downtime caused by the event. Much more difficult is estimating the opportunity costs of strategic events because historical experience is unlikely to provide any guide to the future.

Types of Impact Data

A loss event can affect the balance sheet (by changing the value of the assets and liabilities held by the firm) or the income statement (by causing additional expenses or losses in revenues). It may also have indirect effects by making other loss events more likely. In general, balance-sheet losses are more infrequent but have a greater impact than events affecting the income statement.

Balance-Sheet Impacts   To the extent that the event's impact is through the balance sheet, the impact is basically the product of two values—first, the extent of asset damage, and second, the value of the asset. If the extent of the damage is fixed for a particular event, it follows that the impact distribution should follow the distribution of the asset's value. Estimating the balance-sheet impact therefore requires accurate valuation of the assets—this provides a benchmark estimate for the possible impacts. For traded instruments in liquid markets, a mark-to-market valuation is most appropriate. For less-liquid instruments (such as over-the-counter positions), a valuation model can be developed. Infrequently traded balance-sheet assets and liabilities can make use of book values with all the accounting vagaries that implies FIFO versus

LIFO, and amortization and depreciation schedules, for example. Lacking a market value for the real asset and liability asset, some measure of the firm-specific value should be used. If this is difficult to produce, the asset's replacement value (including purchasing costs) can be used as a proxy.

Income-Statement Impacts There are two components for revenue or expense-related events: first, a "fixed" cost that is imposed each time the event occurs, and second, a random "variable" cost—the cost of the time required to manage (or repair) the event.

The variable cost includes internal direct costs, such as the cost of unplanned overtime, as well as the opportunity costs caused by the inability of staff to do more profitable activities. The variable cost also includes the external indirect costs (unless these are modeled in other causally related events). In mature operational environments, the variable costs of most events will be the relatively minor internal direct costs associated with handling exceptions. However, these apparently minor internal events may lead to some of the massive-impact events if not properly managed.

The fixed costs incorporate standard costing, which would allocate all the costs of the resources associated with handling the potential event, regardless of whether the event occurs or not. Whether fixed costs are included in the impact analysis depends on whether the group handling the event is inherent to the business, because the events themselves can never be designed out of the system. If operational risk management is a preamble to organizational redesign or outsourcing, a complete allocation of costs to events is appropriate. However, if the focus is more short-term and operational, the impact should only include the variable costs.

Box 6.5:   Example — Costs associated with incorrect securities settlement messages

According to a recent benchmarking analysis of securities settlement messages performed by SWIFT, the following costs were associated with handling various settlement-related loss events (Table 6.4).

TABLE **6.4** Errors in Settlement Instructions — Impacts and Frequencies

Impact per event	Event	Approximate frequency
$10	The fixed cost associated with the settlement message	100% of messages
$6	The variable cost of repairing the message	59% of messages need repair and query
$16	The cost of a mismatch	10% of confirmations and statement result in mismatches
$50	The cost of resolving a settlement failure	15% fail to settle on time

Source: SWIFT

Impact Data Sources

In addition to the generic event data sources described earlier, event impacts have their own unique sources. Although most of these historical sources of impact data only record direct historical impacts (for example, additional expenses, losses in revenues, reductions in the value of assets, or opportunity costs) rather than indirect ones (that is, causing other loss events), they can, nonetheless, provide useful benchmark estimates.

Losses Recorded in the General Ledger The starting point for any analysis of direct impacts is usually the various realized loss accounts in the general ledger. Some of these can be adapted and restated to follow a loss-event structure.

Loss Events Log Direct impacts might be recorded here, in particular the time spent handling the event. One should be careful when using the time between loss-event time stamps to determine the staff-hours devoted to handling the event—staff are rarely involved in handling only one such event at a time, so the difference will overestimate the direct costs. Loss event logs also ignore any allocated costs.

Audit Reports These are relevant for major losses.

Senior Management Interviews These can provide subjective estimates that are quite reliable for frequent operational losses that are difficult to prevent.

Scenario Analysis Using Delphi Groups   This is useful for infrequent events that have firmwide implications and multifunctional causes.

External Trade Reports and Trade Data Services   These provide benchmark estimates for operational performance.

Other Issues

When estimating impacts of losses using historical data, a number of caveats should be kept in mind.

Estimate Impacts per Event   The impact of the event usually varies from one occurrence of the event to another, and as a result, losses should be estimated in terms of their effect per individual event rather than in terms of aggregate losses over a time period. There are several reasons for the range of impacts: slightly different causes for the event (although not too different or else it becomes a different event), variations in the skills of the people handling the event, or variations in the time taken to access, diagnose, repair, and verify the event. We can capture the variation in impacts by developing the dependencies between events and an approximate probability distribution of potential impacts should the event occur.

Include Indirect Costs   When making subjective estimates of event severity—the approximate dollar-cost to the "owner" of the affected resource or process—we must be careful to include direct costs (such as loss of processing time), as well as indirect costs (such as the cost of management attention, lost trading opportunities, damage to the firm's reputation with its counterparties, and increased costs).

Avoid Double-counting   What is incorporated under the impact of a loss event depends on two things: first, the precise definition of the loss event, and second, the broader set of causal relations between this event and others. It is critical to be consistent about what is (and is not) included in the impact associated with a particular event or factor. For instance, one may choose to ignore an event's indirect effects if these indirect losses are captured in the direct loss of another event. An impact once allocated to one event cannot be allocated again to a different event.

Capture Net Impacts   Impacts should be estimated net of any loss prevention, loss reduction, and risk transfer if the mitigating factor is not made explicit. For example, this can be used to alter the underlying loss distribution to account for insurance deductibles, policy limits, and call strikes.

Use a Consistent Baseline   Without this, event risks cannot be compared. When estimating the impact, imagine what the cost of the event would be if it occurred immediately. This ignores, for instance, the fact that the costs of handling the event may evolve over time, say, as we gain more experience, or as insurance becomes available. Impact estimation also ignores the likely effects of inflation, which should be incorporated in the aggregate risk assessment (see Subsection 8.1), but not separately in the evaluation of each individual event.

6.6   SUBJECTIVE RISK ASSESSMENT

Multifunctional experts can subjectively estimate operational process risks either individually or as a group. Subjective assessment makes the most sense if:

*   Historical data (either external or internal) is unavailable, too expensive, or of poor quality.

*   Historical data is not readily generalizable to these particular circumstances. This may be because experts believe that the past tells us little about the distribution of losses moving forward or there are major changes in the system that will change the risks affecting a particular process.

It follows that subjective assessment is particularly appropriate for rare, high-impact losses or catastrophic risks for which there is very limited data. The alternative—not analyzing these events—will not make them go away; rather, it will just make the firm less able to deal with them should they occur. Of course, no single approach can guarantee outcomes. The best we can do is improve our expected results.

Qualitative versus Quantitative Subjective Estimates

Most checklist-based approaches to operational risk assessment suffice with just qualitative estimates of the risk (see Subsection 3.2). Subjective assessment of an event's likelihood or impact can remain purely qualitative or it can use the qualitative estimate to provide a quantitative benchmark. Quantified judgments invariably provide more information than informal assessments. They make the assessment easier to understand and communicate to others, and also make it accessible for testing. For example, subjective point estimates can be converted into quantitative estimates by specific ranges as in Table 6.5:

TABLE **6.5** Qualitative Risk Assessment

Likelihood level		Likelihood that the event will occur in the next year
VL	Very Low	Less than 2%
L	Low	2–5%
M	Medium	5–10%
H	High	10–20%
VH	Very High	More than 20%

A more sophisticated approach quantifies the subjective estimates by producing a ranking of the relative frequencies or impacts of the different events under comparison and then scaling the rankings to some probability scale through a calibrated linear model. Rankings can then be mapped to a quantitative scale if the levels of two events' frequencies/ risks/impacts are known.

FIGURE **6.3** Simple Mappings between Rankings and Probabilities

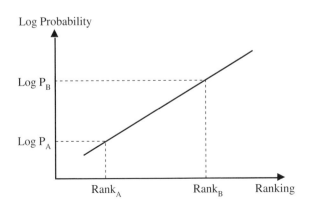

The mapping connecting the frequency/risk/impact (P) of the event and its corresponding ranking (R), given two objectively estimated levels A and B, is given by:

$$\text{Log}\left(\frac{P_{\text{event}}}{P_A}\right) = \text{Log}\left(\frac{P_B}{P_A}\right)\left(\frac{R_{\text{event}} - R_A}{R_B - R_A}\right)$$

Sometimes a third calibrated event is used to test the model. Different experts' rankings can also be integrated using simple averages of the rankings. Just as for direct estimation of probabilities, the extent to which experts are consistent with each other is an indication of the need for more consensus-based group approaches.

With any quantitative assessment, there is always the danger that managers believe they have a better understanding of the risks than they actually do. This can be remedied by performing a sensitivity analysis of any risk assessment, and specifically asking how important additional accuracy in risk estimates is to management objectives. In general however, even an error-ridden estimate of the loss impact and frequency is superior to a purely subjective estimate. Unlike subjective estimates, quantitative estimates can be compared and aggregated, and force managers to focus on the risk exposure rather than hiding behind a bland statement such as, We have a "high" likelihood of the event occurring. Further, quantitative estimates can be used to anchor subjective estimates, whereby techniques such as the *Bayes Rule* can be used to update the forecast to account for new information.

Individual versus Group-based Subjective Assessments

Subjective assessments of a particular impact or likelihood can be performed by interviewing a single individual, polling the views of a number of staff members, or having staff members work together to produce a consensus assessment. Each approach has its own strengths and limitations and needs to be matched to the specific situation if accurate subjective assessments are to be produced.

T_ABLE **6.6** Individual versus Group Risk Assessment

Assessment Type	Advantages	Disadvantages
Individual	Gets line managers involved May be forward-looking May be good at the body of the distribution, assuming expert is close to the losses Identifies risk factors or loss events controlled or realized within the respondent's area	Subject to individual cognitive biases such as availability and threshold biases Lacks understanding of how upstream loss events may affect them Estimates may be inconsistent
Group	Gets functional managers involved Leverages a broad range of expertise and experience May be useful for estimating tail risks May be forward looking Good at focusing on the interfaces between processes where many losses originate Identifies risk factors or loss events controlled or realized within the respondent's area	Subject to cognitive biases such as availability and threshold biases, group-think Difficult to integrate individual opinion with group opinion May be a political process Difficult to select appropriate individuals/groups Estimates may be inconsistent

Consider each of these approaches in more detail.

Individual Assessment

Individual expert opinions regarding specific potential losses can be gathered using detailed questionnaires sent to the business areas. This approach has the advantage of being consistent across different business areas, but some subtleties may be lost because business area staff are not involved in the design and development of the questions posed. Surveys can then be augmented by structured follow-on interviews with business managers to investigate and corroborate potentially important findings. Questionnaires need to be specific enough to catch the relevant events but general enough to apply to different business areas. The longer the survey and the greater the number of irrelevant questions, the less likely a good response will be. Electronic documents can be e-mailed to business managers to fill in and return. An even better approach is to set up an online form on the Web and load the results directly into the risk databases for analysis. Structured interview methodologies can be used in which the risk analyst walks through the questionnaire with the respondent. The latter approach has the benefit of producing better results but requires more resources.

Box 6.6: Individual Cognitive Biases

Individual risk assessment is fraught with challenges; humans are subject to a variety of behavioral and cognitive biases that make risk estimation difficult.

TABLE 6.7 Cognitive Biases Toward Risk

Individual bias	Description and implications	Potential fixes
Threshold heuristic	Events below some threshold of probability disappear from the radar screen of managers who are eager to allocate limited managerial attention. The threshold heuristic causes decision-makers to underestimate shock probabilities.	External risk assessment; analysis of work logs.
Availability bias	Attention is given to the most prominent or most recent example. This leads to the sudden imposition of controls that may actually exacerbate the problem or cause other problems.	Maintaining a history of loss events in the form of a loss log can help extend the manager's memory.
Anchoring	Tendency for future judgments to be made in terms of earlier judgments. For example, experts who were originally asked about the expected impact of an event will anchor subsequent assessments of extreme percentiles around the mean.	Ask for estimates of extremes of the distribution before obtaining the mean or median estimate.
Base rate insensitivity	Focus on relative frequency, not objective frequency. Managerial accounting systems tend to favor high-frequency shocks because the shock occurs so infrequently as not to be captured in the usual reporting period. Activities that appear profitable may not be so when managers realize their exposure to low-frequency shocks.	External loss logs, incident reports, use of extreme value theory to estimate tail loss.
Framing effects	Context changes the impression left by data. Marketing group presents the problem as a marketing problem, insurance group presents it as an insurance issue.	Interfunctional group decision-making.

TABLE 6.7 Cognitive Biases Toward Risk (cont'd)

Individual bias	Description and implications	Potential fixes
Subjective frequency estimation	Infrequent events are overestimated, frequent events are underestimated.	Calibration of group estimates with objective estimates; use of pairwise ranking with objective scales.
Confirmation bias	Tendency to gather more information to confirm initial hypotheses. If we believe a business area is highly risky, we will search longer to find evidence of the risks.	Do not be too hasty to make decisions. Allow divergent analysis in group risk assessment sessions.
Loss-averse but not risk averse	Tendency to gamble on long odds. A problem of trading in particular, where compensation is based on short-term profits without any provision for infrequent losses; thus, the line officers in position to assess the long-term risks are rewarded for ignoring them.	Performance measurement should be based on the risk taken on rather than on the P&L obtained.
Miscalculated probabilities	Only successes are remembered, not the failures. Staff naturally wish to forget problems and as a result are overconfident.	Loss logs. Change organizational culture to allow staff to discuss problems more openly.
Ego	Emotional involvement with outcomes. One's ego and preferences may dictate uncontrollable outcomes.	Depersonalize problems. Use an impartial facilitator in group sessions. Incentives can also be helpful toward removing the bias.
Representative-ness bias	Isolated instances are assumed to be representative.	Use detailed incident reports. Develop detailed event and fault trees toward describe the unique aspect of loss events.
Illusion of control	We assume we can control more than we can.	Test models against actual experience.

There are several important guidelines that should guide the process of individual risk assessment:

Define the Problem It is essential to define the relevant events, factors, and targets including any conditions that are assumed and the nature of the desired forecasts, for example, the time horizon of the forecast. It may also be helpful to summarize to the expert some of the existing relevant studies that shed light on the problem.

Choose your Experts Carefully   Experts, usually business managers or business risk analysts, should be close to the major operating risks in the business unit under analysis. The opinions of individuals regarding the loss events realized and controlled in their own area should *always* take precedence over consensus or other managers' views. Experts should also have a good memory of their own errors and the errors of those staff members who are close to them. Obviously, these will be subject to some biases such as recency effects (which make experts more likely to overestimate the risk of recently occurring events relative to others). The level of experience required of the expert depends on the frequency of the event being evaluated. Of course, there is always the danger that the experience of long-serving staffers is simply no longer relevant if technology or systems have undergone major changes during their terms. Infrequent events may need an expert with 10 years' experience while probabilities of very frequent events could be estimated just as accurately by less-experienced personnel. Another helpful heuristic uses more-senior managers to estimate the impacts and lower level staff to estimate the event frequency. Pairwise comparisons of risks (see Box 6.6) can be used to produce measures of the consistency of individual experts' estimates and suggest whether there is a need for group estimation approaches.

Disaggregate the Problem   A standard approach to improving subjective estimates is to disaggregate the problem so that individual respondents find the task more tangible and therefore tractable. For example, it is easier to estimate the likelihood and impact of common events, and then to use tools such as fault trees to infer the frequency of causally related events rather than have experts estimate the likelihood of infrequent events directly.

Estimate Distributions   Experts' uncertainty over their estimates may make them reluctant to produce anything other than point estimates of frequency and impact. This essentially treats the variables as certainty equivalents, but will decrease the levels of unexpected and catastrophic losses and may have a systematic effect on the levels of expected losses. Point estimates help identify *expected* losses, but to analyze unexpected or catastrophic losses, distributions of frequencies and impacts are needed. Fortunately, there are a number of general distributions (described in Subsection 7.2) that reliably capture many of the characteristics of loss events. Alternatively, estimating a probability distribution can be subdivided into the task of making a number of point forecasts.

Use Simple Probability Models Vose (1996) discusses some of the issues involved in using expert opinions about frequency and impact distributions. Unless there are theoretical justifications for parametric distributions, simple shape distributions such as triangular and uniform, and general distributions should be used for modeling expert opinions.

Experts Should Understand Basics of Probability Direct estimation of probabilities assumes that selected staff can reliably estimate probabilities. Experts should also be comfortable with basic probability theory, otherwise, it may be difficult for them to express their beliefs. Probabilities are difficult for most people to grasp intuitively. Instead of asking for probabilities directly, it may be helpful to ask the expert to choose between two alternatives, one of which has a prior defined probability.

Box 6.7:   Pairwise Comparisons

Another useful technique when dealing with individuals acting alone or within a group is the method of paired comparisons (Hunns, 1982). Experts are generally better at comparing risks than at estimating risks directly. This approach has each expert comparing all risks, two at a time, in terms of frequency or impact, or both. The ranking of these comparisons can then be analyzed for internal consistency (even used as a measure of the experts' competence), for external consistency (against other experts), or quantified using the techniques that have already been described. The difficulty with pairwise comparisons is the possible absence of a natural ranking for the event. This is most likely to be the case for very complex events that are very different than for simpler homogenous events. It is also important that experts evaluate pairs independently of their previous choices. This technique may involve a large number of comparisons ($n(n+1)/2)$) relative to the number of direct probability estimates (n). There are software packages that efficiently support pairwise comparisons.

Group Assessment

For complex loss events with impacts felt far beyond their source, no single organizational actor has a complete picture of the firmwide exposure. For these and other complex risks for which the estimation requires input from a number of areas, a group of staff members can produce better risk assessments than any single individual. This leverages experts' different perspectives toward different parts of the process and the risks that may result. Group approaches are also appropriate for the brainstorming of risk management alternatives and priorities.

Group assessment is no panacea, however. When using a group assessment, interaction between experts must be managed carefully to avoid the biases (Table 6.8) to which groups can be prone such as overconfidence and parochialism.

TABLE **6.8** Group Risk Assessment Biases

Group bias	Description and implications	Potential fixes
Undefined problem	Imprecisely defined loss events. Arguments concerning their experts differing perceptions of events.	Events must be precisely defined so that everyone in the group is evaluating the same problem. Also useful is to group events into subsets with similar characteristics (source, frequency, impacts) so they can be more easily compared. Sometimes, loss events can be broken down into distinct subevents that are better analyzed separately.
Clash of the titans	Experts often have strong opinions that can be disruptive or lead to an unproductive stalemate.	Facilitator should guarantee all parties get some opportunity to voice their opinions.
Group-think and herding	Pressure to follow group or cultural norms; particularly a problem with consensus groups.	Facilitator should be willing to act as devil's advocate. External parties should help in group risk assessment.
Group risk taking	Groups tend to make more risky decisions than individuals.	Risky decisions should not be hurried. Participants should be forced to think through the implications of their assessments.
Unk-unks	It is not the hard-to-measure risks that are the most dangerous; rather, it is the unknown risks that we have not even thought of.	Have as wide a range of experience in the group as possible. Be willing to discuss out-of-the box scenarios.

TABLE 6.8 Group Risk Assessment Biases (cont'd)

Group bias	Description and implications	Potential fixes
Tunnel vision	Different people see things differently (particularly from different functional areas). Organizational structures divide processes into discrete areas and problems fall through the interfaces between areas.	Use consensus approach to counter tunnel vision. Make sure all loss and risk data are accessible firmwide. Use risk-based transfer pricing.
Spaghetti factor	Size and complexity of the situation lead to unexpected or sneak conditions.	Use explicit process maps, well-maintained documentation, fault trees, operational databases.
Latent errors	Many losses are realized over a long period and therefore ignored.	Organizations should have well-developed record management and archives.
Escalating commitment	Good money is thrown after bad; paying attention to sunk costs.	Independent external assessment. Performance measurement should have a limited memory. For instance, traders should be encouraged to trade a flat book as if they have no prior losses or gains.

Critical to effective group risk assessment is a facilitator to integrate perspectives, prevent biases arising from personality differences in the group, and minimize group effects such as overconfidence and the fear of looking foolish. Random polling of different groups of staff is not sufficient, nor is unstructured negotiation between staff because of the potential intrusion of political factors. In general, groups can assess the likelihood and impact of events in the following ways:

- Polling of individual estimates
- Delphi methods
- Nominal group methods
- Consensus methods

The choice of method and line experts should reflect the risks, the structure, and the limitations of the loss data rather than simply the availability of the staff.

TABLE 6.9 Techniques for Impact, Frequency, and Dependency Assessment

Assessment method	To estimate event likelihoods	To estimate impacts	To estimate dependencies
Polling of single individual	Useful for events in the individual's experience, i.e., for front-line staff close to the occurrence of the event	Assumes higher level managers can produce useful impact estimates.	Useful for simple events within individual's area of control
Polling of multiple individuals	Appropriate for external uncontrollable events where experts' knowledge is limited	Assumes different staff members experience different aspects of the impact	
Delphi	Like polling but allows the possibility of oversight (and also the herding of estimates)	–	–
Nominal group	Like consensus approaches, but strictly limits group effects. May also prevent divergent thinking		
Consensus	Useful for complex events with firmwide causes	Assumes group effects are not too limiting (Scenario Analysis)	Useful for complex events with firmwide causes

Polling of Individual Estimates First, individuals make their estimates separately. These estimates are then aggregated in terms of some statistic of the sample estimates. Commonly chosen are the arithmetic mean:

$$P_{event} = \frac{1}{n} \sum_{\text{expert } i}^{n \text{ experts}} P_{event}^{i}$$

or the geometric mean:

$$P_{event} = n \sqrt{\prod_{\text{expert } i}^{n \text{ experts}} P_{event}^{i}}$$

of the experts' probability estimates. These treat different forecasts symmetrically—a reasonable assumption if we have no evidence to assume one forecaster is better than any other. Sometimes, a maximum of the sample estimates may be appropriate, say, for impacts when different staff members experience different aspects of the total impact. If there is evidence that some forecasters are better than others, then we might weigh these forecasts more heavily than the others using a weighted average:

$$P_{event} = \sum_{\text{expert } i}^{n \text{ experts}} w_i \, P_{event}^i \left/ \sum_{\text{expert } i}^{n \text{ experts}} w_i \right.$$

If the errors of forecasters are assumed independent, then the weights should be the reciprocals of the error variances.

Individual polling is easy to do and avoids some of the potential clashes that can result from having many experts in one place. But this is also its major disadvantage, since it prevents experts from learning from one another and developing better estimates than they would have been able to produce individually.

Delphi Methods   This takes the same expert estimates as before, but then distributes all estimates to all experts, which allows them to reassess their estimates. Again, this isO≤elatively easy to perform and provides for some sharing of information between experts, but does not allow any real discussion to take place. Following submission of revised estimates, an aggregate estimate is produced using the geometric mean.

Nominal Group Methods   This takes this information-sharing a step further and allow *limited* discussion between experts to clarify issues, but avoid extensive discussion. The hope is that this prevents both the domination of the group by personalities and the tendency toward group-think that can be the bane of more consensus-based risk estimation.

Consensus Method   At the extreme end is the consensus group, which requires that the group produces an estimate that all members agree on. This can lead to heated discussions that must be carefully managed by a skilled facilitator if the process is not to be biased or get out of control. The group consensus approaches is more appropriate if there is much disagreement among individual estimates calculated using other methods. The use of group techniques to evaluate risks is not just a preamble to risk measurement and prioritization. Developing a forum for discussion—a safe area where managers evaluate practices and operational decisions offline—may be more important than the measurement produced. Subjective assessment by groups of experts is also particularly useful for playing out disaster scenarios, in effect building synthetic data points at the extreme tails of the distributions to counter the natural tendency of data to focus on the body of the distribution. Tail distributions can then be fitted to these points to get a better handle on the potential for catastrophic losses.

Evaluating Consistency Across Experts

Statistical techniques such as *Analysis of Variance* can be used in combination with *pairwise comparisons* (see Box 6.6) to test the consistency of estimation between different experts. This requires estimating the F ratio, that is, the ratio of the variance within individual estimates to the variance across different individuals' estimates, scaled by the ratio of the degrees of freedom associated with the two-variance estimates. See any good introductory statistics text, such as Wonnacott and Wonnacott (1977) for a discussion on Analysis of Variance techniques. If the F ratio is very high across individual estimates, it suggests that there is little consistency between experts and therefore they are developing their estimates using very different mental models of the phenomenon. This would imply a need to get experts together to form consensus estimates.

CHAPTER 7

ESTIMATING POTENTIAL LOSSES — LOSS DISTRIBUTIONS

7.1 ESTIMATING RISK FACTORS

A variety of modeling and forecasting techniques can be used to estimate both the average level and potential range of risk factors for a given time period. Risk factors can be understood in terms of their probability distributions over a time horizon. These distributions are assumed to be stable. More than anything else, the choice of factor model depends on the extent of the time horizon, with very different models useful for short-term and longer term situations. Table 7.1 provides a summary of the issues; readers should refer to Makridakis and Wheelwright (1989) for a more detailed explanation of the different techniques. All of these models are based on two important assumptions. First, risk factors are accurately represented by KRI proxies that have reliable historical data, and second, the patterns revealed in historical data are likely to persist into the short, medium and long terms.

TABLE 7.1 Different Forecasting Models: Strengths and Limitations

Method	Strengths	Limitations
	Short-term models	
Naive forecasts (random walk)	Very simple to use and understand. Can also provide a benchmark to evaluate other models	Ignores almost all the data!

TABLE 7.1 (cont'd)

Method	Strengths	Limitations
Short-term models (cont'd)		
Moving average	Easy to use and understand	Very sensitive to size of look-back period. Takes some time to adjust to major changes
Exponential smoothing	Fairly easy to use and understand	Selection of smoothing parameter
Medium-term models		
Box-Jenkins (ARIMA)	Capable of capturing subtle patterns in the data	Complex for many end users
Single-equation regression	Outperforms most alternatives. Useful for control and operations managers because it suggests interventions	Expensive to develop and maintain; requires large amounts of data
Decomposition	Plausible. May be appropriate for medium term	Little statistical justification
Long-term models		
Trend curves	Easy to use and understand. Appropriate for longer term	May encourage mindless extrapolation of historical trends
Judgmental methods, e.g., scenario analysis	Can be wide-ranging, inexpensive. Appropriate for long-term forecasts	May be inaccurate. Subject to political, individual, and group biases (see Subsection 6.6)

Short-term Factor Models

There is significant inertia in many important risk factors such as volume, price, and staffing levels. This allows us to make relatively accurate short-term forecasts for these factors over periods of a few months to a year. For short-term models, long-term trends or low-frequency cycles in the data are typically ignored. A variety of models can be used to simulate and forecast risk factors (F) over a short time horizon given observed data (X) subject to error (E), including:

- Random walk model
- Moving average model
- Exponential smoothing model

Random Walk Model   This holds that the value of a factor at the end of a time period differs only from its value at the beginning of the time period by a symmetric, zero mean distributed random error. It is written as:

$$X_{t+1} = X_t + E_t$$

The error term E_t follows a probability distribution (typically, normal with a zero mean). The best prediction for the factor's value in the next period is therefore the current factor's value:

$$F_{t+1} = E(X_{t+1}) = X_t$$

Random walk models assume that the data have no memories of the past and therefore that historical data has no value for forecasting.

Moving Average Model   This model, in contrast, estimates the next period value of a factor as a moving average of the last n data point:

$$F_{t+1} = \frac{\sum_{s=t-n+1}^{t} X_s}{n}$$

Selection of the optimal look-back period (n) should be based on historical back-testing according to which parameter value minimizes a particular error statistic, typically the mean squared error or the mean absolute deviation.

Exponential Smoothing Model   Unlike the moving average model, this model has time-decaying weights on earlier data points, making it more sensitive to more recent observations. It takes the form:

$$F_{t+1} = \alpha X_t + (1 - \alpha)F_t$$

where α is a smoothing constant and satisfies $0 < \alpha < 1$.

Medium-term Factor Models

These cover forecasts from a few months to several years. Examples include budgeting, decision-making, and resource allocation and business planning.

Seasonal Models Seasonality refers to a repeated periodic pattern in the data. For instance, a weekly cycle might be expected in securities; Monday mornings and Friday afternoons are generally volatile times. Seasonal cycles may be seen in commodities or around particular periods such as the end of the calendar year or accounting year. Seasonal estimates are produced by dividing the data by seasonal indices that are estimated as a moving average over the seasonal period. Techniques such as *Winter's method* can be used to build a model when the data has both a trend and a seasonal component. Alternatively, more complex *decomposition* models can be developed; these usually model the data as a product of seasonal, trend, cyclic, and random components.

Time-Series Analysis The most general time-series model available is the Box-Jenkins (ARIMA) Model. Although it can be complex, unlike many of the other techniques discussed, it can be justified statistically, and is capable of systematically capturing some very complex patterns in the data. There are three distinct components (p, d, and q) in an ARIMA(p, d, q) model:

Autoregression (p): This describes the linear relationship between current observations and a finite number of historical ones, and can be written as:

$$x_{t+1} = \phi_1 X_t + \phi_2 X_{t-1} + \ldots + \phi_p X_{t-p+1} + E_{t+1}$$

It is estimated by analyzing the autocorrelation function (the correlation of the current observation with historical ones).

Integration (d): Many data series do not have a fixed mean over time. Nonetheless, the data may exhibit some consistencies in its behavior. Integration refers to repeatedly differencing the data (d times) until it exhibits stationary behavior, that is, developing a new data series:

$$X'_t = X_t - X_{t-1}$$

Moving Average (q): Not unlike the earlier moving average models, this describes the relationship between the current observation and historical errors. It can be written as:

$$X_{t+1} = E_{t+1} - \theta_1 E_t - \theta_2 E_{t-1} - \ldots - \theta_q E_{t+1-q}$$

and can be shown to be equivalent to an infinite autoregressive model. As for autoregressive models, moving average models can be identified by using the autocorrelation function.

The Box-Jenkins technique systematically incorporates all three elements into a single ARIMA(p, d, q) model where p denotes the autoregressive parameter, d the level of integration, and q the moving average parameter. For further information on how to develop an ARIMA model, consult Box, Jenkins, and Reinsell (1994). Laycock (1998) discusses an application of ARIMA models to the problem of mishandling losses.

Linear Regression These models try to quantify a logical causal relation between the risk factor and some other more easily identified independent variables. Simple linear regression models fit a straight line between the dependent risk factor and the independent variables. Other variants of regression allow for non-linear functions of the independent variables to be used, or loosen some of the distributional assumptions required (for example, independent errors and constant variance).

Other Techniques *Simultaneous regression models, GARCH,* and *state space models* can be used to model the evolution of whole systems of factors over time; however, these have heavy data requirements and can be very difficult to understand and interpret. There is also little evidence that more complex models such as these outperform simple regression or time-series models. Similarly, data-mining approaches such as *cluster analysis, principal component analysis, neural networks, factor analysis,* and *discriminant analysis* can be used to identify historical patterns if very large databases are available. The best examples of these techniques have been in the retail environment, especially modeling banks' experience with consumer fraud. While such behavioral modeling plays a major role in understanding credit-card fraud and cross-selling, the lack of internal data may limit the use of these techniques for operational risk modeling.

Long-term models

Long-term models cover forecasts of two years or more. They are notoriously inaccurate. Nonetheless, they are used extensively in areas such as strategic planning and capital budgeting. Techniques such as *scenario analysis* and *trend analysis* can be used, subject to some inevitable scope for massive errors. In some cases, such as demographics and technology forecasting, *exponential* or *diffusion models* can be somewhat reliably fitted to the data.

7.2 FITTING PROBABILITY DISTRIBUTIONS

Basic Approaches

Based on historical samples, analysts need to infer more general distributions. There are three basic families of probability distributions used to describe the frequencies and impact of specific events. These are:

- Empirical distributions
- Shape distributions
- Parametric distributions

Empirical Distributions An increasingly popular approach leverages relatively complete internal loss logs to produce an *empirical distribution* as a proxy for the population distribution of event occurrences. The empirical model is easy to use, although not always feasible without sufficient data to fill out the full range of possible values. Empirical models use the actual (sample) loss distribution as a proxy for the projected future loss distribution (population). Monte Carlo simulation tools such as those described in Appendix B allow any empirical distribution to be used and basically mimic the probability density function by the histogram of loss frequencies (similarly for impacts). The empirical approach has the benefits of being objective, of not requiring user-defined distributional assumptions, and of working well if there is extensive historical loss data similar to that likely to be experienced in the future. They have the disadvantages associated with all samples, namely, understating tail events and overstating the importance of the firm's idiosyncratic experiences.

Shape Distributions Distributions such as *triangular, uniform*, and *general* are used with subjective frequency and impact estimates. They have the advantage of being simple and therefore readily understood by staff experts without statistical training. When data are unavailable, they also have the advantage of being easily defensible. Shape distributions have the disadvantages of not capturing the subtleties of the distribution, nor of being borne out by experience with other loss events.

Box 7.1: Probability Distribution — Triangular

Type: Shape, continuous (although not differentiable), and bounded

*Probability
density
function (Pdf)*: Triang [min, mode, max](x)

$$= \frac{2\,(x - \min)}{(\text{mode} - \min)(\max - \min)} \quad \textit{if } \min \le x \le \text{mode}$$

$$= \frac{2\,(\max - x)}{(\max - \min)(\max - \text{mode})} \quad \textit{if } \text{mode} \le x \le \max$$

Mean: $\dfrac{\min + \text{mode} + \max}{3}$

Variance: $\dfrac{\min^2 + \text{mode}^2 + \max^2 - \min \times \text{mode} - \min \times \max - \text{mode} \times \max}{18}$

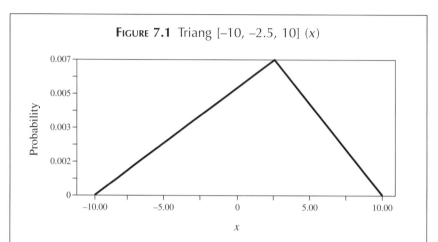

FIGURE 7.1 Triang [–10, –2.5, 10] (x)

Note: The triangular distribution is appropriate when there are a maximum value, a minimum value, and a mode (the most likely value within the range from the minimum value to the maximum), and little historical data. Although it has no theoretical basis, like other shape distributions, it derives its statistical properties from its geometry. It offers flexibility in its shape as well as efficiency in use. However, the triangular shape usually overemphasizes the tails of the distribution and underestimates the "shoulders" in comparison with other more "natural" distributions. The triangular distribution is particularly useful as an approximate probability distribution for event impacts.

Box 7.2: Probability Distribution — Uniform

Type: Shape, continuous (although not differentiable) and bounded

Pdf: Uniform [min, max]$(x) = \dfrac{1}{\text{max} - \text{min}}$ where min $\leq x \leq$ max

Mean: $\dfrac{\text{max} - \text{min}}{2}$ *Variance*: $\dfrac{(\text{max} - \text{min})^2}{12}$

FIGURE 7.2 Uniform [4, 9] (x)

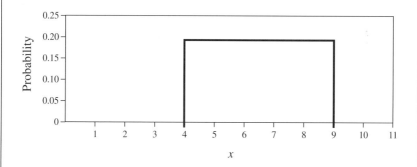

Note: Like the triangular distribution, the uniform distribution is particularly useful for simulating impact. Because all parameter values have the same constant probability density, the distribution does not appropriately reflect the perceived uncertainty of the parameter. However, it maybe useful in highlighting the fact that very little is known of the parameter or that the parameter has been poorly determined. The distribution is most suited as a way to convert qualitative estimates of impact into more quantitative ones for subsequent simulation and analysis.

Box 7.3: Probability Distribution — General

Type: Shape, continuous (although not differentiable), and bounded

Pdf: General $[\{x_i\}, \{p_i\}](x) = p_i + \dfrac{x - x_i}{x_{i+1} - x_i} (p_{i+1} - p_i)$

where $x \in [x_i, x_{i+1}]$

Mean: No closed form   *Variance*: No closed form

FIGURE 7.3 General [{0,1,2,3,4,5,6,7,8,9,10}, {0, 0.05, 0.11, 0.16, 0.22, 0.11, 0.05, 0.03, 0.11, 0.16, 0}] (x)

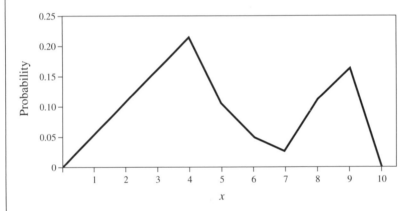

Note: General distributions are often used to represent the subjective opinions of experts, particularly when formed using the method of pairwise comparison.

Parametric Distributions   Unlike shape distributions, parametric distributions require an experienced analyst to choose from a family of distributions and then select parameters that best fit the distribution to a particular data set. Parametric distributions such as *exponential, Poisson, beta,* and *Weibull* make strong mathematical assumptions about the underlying process of events. For example, a Poisson distribution is used to describe the frequency of randomly occurring events whereas an exponential distribution describes the times between such random events. Parametric distributions should be used if:

- There is some theory underlying that particular distribution that applies to the particular problem.

- Internal or external experience suggests that this distribution is appropriate for this type of problem.

- Internal data approximately fits the distribution.

The parametric approach can be particularly useful for evaluating catastrophic operational risks for which we have limited data, because the distribution provides information beyond the range of the sample data. Formal parametric distributions also impose a top-down discipline on the operational loss simulation process. Some banks, for instance, specify *a priori* the distributions that should be used for a given loss event and then collect empirical data to estimate the best parameters for that distribution.

Table 7.2 summarizes each of these approaches to fitting distributions:

TABLE 7.2 Empirical, Shape, and Parametric Distributions:
Advantages and Disadvantages

Distribution	Advantages	Disadvantages
Empirical	Objective, good for large internal loss logs (more-frequent events)	Sample may not be representative, and can be driven by outliers
Shape	Simple, good for subjective estimation (less frequent events)	May not be an accurate representation of impacts or frequencies
Parametric	Complete, useful when theory exists (e.g., Poisson, exponential, binomial)	Complex, demands staff with statistical training

Box 7.4: Probability Distribution — Exponential

Type: Parametric, continuous, differentiable, and partially bounded

Pdf: Exponential: $[\lambda](x) = \lambda\exp(-\lambda x)$ where $x > 0$ and $\lambda > 0$

Mean: $\dfrac{1}{\lambda}$ *Variance*: $\dfrac{1}{\lambda^2}$

FIGURE 7.4 Exponential [0.25] (x)

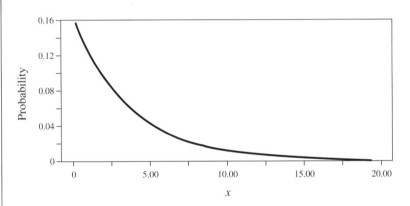

Notes: Exponential distributions are typically used by reliability engineers to describe the times between events that are purely random with a constant probability per unit time of occurrence. In this case, we have a constant failure process with parameter λ—the constant failure rate at which these events occur over time. We can also show that an exponential time between events leads to a Poisson number of occurrences in any particular time interval. The exponential distribution is widely used to model external events recurring randomly in time, for instance, the amount of time (starting from now) until an earthquake occurs or until a new war breaks out.

Box 7.5: Probability Distribution — Normal

Type: Parametric, continuous, differentiable, and unbounded

Pdf: Normal $[\mu, \sigma](x) = \dfrac{1}{\sigma\sqrt{2\pi}}\exp\left[-\dfrac{1}{2}\dfrac{(x-\mu)^2}{\sigma^2}\right]$

Mean: μ *Variance*: σ^2

FIGURE 7.5 Normal [0, 1] (x)

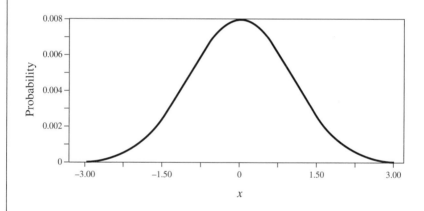

Note: The Normal (or Gaussian) distribution occurs in a wide variety of applications due in part to the results of the *Central Limit Theorem*. Loosely put, it states that the sum of a large number of independent random variables has a distribution that is asymptotically or approximately normal. It can be a useful model of the aggregate impact of a large number of small, largely independent losses, such as small measurement errors.

Box 7.6:   Probability Distribution — Poisson

Type: Parametric, discrete, and partially bounded

Pdf: Poisson $[\lambda](x) = \dfrac{e^{-\lambda}\lambda^x}{x!}$

where $\lambda > 0$ and x is a non-negative integer.

Mean: λ *Variance*: λ

FIGURE 7.6 Poisson [2] (x)

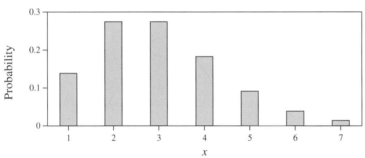

Note: The distribution of frequencies for commonly occurring events is often modeled as a Poisson distribution. Systems modeled with a Poisson frequency or failure rate have a constant failure rate over time, that is, the probability that an event occurs is constant during any short time period. For instance, if a computer system crashes on an average of once every 200 hours of operation, a Poisson [10] distribution will model the number of crashes that could occur during the next 2,000 ($=\lambda t$) hours of operation.

In general, many event frequencies are reasonably well-fitted to the Poisson distribution, although there is a tendency for the distribution to overestimate the low-frequency days relative to the high-frequency days. This is because events in most real-world applications are not independent—when an event occurs, other events tend to occur in tandem. An approximate test of the suitability of the Poisson distribution as a fit for the sample data is how close the sample mean is to the variance. If there is a major difference, other distributions such as the binomial or negative binomial may be more appropriate.

Box 7.7: Probability Distribution — Binomial

Type: Parametric, discrete, and partially bounded

Pdf: Binomial $[p, n](x) = \binom{n}{x} p^x (1 - p)^{n-x}$

where $0 < p < 1$ and n is a non-negative integer

Mean: np *Variance*: $np(1 - p)$

FIGURE 7.7 Binomial [0.5, 10] (x)

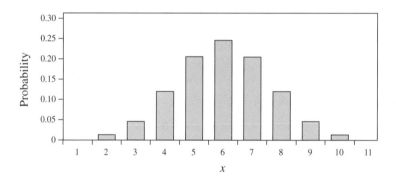

Note: Another commonly used distribution for frequencies is the binomial distribution. Unlike the Poisson, the binomial distribution is appropriate for samples in which the variance of the frequency distribution is less than the mean. This contrasts with the Poisson, for which the sample variance should approximately equal the mean, and the negative binomial, for which the sample variance should exceed the mean. Also unlike the Poisson, the binomial distribution has two parameters—n and p—which give more flexibility to better fit the data. With a binomial, the probability of having exactly x events occurring in a given time period is x, where x is at most n events. Binomial distributions are often used for batch-like processes, with transactions having a constant probability of being rejected. Suppose, for example, that for each transaction there is a 50 percent chance of a mistake. This means that in a batch of 10 transactions, we would expect to see the probability distribution of error-prone transactions as shown in Figure 7.7. Sometimes, binomial distributions (like their continuous equivalents, normal distributions), are often used to model market-related impacts where the number of losses tend to roughly equal the number of gains and where there is always the possibility of very large positive and negative shocks.

Box 7.8: Probability Distribution — Negative Binomial

Type: Parametric, discrete, and partially bounded

Pdf: NBinomial $[p, s](x) = \left(\dfrac{s + x - 1}{x} \right) p^s (1 - p)^x$

where $0 < p < 1$, and s and x are non-negative integers

Mean: $\dfrac{s(1 - p)}{p}$ *Variance*: $\dfrac{s(1 - p)}{p^2}$

FIGURE 7.8 NBinomial [0.5,5] (x)

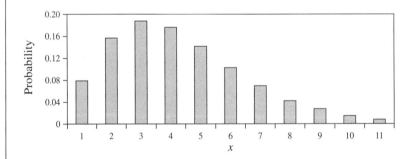

Note: A more flexible alternative to the Poisson distribution is the negative binomial distribution, which estimates the number of failures (or non-events) there will be before the sth success (event) occurs. Unlike the binomial distribution, the negative binomial has no upper limit on the total number of "trials," thus making it more appropriate in circumstances where extremely large losses are possible.

Box 7.9:   Probability Distribution — Pareto

Type: Parametric, continuous, differentiable, and partially bounded

Pdf: Pareto $[\theta,\ \alpha](x) = \dfrac{\alpha\theta^{\alpha}}{x^{\alpha+1}}$ if $x > \theta$

Mean: $\dfrac{\alpha\theta}{\alpha - 1}$ if $\alpha > 1$ 　　　　　 *Variance*: $\dfrac{\alpha\theta^{2}}{(\alpha - 2)(\alpha - 1)}$ if $\alpha > 2$

FIGURE 7.9 Pareto [1, 2] (x)

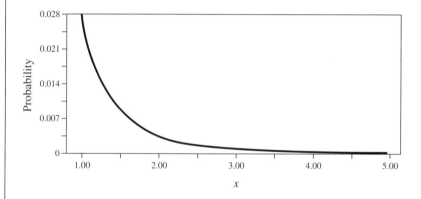

Note: The Pareto distribution (also known as the zeta distribution) is used to describe the likelihood of an impact beyond some minimum value θ; for instance, it is sometimes used to estimate the likelihood of an insurance claim given a changing deductible. Pareto distributions have been used to model the size of companies' stock-price fluctuations and insurance claims.

Box 7.10: Probability Distribution — Log normal

Type: Parametric, continuous, differentiable, and partially bounded

Pdf: Log normal $[\mu, \sigma](x) = \dfrac{1}{x\sqrt{2\pi\sigma^2}} \exp\left(-\dfrac{(\log_e x - \mu)^2}{2\sigma^2}\right)$

Mean: $\exp\left(\mu + \dfrac{\sigma^2}{2}\right)$ *Variance*: $e^{2\mu} \exp(\sigma^2)(1 - \exp(\sigma^2))$

FIGURE 7.10 Log normal [2.8, 1] (x)

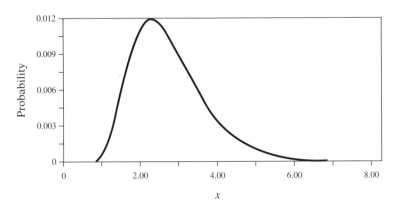

Note: A commonly used distribution for balance-sheet losses is the log normal distribution. As its name suggests, the logarithm of the log normal random variable is normally distributed. Unlike the normal distributions, the log normal distribution does not allow negative values and therefore may be more appropriate for modeling exchange rates or interest rates close to some positive minimum value (say zero). Log normal distributions are often used to simulate impact distributions, particularly for the severity of property and liability losses for which there is no possibility of a positive gain as a result of the event. Repair times (themselves a type of impact) are also often log normally distributed.

Box 7.11: Probability Distribution — Weibull

Type: Parametric, continuous, differentiable, and partially bounded

Pdf: Weibull $[\alpha, \beta](x) = \alpha\beta^{-\alpha}x^{\alpha-1} \exp\left(-\left(\frac{x}{\beta}\right)^2\right)$

where $\alpha > 0; \beta > 0$

Mean: $\frac{\beta}{\alpha}\Gamma\left(\frac{1}{\alpha}\right)$ *Variance*: $\frac{\beta^2}{\alpha}\left[2\Gamma\left(\frac{2}{\alpha}\right) - \frac{1}{\alpha}\Gamma\left(\frac{1}{\alpha}\right)^2\right]$

FIGURE 7.11 Weibull [1, 2] (x)

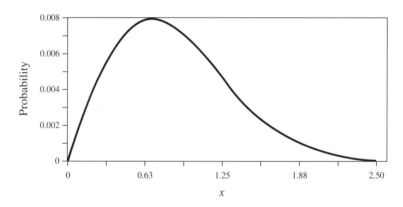

Note: The Weibull distribution provides extra flexibility when an exponential or a log normal distribution might be inadequate, especially when conditions of strict randomness are not satisfied. For example, the Weibull distribution is often used to model the time between event occurrences when the probability of occurrence changes with time. The choice of β, the shape parameter, has a dramatic effect on the shape of the distribution. The Weibull distribution becomes an exponential distribution when $\beta = 1$, and has a similar shape to the normal distribution when $\beta = 3.25$.

The Weibull distribution is extensively used to model the times between events in hardware systems, which, unlike most organizational systems, tend to have non-constant failure rates.

During the burn-in (or learning) phase, the times between failures can be modeled with a Weibull distribution with $0 < \beta < 1$. During the burnout (or forgetting) phase, errors tend to become more prevalent and are modeled with $\beta > 1$.

During the useful life of the hardware (between the burn-in and burnout phases), failure rates are assumed constant and the times between events can be modeled with an exponential distribution (or equivalently, a Weibull distribution with $\beta = 1$).

FIGURE 7.12 Various Weibull Distributions

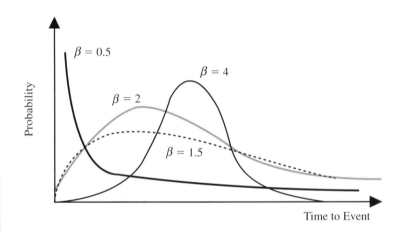

Box 7.12: Probability Distribution — Beta

Type: Parametric, continuous, differentiable, and bounded

Pdf: Beta $[\alpha_1, \alpha_2](x) = \dfrac{x^{\alpha_1 - 1}(1 - x)^{\alpha_2 - 1}}{\displaystyle\int_0^1 t^{\alpha_1 - 1}(1 - t)^{\alpha_2 - 1}\, dt}$

where α_1 and α_2 are positive.

Mean: $\dfrac{\alpha_1}{\alpha_1 + \alpha_2}$ *Variance*: $\dfrac{\alpha_1 \alpha_2}{(\alpha_1 + \alpha_2)^2 (\alpha_1 + \alpha_2 + 1)}$

FIGURE 7.13 Beta $[2, 3]\ (x)$

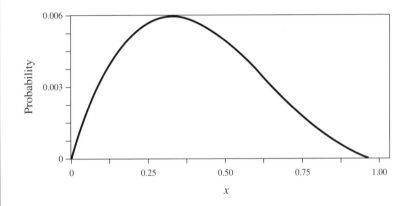

Note: Like the Weibull distribution, the beta distribution has a wide range of shapes. It is most often used for project risk assessment to estimate the impacts associated with time delays in projects or due to repair activities.

Box 7.13: Probability Distribution — Extreme Value

Type: Parametric, continuous, differentiable, and partially bounded

Pdf: $\text{Extreme} [\alpha_1, \alpha_2](x) = \dfrac{1}{\alpha_2} \exp\left(-\dfrac{(x - \alpha_1)}{\alpha_2}\right) \exp\left[-\exp\left(-\dfrac{(x - \alpha_1)}{\alpha_2}\right)\right]$ where $\alpha_2 > 0$

Mean: $\alpha_1 + 0.577\alpha_2$ 　　　　 *Variance*: $\dfrac{(\pi\alpha_2)^2}{6}$

FIGURE 7.14 Extreme [2, 3] (x)

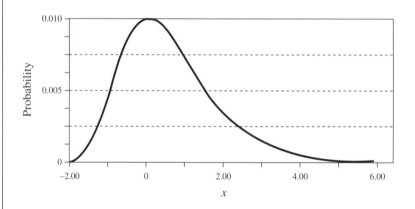

Note: Sometimes known as the Gumbel distribution, the extreme value distribution is used to model the extreme values of some random variable (typically the maximum). It is particularly useful for modeling the extreme losses that could cause some massive catastrophic event that could irreparably damage the system. Extreme value distributions have been applied to estimating the worst-case impact of major storms, fires, and even corporate defaults. The challenge with extreme value distributions is that out of n data points, only the extreme $2\sqrt{n}$ points can be used in the fit. See Box 2.12.

7.3 CHOOSING AN EVENT DISTRIBUTION

Frequency versus the Time Between Events

When analyzing events, we are faced with a choice of whether to model the event's frequency or the time between events. Frequency data, the number of events occurring in a particular time interval, is usually only available for relatively frequent events (events occurring several times a month or more). Modeling frequencies is also appropriate when the frequency is relatively stable during sufficiently long time periods, that is, there appears to be no consistent trend (upward or downward) over time. This is the case when the events are essentially random, their causes deeply embedded in the business process or external environment. For example, actuaries will typically model event frequency when analyzing the occurrence of insurance payouts. Poisson, negative binomial, and beta distributions are often used to model frequency distributions.

For less-frequent, high-impact events—events that occur, say, only a few times a year—less data are available, and it is much more likely that frequencies will change over time. For these reasons, reliability engineers typically focus on times between events rather than the frequency (which is typically renamed the event failure rate). The times between events (t) and failure rates (often denoted by $\lambda(t)$) are related mathematically by:

$$\lambda(t) = \frac{p(t)}{\int_0^t p(t') \, dt'}$$

where $p(t)$ is the probability of a particular event occurring at time t.

Constant failure rate (CFR) processes are therefore those for which the failure rate is constant over time and are equivalent to modeling event frequency. CFR processes are appropriate when the sources of failure are random and usually outside the system, for instance, caused by ongoing random environmental stress. Examples of these range from earthquakes to lawsuits. CFR processes are also appropriate for many ongoing operational loss events. Not all systems exhibit CFRs. Some internal events exhibit *decreasing failure rates* (DFRs) over time with the burn-in and learning associated with the process. Others exhibit *increasing failure rates* (IFRs) over time with burnout of the system or process elements.

Non-constant failure rate processes are often captured mathematically using the Weibull distribution.

Box 7.14: The Bathtub Curve

Sometimes you can't find a theoretical distribution that matches the historical times between failures. In such a case, it may make sense to build a composite of the failure distributions that have the required shape. One commonly used combination is the so-called *bathtub curve,* which exhibits DFRs early in the life cycle (burn-in), CFRs (useful life), and IFRs during the burnout stage of the life cycle.

FIGURE 7.15 The Bathtub Curve

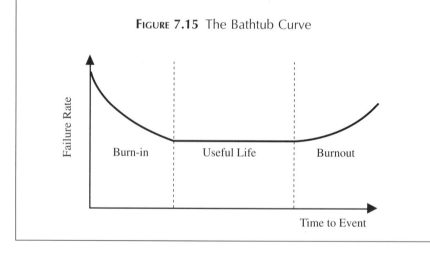

We have seen that risk analysis should have clearly defined objectives such as efficiency, capital management, or growth. A focus on efficiency usually demands models of event frequency. A focus on capital management, however, requires a longer term perspective considering less frequent events, in which case modeling the times between events is usually more appropriate. In general, it does not make sense to incorporate both very infrequent events and much more frequent events into the same model. For example, combining the effect of very different types of events (such as a hurricane and daily operations failures at a data center) only confuses analysis because their effects tend to be unrelated.

Box 7.15: System Reliability and Failure Rates

Reliability engineers are often interested in estimating the probability that a system will function without failure over a time period (t). This is the *reliability* of the system, and is given by the continuous (an integral) sum of the probability of failure $p(t)$ over all the possible times to failure up to the time t. It is written mathematically as:

$$R(t) = 1 - \int_0^t p(t')\, dt'$$

or equivalently
$$p(t) = -\frac{dR(t)}{dt}$$

The *failure rate* can then be defined as the ratio of the probability that the event occurs in a particular time period divided by the reliability of the system at that time. More formally, it is given by:

$$\lambda(t) = \frac{p(t)}{R(t)}$$

or equivalently
$$R(t) = \exp\left(-\int_0^1 \lambda(t')\, dt'\right)$$

Choosing Impact Distributions

Just as for frequency distributions, theoretical distributions can be fit onto samples of historical impacts, or if the sufficient data is available, we can directly use the empirical distribution. Although many of the issues that are important for estimating frequency and time-between-event distributions are also relevant for estimating impact distributions, a very different set of parametric distributions tends to be used. This is due to the tendency to have a large number of small losses instead of a small number of small losses. For this reason, Weibull or exponential distributions are most often used. Impact distributions are usually continuous rather than discrete, and are often at least partially unbounded since they may have both negative and positive legs to the distribution. Unfortunately, sometimes impacts are worse than that. Actuaries often distinguish between impacts that have well-behaved probability distributions and those that have heavy tails. The latter pose so-called *dangerous risks* because it is difficult to estimate them based on information from the body of the distribution; for example, log normal and some parameterizations of Weibull and Pareto distributions. Pareto distributions are often used for modeling insurance claims for fire damage. For credit-related losses on the balance sheet, the loss distribution has a very non-normal structure with many small losses but a few very large losses. This is often modeled using the Weibull distribution. Those impacts that are mainly the result of repair tasks that take a variable amount of time can be modeled in the same way as times before failure, that is, using exponential and Weibull distributions. Impacts that depend on some external factor such as interest rates or market rates should be modeled using the distribution most appropriate to that factor, typically log normal or normal for market-related losses.

Box 7.16: Example — Mishandling Events in a Insurance Company

An insurance company records the following history for 100 recent small mishandling expenses gathered during a six-month period. Estimation begins by plotting the size of the impact for each individual occurrence of the event rather than aggregating them over a time period.

FIGURE 7.16 Impact Time Series

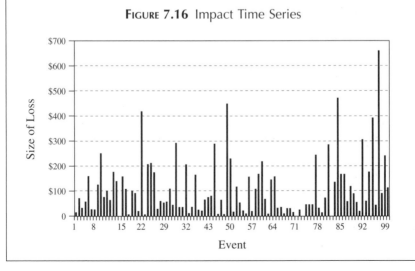

The insurance company finds that a Weibull distribution fits the loss data. To parameterize and test this model one would use the same transformations and goodness-of-fit criteria (to be discussed later in this section).

FIGURE 7.17 Fitting a Weibull Distribution to Impacts

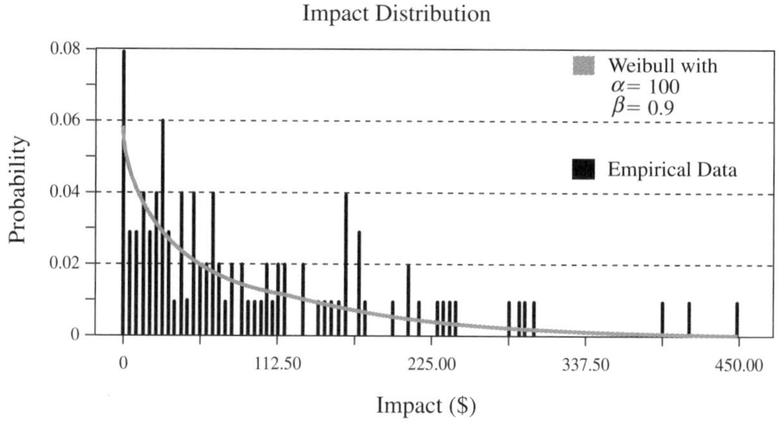

Impact Distribution

Building a Distribution

In general, four steps are required to select and parameterize a distribution for shape and parametric distributions.

1. Build a histogram of loss frequencies, times between events, or impacts.

2. Identify the candidate distributions.

3. Estimate the parameters of the distribution.

4. Test the goodness-of-fit between the data and the theoretical distribution.

By contrast, if we use empirical distributions, only Step 1—build the loss histogram—is required. Consider these steps in more detail:

Build the Loss Histogram The first step is to choose an appropriate time scale for analysis. This might be calendar time, batch number, operating time, or the number of transactions. A good choice of time scale can dramatically simplify subsequent analysis by removing one source of the loss variation (usually a major, at least partially controllable, risk factor). Once we have identified the time scale, we must build buckets for allocating the events. For example, during a one-year period, a major commercial bank was found to have mislaid transactions (a major loss event for it) at the following times: t_1, t_2, t_3, ... t_n (measured in days from January 1, 2000).

TABLE 7.3 Example of Event Times Data

Event Times (in days)									
5.1	10.3	16.3	25.2	34.6	44.3	44.7	45.3	46.1	78.7
117.4	138.3	139.3	141.3	144.5	148.9	153.4	158.0	161.8	165.7
170.1	176.1	182.1	188.4	198.8	210.1	221.6	229.1	237.5	246.3
258.8	275.0	291.6	322.6	348.8					

Modeling Frequencies: If we choose to model frequencies, we must count the number of occurrences (frequencies) of the event in different time periods. The resulting *checksheet* logs the number of events that have occurred during a particular time period. From the checksheet, we can produce a histogram of loss occurrences over time that gives us general information about the presence of trends in the data and therefore the general reliability of the data for projecting the future. In Figure 7.18, we see that the number of events occurring each month varies over time; just one event occurred in April, whereas six events occurred in June.

FIGURE 7.18 Example — Monthly Event Count

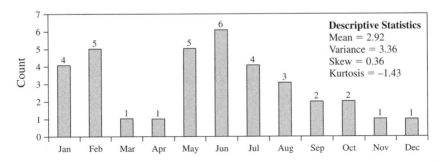

If we plot the number of months for which we have n events, where n = 0, 1, 2, 3, and so on, we can produce a frequency histogram to which shape, empirical, or parametric frequency distributions can then be fitted. This is done by rank-ordering the months according to the number of events occurring that month, and then counting the number of months with that number of event instances.

FIGURE 7.19 Example — Frequency Histogram

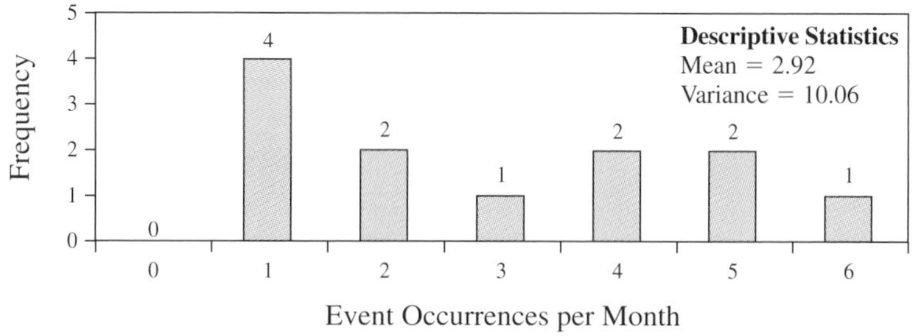

The precise number of time buckets used in the frequency histogram is important—too many classes and the data are too sparse, too few, and too aggregated. One rule of thumb is *Sturges' Rule*, which holds that the number of classes should be the integer part of

$$(1 + 3.3 \log_{10}(\text{\# of points in sample}))$$

In the above example, this is

$$1 + 3.3 \log_{10}(35)$$

which is slightly more than 6.

Modeling Times Between Events: If we are modeling times between events, this requires estimating the inter-event times: $t_{i+1} - t_i$ (also measured in days), and then rank-ordering them.

TABLE 7.4 Example of Inter-event Time Data

0.4	0.6	0.7	1.0	2.0	3.3	3.8	3.9	4.4	4.4
4.5	4.6	5.2	6.0	6.0	6.0	6.3	7.4	8.4	8.9
9.0	9.4	9.8	10.4	11.3	11.6	12.4	16.3	16.6	20.9
26.2	31.0	32.6	38.7						

With this data, we can build a histogram of the times to failure for the event (Figure 7.20).

FIGURE 7.20 Example — Times Between Events Histogram

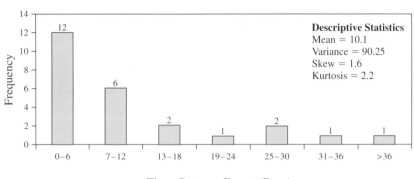

Times Between Events (Days)

Identify the Candidate Distributions Based on the histogram, we can make some preliminary guesses as to the most appropriate distribution. The two most immediate criteria for identifying candidate distributions for a sample are whether the distribution is discrete or continuous, and whether the distribution is bounded, partially bounded, or unbounded.

Discrete versus Continuous Distributions Discrete distributions take a set of discrete values, each of which has a particular probability of occurring. Frequency distributions should be discrete if a relatively small number of events occur per time period. Discrete distributions include binomial, Poisson, and negative binomial. Continuous distributions describe random variables that could take any value within some range. Continuous distributions are appropriate for modeling impacts or the times between events. Continuous distributions such as exponential, normal, log normal, beta, Pareto, and Weibull should only be used for frequencies if a sufficiently large number of events occur per time period.

Bounded versus Unbounded Distributions Unbounded distributions range from minus infinity to plus infinity. Examples include normal, logistic, and extreme value distributions. Bounded distributions include uniform, triangular, beta, and binomial. Partially bounded distributions are bounded at one end; examples include exponential, Poisson, Weibull, and Pareto.

Another useful tool for identifying distributions is the sample's descriptive statistics, such as mean, median, skew, and kurtosis. For Poisson distributions, for instance, the mean of the frequency distribution is approximately equal to the variance. For binomial distributions, the mean is greater than the variance, whereas for negative binomial distributions, the mean is less than the variance. If the failure times come from a symmetric distribution such as a normal or a Weibull with a high shape parameter, then the data will have a mean approximately equal to the median, zero skew, and a kurtosis of around 3. If the mean is much greater than the median and the data is skewed to the right, then the exponential, log normal, or Weibull distributions may provide a better fit to the normal. If the mean is approximately equal to the standard deviation, then an exponential distribution might be most appropriate.

Recall our earlier loss data. For this monthly frequency distribution, the mean is 2.92 and the variance is 10.06, which suggests we use a parametric distribution such as a negative binomial. If, on the other hand, we choose to estimate the weekly frequency distribution, we would have a very different distribution, much more consistent with a Poisson distribution.

FIGURE 7.21 Event Occurrences per Week Frequency Histogram

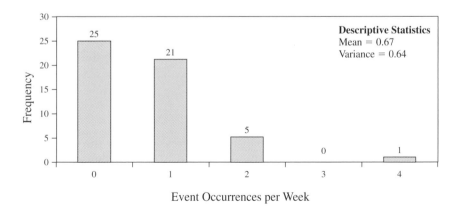

This is typical, since real-world events tend to have more interdependencies over short time periods and much greater variance over longer time periods than predicted by a strict random Poisson process.

In contrast, the time-between-event data is heavily skewed to the right, so an exponential distribution may be appropriate.

TABLE 7.5 Commonly Used Probability Distributions

Frequency	Poisson, beta, binomial, negative binomial
Time between events	Exponential, Weibull, beta
Impact	Uniform, triangular, general, exponential, Weibull, binomial, normal, Pareto, log normal, beta, extreme value

Estimate the Parameters   There are several ways to estimate the parameters of a particular distribution. The simplest approach matches the moments (or percentiles) from the empirical distribution to moments (or percentiles) of the theoretical distribution and then solves for the theoretical distribution's parameters. For example, fitting an exponential distribution to the times between events in our previous example, we have the mean $= 1/\lambda = 10.1$, which leads to a $\lambda = 0.10$ or the standard deviation $= 1/\lambda = 9.5$, which leads to a $\lambda = 0.11$. In either case, the exponential probability density function becomes $0.1\exp(-0.1t)$.

Another way to estimate parameters is by using *probability plots*. This also provides an informal test of the goodness-of-fit between the data and the theoretical distribution. Using rescaled graph paper, we can plot the data against an appropriate transformation of the sample's cumulative probability distribution:

$$F(t) = Pr(T \leq t)$$

A straight line can be fitted using linear regression, with the slope and intercept providing estimates of the parameters of the distribution and the regression's R-squared being a measure of the quality of the fit.

TABLE 7.6 Probability Plots for Various Distributions

Distribution	X axis	Y axis	Parameter
Exponential	t_i	$\log_e (1/(1-F(t_i)))$	Slope of the line equals the failure rate λ
Weibull	$\log_e (t_i)$	$\log_e (\log_e (1/(1-F(t_i))))$	θ parameter estimated by $\exp(-a/\beta)$ where a is the intercept and β is the slope
Normal	t_i	$\Phi^{-1}(F(t_i))$ $\Phi(x)$ is the cumulative normal probability distribution function	σ is estimated by $1/b$ and μ by $-a/b$ where a is the intercept and b is the slope
Log normal	$\log_e (t_i)$	$\Phi^{-1}(F(t_i))$	The shape parameter s is $1/b$ and the median t_{med} is $\exp(-s \times a)$

For instance, using our previous example, we can plot the $\log_e (1/(1-F(t_i)))$ against the times between events. Running a simple least-squares linear regression produces a line with slope 0.12 and an intercept of 0.16. With that, 96 percent of the total variance is explained, indicating a good model fit.

Figure 7.22 Example: Exponential Probability Plot

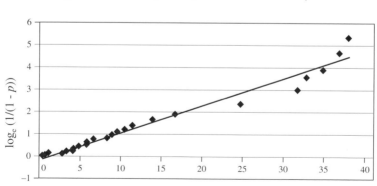

Time Between Events

For more details on probability plotting techniques, see Chapter 6 of Meeker and Escobar (1998).

Finally, we can use *maximum likelihood* estimators to maximize the fit over different parameter settings. For details on how to use maximum likelihood for reliability data, refer to a good text on reliability engineering such as Ebeling (1997). Maximum likelihood methods fit models to data by selecting combinations of models and parameters for which the probability of the data is large. These combinations are more plausible than those combinations with low probability. Likelihood methods, unlike more specific techniques such as linear regression, are more robust and can be applied with a wide variety of distributional and data assumptions. The total likelihood can be written as the joint probability of obtaining the data given the parameters and models. We can then estimate the parameters by maximizing this likelihood over the possible parameter values.

Test the Goodness-of-Fit   Formal goodness-of-fit tests such as the *chi-square* (for general distributions), the *Bartlett test* (for testing exponential distributions), *Mann's test* (Weibull), and *Kolmogorov-Smirnov tests* (normal and log normal) can be used to evaluate the quality of fit between the data and the distribution. The details of these tests are beyond the scope of this text but can be found in a good text on statistics or reliability engineering such as Ebeling (1997).

7.4   ESTIMATING DEPENDENCIES

Subsections 5.3 and 7.1 looked at the identification and estimation of risk factors, primarily in terms of their direct impact on operational targets. In this section, we estimate the indirect impact of events and risk factors by analyzing the dependencies between different events and between risk factors and events.

When Are Dependencies Appropriate?

It is important to maintain discipline over this process of developing dependencies. Adding dependencies to a model significantly increases its complexity and can only be justified when it improves our ability to achieve the objectives of the analysis. For instance, if our objective is efficiency, we should focus on identifying the causal drivers (rather than correlations) of the more frequent events and, in particular, analyzing and predicting those events that cause other downstream events. If our objective is growth, then managing impacts and asking what risk factors drive the high-impact events should be a priority. If the focus is capital management, then identifying the correlations between high-level risk factors is essential if we are to find any natural hedges between risks.

TABLE 7.7 Business Strategy and the Use of Dependency Models

Objective	Type of risk	Useful dependencies	Management focus	Approach
Efficiency	Expected losses	Causation of high-frequency events by controllable factors and events Find common factors and events	Risk prevention	Lower event frequency
Growth	Unexpected losses	Causation of high-impact events General functions affecting impacts	Loss mitigation	Limit impact
Capital management	Catastrophic losses	Correlation of factors with target variables and causation of high-impact events	Risk financing	Finding hedges Capital buffer and offsetting risks

Developing Dependency Models

There are three steps to building dependencies that add value to the operational risk model rather than merely complicating it.

Identify the High-risk Events We Wish to Explain   Analysis can never capture all the potential dependencies. Analysis should not be distracted by extraneous data; the mere existence of data about a possible dependency does not justify including it. Focus on explaining only those high-criticality (high-frequency or high-impact) events that make a difference. Building complex dependency models for low-criticality events is invariably a waste of time.

Identify the Events and Factors That Affect the High-risk Event   Using workshops and structured follow-on interviews, middle and line management can provide detailed information about the events they believe drive loss events. These beliefs can be captured informally through brainstorming and negotiation in consensus group settings (see Subsection 6.6).

Quantify the Relation Between the Independent Events/Risk Factors and Dependent Events Subsection 2.8 discussed the use of statistical and causal models to analyze dependencies. Data from incident reports and direct observation, and follow-up of real-life problem cases can be used to justify statistical dependency models. Using data-mining tools on existing data can identify statistical patterns in historical loss data that may be important. Some of these patterns may be spurious, but at least they force analysts to focus on broader risk factors that are too much part of the scenery to be perceived by busy operational managers. If a reliable relationship is found, better data sources can be developed. Alternatively, causal models can leverage informed judgment about the dependencies. Causal models are particularly useful to operational managers with efficiency and growth objectives because they focus on the causes of problems rather than the symptoms. While statistical models are best used for capturing dependencies between risk factors and event frequencies, impacts, or aggregate losses, causal models are useful to capturing the relations between events. In practice, causal models are used to infer the likelihood of (usually much less frequent) implied events given the likelihood of causally related events.

Box 7.17: The Causes of Computer Downtime and Data Loss

One of the most potentially troublesome operational event is computer downtime and the resultant corruption of the firm's databases. Fortunately, many industry surveys have identified that the most common sources of computer downtime. For instance, based on 5,320 incidents reported in the US from 1982 to 1994, Jackson Higgins (1996) suggests these following causes: power outage (27.7 percent of causes), storm damage (11.7 percent), flood (9.6 percent), hardware error (7.7 percent), bombing (7.2 percent), hurricane (6.3 percent), fire (5.6 percent), software error (5.4 percent), power surge or spike (5.1 percent), earthquake (4.9 percent), network outage (2.1 percent), human error (2.0 percent), heating, ventilation and air-condition (HVAC) failure

(1.4 percent), burst pipes (1.0 percent), employee sabotage (0.8 percent), and other (1.5 percent). Another survey, Sullivan (1993), based on a different sample of 2,428 incidents, concluded the following sources of data loss at computer installations: power failure (35 percent), power surge or spike (10 percent), storm damage (9.4 percent), fire or explosion (8 percent), hardware error (7 percent), flood or water damage (7 percent), earthquake (5 percent), human error (3 percent), and HVAC failure (2 percent).

Causal Modeling

There are several types of causal models, ranging from the simple *Fishbone Analysis* and *Barrier Analysis*, to more the complex *Fault Trees*, *Event Trees*, and *Bayesian Belief Networks*. They all provide different lenses with which to understand how events affect other events.

Box 7.18: Fishbone Analysis

A simple notation commonly used by engineers to identify the events and factors that cause expensive errors is the Fishbone Analysis. Much like a qualitative version of a Fault Tree, it represents each potential problem as an arrow, which leads into another more troublesome problem, also represented as an arrow. The result is a complex fishbone-like structure of the causes of operational problems. For example, the settlements group of a major bank produced a Fishbone diagram of the potential problems affecting the content of a settlement instruction (Figure 7.23).

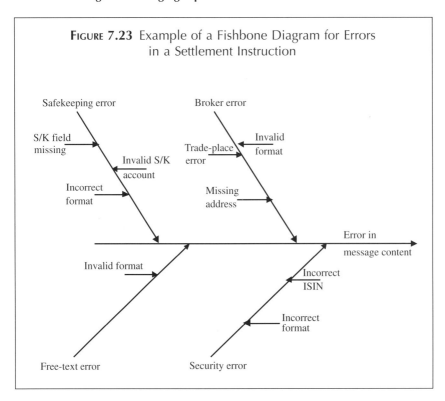

FIGURE 7.23 Example of a Fishbone Diagram for Errors in a Settlement Instruction

All causal techniques involve building a hierarchy of events and factors in which some critical root "top" event is caused (or at least made more likely) by a combination of other simpler events. Classic examples of root-cause analysis are described in Pew (1981), Vaughan (1996), McConnell (1987), and Allison (1971). Wilson (1993) provides an excellent review of techniques for analyzing the root cause of events. Typically, in tools that utilize causal modeling techniques, such as Algorithmics WatchDog™ (see Appendix B), users specify the likelihood of underlying events and use the causal model to infer the likelihood of the top event. In some cases, the process can be reversed, with the likelihood of top events used to infer the likelihood of lower level events.

Box 7.19: Fault Tree Analysis

Fault tree analysis (FTA) focuses on specific (usually catastrophic) events and analyzes possible causes in terms of a top-down causal structure of AND and OR events. Correctly constructed, fault trees help risk managers pinpoint and rank all the different routes through which a particular (root) event could occur. Analysis of historical data, experience, and judgment can all be used to identify fault tree structures. FTA can be qualitative, quantitative, or both depending upon the application. The result of FTA can be a qualitative listing of the possible combination of events that can culminate in the critical system event or the quantitative probability that the critical event will occur in a specified time interval. Typically, the focus of a qualitative FTA is diagnostic and corrective in that we are interested in finding all possible paths that could lead to the critical event occurring. In the context of operational risks, fault trees usually categorize the events leading to the top event failure in terms of general failure areas such as personnel, procedures, or systems.

FIGURE 7.24 Simple Fault Tree Structure

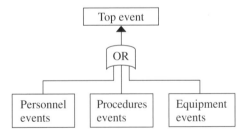

Application

A fault tree analysis is carried out in the following steps:

1. Define the problem and boundary conditions

2. Construct the fault tree

3. Identify the minimal cut-and-path sets

4. Perform qualitative analysis of the fault tree

5. Perform quantitative analysis of the fault tree

Define the problem and the boundary conditions   This step can be crucial if the FTA is not to lose its focus and become bloated. The critical event or the TOP event to be analyzed must be given a clear and unambiguous definition. The definition of the top event should describe the type of event that occurs, where it occurs (which business process or resources is affected, for example, back-office operations), and under what conditions it occurs (for example, during batch runs). To prevent sprawling analyses, the scope should be defined: Which parts of the system are included in the analysis and which are not? What level of external risk factors or stresses should be included in that analysis (should we include sabotage, hacking, virus attack, war, or earthquakes)? Does the quality of the available data justify this level of analysis?

Construct the fault tree   Fault trees should be built in a top-down, recursive fashion. The "daughter" events that cause the root or TOP event must be treated in the same fashion as the TOP event as the analysis moves downward. The daughter events are linked to each other through logic gates like AND and OR. An AND gate signifies that the TOP event occurs if all the daughter events linked by the gate occur at the same time. An OR gate signifies that the TOP event occurs if any one of the events linked by the gate occurs at a given time. It is not necessary to follow all events to the same level of resolution. Some events may remain undeveloped—reflected in a lack of data about or lack of interest in them. Some events may terminate in risk factors as their underlying causes rather than other events, as in Figure 7.25.

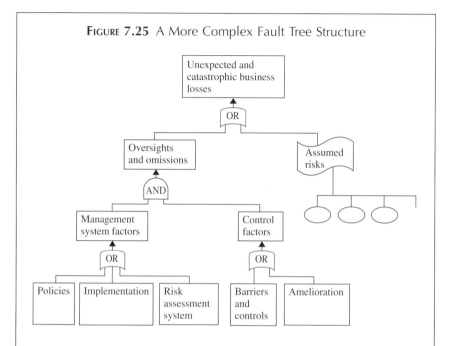

FIGURE 7.25 A More Complex Fault Tree Structure

Identify minimal cut and path set Fault trees provide information about the possible combinations of events that result in the TOP event. A *cut set* is a set of daughter events whose simultaneous occurrence ensures that the TOP event will occur. A cut set is minimal if it cannot be reduced without losing its cut-set status. A path set is an analogue of the cut set that defines a set of basic events whose non-occurrence ensures that the top event will occur. It generally corresponds to failure of embedded control systems. Cut and path sets are computed using logic rules through algorithms like *MOCUS* (Method for Obtaining Cut Sets). Computer programs are available for doing this analysis (see Appendix B).

Perform qualitative analysis of the fault tree Qualitative evaluation of information in fault trees is carried out on the basis of minimal cut sets. The lower the order (number of elements) of the cut set, the more critical is that event for bringing the process down. The risk manager would devote more energy on dealing with low-order cut sets. Equally important, of course, is the type of event in the minimal cut set that gives an indication of the type of action required to control it. For example, a daughter event in the minimal cut set could be due to human error, fraud, or software/hardware error. Each of these requires different strategies to control it.

Perform quantitative analysis of the fault tree   Quantitative analysis of fault trees relies on assigning probability values to the reliability of individual events, resulting in an overall probability of the TOP event occurring during a particular time interval. All (leaf) events are assumed to be independent of each other. The basic approach in fault tree analysis is that events under an OR gate have their probabilities added together, whereas events under an AND event have their probabilities multiplied together. For example, consider the simplest case of two events, A and B, which cause a third event C if both A AND B occur, and a fourth event, D, which occurs if either A OR B occurs.

FIGURE 7.26 Venn Diagram

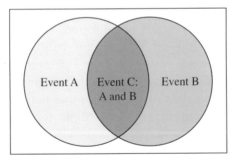

In this case, the probability of C is:

$$P(C) = P(A \text{ AND } B) = P(A) \times P(B)$$

if A and B are independent. The probability of D is:

$$P(D) = P(A \text{ OR } B) = P(A) + P(B) - P(A)P(B)$$

Extrapolating from the fault tree to the dependent event's implied frequency distribution is, in general, quite complex. However, if the events all have the same form of constant failure rate distribution (as is usually the case), then the failure rate (λ_{OR}) of the OR combination is also a constant and is just the sum of the failure rates of the individual events:

$$\lambda_{OR} = \lambda_A + \lambda_B$$

For an AND structure, *all* the events need to occur to cause the top event to occur. Unlike the case with OR systems, constant failure rate components in AND combinations do not produce constant failure rate systems; however, we can approximately write:

$$\frac{1}{\lambda_{AND}} = \frac{1}{\lambda_A} + \frac{1}{\lambda_B} - \frac{1}{\lambda_A + \lambda_B}$$

It is important to bear in mind that analytical approaches such as these are valid only if the different events are independent. If there are changing failure rates or dependencies between components, we must use more powerful techniques such as *Markov Analysis* or *Monte Carlo simulation* to analyze a fault tree. Monte Carlo simulation proceeds by assigning probability distributions to the leaf events and by simulating to estimate the likelihood of the TOP event.

When Are Fault Trees Used?

Fault trees are most appropriate for analyzing the causes of a particular known event involving a critical risk. Fault trees do not depict the passage of time (unlike event trees) and are therefore best suited for events that are essentially random (that is, Poisson frequency distributions) and ongoing. This usually means the events have few human components because of the ability of humans to be reflexive. Fault trees offer an extremely flexible and extensible approach incorporating qualitative, quantitative, or simulation-based solutions. FTA is analytically well-defined, so that given a fault tree, the solution is analytical and repeatable. It can be used both for one-shot analysis or periodic monitoring of operations.

Like all risk measurement techniques, fault trees have their limitations. There are no clear rules about the level of analysis to be performed. Often the data dictates the practicality of analysis. Huge fault trees are frequently the result of analysis that is over the budget and that run out of time. There can be a great deal of disparity between the levels to which different events are developed. Leaf events may *not* be independent (as assumed in quantitative analysis). Simulation may (partially) address the problem by capturing rank correlations between risk factors (see the discussion of Monte Carlo simulation in Subsection 8.2).

In many applications, however, the primary benefit of FTA is not quantitative analysis, but developing a representation of clearly defined events and their interdependencies and then sharing this information organization-wide.

Further resources: For a useful guide to fault tree techniques, see Henley, E. J. and H. Kumamoto (1991), *Probabilistic Risk Assessment—Reliability Engineering Design and Analysis*, New York, IEEE Press.

Box 7.20: Event Trees

Event tree techniques quantify how mismanagement can accentuate an event's direct impacts and cause a host of other unexpected events—how problems can snowball out of control. Event trees are useful for suggesting the precise timing of control interventions that can prevent events from developing into much greater losses. Event tree analysis (ETA) has been used extensively to evaluate the reliability of complex systems used in chemical plants, nuclear power stations, and aircraft. Event trees map a sequence of activities, left to right in a chronological order, showing how one event or activity leads to another in time.

FIGURE 7.27 Generic Event Tree

Time Progression ▶

Event occurence	Event detection	Response identification	Response implementation	Outcome
External event occurs	Staff detects event	Staff correctly diagnoses response	Staff implements appropriate response	Success
			Staff implements inapropriate response	Failure
		Staff misdiagnoses response		Failure
	Staff fails to detect event.			Failure

Just as for fault trees, simple Boolean logic can be used to estimate the probability of compound events given the probability of different intervening responses and events. Figure 7.28 shows an example.

FIGURE 7.28 Probabilities in an Event Tree

Time Progression ▶

A	B	C	D	Probability
P(A)	P(B)	P(C)	P(D)	P(A)P(B)P(C)P(D)
			$1-P(D)$	P(A)P(B)P(C)(1−P(D))
		$1-P(C)$		P(A)P(B)(1−P(C))
	$1-P(B)$			P(A)(1−P(B))
$1-P(A)$				(1−P(A))

When Is ETA Used?

ETA is used when understanding of the progression of the event over time is crucial. It is most helpful when long time-lags prevent events from being quickly discovered or when the event's impact increases with time. Event trees are especially useful for dynamic situations when human actions are dependent on previous actions. ETA is also relevant following major organizational changes such as new systems, new processes, new clients, and new businesses. These changes to the organization introduce new events, the implications of which can ripple downstream to other business areas. ETA helps focus management attention and chart these downstream effects. They are most relevant when we are concerned about the implications of events—often in another part of the organization out of our immediate control—on those processes and resources that *are* under our control and responsibility.

Unlike FTA, the focus of event trees is the *effect* (not the cause) of a particular event. ETA is divergent and inductive rather than convergent and deductive, inferring on the basis of historical experience the implications of some specific event. Event trees, therefore, should be viewed as a complement to, rather than a substitute for, FTA. Some have tried to integrate FTA and ETA into a hybrid called *Cause-Consequence Analysis* (CCA). This is used to identify chains of events that can result in undesirable consequences. With the probabilities of the various events in the CCA diagram, the probabilities of the various consequences can be calculated, thus establishing the risk level of the system.

In practice, one difficulty of using event trees and faults trees is the existence of dependencies between events. For example, if a staff makes a check of a transaction and the *same* person does a follow-on check the said transaction, the probability of error is very different than if a different person performs the follow-on check. Although dependencies can be captured formally by developing contingent probabilities (that is, the probability of a correct check given another check previously performed by the same person), such dependencies are hard to capture and add greatly to the complexity of the model. Another type of dependency that is often not captured in fault and event trees is *common-cause failure*. These are events or factors that would cause a large number of subsystems to fail. Examples include multiple reports that are corrupted by the same database errors or a wide range of operations disrupted by major damage to facilities.

Further resources: See Wilson's (1993) book on root cause analysis and Ebeling's (1997) book on reliability engineering.

Box 7.21: Bayesian Belief Networks

Bayesian Probability Theory allows additional information to inform the probability of events. Bayesian Belief Networks (BBNs) consist of nodes representing variables, and arcs between them representing the conditional probabilities linking these variables. In the context of operational risk applications, the variables are events, and the links are the probabilities that another event occurs given that the first event has occurred. One of the strengths of BBNs is that unlike traditional event trees and fault trees, BBNs can be run in either direction. In other words, many different subsets of all the events can be used to infer the probabilities of the other events in the model. A simple BBN might relate the loss associated with an event (say incomplete transaction) to other factors or events, such as the product, the counterparty, the origin of the counterparty.

FIGURE 7.29 A Simple Bayesian Belief Network

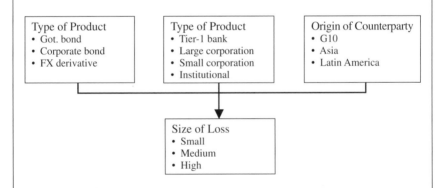

BBNs have been used in tools such as Algorithmics WatchDog™ (see Appendix B) to predict events such as failed transactions before they occur. BBNs also offer an alternative means to simulate events in order to estimate the correlations between events. For further information on BBNs refer to F. V. Jensen, 1996, *An Introduction to Bayesian Networks*.

Statistical Dependencies

There are two forms of statistical dependency.

1. Between risk factors and event frequency, or more precisely, the number of occurrences of an event during the time period versus mean level of risk factor during the same time period. For example, in investment banks, staff turnover is closely related to the level of the end of year bonuses.

2. Between risk factors and event impacts, or more precisely, the mean impact per event during the time period versus mean level of risk factor during the time period and the number of occurrences of the event during the time period. For example, sales staff replacement costs might be related to the sales produced by that individual.

Plot Time Series For both types of dependency, a simple time-series plot of dependent and independent factors and events is usually the first step to building the dependency model, as in this plot of the event frequency against the factors over time Figure 7.30.

FIGURE 7.30 Average Volume and Reworked Transactions Over Time

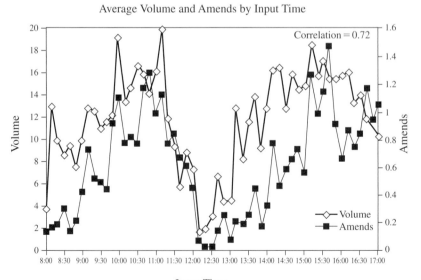

Input Time

Time-series plots show the strength of the relationship, which if worthy of analysis, should be immediately visible from the time series. It also suggests other potentially more important factors that should be analyzed. For instance, in this case, we see that both volumes and amends vary systematically with the time of day. Is time of day a more useful indicator of amends than volumes, *per se*? Alternatively, we may wish to incorporate both dependencies into a single model of amends.

Build a Scatter Diagram   Time-series plots should be followed by a scatter diagram of the number of occurrences or mean impact of a particular event during a particular time period plotted against the mean level of risk factor during the same time period. For example, different clerks vary to the extent to which they have experience performing a particular type of manual-checking. The same clerks also vary to the extent they make errors. In this case, the risk factor is the mean extent of the clerk's experience (months in the job) and the dependent event is the number of errors during that month.

TABLE **7.8** Experience and Error-Rate data

Experience (months)	1	3	3	4	4	5	6	7	7	8	13	14	23	26
Error rate (no.)	11	14	9	8	12	9	8	8	3	5	2	3	1	2

Plotting these in a scatter diagram reveals some important patterns (Figure 7.31).

FIGURE 7.31 Typical Scatter Diagram for Experience and Errors

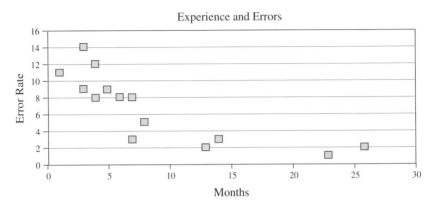

Like most experience curves, error rates start very high but fall off dramatically after a few months. After this, they stabilize at a low level, until eventually they may increase as staff get older or become less motivated. This might be modeled as a negative linear or non-linear relation. Figure 7.32 shows a few of the potential relationships between interdependent variables that can be revealed in scatter diagrams.

Figure 7.32 Simple Patterns Found in Scatter Diagrams

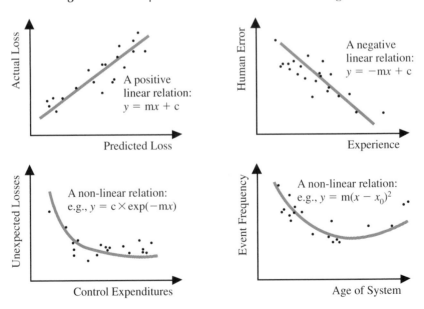

Box 7.22: Statistical Experiments and Descriptive Methods

Statistical experiments can be used to verify and estimate the causality between risk factors and the events they affect indirectly, and the business and process outputs they affect directly. If the risk factors are controllable, designed experiments can also be used to estimate the optimal level of the risk factor (either in terms of the expected or unexpected loss or both). For controllable factors, experiments involve a change in one independent variable (say staff turnover) and then analysts measure the effect of the change on the dependent variable (such as error rates). A variety of potential experimental designs can be used corresponding to selecting *test groups* with different levels of a single independent risk factor, to *factorial designs* involving more than one independent variable. For non-controllable factors, for which researchers cannot manipulate the independent variable, purely *descriptive methods* such as observation and surveys can be used and any correlations between factors and events observed.

For example, managers might wish to test whether losses due to human error was affected by the use of computer support tools. Analysts might perform a statistical experiment that divided the staff into four groups based on their level of experience and the extent of computer support.

TABLE 7.9 Errors Associated With Computer-Supported and Manual Processes

	Low experience	High experience
Computer supported	34	23
Manual	47	21

Analysis of the data begins with *scatter diagrams* to identify possible relationships between risk factors. Any correlations found suggest but do not imply causation. The next stage is comparing the differences between groups in terms of their means and ascertaining whether the difference between means is due to random effects.

Simple statistical techniques such as *Analysis of Variance* (ANOVA) can then be used to detect whether different levels of factors affect the mean level of some particular event frequency. Formally, this requires comparing the variance of each of the subsamples with the total variability in all the samples. Test statistics are essentially the ratio of variances, which should satisfy an F distribution. The details are found in any elementary text on statistics such as Wonnacott and Wonnacott (1977), and Schlaifer (1987).

Other related techniques can be used to integrate and apply statistical experiments and other qualitative approaches. For instance, *meta analysis* techniques can be used to evaluate and integrate loss studies from very different contexts. *Taguchi methods* have also been used to identify the important factors involved in process or product design, and reduce the variation associated with the important factors by tightening tolerances and increasing the slack associated with the other less important factors to reduce cost.

Defining a Dependency Model Although scatter charts may suggest the basic form of a dependency model, the analyst is still faced with choosing from among several ways to implement the model. This usually involves either:

- Rank correlations

- Linear regression and its many extensions

- General mathematical functions to estimate the impacts (usually with a stochastic component)

Rank Correlations: If we have a historical database of the independent risk factor and the dependent frequency, impact, or aggregate loss, we can estimate the Spearman's Rank Correlation. As mentioned in Subsection 2.8, rank correlations are calculated by first replacing the n observed values for the two random variables X and Y by their ranking, with the largest value having rank 1 and the lowest with rank n. Then we calculate the rank correlation as:

$$\rho_{x,y} = 1 - \frac{6\sum_i (x_i - y_i)^2}{n(n^2 - 1)}$$

where x_i and y_i are the ranks of the ith pair of X and Y variables. $\rho_{X,Y}$ lies between -1 and $+1$ with either extreme denoting a negative or positive relation between the variables, respectively. The value of $\rho_{X,Y}$ can be tested for significance using the test statistic:

$$t = \rho\sqrt{\frac{n-2}{1-\rho^2}}$$

which roughly follows a t distribution with $n-2$ degrees of freedom.

Alternatively, rank correlations can be subjectively estimated. Experts might rank the relative importance of the various risk factors for a particular loss event. Starting with the least important factor (say, quality of procedures) and giving it a weighting of 1, experts would then estimate how many times more important the next factor (say, training) is. Assume, for instance, that it is three times more important, and then repeat the exercise for the other factors. The result is seen in Table 7.10.

TABLE 7.10 Subjective Assessment of Rank Correlations

Risk factor	Unadjusted weighting	Importance weighting (sensitivity)
Volume	7	7/16 = 0.4375
Transaction complexity	5	5/16 = 0.3125
Training level	3	3/16 = 0.1875
Quality of procedures	1	1/16 = 0.0625

Rank correlations can then be scaled to reflect this weighting; in the cases when we have more objective correlations, the rank can be rescaled to be consistent with these correlation levels.

The use of rank correlation is appropriate when all of the following conditions hold:

- There is a logical but hard-to-formalize relation between the factor and event frequency/impact.

- There is insufficient data to justify a more-detailed model of the relation between the factor and frequency/impact.

- Correlations make a difference to the analysis. This can be tested by comparing the results of two simulations, one assuming a correlation of 1 and the other assuming a correlation of -1. Is there much difference between the simulations? If not, correlations are not a major issue in the analysis.

Unlike other techniques such as linear regression, rank-order correlation does not assume any particular mathematical relation between the variables nor any distributional assumptions about these variables. This makes it particularly useful for loss modeling when loss distributions are typically non-normal and it is difficult to justify any particular functional relation between the variables. Unlike Pearson-correlated variables, most simulation packages can simulate rank-correlated variables with general distributions using the technique first described by Iman and Conover (1982). Variables with Pearson correlations can only be simulated using *Cholesky decomposition* if they have joint normal probability distributions, which can be very restrictive.

Although estimating the rank-order correlation is a simple way to incorporate dependencies into the losses and is distribution independent, it has some problems. Like all correlation-based dependencies, it is essential to maintain consistency between rank-order correlations. For example, if some human errors are positively correlated with volumes and the same errors are positively correlated with some measure of transaction complexity, then the complexity cannot be negatively correlated with the volume. Mathematically, this means that the correlation matrix must be positive definite, that is, it has no negative eigenvalues. Such inconsistencies become likely as the number of correlated variables increases. Good simulation software should highlight ineligible entries and suggest ways to change the values to be consistent.

For further information on rank correlation methods, see Kendal (1990).

Linear Regression: Multiple linear regression models are commonly used mathematical techniques and can be used to test the relation between sampled risk factors and the number of occurrences of an event or between risk factors and the mean event impact losses. A line of best fit between inputs and outputs is then built by minimizing the sum of the squared deviations between the y variables (losses) and a linear combination of risk factors. The sensitivity of the losses to risk factor changes is then the beta coefficient of the factor. The t score of the parameter can be used to test the significance of the factor. Insignificant factors should, of course, be removed from the model. The extent to which the regression captures the variation in the losses is captured by its R-squared and the significance of the model as a whole can be analyzed using its F statistic. The downside of the ability to perform analytical tests of significance is the need to make several assumptions, including:

- Model form: There is a linear relationship between variables—this can be loosened by transforming the x or y variables. Although the assumption of a linear relation is usually reasonable over short time periods, it can break down as when there is the possibility of structural change or for assets with extensive optionality, for example, fixed-income portfolios with high convexity.

- Error terms are independent and identically normally distributed. This is often a reasonable assumption when analyzing the effect of risk factors on either impacts or aggregate losses. However, frequencies are rarely normally distributed. Frequency regression models can be developed by transforming the frequencies (or alternatively, the times between events) into a new variable, which is normally distributed. For example, in the case of CFR processes, we might regress risk factors against the log of the failure rate. Alternatively, model parameters can be estimated using maximum likelihood techniques.

- Risk factors are measured without any error. This can be a problem for continuous risk factors with time lag, but noisy risk factors are rarely appropriate for inclusion in the model anyway. Less problematic are the many categorical (0,1) risk factors, which are typically much less error prone. Examples of these include the type of transaction or the office, location, or system.

Box 7.23: Logit and Probit Models

Another approach uses *logit* or *probit* transformations of the dependent variable of the linear regression into a continuous probability lying between zero and one. This can then be used to predict the probability of a particular event occurring over a given time period. Bankruptcy and credit models have made extensive use of logit and probit models. Writing in the *Economic Review*

(Federal Reserve Bank of Cleveland, 1987 Q4), Avery and Belton used a logit model to predict bank failure. Based on Bank Call report data from the early 1980s, they developed a logit model with three major risk factors: the percentage ratio of primary capital to total assets, percentage ratio of loans more than 90 days past due to total assets, and the percentage non-accruing loans to total assets. These models appeared to be able to discriminate between high- and low risk banks.

There are many other practical issues involved in developing an effective regression model. The most common problem is that of overfitting the data. The number of data points should be much more than the number of parameters and variables used in the analysis. Overfitting the data can be a major concern; although it may improve the fit of the model to the historical data, it is unlikely to improve prediction of the future losses. Simply choosing the model that best fits the data often leads to overfitting. A better approach is to use a standard model that fits the context being studied and provides an adequate fit rather than necessarily the best fit. Simple models are always preferred to more complex ones when the simpler model provides almost as good an explanation. Another important issue is the importance of data cleaning. Regression models are very sensitive to outliers; just one major outlier can have a major effect on the regression model. For a more detailed analysis of both regression and other econometric estimation techniques, see, for example, Neter et al. (1996) and Pindyck (1991).

Discriminant Analysis: This method can also be used to extract a few quantitative risk measures from many qualitative risk assessments. Similar techniques have been used in bankruptcy analysis, where a small number of key risk indicators is selected from a much larger number of financial ratios. The basic approach develops a factor model of those qualitative factors that drive variance in some well-defined quantitative measure of risk. See Cruz et al. (1998) for more details.

Mathematical Function: More general mathematical functions can be developed for how risk factors affect events. These are usually stochastic, although deterministic models (the so-called *Physics of Failure* approach) can be applied. Stochastic models often use linear regression that can be augmented with path analysis or structured regression techniques. In some cases, we can use the *proportional hazards model,* which has the general time-varying failure rate:

$$\lambda_0(t) \, \exp \, (\beta_1 z_1 - \beta_2 z_2 + \dots \beta_n z_n)$$

General mathematical models such as this quickly become too complex to interpret and explain, and can be difficult to justify given the paucity of operational data.

Box 7.24: Example — Size and Operational Losses

Are big firms more likely to have larger impact loss events than smaller firms? The European Commission recently proposed that capital charges might be based on firm size and business income. A recent study by PricewaterhouseCoopers (*Operational Risk Newsletter,* Jan. 2000) suggests that size accounts for only about 5 percent of the variance in loss severity. It also appears that there is a non-linear positive relationship between the size of operational losses and the size of the firm. The study suggests that revenues drive more of the variance in event impacts than do other scale variables such as assets or manpower. They tested a model of the form:

$$L = R^\alpha F(\theta)$$

where L is the loss impact, R is the revenue of the firm where the event took place, α is a scaling factor, and $F(\theta)$ is a residual risk component. Ordinary Least Squares Regression was used to parameterize the model and test the fit. The results produced a low R-squared, about 5 percent, suggesting that most of the event impact was driven by the residual risk component, and a scaling factor α of about 0.15.

7.5 BUILDING THE OPERATIONAL RISK DATABASE

The end result of risk identification and measurement is a body of accumulated knowledge about loss events and risk factors. This should be stored in an operational risk database for use in subsequent risk analysis and resource allocation. The operational risk management database fulfills several important functions:

- It provides a consistent firmwide basis for estimating existing operational risks in processes and resources in different business areas.

- It supports the development process for new products, new systems, and new businesses by realistically estimating potential risks before development rather than accepting them after the fact. This can suggest improvements in the design of new products and systems, leading to a spiral of ongoing process improvement.

- It allows aggregation of risks to different organizational areas, processes, or resources.

- It provides a central resource to diagnose the causes of failure and determine corrective action.

- It may be used to validate a firm's operational competence to internal and external parties. For example, a complete analysis may provide legal evidence and could confirm compliance.

To perform these tasks, the database needs to be closely coupled with the historical and subjective data used to infer factor and events' frequency, impact distributions, and any causal relations with events.

FIGURE 7.33 The Operational Risk Database

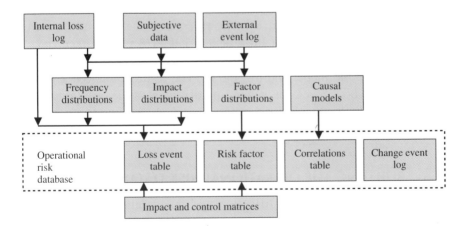

Box 7.25: Failure Modes and Effects Analysis

Many industrial organizations develop risk databases to capture the reliability of their systems and facilitate ongoing improvement in their processes. These are often called Failure Modes and Effects Analysis (FMEA) databases, which generalize from specific individual failures to generic failure modes or risks. FMEA approaches start with the individual elements of the process and investigate the various events that may happen. This contrasts with the top-down approach taken by fault tree analysis. Both are useful. One difference between risk databases and FMEA databases is that in the latter, the unit of analysis is the particular physical component that can fail. In an operational risk database, the unit of analysis is the event itself, which might not be associated with a specific asset or part of the organization. Additional information on FMEA and its related technique, Failure Mode, Effect and Criticality Analysis (FMECA), is described in *Military Standards: Procedures for Performing a Failure Mode, Effects and Criticality Analysis* (1980).

Loss Event Tables

The most important component of the database is the loss event table. Event details, including distributional information about event frequencies and impacts, should be stored in a static loss event table with information about event prevention, mitigation, and financing actions. The loss event table may also contain information about the control and impact structure connecting processes, loss events, and risk factors. A loss event table might contain the following fields:

- Event code—Events should be tagged with a standardized alphanumeric code (described in the event dictionary) to enable easy access to event information.

- Loss description—As precise a description as possible of the loss event.

- Event time line—A generic time line showing the typical occurrence of subelements of the event such as prediction, duration, impact, realization, and mitigation. This would help managers understand the likely evolution of events and where they should focus their efforts for prediction, control, and mitigation. This would include the typical duration, the length of time over which the event occurs, and the typical time lag—how long it may take between the occurrence of the event and the discovery of the event.

- Sources of further information—Include internal experts, managers with experience in dealing with this event, or external experts on the techniques or tools used to manage the event. The latter is particularly important in the case of infrequent events for which it may be crucial to get fast access to firefighters.

- Frequency distribution information (only for loss events, not risk factors).

- Impact distribution information—Impacts should include direct and opportunity costs (approximations). Indirect costs should not be captured if they are included in the direct impacts of impacted events (only for loss events, not risk factors).

- Risk distribution—This combines the frequency and impact fields used by loss events into a factor distribution for the upcoming time period. This field may be updated by external models for predicting market volumes and market levels (risk factors only).

- The higher level processes/resources immediately impacted by this loss event.

- Processes or resources that control the event. This data is obtained from the control matrix (Boxes 5.7 and 5.8). These processes and resources may be external to the firm. Specific individuals may be designated responsible for the event.

- The events immediately caused or made significantly more likely by the occurrence of this loss event. Many events in a loss database may have no impact in themselves but are included because of their effect on other high-impact loss events.

- Event causes. These may be other events or risk factors such as revenues and product complexity. Alternatively, this may be used to capture the causal structure. A separate correlations table may also be used. From the perspective of risk estimation, including both causal structure and correlations is redundant, but event causation does help identify effective management responses. If several events are possible causes, we might also include the approximate extent to which an event causes another event (conditional probabilities).

- Lessons learned from recent occurrences of the event. Ongoing actions that may affect the occurrence or management of the event.

- Generic risk category to which the loss event belongs.

- General actions that may mitigate the loss after the event has occurred. For major events, this might include details of contingency plans and the staff responsible. May also include a description (including estimate of the cost) of the *resources required to repair the damage* after the event has occurred.

- General actions that may mitigate the loss before the event occurs.

- Actions that may prevent the event. May also include a description (including estimate of the cost) of the *resources required to lessen the risk* before the event occurs.

- Other comments.

Part of a typical loss event table is shown in Table 7.11.

Other Components of an Operational Risk Database

If our focus is resource allocation and capital management, it can be useful to produce a *correlations matrix* relating external and internal risk factors and aggregate event losses. This matrix would contain only significant correlations defined at discrete intervals (say −1, −0.7, −0.3, 0, 0.3, 0.7, 1) between risk factors and event impact, frequency, or aggregate losses. Correlations between event impacts, frequencies, and risk factors can be inferred from the dependency structure (say, using Bayesian networks or discriminant analysis) or estimated subjectively.

TABLE 7.11 A Typical Loss Event Table

Event ID	Description of loss event	Event drivers	Prevention resources and actions	Repair resources and actions	Impacted events
10101	Unreconciled confirmations caused by lateness, inaccuracies, or through disagreement	Complex structured transactions, high volumes, manual entry of deals, use of fax	Use of the SWIFT system to provide for automatic matching of confirmations	Face-to-face exchange of outstanding lists with counterparties	Failure in confirmation process
10102	Inadequate external authorization	New and unfamiliar counterparties, complex structured instruments	Written limits describing counterparty staff authorized to trade, by transaction type, amount, P&L	Report exceptions to management immediately	Failure in confirmation process
10103	Inadequate management reporting of confirmation risks	Skills of operator, number of trades	Automated management report generation after five days	Letter sent out within four working days explaining mistake	Failure in confirmation process
10104	Deal entry errors	Incorrect deal entry: incorrect or incomplete terms, missing deals	Dual entry of deals	Correct deals and post deal change report	Failures in risk management process
10105	Model errors	Exotic instruments, end-user model development	Centralized model management, model release process	Utilize standard back-up models	Failures in risk management process
10106	Software errors	End-user model development	Extensive testing program, regression testing	Isolate and remove software bugs	Failures in risk management process
10107	Lack of price and volatility verification	Exotic instruments, illiquid markets, over-reliance on internal models	Develop procedures to cover which volatilities to use in which circumstances	Get quotes from counterparties if available	Failures in risk management process

TABLE 7.12 A Typical Correlation Matrix
(Blank entries assumed to be zero)

	External factors			Internal factors			Loss events' impacts			Loss events' frequencies		
External factors		0.3										
									0.3			
					0.3							
Internal factors							–0.7					
						0.3						
									–0.3			–0.3
Loss events' impacts												
											0.3	
												0.3
Loss events' frequencies												

Other elements of an operational loss database system might include:

- A change log of forthcoming change events that might cause losses in the immediate future
- Model base of acceptable aggregation and risk calculation procedures
- Automatic audit trail to make sure that any changes to static data are transparent to users
- Explanation facilities built on top of the event structure table to enable managers to explain events as they occur
- Report generators to produce management reports
- Internet and intranet read-only access

For operational risk management to be successful, the risk database must be updated in a timely fashion and used before new processes and systems are introduced into the business. Although maintaining the database must be a business-wide effort, the operational risk management group should be responsible for its preparation and management.

7.6   INTEGRATING WITH MARKET AND CREDIT RISKS

One can go beyond partial periodic risk reports to develop aggregate estimates of the total risk for the entire organization. This means integration with existing market and credit risk models for aggregate risk assessment. Given the general framework we have developed for loss events and risk factors, this becomes relatively straightforward. Market risk assessment is really a special case of the above analysis with a financial portfolio as a resource affected by continuous market factors rather than discrete loss events. Simulation of correlated risk factors makes possible the integration of market, credit, and operational risks. Indeed, traditional parametric models of market risks are just a special case of the approach outlined above. For instance, the market VaR is just a multiple of the variance of a portfolio resource calculated as a weighted sum of the variances associated with a number of continuous market factors. This is an important advantage of a correlation-based methodology since it allows firms to extend existing market risk measures to painlessly include non-market risks. Another special case of the above analysis is credit risk measurement, which focuses on the likelihood of default events and the likely impacts of those events (recovery).

FIGURE 7.34 Integrating Operational Risk with Market and Credit Risk databases

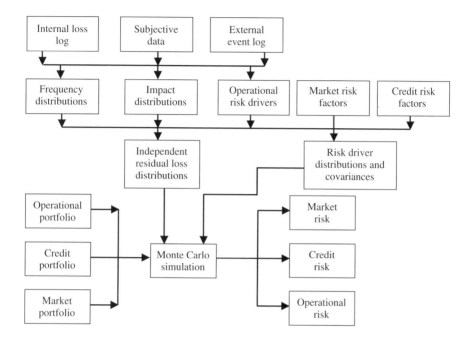

CHAPTER 8

ANALYZING RISKS

So far we have built a profile of the different risks faced by a particular operational unit. Analyzing this profile involves a number of different steps, including:

1. Aggregating the risks
2. Identifying risk management alternatives
3. Analyzing individual loss events
4. Analyzing risky processes and resources
5. Analyzing key risk factors
6. Evaluating the different risk management interventions

These steps are discussed in more detail in the pages that follow.

8.1 AGGREGATING RISKS

To prioritize risks, efficiently allocate resources, and consistently assess performance, managers need to aggregate risks over the different events/ factors that affect different business areas both within a single time period and over different time periods. If the objectives of risk analysis are to minimize the volatility of earnings, income statement protection, and the estimation of EaR, then risk aggregation is an issue only within the current reporting period. If, on the other hand, balance-sheet protection and the estimation of VaR are the focuses of analysis, and operational risks are likely to change over time, then risk aggregation should extend beyond the current reporting period. Consider first the problem of risk estimation within a single time period.

Aggregation Over Events Within a Single Time Period

The aggregate loss in a single time period is the sum of a random number of individual losses from different events:

$$\sum_{\text{event } i} \sum_{j=1}^{\tilde{n}_i} \tilde{I}_{i,j}$$

where n_i is the number of occurrences of event i with impact $I_{i,j}$ in a given time period.

Analytical Approximation When we have a large number of relatively similar loss events, such as those found in a credit or insurance portfolio, we can use analytical techniques (see Klugman et al., 1998, and Rolski et al., 1999) to estimate the aggregate loss. These actuarial approaches generally assume that all the losses have identical or independent loss distributions; while appropriate for large portfolios, they are hardly valid for most operational loss models. For example, if we assume that the impacts are independent and identically distributed random variables with mean μ *and* the number of occurrences of the event is independent of the impacts, then the mean of the total loss L during the time period is just the product of the mean impact I and the mean number of occurrences during the period. Mathematically, this is known as *Wald's equation* and states that if

$$E[I] = \mu \text{ and } \sigma^2[I] = \sigma^2 \text{ (a constant)}$$

and the constant failure rate is λ in a time period t, then:

$$E[L] = \mu \lambda t$$

Wald's equation also implies that the variance of the cumulative impact during the time period is given by:

$$\sigma^2[L] = \lambda(\mu^2 + \sigma^2)t$$

Using Monte Carlo Simulation When an analytical approach is not viable, Monte Carlo simulations are used to estimate the total set of losses for an entire business or operating unit. Subsection 8.2 looks at the use of simulation techniques in more detail. Basically, a simulation requires that two steps be performed for each event:

1. Simulate the number of instances of a particular event (n) that will occur within a particular time period. This is done by sampling from the event's frequency distribution.

2. Sample the event's impact distribution n times. The sum of these impacts is an estimate of the aggregate cash flow during the time interval.

Doing this repeatedly produces a distribution of cash flows within the period from which the expected loss (mean), unexpected loss (standard deviation), and catastrophic loss (extreme percentile) can be estimated.

Aggregation Over Multiple Time Periods

Given estimates of the aggregate cash flows from a loss event in different periods, we need to develop a model of how loss events should be priced.

FIGURE 8.1 Loss Event Cash Flows

Most pricing models are variants of the standard formula for net present value (NPV), discounting (at a rate r) the expected cash flows $E(C_t)$ in each time period (typically a year) up to a time horizon (T). This time horizon would typically be the economic life (in years, for example) of the resource or asset that gives rise to the loss event.

$$\text{NPV} = \frac{1}{(1 + r_1)} E[C_1] + \frac{1}{(1 + r_2)^2} E[C_2] + \frac{1}{(1 + r_3)^3} E[C_3] + \dots$$

$$+ \frac{1}{(1 + r_T)^T} E[C_T]$$

From a simulation perspective, there are three important things to notice about this formula. First, NPV is the discounted sum of *expected* (not simulated) cash flows. Second, it is a *single number* (not a random variable) that describes the economic value and captures all the risk of a series of future cash flows. Third, if the risks and the expected cash flows are constant over time, then the formula simplifies to that for an annuity.

The analytically correct way to estimate NPV simulates cash flows in multiple time periods, takes expectations within each time period, and discounts them at a discount rate that reflects the risk of the cash flows, that is:

$$NPV = \sum_{t}^{T} \frac{E[\tilde{C}_t]}{(1 + r)^t}$$

Unfortunately, the NPV figure on its own tells us nothing about the shape of the distribution or the associated risks. There are ways around this.

Use the Single-Period Model The simplest approach treats the different time periods as a single long period and simulates the in-period cash flows rather than their discounted values.

As explained in the single-period case, doing this repeatedly produces a distribution of cash flows within the period from which the expected, unexpected and catastrophic losses can be estimated. The problem with this is that it fails to capture the time value of money and only captures the risk in the current time period. Given the changing nature of risks and the difficulties of forecasting beyond a single period, this might be all that is required.

Discount Simulated Cash Flows at Risk Adjusted Rate Some simulation models discount every simulated cash flow (rather than the expected cash flows) at a risk adjusted discount rate, and repeat over multiple scenarios to produce a distribution of possible NPV values:

$$N\tilde{P}V = \sum_{t} \frac{\tilde{C}_t}{(1 + r)^t}$$

From this distribution, statistics representing the expected, unexpected, and catastrophic losses can be obtained. The discount rate can be assigned by subjectively comparing the distribution of the cash flows with those of other projects in the organization. The most fundamental problem with this approach is that the NPV is a single number that already captures the risk; therefore, looking at distributions of NPVs to estimate the risks (unexpected and catastrophic losses) is strictly speaking, incorrect because the risks are then double-counted. Another difficulty is that these cash flow distributions may be asymmetric with fat tails and therefore present a challenge to would-be assessors of the risk. A more complex—but theoretically sound—estimate of the risk adjusted discount rate could incorporate the aggregate loss's risk factor loading of priced risk factors (that is, factors that drive the firm's stock returns). Rather than assume all operational risks are diversifiable, this approach argues that non-diversifiable operational risks exist because there are unexpected events that affect the value of most firms.

Discount Simulated Cash Flows at Risk-Free Rate   Alternatively, one can consider multiple time periods and discount individual simulated cash flows back to the present at the risk-free rate r_f rather than the risk adjusted discount rate r:

$$N\tilde{P}V = \sum_t \frac{\tilde{C}_t}{(1 + r_f)^t}$$

Doing this repeatedly also produces a distribution of present values from which the expected, unexpected, and catastrophic losses can be estimated. This avoids the problem of double-counting the risk but it can be difficult for managers to interpret. This approach is adopted in the simulation described in the next section. Discounting at the risk-free rate assumes that the operational risks are all diversifiable. This is a reasonable assumption because the frequency and severity of many purely internal losses are not likely to be correlated across different firms. Hence, these firm-specific risks can be diversified away by shareholders and, therefore, should not affect the firm's cost of capital. This acknowledges that mere variability of the cash flows does not in itself lead to a higher discount factor. What does lead to a higher discount rate is the extent to which investors cannot diversify away the risk by holding a broader portfolio of risky assets.

8.2   MONTE CARLO LOSS SIMULATION IN PRACTICE

The Monte Carlo simulation of potential losses is one of the powerful tools for risk analysis. Useful introductory guides to simulation in risk analysis are provided by Evans and Olson (1998) and Vose (1996).

Advantages of Simulation

The Monte Carlo simulation has a number of important advantages that make it highly effective for risk analysis.

- It is flexible enough to allow a range of very different distributions for event frequencies and impacts.

- Correlations and causal dependencies can be modeled. These allow identification of natural hedges, which can dramatically decrease both net operational exposures and the risk management required.

- Greater levels of accuracy can be obtained by increasing the number of iterations (assuming of course, that the model is sound to begin with).

- Sensitivity analysis is easy to perform.

- Software is available (some commonly used tools are described in Appendix B).

- The simulation allows users to run "what-if" scenario analysis to assess the impact of system or control changes (for example, new hires, new insurance, and hedging policies) on the aggregate risk.

Limitations of Simulation

Simulation is not a panacea; it has a number of limitations.

Model Risk   Loss simulation is only useful to the extent that the assumptions and estimates regarding the loss and frequency distributions are reasonable. It follows that the main limitation of the technique is *model risk*. Model risk for simulations has two important elements—first, our uncertainty regarding the choice of underlying distributions, and second, our uncertainty regarding the parameters of those distributions. Parameter uncertainty in the distribution can be incorporated into the distributional assumptions; both types of uncertainty have the effect of increasing the standard deviation of frequency and impact distributions (that is, increasing unexpected losses).

Derman (1996) discusses a number of guidelines for managing model risk in financial models, many of which are applicable here. The most useful advice for managing model risk is to *keep the model simple.* Nowhere is this more important than in the treatment of dependencies; the complexity of the model increases dramatically with the number of dependencies. Analysts should test the need of a dependency by estimating the effect on the model's results of extreme perfectly negative or positive correlations ($\rho = -1$ or 1) *before* incorporating it into the model. The secondmost important piece of advice for developing simulation models is to perform *systematic sensitivity analysis* of assumptions. Sensitivity analysis tests the effect of different assumptions (different parameters, different distributions, or, perhaps, additional dependencies) on aggregate risk; the larger the effect, the more attention should be directed to gathering further data, soliciting more opinions, and performing additional analysis.

Another issue that has prevented the widespread use of simulation techniques is their heavy use of computing resources. This is becoming less important as massive computing power is more widely available. In addition, techniques such as *Latin hypercube sampling* can be used to dramatically improve the efficiency of the Monte Carlo simulation.

Box 8.1: Estimating the Number of Simulation Runs

Just how many simulations are required to produce an estimate with a given level of accuracy (say, 95 percent within the correct value) can be estimated by invoking the Central Limit Theorem. It argues that the sample estimator will tend to asymptomatically converge to a normal distribution as the sample size n (the number of runs) increases. For example, to have a 95 percent confidence that our estimate $\bar{x}$ lies within 1% of the true mean μ, requires:

$$0.95 = \Pr\left(0.99\mu \leq \bar{x} \leq 1.01\mu\right)$$

If the sample mean is normally distributed with mean μ and standard deviation $\sigma\sqrt{n}$, this produces a sufficiently accurate simulation when:

288 ■ Measuring and Managing Operational Risks in Financial Institutions

$$\frac{0.01\mu}{\sigma/\sqrt{n}} \leq 1.96 \text{ or } n \geq \left(\frac{0.01\mu}{1.96\sigma}\right)^2$$

Not knowing μ or σ, we must estimate them with $\bar{x}$ and the sample standard deviation s. Simplifying, this leads to:

$$n \geq \frac{38,416s^2}{\bar{x}^2}$$

Other percentiles can be estimated similarly. In practice, several thousands of simulation runs will typically be needed for real world simulation models depending on the required level of accuracy. Fortunately, with high-powered server technology, these simulations can be completed quickly, often in less than an hour.

Difficulties Combining Very Different Events Loss simulations (like any other model) are problematic when used to capture very different phenomena. For instance, combining extremely low-frequency events in the same model with much higher frequency events is unlikely to produce good results. This is because the required number of simulation runs must satisfy two conflicting constraints—the granularity of the simulation and its accuracy. The simulation must have sufficient granularity (the time between events) to capture the most frequent events, and yet have the accuracy (which is a function of the number of runs) to estimate the risks of the least frequent events. A wide range of event frequencies in the same model means that a vast number of simulations would be required to produce sufficient accuracy in the low-frequency events. In any case, less frequent operational events (for contingency planning) are usually best analyzed offline from the operational risks that are our focus here. Furthermore, there are few benefits to an all-inclusive simulation model because there are unlikely to be useful dependencies between very infrequent events (such as natural disasters) and more frequent events (such as employee fraud). Hence, simulation is most effective for the more frequent events within a similar, although still relatively broad, range of frequencies.

Simulation Focuses on Variance   Simulations focus on unexpected and catastrophic losses. Simpler analytical techniques can be used for expected losses. Loss simulation adds little to simpler analytical techniques if it focuses only on expected losses. Simulation is most appropriate when there is a great deal of variance (high unexpected losses) in the losses associated with a particular event. This is especially likely if there is a great deal of uncertainty regarding event impacts, as is the case with, for example, data-entry errors.

How Does it Work?

All Monte Carlo simulations for losses involve the following steps:

1. Build a model for cash flows that depends on factor moves, event frequencies, and impact random variables $x_1, x_2, x_3, ..., x_n$ where their distributions and any dependencies between them are defined.

2. Generate pseudo-random values $x_1, x_2, x_3, ..., x_n$ representing event occurences and factor changes, and then generate the cash flows from step 1.

3. Map the cash flows to different business or process areas where they are aggregated. The probability density function of mapped losses is then approximated by the empirical frequency histogram based on the random sample. Sample statistics are used to estimate the expected loss (mean), unexpected loss (standard deviation), and catastrophic loss (some extreme percentile).

The most common challenge with simulation is ensuring that every scenario evaluated in a model is a plausible one. This means that the structure of the simulation must follow as closely as possible the causal structure of how events and factors unfold over time. For instance, the following operational loss model focuses on the unexpected losses associated with business cash flows resulting from loss events and risk factors. Of course, by using a different set of event impacts and risk factor shifts, similar simulations can easily be used to focus on unexpected losses in other target variables such as P&L, return on investment (ROI), or Economic Value Added (EVA™).

The model involves the following sequence of activities. First, for a given time period, we must simulate any risk factors and estimate the number of events that will occur. Then, we must sample the impact distribution that many times to produce an estimate of the aggregate loss during the time interval. Finally, after discounting the cash flows to the present, we need to allocate these present values to any specific risk categories that we have predefined.

FIGURE 8.2 Simulating Loss Events and Risk Factors

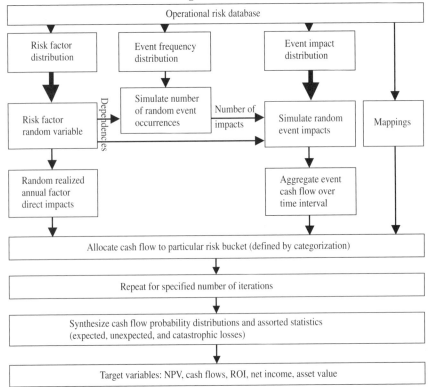

Let's explore this process in more detail.

1. Start with the user's time horizon T (say, 3 years), during which we aim to estimate the risk. Divide this time horizon into $T/\Delta t$, that is, time intervals each of length Δt (say, 1 year). Set $i = 1$ and $t_i = 0$.

2. Iterate the following steps over different time intervals until we reach the time horizon, that is, from $i = 1$ to $T/\Delta t$. Note that this is not necessary if all the events have constant failure rates and there is

no dependencies on non-stationary risk factors, in which case we can take the first time interval as typical and assume similar cash flows in later time intervals.

2.1 For a given time interval $[t_i, t_i + \Delta t]$:

- Randomly sample all the firm's external risk factors from their user-defined distributions over the time interval. For instance, a factor F might be modeled as a discrete stochastic process such as:

$$\Delta F_i = \mu_i F_i \Delta t + \sigma_i F_i \varepsilon_i$$

where $\varepsilon_i \sim N(0, \sqrt{\Delta t})$

Factors should incorporate any correlation-based dependencies, either user-projected or based on historical data (Subsection 7.4).

- Estimate the mean level of the factor over the time interval $[t_i, t_i + \Delta t]$; in this example, this would be:

$$F + \Delta F/2$$

This level of the factor may have direct impact on various business targets or indirect impact through influencing event frequencies or events' aggregate losses over the time interval $[t_i, t_i + \Delta t]$ (Subsection 7.4).

- Estimate any direct impact of these factors (Subsection 7.1).

- For each non-causally implied event k:

  ○ Estimate the event's frequency: Based on the simulated level of the risk factors, and any dependencies between these and the number of event occurrences over the time interval, randomly sample the number of times (n_k) that an event occurs during the time interval $[t_i, t_i + \Delta t]$.

  ○ Estimate the aggregate impact based on the simulated mean level of the risk factors, the frequency of events during the time interval, and any dependencies between these and the aggregate event impact. Take a random sample of size n_k from the impact distribution. The sum of these impacts in the sample:

$$\sum_{p=1}^{\tilde{n}_k} \tilde{I}_p$$

is the loss associated with the event over the time interval.

- For each causally implied event k:

  ○ Estimate the number of times n_k that an implied event occurs in the time interval given the number of non-causally implied events that have occurred (Subsection 7.4).

  ○ Take a random sample of size n_k from the impact distribution. The sum of these impacts in the sample:

$$\sum_{p=1}^{\tilde{n}_k} \tilde{I}_p$$

is the loss associated with the implied event within the time interval.

- Discount event and factor cash flows back to the present. If we have events with non-constant failures rates, and are simulating over multiple time intervals, this is simply the product of aggregate cash flow over the interval and:

$$\frac{1}{(1 + r_f)^{(t_i + \Delta t / 2)}}$$

where $t_i + \Delta t/2$ is the midpoint of the current time interval, and r_f is the real risk-free rate.

- Use the mappings developed in Subsection 5.5 to allocate the loss events and/or factor losses' simulated present values over the time interval to the processes and business areas that control and are impacted by them.

    2.2 Repeat step 2.1 over a large number of different iterations over the same time interval until we reach a desired level of accuracy (see Box 8.1). This usually requires from several hundred to several thousand iterations, depending on the number of events and the degree of accuracy required.

    2.3 Set $t_i = t_i + \Delta t$.

3. Repeat Step 2 for subsequent time intervals $[t_i, t_i + \Delta t]$ until we reach the time horizon. This is only necessary if we are dealing with non-constant failure rate events, in which case different time intervals may have different frequency and impact distributions. An alternative to this approach simulates times to failure rather than changing event frequencies over different time intervals. This requires generating the random times between events' occurrences until their sum exceeds some predefined time horizon.

4. Estimate the statistics of the aggregate NPV distribution associated with an event, process, or business over the time horizon—the mean, standard deviation, and, perhaps, the 95th percentile correspond to the expected losses, unexpected losses, and catastrophic losses. If these risks seem too high, do not assume the estimates are wrong; instead, focus more on the analysis.

5. Develop confidence intervals based on sensitivity analysis by asking the question: What would be the effect on our decision-making if we have made major errors in our distributional and dependency assumptions? This tests the robustness of the analysis by testing alternative assumptions concerning dependencies and distributions. Sensitivity analysis should be performed with any risk estimate.

6. Perform "what-if" scenarios of loss prevention, risk transfer, and loss reduction according to their impact on events' expected, unexpected, and catastrophic losses. What-if scenario models can be used to evaluate the risk reduction effects of a particular organizational process relative to its costs, the impact of a new transaction or service, or the effect of new systems and policies on the organization's risk profile. Simulation models such as this can even be used for analyzing M&As, and divestments to see the effect on the distribution of future P&L (or a similar target variable).

Box 8.2: Modeling Firmwide Risk Related Costs

As discussed in Subsection 2.2, there are additional economic losses associated with having extensive operational risks such as the pressure to decrease debt, bankruptcy costs, tax effects, and expensive visits to the capital markets. If high-level capital management and corporate financing is the objective of the risk analysis, then these can be usefully modeled on a firmwide basis given the aggregate level of unexpected losses. For instance, one of these effects—the tax effect of the debt load—is discussed below.

Operational losses can affect the risk of the firm, which in turn affects the debt utilization. Debt financing is usually cheaper than equity-based financing because interest expenses on debt, unlike stocks' dividends, are tax deductible. Carrying additional risky operational assets increases the likelihood of bankruptcy and requires a decrease in the debt level that is required to support that risk if firms wish to maintain a given credit rating. These tax effects can be stated as an adjustment to the value of the firm's operations as a whole. This adjustment would be:

$$\frac{(1 + r)^T - 1}{(1 + r)^T r} C(\Delta D)(1 - T_c)$$

where C is the coupon rate, T is the time horizon, and T_c is the marginal tax rate. ΔD, the marginal debt foregone as a result of carrying the additional operational risk, is the extent to which the level of loss associated with the probability of default (associated with the current credit rating) decreases because of the increased operational risk. This can be calculated, as shown in Subsection 16.2.

8.3 IDENTIFYING RISK MANAGEMENT ALTERNATIVES

After analyzing the risks of and processes responsible for different events, risk managers working with line operations must identify the possible ways of managing these risks. Disciplined and centralized risk analysis comes into its own here because it forces a structured approach to alternative identification, analysis, and decision-making.

A Portfolio View

Management actions seek to change the risk profile of individual events and, therefore, the risks of resources and processes. However, operational managers should not be concerned solely about specific events; rather they should focus on entire *portfolios* of risky processes and how to best manage them. It is dangerous to give in to the temptation to treat each loss event separately. Individually managing the risks of loss events, may succeed in solving the problem of each loss event, but often results in needless complexity and other unintended consequences. Remedial actions for one event may exacerbate the losses associated with another event. For instance, outsourcing may swap operational loss events for legal and credit losses, or overly restrictive control systems may demotivate line staff. One of the most important benefits of a whole systems approach to operational risks, is the ability to avoid the silo mentality that is the cause of many of the risks in the first place. There may also be some natural hedges between exposures and synergies across many organizational risk and control practices. Fortunately, by knowing the major risk factors and loss events that drive the aggregate losses, we can predict many of these portfolio effects.

Avoid Functional Thinking

Premature identification of management approaches to handle local exposures can be a major problem. For instance, risk managers trained in insurance tend to see the world as an insurable portfolio; financial risk managers see it as a hedging problem; and planners are interested in developing strategic resources and outsourcing support areas. Section III can help risk analysts and managers break free of functional constraints in their thinking. It provides an impartial view of the relative advantages and disadvantages of various risk prevention, mitigation, and control activities that constitute the broadly defined practice of risk management.

Level of Risk Management Solution

Furthermore, analysts should start with the obvious solutions, which usually address specific events, and try to branch the various solutions to consider more alternatives, thus making these solutions address more general problems. Usually, it is less costly to manage risk exposures at higher levels of the organization than at lower levels. This is because many exposures net out, are uncorrelated, or have offsetting revenues or cash flow. Much of financial risk management assumes centralized aggregation of exposures for precisely this reason. Unfortunately, generalized approaches can also be the least effective way to address particular risks because they are so far removed from the exposure. This is especially important for some idiosyncratic operational risks, which may require operational solutions delivered by those close to the underlying exposure. While we ultimately only care about the aggregate exposures facing the firm as a whole, focusing immediately on net effects also gives premature attention to risk transfer approaches before considering possible operational solutions to operational risk exposures.

This trade-off between producing risk management solutions tailored for specific low-level exposures and the more cost-effective, firmwide solutions means that both bottom-up and top-down approaches should be used to identify promising methods for managing particular risks.

FIGURE 8.3 Levels of Risk Management

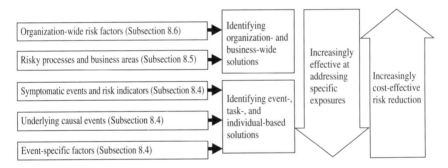

8.4   ANALYZING LOSS EVENTS

While every risk analysis is unique, there some general steps that every systematic analysis should follow.

1.   Analyze the event's risk profile

2.   Understand the chronology of the event

3.   Identify any time trends

4.   Determine any causal events

5. Identify common risk factors

6. How controllable is the event?

Let us consider each in more detail.

Analyze the Event's Risk Profile

Based on the data and models developed earlier, risk analysts can begin to prioritize and suggest appropriate mechanisms to deal with the risks. The most useful analytical tool is a breakdown of the events according to their approximate likelihood and impact, but the loss distribution too suggests risk prevention, control, mitigation, and financing alternatives.

Likelihood and Impact The risks of individual loss events are easiest understood in terms of their likelihood and impacts. The most worrying events, of course, are those with high impacts and a high likelihood of occurrence. Knowing where the loss lies on the likelihood/impact continuum gives us an immediate focus for our actions. Throughout the book, we have emphasized that remedial efforts for high-frequency, low-impact events should aim to decrease the event's likelihood by managing risk factors and loss prevention. Similarly, once-in-a-lifetime events should be dealt with by reducing impact through loss control, loss reduction, and contingency planning. Loss prediction and factor management techniques can be used to affect either impact or likelihood.

FIGURE **8.4** Likelihood and Impact Revisited

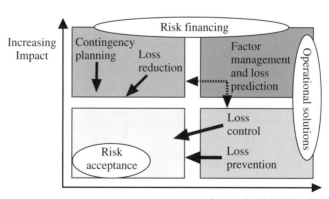

Loss Distributions Focusing on just the event likelihood and impact is a useful guide to the expected losses associated with events, but it tends to downplay the unexpected losses. For this reason, it is also helpful to analyze the event's contributions to expected, unexpected, and catastrophic losses. Furthermore, loss distributions can be used for risk aggregation and subsequent capital allocation.

Expected Losses: The various expected losses controllable by a business area should be compared quantitatively or rank-ordered using a *Pareto chart*. This shows us the relative importance of the exposure and suggests, all else being equal, where the risk reduction activities should focus. High expected losses that are largely controllable suggest the need for major structural changes through operational techniques such as *process reengineering, automation, enterprise resource planning,* or sometimes better *training* (see Chapter 11). If the loss is largely uncontrollable, then expected losses can also be compared with any existing loss provisions (see Subsection 16.1). A discrepancy between loss provision and expected loss may suggest a need to increase the loss provision. This should not be done without checking the precise scope of the loss provision to see if it coincides with that of the loss event definition. Provisions often reflect accounting conventions rather than economic reality. They also tend to be more often used for frequent, low-impact losses for which it is relatively easy to justify the accounting treatment.

FIGURE **8.5** Provisioning for Expected Losses

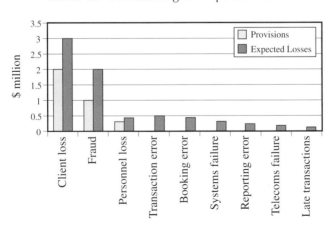

Unexpected Losses: Often, just because an event has low expected losses does not necessarily imply it will have low unexpected losses, particularly if the event has a wide range of potentially high impacts. This can be seen more clearly if we plot expected versus unexpected losses for a particular set of loss events.

FIGURE 8.6 Expected and Unexpected Losses

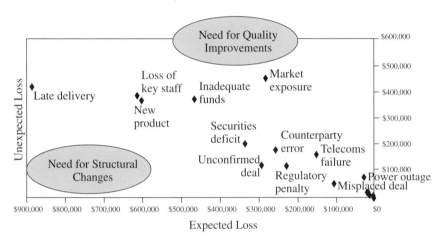

Events with low expected losses but high unexpected losses typically result from poor implementation of a basically sound operational structure and suggest a need for improving the quality of inputs or the resources used to process them. For this reason, decreasing unexpected losses often involves managing the factors that cause the risk by using techniques such as *quality assurance, personnel selection,* or *human factors* engineering techniques as ergonomics, improving motivation, and better working conditions (see Chapter 9). Major structural changes usually are not appropriate unless high unexpected losses are also accompanied by high expected losses. Other techniques used to reduce controllable unexpected losses target loss prevention and loss control activities such as *standardization, buffering, redundant design, flexible work systems,* and *work and job restructuring* (see Chapters 11 and 12). If the losses are largely uncontrollable, the result of external variability, then risk financing techniques (see Chapter 14) are more appropriate.

Catastrophic Loss: Subject to the many limitations imposed by data, we can also use loss simulations to evaluate catastrophic risks. When looking at catastrophic risks across different events, a pattern tends to emerge. Most events, being relatively low level, have low catastrophic losses. A handful have huge catastrophic losses.

FIGURE 8.7 Catastrophic Losses

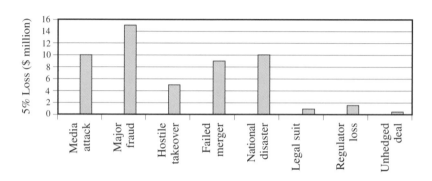

Catastrophic losses that are at least partially controllable are usually best managed through the impact (usually the indirect impacts) rather than through their likelihood. All catastrophic losses have reputational effects that can be mitigated by responsive management. This implies that loss reduction and contingency management techniques (see Chapter 13) such as *facilities management, contingency planning, crisis management,* and *public relations* should be used to limit the damage. In general, these approaches are only partial and take some time to put into effect; meanwhile, the firm is exposed. Often this residual exposure is best managed using risk transfer of the uncontrollable aspects through hedging, insurance (for example, fidelity, D&O), and other forms of contractual risk outsourcing while a more operational solution (if available) is developed for the longer term.

To summarize, managers should adapt their risk management responses to suit the nature of the risk as shown in Table 8.1.

TABLE **8.1** Risk Management Measures for Expected, Unexpected, and Catastrophic Losses

	Expected losses	Unexpected losses	Catastrophic losses
Controllable	Loss-prevention measures (Chapter 11). e.g., Process redesign	Factor management (Chapter 9), e.g., quality management	Loss control and reduction (Chapter 13), e.g., contingency planning, reputation management
Uncontrollable	Risk financing (Chapter 14) and especially loss provisions (Subsection 16.1)	Risk financing (Chapter 14) and the use of risk capital (Subsection 16.2)	Risk financing (Chapter 14) e.g., insurance, contractual outsourcing, hedging

Understand the Chronology of the Event

Events go through a number of stages, each of which can be the focus of risk management prevention, control, and mitigation strategies. Particularly for contingency planners and crisis managers dealing with more complex events—usually infrequent events with many indirect impacts—understanding the event's chronology can help direct scarce risk management resources to the most crucial stage. Consider the typical time line of a complex event (Figure 8.8).

FIGURE **8.8** Analysis of Loss Event Structure

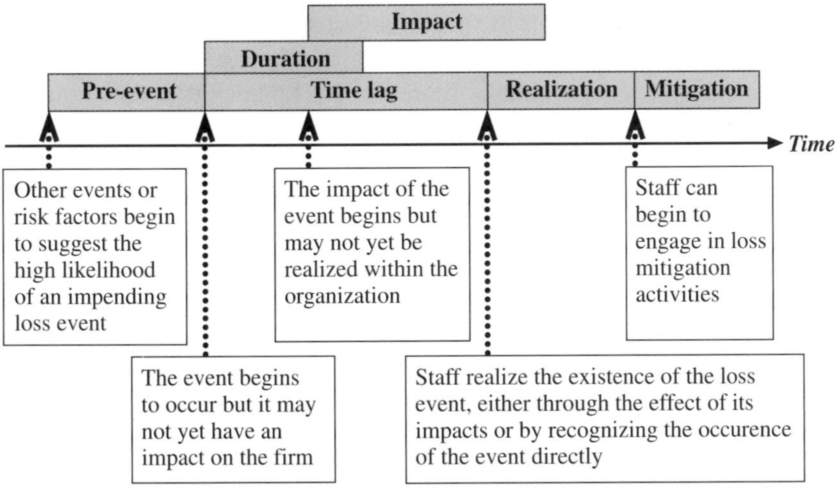

Pre-event   Events may be preceded by events or risk factors that, without causing a loss in themselves, are suggestive that a loss event is imminent. For these events, *loss prediction* techniques such as *Regression, Discriminant Analysis* or *Bayesian Belief Networks* can be used (see Subsection 7.4). For example, in the case of employee fraud, most cases are perpetrated by repeat offenders, indicating the need to screen employees extremely carefully before placing them in positions of trust. Political instability in a region might suggest retrenchment or reduced work loads in a particular office. High trader volumes with a particular counterparty in a particular country might make failed transactions much more likely.

Duration and Impact   Prediction is followed by the actual occurrence of the event itself, which may or may not be contemporaneous with the event's impact. For some events, the length of time during which the event has an impact is important. For example, the impact of power-related failures, blackouts, and brownouts is dependent on the length and intensity of the event's duration. A telephone system may be able to handle an outage of two seconds with no ill effects, whereas digital data transmission may be corrupted after only 20 microseconds. For such events, there should be an absolute minimum of time-consuming human intervention; instead, automated rapid response cut-ins should be used to detect the event and intervene.

Time Lag   The realization that the event has occurred may itself be delayed for some time after the beginning of the event's duration and the commencement of its impact. Time lag can be an important factor, because many events' impacts increase the longer the event remains undetected. A long time lag is often the result of obtaining resources and other assets, the quality of which is unclear to the owner at the event onset and is only revealed over a long time. For instance, poorly designed software can have errors that take time to discover. Many cases of management fraud have had long incubation times characterized by a number of predictive events that were ignored (see the later discussion on fraud prevention). Events with long time lags also tend to have a wider range of possible impacts. Management may be lulled into a false sense of security by the likely impacts of long time lag events, which are often quite low. However, the occurrence of even these near-miss events is a good predictor of potentially much more devastating events down the line. Sometimes, latent failures (usually with low impact) that remain ignored may become part of the scenery and, therefore, hard for internal management to detect. Events with high impact and a long time lag require more time spent up front in *monitoring, prediction, sampling, quality assurance, personnel selection,* and *relationship management.*

Realization   The time taken to realize the significance of the event can be the major bottleneck. This is especially so for historically successful management because complacency, poor communications, faulty organizational norms, and long incubation times can impair the process of disaster response and recovery. "It cannot be happening here," goes the refrain, thus leading to a critical delay. Decreasing this delay requires two components: good control systems and a risk aware culture with an openness to acknowledge problems and act quickly. Various forms of *audit procedures, diagnostic control systems, limits,* and *alarms* can be used to detect a problem and accelerate a management response. Unfortunately, there is always the tendency to shoot the messenger who brings bad news. In an effort to prevent this, some firms have adopted so-called whistleblower charters to bring problems into the open without fear of retribution. Failing to manage organizational denial leads to executives trying to hide information rather than solve the problem. Invariably, external stakeholders will see through this and will penalize the business still further in the form of decreased lines of credit, falling stock prices, and lost customers.

Mitigation   Sometimes the mitigation of the event occurs immediately after the control staff realize the event has occurred. More often, mitigation activities themselves require freeing up additional resources, which in turn delays the completion of the mitigation process. Critical staff and other resources may be off-site. Facilities may take time to be brought online. *Contingency planning,* rather than *crisis management,* can make sure that time is not wasted identifying and analyzing the crisis rather than resolving it.

To summarize, managers need to capture the key stages in the progression of a high impact event, and identify which stages offer the most opportunity for risk management intervention.

TABLE **8.2** Risk Management Measures For Different Event Stages

Stage of event	Pre-event	Duration and impact	Time lag	Realization	Mitigation
Management focus	Prediction of underlying risk factors and causal events	Rapid response through early warning systems and automation	Loss control systems, quality management	Loss control systems, clear organizational structures, risk aware culture and incentives, strong audit	Contingency planning, crisis management, public relations

Identify Any Time Trends

Most subjective measures of risk are best thought of as relative measures, so it matters less *where* a company starts in the risk coordinate system than *how its risk changes* within it in time. Any trends will take time to reveal themselves and so are only relevant for more frequent events and volatile risk factors. Managers should be extremely wary of reading too much into limited time samples of events. Managers should ask whether a trend is the result of some identifiable change in an internal or external risk factor (rather than just wishful thinking) and whether that change is likely to be permanent. If the number of events occurring per unit time is decreasing, additional remedies are probably unnecessary and may even be counterproductive, unless, of course, more trouble is being stored up for some massive loss event in the future (particularly for events with a long time lag). If the time trend is negative, simple extrapolation should suggest the urgency of the problem and the need to allocate further resources. Formal statistical trend analysis techniques (such as time-series analysis and control/probability charts) can be used to test the validity of loss trends. Simulation models can incorporate these trends by modeling any factor dependencies or using non-constant failure rate distributions (see Subsection 7.3). In some cases, fundamental models can be developed, as with learning-curve or diffusion-curve models.

Determine Any Causal Events

Event analysis should be directed toward event causes rather than their symptoms. Causes can be other events or risk factors. Addressing the ultimate source of the loss is usually much more cost-effective than dealing with the symptoms of the loss or the structural path by which one loss leads to another. Attacking the underlying source of the risks by redesigning the process or system to "design out" the risk can be done using loss prevention techniques such as *process reengineering, redesign,* better *training,* and *TQM* (see Chapter 11). For example, losing a client might result from specific events and factors such as late and inaccurate transactions, high charges, or unresponsive help-desk facilities. High charges may reflect underlying interest rates and be uncontrollable, but redesigning the process of producing and validating transactions could limit the frequency of late or inaccurate transactions and thereby decrease client loss. Unfortunately, designing out the risk may be too expensive or may mean designing out the functionality. In this case, the next best approach is to provide a risk control on the causal "path" that links the ultimate (or most significant) cause and impacting event. Pareto charts can be used to direct attention to more common causes of particular events. Causal techniques (Subsection 7.4) such as *Fishbone analysis, fault trees* and *barrier analysis* can identify how events cause one another and what can be done to limit the spread of events. For example, many major loss events result from a combination of transactional process failure and a failure of control or monitoring. Fault trees would model this as an AND event. Other than changing the risk of the component events, AND events can be made less likely by adding redundancy (Subsection 12.2), perhaps by additional controls to prevent faults rising up the fault tree. Barrier analysis, as the name suggests, views events as threats to some critical internal asset and builds various barriers to prevent events from progressing further. This is the perspective to risks adopted by security professionals, for example, network firewalls, access cards, and master keys (Subsections 12.6 and 12.7).

Identify Common Risk Factors That Drive the Event

What do most occurrences of this particular loss event have in common? It may be that they result from similar market conditions, the same type of system, the same office, or even the same individual. For more controllable risk factors, techniques such as *ANOVA* and *statistical experiments* can be used to evaluate whether a particular source of risk is different from the other sources of risks. If it is, remedial actions that reflect the type of variation can be put in place. The analyst should drill down until the highest common risk factor in all the problem cases is discovered and focus management activities on that. For example, if a particular office differs from all other offices, it may be a problem of internal control, morale, or systems within that office. If transactions entered using a particular system tend to show higher error rates, then there may be a problem in the system, the training, or the staff using it.

The most important risk factors that drive specific event losses are price and volume effects. Aggregate losses that increase with the volumes or prices of transactions are particularly important because they have a much higher marginal effect on the total costs and, therefore, the overall level of processing. Within a normal operating range, increasing volumes make errors proportionately more likely per unit time and therefore lead to increased aggregate losses over the time period. However, for firms with flexible operational workflows, it is the changes in the (usually externally determined) transaction prices that are most critical during this normal operating range. Outside this range, many human and computing-related errors become important. For example, beyond the normal operating range, even a small increase in volume can produce a major increase in error events. This may be because of increased stress levels or system constraints that cause even more errors to occur. In some circumstances, too little volume can also be problematic, since sagging motivation causes performance to suffer.

FIGURE 8.9 Volume Effects

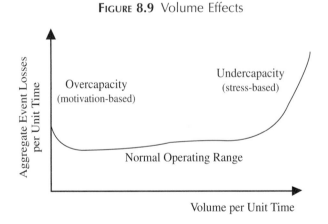

Operating flexibility should reflect the variation in volumes and tasks should be redesigned to keep operational resources working within their normal operating range for as much of the time as possible (see Chapters 11 and 12 on loss prevention and control, in particular, the discussions on Work and Job Restructuring, and Inventory Management).

How Controllable Is the Event?

Related to the issue of causation is the degree to which we can control the event. Just how easy is it to change frequencies and impacts? The range of feasible risk management actions varies depending on whether the loss is controllable (generally those within the company's scope of operations), influenceable (those involving other entities, such as customers and competitors), or uncontrollable (those that are outside the company's control entirely, such as foreign exchange and interest rate fluctuations). For example, the more controllable the event, the less appropriate is risk financing, which is only possible for the firm's residual diversifiable risks. Another issue is the degree of control relative to competitors. The more controllable the event relative to other firms (particularly if it is a priced risk factor), the greater the possibility that this may provide a competitive advantage for the firm, making risk transfer less appropriate.

TABLE 8.3 Event Controllability and Risk Management Responses

	Prevent the loss	Decrease the impact
Controllable loss events	Loss prevention (e.g., process reengineering, ERP, work and job restructuring, automation, compliance)	Loss control (e.g., buffering, diagnostic control systems, audit, boundary systems)
Influenceable loss events	Factor management (e.g., TQM, personnel selection, relationship management)	Loss reduction (e.g., corporate diversification, legal asset protection, contingency planning) Risk financing (e.g., project financing, insurance, securitization)
Uncontrollable loss events	Loss prediction (e.g., business planning, market intelligence, project risk management) Reduced risky activity (e.g., business exit)	Crisis management, risk transfer, reduced risky activity

8.5   ANALYZING RISKY PROCESSES AND RESOURCES

In practice, analyzing risk management alternatives cannot be done only at the event level. While event analysis can suggest specific approaches for dealing with exposures, the aggregate effect of events on particular processes and business areas must be considered if controls are not to be piecemeal or ineffective. Maps of process risks can produce a systemic perspective on the entire organization and emphasize organization-wide optimization rather than suboptimization at the level of individual business unit.

Performing an analysis of the risks associated with different processes and resources is not unlike the previous analysis of loss events, but there are some additional guidelines that can help.

1.   Prioritize and begin by spotlighting the most risky processes and resources. Within these processes, focus on preventing or mitigating the major loss events.

2.   Compare process risk and the value added by different processes. Is the process risk commensurate with the value added by the process? Should we even be doing this process? Can we contract the process or resource to external vendors?

3.   Analyze risk allocation within the organization. Are risks controlled by one business area and impacting other business areas without any compensating resource flows?

4.   Intervene. Develop process-wide interventions to design out or mitigate the risk. Assess any potential organizational barriers to implementation.

Prioritize by Spotlighting High-Risk Processes and Resources

Where are risks found within the organization? Using the models developed earlier, we can build Pareto charts of the level of (un)expected losses resulting from different business processes. Alternatively, color-coded process maps of the risks can be developed directly from the estimates of the aggregate risks (expected/unexpected/catastrophic) associated with different resources and processes. A traffic-light scheme is often effective (red, amber, green) and can be used as part of a broader balanced scorecard.

FIGURE **8.10** Color-Coded Process Risk Map

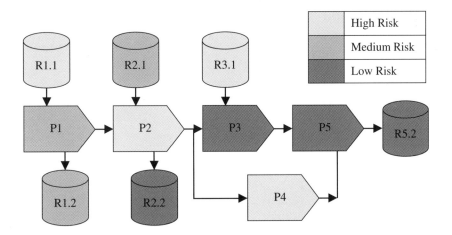

Bear in mind that the impact of different events and risk factors also includes the indirect impacts on business continuity, specifically the effect of any resultant downtime on P&L. (For more critical processes, much of an event's catastrophic impact is likely to be its effects on business continuity.)

For each element of the process risk, we can estimate which loss events and risk factors make the largest single contribution and make these the focus of event loss analysis described in the previous section.

Compare Process Risk and Process Value Added

Value added is the wealth that the process or business unit is able to create from its own efforts. Each subprocess of a firm's value chain adds value, that is, increases the value of its outputs relative to its inputs. The sum of these in-process "value-added" components (both tangible and intangible products and services) is essentially the firm's net income. Value added can be understood in terms of the expected income associated with the business unit, or it can include risk capital costs as in Economic Value Added (EVA™) calculations (see Subsection 16.2). Without a ready market for these in-process goods and services, valuation can be difficult. So, as an alternative, the firm's net income can be allocated back to the various organizational units responsible for producing it. This can be done simply (although only approximately) in terms of some common basis such as headcount or net expenses. Any expected losses associated with the process should also be incorporated into the value added. The approximate value added can then be compared with the (un)expected losses associated with that business area or subprocess, as in Figure 8.11.

FIGURE **8.11** Process Value Added versus Unexpected Losses

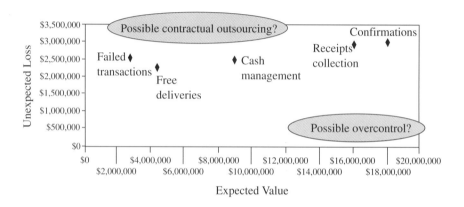

Assuming that any high risk events within these processes have already been dealt with, a very high level of unexpected losses relative to expected value suggests that the business area or process might be a good candidate for *contractual risk transfer* techniques (see Subsection 14.7). For example, in the above example, the internal processes for cash management and handling failed transactions might be appropriate for contractual outsourcing. Conversely, processes that add a great deal of value without significant levels of unexpected losses may be overcontrolled and ripe for a reallocation of scarce control resources.

Analyze Risk Allocation Within the Organization

It is important to distinguish between the locus of event impacts and the locus of control of those events (see Subsection 2.7). As realized losses in one process are mapped to the business areas that can control them, a true economic picture of the risk sources and sinks becomes apparent. Major discrepancies between realized losses and controlled losses demand, at minimum, more cross-process cooperation and coordination, and even suggest the need for transfer pricing to account for any discrepancy. One typical example of this is found in the downstream subprocesses of a broader value chain. In their eagerness to cut costs, upstream process areas may be tempted to produce poorer quality outputs that then become inputs to the downstream subprocess. The downstream process thus takes on a risk that can only be controlled upstream.

Within interdependent processes, operational risk mitigation is often organizationally difficult because the different parties may be unwilling to take ownership of the risk. In general, the responsibility for the risk should lie with the agency that initiates or controls it rather than where the impact of the risk is realized for fear of moral hazard. Alternatively, moral hazard can be alleviated by transfer pricing based on the discrepancy between risk control and realization. The challenge with such transfer pricing schemes (particularly if based on quantitative risk assessment) is maintaining transparency to all parties within the organization. For this reason, any risk transfer initiative should build on existing internal (and presumably accepted) efforts to improve cost allocation, such as activity-based costing.

Intervene

First, managers should develop process-wide interventions to design out or mitigate the risk. If most process losses result from the causal interactions between different events, or if no small group of events seems to contribute to most of the loss, process-wide solutions will be more appropriate than managing the risks of individual events. If there is patience for a longer term solution, management of organizational factors (for example, through better training, personnel selection—see Chapter 9) and loss prevention approaches (such as reengineering or ERP—see Chapter 11) can make a massive difference, particularly to expected losses and, to a lesser extent, unexpected and catastrophic process losses. In some cases, the complexity of the system as a whole causes the catastrophe, in which case massive reengineering of operations may offer the only means to dramatically limit the risk (Subsection 11.1). Lacking patience for such a solution, loss control (Chapter 12) and reduction (Chapter 13) practices can be put in place across the board to limit the risk. The easiest of these control measures for process losses is to build in extensive redundancy (Subsection 12.2), for example, through back-up processes, reciprocal agreements with other firms, cross-training, double-checking, and separation of duties.

In the case of catastrophic process losses, managers are faced with several choices: reduce the indirect impacts of the disaster (the most important of which are business and process continuity and their effects on the firm's reputation), accept the risk and allocate more capital, or leave the business altogether. Loss reduction through contingency planning and effective crisis management can dramatically limit catastrophic losses. Risk transfer and financing techniques (Chapter 14) such as hedging, insurance (internal and external), internal capital, and lines of credit offer ways to alleviate impact of major losses by passing risks to external parties better able to handle the risks. Of course, there are limits to what loss reduction and risk financing can do. While loss reduction may reduce risks in autonomous subsystems, they sometimes have little impact (or even increase risks if there is morale hazard) on the complete system. Risk financing is also limited in its effects; for instance, insurance companies have a vested interest in delaying and avoiding payments, moral hazard and adverse selection cause them to increase their premiums, and hedging programs assume limited-basis risks. Some processes involve such potentially catastrophic reputational losses that management might be advised to abandon the process altogether. This is particularly true if the process is only tangential to the firm's core competence.

8.6 ANALYZING RISK FACTORS

Firmwide risk factors (for example, level of the stock market) directly affect the volumes demanded or the prices charged for services and, therefore, the firm's revenues. Risk factors may also directly affect the prices of various inputs and thus the costs of resources used to generate these revenues. Most direct risk factors are outside the firm's control and if they are priced in some external market, we can look to insurance providers and financial markets to cover the risk. Of course, just because a risk can be transferred externally does not imply that management should do so. If the external risk factor is priced into the firm's stock returns, then we may wish to keep the exposure (it is presumably a risk to which investors wish to be exposed).

Risk factors may have indirect effects by making loss events more likely (increasing frequency) or more severe (increasing impact). For instance, when loss events are caused by human error, we might investigate the factors that drive errors. There might be a lack of experience or training, or perhaps there are environmental factors that play a role. Statistical experiments, regression, factor analysis, and ANOVA can be used to further evaluate these factors. A relatively small number of business-wide risk factors can affect many different events. Organizational policies, capacity, staffing, location, process structure, and technology all can determine the baseline for many operational exposures. For this reason, and for maximum effectiveness, risk factors should be systematically managed over the range of events they affect and in the business areas where they are realized. Understanding how the entire portfolio of loss events maps to a small number of loss factors helps focus management attention on the underlying systemic factors that drive losses such as operational leverage, culture, complexity, or volatility of the environment. These infrastructure-related risk factors are often difficult to justify precisely because their impacts are so diffused throughout the organization. In addition, by knowing how risk factors affect events, we can project the potential benefits that would result from better managing the risk factors.

Factor Management

If the risk factors are at least partially controlled by the business, then we may wish to better predict the risk factor, decrease the level of the risk factor, change the distribution of risk factor (perhaps decreasing its variance), or internally offset the risk in some way. Factor prediction can use standard forecasting techniques such as Box-Jenkins time-series models or neural networks if sufficient data are available (as in many retail banking applications). These can be used for predicting future demands and, therefore, the expected level of loss events. Shifting the distribution of a risk factor invariably requires major organizational and structural change, for example, change of business culture, organizational redesign, process reengineering, or ERP. Decreasing the variance of the risk factor usually involves improving the quality of various organizational resources, for example, personnel selection, training, or TQM.

For instance, business alternatives for dealing with these common risk factors include, in decreasing order of controllability (Table 8.4):

TABLE 8.4 Risk Factors and Risk Management Approaches

	Type of risk factor	Risk management approach
Design and complexity factors	Organization	Organization design (Subsection 9.6)
	Technology, products, and processes	Reengineering (Subsection 11.1)
	Divergent goals and constituencies	Reduce level of activities through divestment (Subsections 9.1 and 14.3)
Individual behavior factors	Competence	Improved resource quality through personnel selection, training (Subsections 9.3 and 9.4)
	Honesty	Culture management (Subsection 9.5), personnel selection (Subsection 9.3), better incentives (Subsection 14.7), fraud detection (Subsection 11.6), shift rotation (Subsection 11.2) , mandatory vacations, boundary systems for incorrect and risky behaviors (Subsection 12.4)
	Motivation	Culture management (Subsection 9.5), boundary systems (Subsection 12.4), incentives, warnings
Cultural factors	Organizational culture and administration	Culture management (Subsection 9.5) through aligned incentives, boundary systems (Subsection 12.4), audit (Subsection 12.8), policies (Subsection 4.6)
	Leadership	Change in leadership, training (Subsection 9.4), personnel selection (Subsection 9.3)
	Morale and communication	Human factors engineering (Subsection 11.5), work and job restructuring, job enlargement (Subsection 11.2), communication processes and tools
Change and volatility	Industry/environment	Business and market intelligence (Subsection 10.3), organizational learning and knowledge management (Subsection 10.2)
	Organization/ operations	Project risk management (Subsection 10.4), change management
	Technology	Redundant design (Subsection 12.2), modularity and flexible open systems (Subsections 11.2 and 11.3)
Economic and financial factors	Revenue sensitivity	Diversification (Subsection 14.3)
	Operating leverage	Contractual risk transfer (Subsection 14.7)
	Financial leverage	Financial restructuring (Subsection 14.1)
	Transaction Exposures	Hedging using derivatives (Subsection 14.6)

Limitations of Risk Factor Management

Although potentially highly effective, factor management approaches unfortunately take a long time to enact. For example, organizational restructuring, reengineering, and cultural changes typically take several years to implement. The positive effects of training do not happen overnight, and may wear off over time with turnover of personnel. Long-term solutions often need to be bolstered with short-term fixes to reduce potential losses involving techniques such as outsourcing, control systems, limits, automation, temporary staff, insurance, or financial hedging. For example, if internal fraud is a major concern, but internal control systems are overstretched and it is too disruptive to quickly replace them, short-term traders' insurance can be obtained before the necessary internal changes are implemented. Factor management must also be tempered with the realization that risk factors and the events they affect may change, thus potentially making any long-term solutions obsolete.

8.7 EVALUATING RISK MANAGEMENT INTERVENTIONS

Most risk management interventions incur costs or have other negative side-effects. Understanding the extent of these costs and comparing them with the benefits of risk management determines the magnitude of the risk management investment or whether there is a need for any such investment.

The Costs of Risk Management

Reasonable and practical risk measures are usually understood in terms of the trade-off between cost and risk reduction. But this is not always true. There *are* situations when cost is not a relevant criterion; for instance, when safety is involved or when regulatory guidelines impose actions on a firm. In such cases, risk management is a cost of being in the business and the only alternative is leaving the business.

The cost of risk management has many elements (Table 8.5).

TABLE **8.5** Costs of Risk Management

Risk management approach	Costs
Loss prediction	Opportunity costs of loss prediction: lost profits Costs of data and analysis
Loss prevention	Opportunity costs of loss prevention: lost profits Direct cost of infrastructure and controls: training, development, utilization, review
Loss control/reduction	Opportunity costs of loss reduction/control: lost profits Costs of redundancies and back-ups Costs of planning and organization
Loss financing	Opportunity costs of loss financing: lost profits Transactions costs Cost of self-insurance Loading in insurance premiums
Acceptance of the loss	Effects on shareholders: through its effects on customers or suppliers being unwilling to pay for the firm's products Political costs: effects on other stakeholders

Marginal Costs of Risk Management

Although aggregate losses generally fall with increases in well-designed risk management expenditures, beyond some level, the extent of additional risk reduction (the marginal benefit) from additional expenditures in risk management begins to decrease. For this reason, complete elimination of risk is rarely a possibility. To minimize the total cost of risk—namely, the sum of the costs of the underlying risks plus the costs of the risk management efforts—investment in risk management should proceed until the marginal cost of risk management exceeds the marginal cost of the losses. The precise marginal costs will vary with different events, the scale of operations, and the type of risk management intervention.

FIGURE **8.12** The Varying Costs of Risk Management

There can be some major economies of scale in risk management. For instance, the cost of information-gathering and analysis can be significant, and for small businesses it may not be worth their effort to precisely estimate the losses associated with particular event. The information that they gather would have little impact on the decision of how much risk they should retain. For large firms, however, the value of information gathered from additional statistical analysis is very likely to exceed the cost of undertaking the analysis (the cost of data collection, analysis, and interpretation).

Extent of Risk Reduction

Presumably, the risk management intervention reduces the expected, unexpected, or catastrophic losses of a subset of risk factors and loss events. It does this by changing the frequency and impact distributions of loss events and also by changing the firm's sensitivity to particular risk factors. In terms of our earlier simulation models, risk management changes the nature of the impact and frequency distributions associated with different events and factors. For instance, we might assume that losses and frequencies are changed by some fixed percentage as a result of the intervention.

TABLE **8.6** The Effects of Risk Management Interventions

Action description	Action cost	Estimated % Reduction in Event Frequency Caused by Action							
		Unconfirmed deal	Misplaced deal	Inaccurate confirmation	Late confirmation	Power failure	Unauthorized deal	Regulatory error	Document error
New dealing room	$10,000,000	–50	–50	–90	–50	0	–50	–50	–50
Process redesign	$200,000	50	40	30	20	0	–50	0	0
Increased staffing	$150,000	0	50	0	0	0	0	0	0
Margin controls	$250,000	10	10	10	10	0	10	10	10
Insurance	$400,000	–50	–50	–90	–50	0	–50	100	–50

In this example, we simulate the effect of different risk management interventions on the frequency of specific events. A similar table could be drawn up for actions' effects on events' impacts. For instance, a new control system might be expected to reduce the number of unconfirmed deals by 50 percent and the number of misplaced deals by 40 percent. In the case of interventions that have revenue implications (for example, new dealing room), we will need to specify the expected revenue increase.

Some interventions will have negative side-effects (increases rather than decreases in event frequency), for instance, automation may lead to de-skilling, or insurance may cause moral hazard problems, or control systems may take more processing time and cause the number of late confirmations to actually increase. One of the rationales for systematic approaches such as this is that they track potential unintended consequences that tend to dog piecemeal approaches to risk management.

Valuing Alternatives

Like all capital investments, the decision to invest in risk management should be based on an estimate of the NPV of the intervention. Subsection 8.1 discussed the calculation of the NPV of an entire portfolio of loss events. Introducing the risk management intervention into the business, changes that NPV. If an improvement, it suggests the project adds value and therefore should be followed through; otherwise, the project should be dropped. If the intervention is ongoing, rather than a one-time decision, then risk-based performance measures (such as EVA™, RAROC, and RORAC) as described in Subsection 16.3 can be used instead of a strict NPV. Within a single period, evaluation of any risk management investments boils down to a trade-off between expected and unexpected losses. This can be shown most clearly by allocating the annualized cost of the risk management intervention to the expected loss of the events that it is designed to mitigate, prevent, or control. Comparing this with the extent to which unexpected (or even catastrophic) losses are reduced produces the following graphic analysis of the effect of different interventions.

FIGURE 8.13 The Effects of Risk Management Interventions

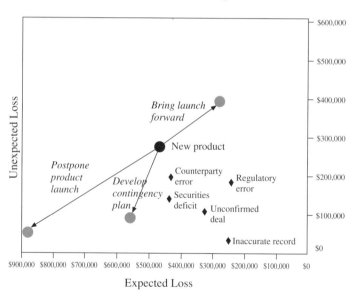

Typically, events in the top right quadrant are ripe for reduction of their unexpected risks, usually through impact reduction. Conversely, events low in the bottom left quadrant may actually require increases in the level of risk because they are being controlled at too high a price. Remembering that many control interventions will affect multiple events, simulation models such as the one that derived this analysis can be very helpful in disentangling aggregate effects.

Section III
RISK MANAGEMENT ACTIONS

Following risk identification, measurement, and analysis, management must take action. The range of possible management interventions to predict, prevent, reduce, and finance a risk is enormous, and inevitably many interventions are beyond the familiarity of individual line and functional specialists. Nonetheless, operations managers should aim to apply the *most appropriate* response; this is not necessarily the response that the manager is most familiar with. This is especially important for operational risks because, unlike insurable or market risks, no single technique can be used to mitigate the effects of all the potential exposures.

This section summarizes a wide range of risk management interventions, explains how they work, and suggests when they are most appropriate. This section builds on an often overlooked classic, *Risk & Risk Bearing* by Charles Hardy, 1st edition (October 1999) Risk Books. Back in 1923, Hardy's contention was that all managers in the business enterprise must regard themselves as risk bearers and risk managers dealing with everyday variances in their commercial environment — foreshadowing by 70 years the concept of enterprise-wide risk management. According to this view, effective risk management begins with a careful categorization of the risks, followed by a systematic and informed analysis of precisely how to respond most effectively to that risk. Although there is no single best categorization of risk management techniques, most interventions seem to fall into several distinct groups:

Risk avoidance (Chapter 9) by not engaging in activities that lead to risk.

Factor management (Chapter 9) of the systematic risk factors that give rise to risk.

Loss prediction (Chapter 10) of the events that may cause future losses.

Loss prevention (Chapter 11) by preventing loss events.

Loss control (Chapter 12) by changing the causal path by which high-impact events occur.

Loss reduction (Chapter 13) by reducing the impact of a specific event.

Contingency management (Chapter 13) of the firmwide aftermath following major loss events.

Risk financing (Chapter 14) to ensure that the firm is able to finance the loss.

These different responses affect different stages of an evolving risk.

FIGURE III.1 Generic Risk Management Interventions

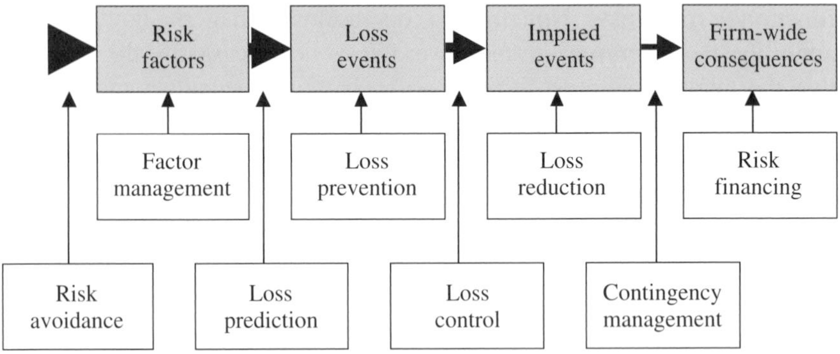

Before we launch into this section, a few words of warning. What follows is only an introduction to a wide range of risk management techniques. Based on the belief that the biggest challenge for operational risk managers is communication and the absence of a common language about risks, this section aims to provide the shared context for each of these activities. Inevitably, some of the material will be introductory to the staff specialists responsible for these areas. Each of these topics deserve entire text books to do them justice. Where possible, managers should check the references at the end of each topic, for more specialized resources that go into far greater detail than can be done here.

CHAPTER 9

RISK AVOIDANCE AND FACTOR MANAGEMENT

In this chapter, we will discuss two related techniques for risk management: risk avoidance and factor management. Risk avoidance involves the decision to reduce the levels of some risk activity, or exit the business entirely. Factor management modifies the operating environment in which loss events tend to arise, by decreasing the level of the risk factor, changing its distribution, or changing the sensitivity of the firm to the factor. Most factor management techniques try to improve the quality of resources used to identify, analyze, and manage loss events. Although not all techniques fit naturally into a single category (for example, financial hedging, and asset–liability management could arguably be discussed here or under risk financing), the following factor-management techniques are discussed here in greater detail:

- Quality management
- Personnel selection
- Training
- Culture management
- Organizational design
- Relationship management

9.1 BUSINESS EXIT AND REDUCED LEVELS OF RISKY ACTIVITY

Firms can always choose to avoid potential exposures to loss by reducing the levels of their risky activities or abandoning the business entirely.

Abandonment may be of business lines, services, internal processes, or even customer groups; for example, firms might choose to not sell insurance products to high risk customers, or cease their proprietary trading activities. The decision to exit a business or reduce the levels of risk activities is often fraught with issues from a variety of business stakeholders. Systematic risk management techniques offer a means to lift the discussion from the level of turf battles and management instincts to more objective (and hopefully transparent) criteria based on risk-based performance measures.

Need for Risk-Based Performance Measures

Typically, internal businesses are not evaluated on a risk adjusted basis, for example, when corporate treasurers assume a firmwide cost of capital. As will be discussed in Subsection 16.2, the diversified or marginal risk of the business consumes several critical firmwide resources, the most important of which is capital. It follows that performance measures must be risk adjusted if managers are to evaluate whether a particular business area creates or destroys shareholder value. At issue is whether the firm has a comparative (not necessarily an absolute) advantage in managing the risk than its customers, counterparties, and competitors, and that the risk is thus most controllable by the firm in question. The more uncontrollable the risk, the less likely is high risk adjusted performance and the more likely the firm will want to avoid the risk. However, if the markets are rewarding the firm for taking the risk—perhaps because it is an integral part of the value chain or involves a critical part of the firm's core competence—then risk avoidance is probably not appropriate.

Business Exit

Business exit or abandonment (rather than just decreased levels of business) is a momentous decision and should be justified in one of three ways. The first is a business' inability to produce profits to cover expected long-term average costs. This is especially likely to be an issue for businesses with high fixed costs for which reduction of risky operations is unlikely to make a great difference. The second is the absolute level of risk—does the firm's current level of capital allow it to handle this absolute catastrophic risk exposure? Do potentially catastrophic losses threaten the viability of the organization? Finally, exit can be justified on the basis of risk-based return; in other words, even if we can handle the exposure, the marginal risk—the difference between the stand-alone risk of the firm with the business minus that of the firm without the business, should be justified by the return (Subsection 16.3).

Reduced Levels of Risky Activities

Less extreme than business exit is the decision to reduce the levels of the risky activity. This makes more sense for investments whose marginal costs of additional transactions or customers are relatively high, uncontrollable, or uncertain. Basic microeconomics suggests that if the marginal cost of an additional customer or transaction exceeds the marginal revenue of the transaction, then the level of that activity should be reduced. These marginal costs should include the risk capital costs associated with the transaction's marginal effect on the stand-alone risk of the firm (Subsection 16.3). Another component of the marginal cost is the degree of operational flexibility within the firm, which makes it easier to change the activity levels. Managers should also consider alternatives to reducing the level of the risky activities, typically by transferring the risks to other parties, for example, to customers through risk-based pricing (Bessis, 1998), or to financial institutions through hedging, or the business line be exited.

Need for Cost and Risk Information

The decision to exit a business or decrease the levels of risky activities requires estimates of costs and risks for that business line or risky activity. Surprisingly, few firms know the added value that is provided by specific customers or transactions, and even fewer evaluate a risk adjusted return by incorporating the marginal or diversified risks inherent in the transaction or customer. Estimating the true value of a customer or a transaction obviously depends on how all the costs (including risk capital) have been allocated to it. Techniques such as *Activity-based Costing* (ABC) can be used to more accurately allocate costs according to the cost drivers (essentially the same as risk factors in this discussion) relevant to that activity. Operational risk modeling can even be viewed as an extension of ABC that adds risk capital, determined by the unexpected costs, to the allocated expected costs. The challenges and rewards of ABC are described in *Cost & Effect: Using Integrated Cost Systems to Drive Profitability and Performance* by Robert S. Kaplan and Robin

Cooper (November 1997), Harvard Business School Press. Taking the perspective of ABC in financial institutions, see *Activity-Based Costing in Financial Institutions: How to Support Value-Based Management and Manage Your Resources Effectively* by Julie Mabberley, 2nd edition (February 1999), Financial Times–Prentice Hall Publishing.

Costs of Risk Avoidance

The direct cost of business exit is, of course, the foregone income (presumably high on a non-risk adjusted basis) that would have been obtained from that activity. There are other costs, not the least of which are organizational or strategic. Marketing and sales may resent giving up a risky but potentially profitable business line, leading to a possible loss of staff. Important stakeholders (unions, managers, and government) other than the shareholders might have legitimate concerns about exiting a particular business area and use their political power to prevent business exit. There could also be hard-to-quantify strategic costs associated with business exit. Unreasonably high levels of risk might be tolerated in the short term because management may believe returns will increase or that risks will decrease as the firm and its customers learn to better manage the risks over time. Economies of scale and learning may be more important than backward-looking risk, cost, and profitability measures. There may be synergies across different business areas that would be lost if the business were abandoned. The decision to avoid a risk may cause other risks (such as legal liabilities). Another concern with dramatically reducing the level of the risky activity is the speed with which the reduction occurs. The time lag associated with the change, if too great relative to the fluctuations in price that drive marginal revenues, can actually amplify the fluctuations and increase the risk.

If possible, the benefits and the costs of risk avoidance should be captured in a formal model of the risks and returns over a sufficiently long period so they can be more objectively evaluated by a number of analysts. NPV models, although effective for new projects, are less useful for evaluating existing businesses and strategic or synergistic investments. Metrics such as EVA™ (Subsection 16.3) can be used to evaluate the performance of existing business areas, while real options models extend NPV models to capture strategic effects. Synergistic considerations can be captured if the firm understands the correlations between its different businesses. Systems and control theory models

(Senge, 1990) can be used in this context to understand the sensitivity of outputs to time lags and fluctuations in inputs.

Further information: For a general discussion on how firms respond to decline, see the classic reference *Exit Voice and Loyalty: Responses to Decline in Firms, Organizations, and States* by Albert O. Hirschman (September 1972), Harvard University Press. At the other extreme is *Voluntary Corporate Liquidations* by Ronald J. Kudla (September 1988), Quorum Books, which evaluates the use of liquidation as a corporate strategic planning tool.

9.2 QUALITY MANAGEMENT

What Is Quality Management?

Quality management changes the risk profile of operational processes and resources by improving the availability, quality, relevance, flexibility, reliability, conformance, and sustainability (Garvin, 1988) of various process inputs and outputs. For example, service availability might be improved by developing a 24/7 help desk, utilizing an intranet solution, or assigning "on-call" personnel. Resource quality can be developed by more inspection (for example, checks on data quality) or improved hiring and training. The relevance of the resource depends on whether the focus and direction of the resource are relevant to the firm's strategy or bottom-line. The same resource often can be leveraged to provide other services. On the process side, performance measures such as primary operating characteristics like throughput and downtime are obviously important. Process flexibility—the ability to handle a variety of different input situations (different trading instruments, different offices, different people)—can be important in volatile business markets. Process reliability—the frequency of downtime from major loss events— can be dramatically improved by cross-functional training (for example, by getting operations staff to spend time on trading desks), using multiple vendors (for example, for data feeds), and improving employee relations and retention efforts. Process sustainability—the process's ability to continue in the indefinite future—can be an important target if there is a limited supply of raw materials being used in the process.

Quality and Risk

Obviously, operational risk management has much in common with TQM. Their basic steps are no different and they share many same techniques. Risk, like quality, captures variance of process outcome. Unlike quality-management approaches however, the risk management approach tries to tie variation to financial costs rather than just be the baseline for continuous process or product improvement. Risk management approaches also differ from TQM, in not assuming variance to necessarily be a bad thing. Risk management generally focuses on the trade-offs between different types of risk. In contrast, quality management does not accept that trade-offs are deeply embedded in operations management and therefore need to be managed explicitly.

Stages of Quality Management

Most quality management processes, such as Motorola's six-sigma approach, have three basic stages. First, internal staff needs to be motivated and empowered to make informed decisions about quality and risk management. This is followed by widely publicized benchmarking against best-practice levels of quality within the organization or elsewhere. For example, quality awards such as the Malcolm Baldrige Award or ISO 9000 give detailed criteria for process quality at all stages of process creation (new processes) and process delivery. The final stage is one of incremental improvement by identifying barriers to quality, usually by staff close to operations. TQM has facilitated this process through the development of integrated metrics to assess the performance of particular transaction-based processes and encouragement of continuous improvement within the process.

Techniques

Quality management comprises several distinct techniques such as inspection, statistical quality control, quality assurance, and strategic quality management.

Inspection This emphasizes product or service uniformity. Firms can always allocate more resources to inspect process outputs to make sure that it meets certain predefined standards. This has two effects. First, it checks the quality of past transactions and second, it prevents much larger downstream losses in the process. Unfortunately, inspection activities are expensive and are themselves error-prone. To avoid this cost, complete inspection of all transactions is rarely performed; for this reason, sampling techniques are often used whereby the overall quality or variance of transaction processing is evaluated using a random sample. For high-volume transactions, various types of sampling of process outputs (such as random, stratified, and clustered sampling) can be used to efficiently obtain a measure of output quality.

Statistical Quality Control This analyzes the process of inspection over time. In particular, statistical control charts (Subsection 15.4) are commonly used to show the variation over time intrinsic to a sampled variable under analysis, and suggest if the distribution of this variable has changed either in terms of level, range, or form. Any such change indicates that the process is no longer "in statistical control." Depending on the distributions ascribed to the variables under study, limits demanding management control interventions can be defined. Control charts have three basic parameters: the sample size, the frequency of sampling, and the width of the control limits. These are all related; as frequency increases, sample size decreases, and control limits become wider. Managing the trade-off between these three parameters lies at the heart of developing effective control charts. Statistical quality control is particularly appropriate for high-volume financial services, where data are available and operations are increasingly under centralized scrutiny.

Quality Assurance This forces a process perspective to quality by building quality into the resource or process from the start. Quality circles, continuous self-assessment, checklists (Subsection 3.2), quality awards, and the Taguchi methods are all relatively painless organizational initiatives that emphasize continuous and directed improvement of resource and process quality. The only issue with quality assurance is that such decentralized control may be appropriate for small branch offices that are unable to take major exposures anyway, but more critical and obtrusive controls are required when the risks become significant.

Strategic Quality Management This seeks to understand the various dimensions of quality — product-based, user-based, manufacturing-based, and value-based. The objective is to position products and services along the particular dimensions of quality demanded by the customer. For instance, customers on a retail bank's electronic trading initiative will value reliability more highly than would end users of financial data services.

Other tools   Just as for operational risk management, other analytical tools such as Pareto analysis (Subsection 6.2), fault tree analysis (Subsection 7.4), fishbone diagrams (Subsection 7.4), and process maps (Subsection 5.1), have all been used to facilitate quality management.

When Is TQM Appropriate?

TQM typically assumes that managers control process outputs through the careful selection of the inputs and that many loss events are the result of a poor-quality resource or process. For example, TQM techniques can be applied to human resources, and is particularly important in financial services, where highly leveraged staff make up most of the operating costs and cause most internal loss events. An emphasis on quality is also generally best suited to more mature business areas with well-developed benchmarks and risks. TQM is not appropriate for handling problems within rapidly evolving processes or resources in a dynamic environment. TQM is generally inappropriate for those risks that are infrequent and externally driven.

Nor is quality management without its costs. Joseph Juran once observed that the costs of achieving a given level of quality could be divided into avoidable and unavoidable costs. Avoidable costs are the opportunity costs from allowing the loss event to occur. Unavoidable costs are the costs associated with the risk management effort itself. For new businesses, avoidable costs tend to be much greater than unavoidable costs and so quality is essentially "free." For more mature systems and processes, however, higher quality (lower supplier risks) means higher costs. So, the increased costs must be carefully weighed against the potential benefits, that is, the reduction of risks.

There are several major organizational pitfalls that may threaten a quality initiative. Although quality awards such as the Malcolm Baldrige Award or ISO 9000 have codified many quality-related practices, some have argued that firms are more interested in obtaining awards than in genuine improvement, in which case improvements will be fleeting and tangential. There is also some question as to just how helpful TQM can be in providing a boost to the bottom-line. For instance, one of the main issues is employee empowerment — there is evidence that quality management is only helpful in high-performing organizations with motivated employees.

Further information: For further information on quality management practices in staffing, see the sections on personnel selection and training. For an excellent overview of quality management, refer to *Managing Quality: The Strategic and Competitive Edge* by David A. Garvin, (January 1988), Free Press. A groundbreaking book on quality management is *Quality Is Still Free: Making Quality Certain In Uncertain Times* by Philip B. Crosby (October,1995), McGraw-Hill. It provides a methodology for developing, maintaining, and measuring a comprehensive quality improvement program. Alternatively, read Joseph Juran's famous reference compilation, *Juran's Quality Handbook* by Joseph M. Juran (Editor), A. Blanton Godfrey (Editor), 5th edition (March 30, 1999), McGraw-Hill Text. For a more technical discussion on sampling and probability, control charts, designed experiments, and other statistical process control tools, see the *Introduction to Statistical Quality Control* by Douglas C. Montgomery, 3rd edition (August 1996), John Wiley & Sons. In a similar vein is *Implementing Six Sigma* by Forrest W. Breyfogle III (1999), John Wiley & Sons. Most of the material on quality management focuses on manufacturing. For a detailed look at the implementation of quality programs in service businesses see *Commit to Quality* by Patrick L. Townsend, Joan E. Gebhardt (Contributor), 1st edition (March 23, 1990), John Wiley & Sons. For a look at how quality improvements can affect a financial service industry, in this case insurance, see *Insuring Quality: How to Improve Quality, Compliance, Customer Service, and Ethics in the Insurance Industry* by Hedy Abromovitz, Les Abromovitz, (October 1997), CRC Press.

9.3 PERSONNEL SELECTION

Effective personnel selection for hiring and promotion is critical for the management of the most important risks faced in many financial-services organizations, the risk of poor work performance, staff turnover, and employee fraud.

Poor Work Performance

In many financial services organizations, personnel selection for hiring (and sometimes even internal promotion) is usually based on large numbers of interviews with managers who are guided by their instincts and biases rather than their reason. Interviews are notoriously unreliable — several studies even suggest that interviewing is of no value in predicting the future performance of candidates and may even distract from more objective assessments of the candidate's intelligence, personality, and attitudes. Nonetheless, most interviewers generally believe that they are capable of successfully using interview techniques despite their lack of training and experience, and reasoning that is often heavily biased.

Adequate staffing depends on maintaining a good fit between two changing factors — the characteristics of the employee and those of the job. Effective personnel selection for hiring and promotion first requires a thorough analysis of the tasks that need to be performed (and not those performed in the candidate's previous position). This must be combined with an understanding of the relevant attributes of those who have performed the tasks well in the past. This understanding then forms the basis for aptitude tests to predict a candidate's potential ability. These tests begin with a careful analysis of the demands of the activity and pose test items that relate to some aspect of the job. These tests should be validated by staff already known to possess skills in the required work area. Aptitude tests, along with intelligence tests, achievement tests, and personality measures have all an important role for different types of personnel selection but unless carefully selected, may result in wasted resources, or at worst, may be discriminatory and illegal.

Staff Turnover

Poor personnel procedures inevitably lead to high staff turnover, one of the major risk factors affecting highly paid staff in the financial services. Staff replacement is very expensive and, in the case of higher level staff, usually costs around 80 percent of the annual salary of the staff member. Training and acclimatizing staff to the new working environment also takes several months, during which errors are far more likely to be made. Furthermore, high turnover also encourages the rest of the staff to look for other positions, which exacerbates the seasonal pattern of turnover following annual bonuses. It is also important to break down turnover rates by the level of experience (either within the firm or elsewhere). In most firms, less-skilled employees have a turnover rate that is higher than their skilled counterparts, female staff have a higher rate than male staff, and younger workers have a higher turnover rate than older ones. High turnover in junior positions is less critical than high turnover in senior management or technical positions. If staff turnover is high but constant in all business areas and categories of staff, there are probably some fundamental problems with HR policies with respect to pay, recruitment, training, and promotion. High turnover for some particular area or employee class would suggest that the nature of the work performed is a key factor.

Employee Fraud

Evidence suggests that a large number of white-collar criminals are repeat offenders. Systematic vetting of prospective personnel can help catch these repeat offenders. Performing background checks, checking qualifications and dates, and looking for evidence of falsified identity or invented/exaggerated experiences need to be an essential part of corporate security. The firm should develop consistent formal guidelines to help determine grounds for rejecting an applicant to avoid any allegations of discrimination by the company. See Subsection 11.6 for further information on other measures to prevent and detect internal fraud.

Further information: For further information on personnel selection, see *Competency-Based Recruitment and Selection* (The Wiley Series in Strategic Human Resource Management) by Robert Wood, Tim Wood, and Tim Payne (April 1998), John Wiley & Sons Ltd.

9.4 TRAINING

Training is so general a term that it needs to be immediately qualified. In this context, training denotes the combination of giving information about potential losses and developing of the skills to measure, analyze, and manage the risk. The skills and knowledge of front-line staff are the first defense to all operational risks. For example, training staff to recognize potential client fraud can save a bank millions. Skilled risk management staff allow a bank to take on positions that less-skilled competitors could not touch.

Structure of Training Programs

Training has several roles — to inculcate organizational risk policies and practices in the minds of new employees, to help staff acquire the skills and information to perform their jobs well, and to train them for other positions (either for promotion or job rotation). The content of substantive risk training programs should target specific risks that affect particular tasks, businesses, or even particular levels of the organization, or management strategies for dealing with a range of risks. The scope and size of the selected audience for these programs depends on the tasks currently performed by staff, their current levels of skills, and the expected need for skills in this area.

Training Guidelines

Training covers such a broad area that it is difficult to produce hard-and-fast principles of effective training. However, some general guidelines have been observed:

- Motivation is the most important driver of effective learning. It may take the form of monetary incentives such as cash rewards, promotion, or intangible incentives such as status and recognition.

- Developing and maintaining these skills require the firm to make an explicit commitment to training its staff at its own expense.

- Firms should make use of industry-wide training forums and courses to expose their staff to the leading edge risk concepts and approaches.

- Information and skills transfer must be cumulative and systematic. Learners need to embed their knowledge in a broader context that should be made explicit. Structured tools such as in-house risk intranets can facilitate this.

- In general, learning is best performed in relatively brief periods followed by a break when the student can assimilate the material. Feedback about students' performance should also be made available to them.

Further information: For further information on training programs and how they can contribute to a firm's bottom line, see *Training for Impact: How to Link Training to Business Needs and Measure the Results* (The

Jossey-Bass Management Series), by Dana Gaines Robinson and James C. Robinson (Contributor), 1st edition (June 1989), Jossey-Bass Publishers. A number of vendors offer specialist risk management training courses, for example, Euromoney, Risk Publications, IQPC, as well as some universities, banks, and consulting firms.

9.5 CULTURE MANAGEMENT

What Is a Business Culture?

A common view of organizational culture holds that it is a shared system of beliefs and norms used to inspire and direct the search for new opportunities. A belief system is the set of organizational definitions that senior managers communicate formally (say through new staff induction or through corporate policies) and reinforce systematically to provide basic values, purpose, and direction for the organization. Norms are a set of specific behaviors expected of members in a particular social group as a result of their holding these common beliefs. Norms facilitate group action and cohesion and are communicated on the job as new employees emulate other staff members. It follows that norms are most rigorously enforced by members when the group believes itself under threat, perhaps from violation or from external forces. Many violations (such as fraud) often result from an individual not feeling sufficiently constrained by group norms. Unfortunately, in an age of high turnover in the financial-services profession and extensive international postings, the traditional norms provided by country, class, race, company, and staff function are losing their ability to constrain behaviors. This is one reason why many major losses (for example, Daiwa, Barings) have resulted from expatriates not feeling themselves bound by the same norms as do local employees.

Need for Culture Management

Risk management depends on the positive attitudes of staff at every level of the organization. Such attitudes can be fostered by risk aware culture or hindered by an overfocus on short-term profits. Unfortunately, a dysfunctional culture is common in many trading firms where individuals compete against each other more fiercely than they do against competitors. *Investment Dealers Digest* quotes a typical attitude on the part of trader: "Your ability to trade is your franchise. You're not interested in sharing how you make money." This attitude is strongly reinforced by the reward system in which traders see that their only sense of value and reputation is in the P&L. The result is a star system of individuals acting alone and unconcerned about the negative long-term effects of their actions on the firm as a whole. Management of organizational culture is usually kept in the background, only to surface when some massive loss causes the organization's reputation to fall, or when the firm faces difficulties hiring and keeping skilled staff.

Changing a Culture

Changing the culture of an organization is a slow process because the existing culture is likely to repel any attempts to change it. One classic model of organizational change (Schein, 1986) involves three stages: unfreezing, changing through cognitive restructuring, and refreezing. A crisis is invariably the prelude to a firm's senior managers acknowledging the need to unfreeze a firm's existing culture. Unfortunately, senior managers are usually the first casualty of any such crisis. Restructuring an organizational culture employs a variety of different mechanisms that must be implemented in a way consistent with the firm's strategic goals and aspirations. These mechanisms often involve a change of leadership, improved status, changes in rewards and incentives, recruitment and promotion policies, measurement and control systems, and communications programs. Management levers such as these are inevitably broad-brush and slow and must be coordinated firmwide from the highest levels of senior management and the board. These levers are clumsy but, in the long term, highly effective. They provide basic values, purpose, and direction for the organization, without which all organizations lose their innovative drive. The coherence of a firm's culture has implications not only for staff morale and motivation, but also in the longer term may have effects on productivity and the levels of operational risk.

The Costs of Change

Major changes in an organization's culture are inevitably traumatic. Staff has invested too much in the old culture, and the wrenching change will invariably lead to some loss of key personnel. Also, different organizational units may have well-defined but antagonistic subcultures. An example might be the schism between support and line, or between back and front office, or between head office in one country and branch offices elsewhere. Managing these different subcultures while sending consistent signals to other parts of the business requires that managers walk a dangerous tightrope.

Further information: For illustrations on the role of culture in risk management, see Marshall (1996). For further information on managing organizational cultures, refer to *Organizational Culture and Leadership* (Jossey-Bass Business & Management Series) by Edgar H. Schein, 2nd edition (January 1997), Jossey-Bass Publishers. This provides an analysis of the components of culture and the levers that can affect it. Also useful is *Diagnosing and Changing Organizational Culture: Based on the Competing Values Framework* (Addison-Wesley Series on Organization Development) by Kim S. Cameron and Robert E. Quinn (August 1998), Addison-Wesley Publishing Co.

9.6 ORGANIZATIONAL DESIGN

Matching Form, Function, and Risk

The formal reporting structure of an organization has important implications for its ability to handle risks. For example, pyramid-like reporting structures with a large number of rigid levels — although appropriate for mature process technologies with well-defined subdivisions between work tasks — are particularly prone to inflexibility in dealing with unexpected events. The growth and increased cost of expertise in staff functions has typically led to such functions being separated from mainline organizations. However, separate staff and line structures increase the cultural and organizational rifts between those who do and those who support. This rift is often exacerbated still further by very different career and incentive packages for staff and line functions (as seen for example in the front and the back office). A typical compromise for large mature multiline businesses is the matrix organization. These combine functional reporting lines with operational reporting, resulting in staff members having multiple reporting responsibilities. Unfortunately, staff in matrix organizations are often confused about who precisely they should report to, a problem exacerbated in new businesses or offices, and one that can lead to the opportunities for internal fraud (Barings organization structure in 1994 being an obvious example).

Massive volatility in the marketplace, the increased importance of differentiated niche services, and the decrease of many scale economies have made small nimble firms more able to compete. For these businesses, ongoing repetitive tasks are being replaced by one-off projects as the elemental unit of work. In response, many of these firms have developed flat or free-form organizations with strictly limited structure on top of operational lines. Free-form organizational structures are the most flexible and responsive to unexpected events and are particularly suitable for project-based organizations where innovation and rapid change are critical to success. For these firms, project risk management and personnel selection is more critical than operations management, because history counts for less when each project is a new experience, and highly skilled staff must have strong incentives not to walk out the door with the firm's intellectual capital.

Further information: For further reference, see *Organization Theory and Design* by Richard L. Daft, 6th edition (October 1997), South-Western Pub. Taking much more of a risk-based view of how organizations develop is *Complex Organizations: A Critical Essay* by Charles Perrow, 3rd edition (January 1986), McGraw-Hill College Division.

9.7 RELATIONSHIP MANAGEMENT

Need to Manage Relationships

For many firms, their most serious business risks involve their long-term relationships with parties outside the central core of the organization. These external parties might be shareholders, creditors, customers, counterparties, clients, partners, competitors, regulators, insurance providers, media groups, and even one-issue pressure groups. A business needs to manage its long-term relationship with each. Relationship management should begin with an understanding of the different objectives of each party and a realization of the potential for disruption that could be caused if the partner fails to secure its objectives.

TABLE **9.1** Stakeholders' Objectives and Their Sources of Power

Stakeholder	Objectives	Source of power
Customers	Product quality, low cost	Purchasing decisions, legal fines
Employees	Good compensation, job security, job satisfaction	Staff turnover, low morale, strike action, low performance, high operational risks
Suppliers	Business continuity, regular cash flows	Working with competitors
Shareholders	Dividends, capital growth, safe capital	Voting rights, buy and sell decisions, class actions
Creditors	Interest payments, safe capital	Calling in loans, refusing to make loans, class actions
Insurance providers	Low financial and operations risks	Refusing to provide coverage, high premiums, canceled contracts
Regulators	Low systemic risks, competitive playing field	Legislation, regulatory penalties
Media	Fair information	Bad publicity

Building a Relationship

Preventing these stakeholders from exerting their power to the detriment of the business, requires first making these stakeholders realize that they have a bilateral ongoing relationship with the business and that unilateral actions can only hurt both parties in the long term. It follows that relationships should be carefully managed at every stage of their life cycle, from partner selection and relationship development to maintenance and conflict resolution. If possible, careful screening and selection of would-be stakeholders (through credit ratings, background checks, interviews, informal socialization) can avoid major problems later. Managers must understand that each party is trying to lock its partners into what it expects are beneficial relationships while trying to maintain flexibility with relationships that are more equivocal. Locking in a relation can be done, in part, through formal contracts but more importantly through an investment in shared processes (for example, just-in-time processes), procedures (for example, common master agreements), and systems (for example, e-commerce and electronic data interchange). Flexibility in relationships is easiest accomplished through redundancy; for example, using multiple vendors, having a broader customer base, renegotiation clauses in contracts, or performance clauses supported by partner tracking. Partner selection is often based on potential synergies, but firms should be willing to view even their competitors as partners in a broader endeavor to build new or ill-developed markets. Trade and standards associations can also play a similar role. Strategic alliances within the industry are especially important for managing the risk of competitor entry or exit. Relationships between parties with unequal power bases tend to be unstable and should be avoided because the more powerful party might be tempted to gouge the weaker one, eventually leading to a breakdown in the relationship.

Maintaining a Relationship

Once a stable relationship has been developed, it must be maintained. This is critical because there is often a prohibitively high cost associated with developing a new relationship or repairing a failed relationship. Maintaining a relationship requires a firm to understand and appreciate the changing needs and issues affecting the other business partner. Business and market intelligence activities (Subsection 10.3) supported by well-maintained customer relationship management systems, and data-mining tools can facilitate this by tracking staff members, institutions, deals, news items, and seminars that are of importance to the partner. Risk-based profitability measures of different customer relationships (Subsections 9.1 and 16.3) should also be used to evaluate customer profitability on an ongoing basis so that negative trends can be identified and rectified quickly.

Relationships in Crisis

Relationships can be severely tested in times of crisis. Crises tend to break relationships apart as they sharply reveal differences in objectives and power bases and as both parties' instinctive response is to isolate and control any damage (for example, poor quality, decreased availability, worsened terms, loss of reputation) caused by the crisis. Stakeholders and, in particular, investors also look to crises as a test of the quality of the firm's management; it is management's *response* to the crisis (rather than the crisis itself) that affects stakeholders' evaluation of management and their willingness to continue working with the firm.

This means that management should seek to resolve crises expediently and openly. Acknowledgment of the crisis is often the first and most painful step (see the discussion on crisis management in Subsection 13.4). Public relations firms and industry associations can be helpful in framing and communicating organizational activities and objectives in a favorable light. In many cases, securing rapid resolution of the situation, thus preventing the opportunity costs of a failed relationship, should be a priority. Most of the time, the worst outcome for both parties is a breakdown of the relationship.

Limitations of Relationship Management

Relationships are not a panacea. Relationships require long lead times. In a period of radical business change, relationships can become irrelevant as short-term, transaction-based interactions take their place.

Further information: For further information regarding the basic issues in relationship management, refer to the groundbreaking book, *Exit Voice and Loyalty: Responses to Decline in Firms, Organizations, and States* by Albert O. Hirschman (September 1972), Harvard University Press. More recently, the book *Relationship Dynamics: Theory and Analysis* by James Musgrave and Michael Anniss (Contributor), (August 1996), Free Press, discusses how relationships within groups, teams, and organizations can be more effectively managed. For an important discussion on how to manage conflict between different partners, see *Getting to Yes: Negotiating Agreement Without Giving in* by Roger Fisher, William Ury, Bruce Patton (Editor) 2nd edition (December 1991), Penguin USA. A more recent work that focuses on the role of negotiation in managing crises is *Managing Outside Pressure: Strategies for Preventing Corporate Disasters* by Matthias Winter and Ulrich Steger (September 1998), John Wiley & Sons.

CHAPTER 10

LOSS PREDICTION

Whether the problem facing operational managers is one of choosing an office location, staff promotion, refunding a bond, or developing an e-commerce strategy, the wise manager will gather more information to avoid some of the biases that tend to plague individual decision-making under uncertainty. For instance, human beings are naturally disposed to underrate risks and overstate the benefits of any activity. Loss-prediction techniques allow managers to better estimate the frequency and impact of future losses, improve their assessments of the major risk factors, or learn about the causal or statistical dependencies that make errors more likely.

Effects of Loss Prediction

Unlike loss prevention and reduction activities, which focus on expected losses, the goal of loss prediction is to reduce the uncertainty surrounding losses, that is, decrease the catastrophic and unexpected losses.

FIGURE 10.1 The Effects of Loss Prediction

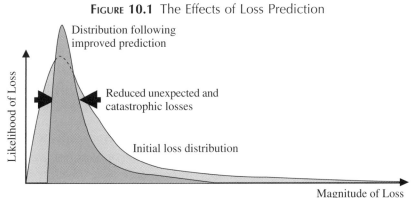

Prediction does not only mean prediction of the expected level of losses or of a risk factor. Equally useful and often easier to obtain are better predictions of the volatility of risk factors or of the range of possible impacts. Similarly, estimation of the trends of risk factors and their future volatilities can help decrease the variance (and thus the unexpected losses and associated risk capital) associated with risky operations.

Predictive models allow managers to anticipate forthcoming operational risks given changes in the underlying risk factors that drive those risks. For example, if a particular business area is losing skilled staff, experiencing high volumes or volatility, engaging in new activities or new systems, or faced by changing legal requirements, it is almost inevitable that it will have more operational problems. If a particular trader, or a particular counterparty operating in a particular sovereign nation, are individually prone to errors, then it is not difficult to project a high likelihood of errors when that trader engages in a transaction with that counterparty. These problems could have been predicted if management had tracked (for instance, through loss logs or change event logs) the current status of various risk drivers (events or risk factors). Anticipating the risk, operational risk managers can then go to the business area involved and develop scenarios, stress tests, and contingency plans to deal with the probable future problems. For example, knowing operational problems are more likely with particular counterparties, a bank might wish to monitor the transaction more closely, or insist on further collateral, third-party guarantees, and so on.

Types of Prediction Activities

Prediction can be qualitative, as in marketing research on the possible demand for different new products, or quantitative, as in forecasting future market prices. Quantitative prediction is only viable for events for which either the causes are at least partially understood or are relatively frequent (therefore, for which we have large amount of data). As discussed in Subsection 7.4, we can develop useful causal models to help identify the likelihood of problems; for example, using simple fault tree models to analyze the events leading to failures. Alternatively, time-series and regression models can be used for prediction, as in the case of financial, labor, and product markets. In both cases, effective prediction typically requires an extensive investment in information to obtain superior forecasts. For a further discussion of the use and relevance of different quantitative prediction techniques, see Subsection 7.1. More qualitative business techniques that utilize various forms of loss prediction include:

• Strategic and business planning

• Organizational learning

• Business and market intelligence

• Project risk management

These are discussed in more detail in this section.

10.1 STRATEGIC AND BUSINESS PLANNING

What Is Strategic and Business Planning?

Strategic and business planning techniques run the gamut from financial planning through business demand forecasting, from Strengths, Weaknesses, Opportunities, and Threats (SWOT) analyses to scenario analysis and real options. Its remit ranges from merely meeting budgets to predicting the future, from thinking strategically about possible opportunities and threats to creating the future. In all cases, strategic planning seeks to develop a long-term direction for the business by creating a consistent and unified vision of the future. This vision inevitably makes strong statements about the risks and opportunities in the firm's external environment and the ability of the firm's internal resources to respond to them. Strategic analyses typically focus on technological, economical, demographic, social, and political changes, and may incorporate those legal and ecological issues that affect the business. Understanding and interpreting these long-term changes are essential if an effective business—and, therefore, operational strategy—is to be put in place.

Strategy and Risk

Strategic plans are developed with an eye to future profits. The hope of profits, much like a lottery, makes people more disposed to taking on the risk. In any case, there is no requirement that expected profits of any venture are in proportion to the risks incurred. Furthermore, businesses are naturally disposed to underrate risk that only exacerbates their difficulty. Formal risk analysis seeks to limit the effect of this bias. However the presence of risk does tend to keep others out of that activity, which in turn reduces competition and increases the likelihood of excess returns.

Different strategies lead to different business risks. For example, the Boston Consulting Group's business matrix specifies that product and service lines require very different management approaches at different stages of their life-cycle because of the very different risks and opportunities involved. Thus, emerging business lines require tightly specified products, extensive inputs from consumers and marketing, lots of forecasting, and extensive logistical support. Growth businesses, by contrast, require superior customer service, extensive capacity development, careful extension of distribution channels, and organized promotion policies to capture market share. As the business matures, there is greater segmentation of the market, more service features, and more focus on cost management and efficiency improvement. As the business declines, there is rationalization of all costs and greater subcontracting.

Other strategic models—such as Michael Porter's five forces model (Porter 1998)—argue that the returns and risks in an industry depend on managing five competitive forces. These forces are the threat of new entrants, the threat of substitute products or services, the bargaining power of both suppliers and buyers, and the rivalry between existing competitors. The risks, too, are posed by unexpected shifts in these forces, customers changing their purchasing decisions, key employees choosing to leave, competitors introducing new services, clients defecting to competitors. Porter suggests that to successfully deal with these forces, businesses must consistently adopt either a low-cost or differentiated strategy. Low-cost strategies are notoriously risk prone because purchase decisions are based on a single, and partially uncontrollable, aspect of the product or service.

Business versus Strategic Planning

Given a firm's strategic direction, business planners seek to imply specific tactics by business line. Business planning focuses on managing the process of business growth. Taking a more tactical viewpoint than strategic planning, it focuses on those episodes in the life of a business that, if mishandled, can spell disaster for the firm. For example, business planners have developed a variety of checklists to identify the possible risks that threaten the success of a merger or acquisition, as well as checklists of new product/service/system risks. These are typically structured in the form of a matrix with very different risks in each cell. For instance, risks vary dramatically depending on whether firms introduce new or existing products/services/systems into new or existing markets.

Further information: For further information on strategic and business planning, refer to the groundbreaking *Theory of the Growth of the Firm* by Edith T. Penrose, 3rd edition (July 1995) Oxford University Press. A more recent and comprehensive review of strategy is provided by *Corporate Strategy: A Resource-Based Approach* by David J. Collis and Cynthia A. Montgomery, (October 1997), Richard D Irwin. Despite the best-laid strategic plans, crises are inevitable in business. Hence, an important role of business planning is developing contingency plans for crisis management. See Subsection 13.3 on contingency planning and Subsection 13.4 on crisis management, which focus on specific events that, although hard to predict because they are not the result of explicit trends in the business environment, are nonetheless plausible and can have major if not devastating impacts.

10.2 ORGANIZATIONAL LEARNING

Leveraging Individual Learning

With increases in business scale, scope and cumulative volumes, individual staff members learn about the operational risks and the events and factors that cause those risks. The challenge faced by businesses is leveraging this individual learning for the benefit of the organization as a whole. In an era of rapid change, the firm does not have time to rely on the natural learning processes about risks and must jump-start the process through more formal operational knowledge management activities. Firms can accelerate the process of operational learning through a variety of organizational and technological mechanisms. These initiatives typically help generate new knowledge, codify existing knowledge, and transfer knowledge from one part of the organization to another. On the organizational side, in addition to ongoing training, firms can develop online directories of internal and external expertise supported by dedicated help desks to handle more complex problems. Technology too plays an important role; document management systems structure the mass of legal and administrative paper work, exception reporting systems automate error handling, while intranets and collaborative groupware help generate and share hard-earned knowledge and skills about problems and the ways to deal with risk. Once the knowledge has been made explicit, it should be embedded in databases, policy manuals, processes, and procedures for future reference firmwide.

Potential Side Effects

Organizational learning and knowledge management are, at best, long-term solutions for some technically controllable events. In addition, learning is not necessarily always a positive factor. Staff may learn to sidestep controls and policies, evade detection, and bamboozle their superiors.

Further information: For further information on the development of knowledge resources within business and operational environments, see the sections on business and market intelligence (Subsection 10.3) and culture management (Subsection 9.5). For an overview of the basic elements of knowledge management, see *Knowledge in Organizations* (Resources for the Knowledge-Based Economy) by Laurence Prusak (Introduction) (April 1997), Butterworth-Heinemann (Trd). Also useful is *Knowing in Firms: Understanding, Managing and Measuring Knowledge* by George Von Krogh (Editor), Johan Roos (Editor), Dirk Kleine (Editor) (January 1999), Sage Pubications. For a discussion on the relation of knowledge management to risk management, refer to Marshall (1996).

10.3 BUSINESS AND MARKET INTELLIGENCE

Need for Systematic and Proactive Intelligence

For those risks that derive from the beliefs and activities of the firm's customers, suppliers, competitors, and regulators, traditional market research can be an important tool. However, the challenge for most businesses is not merely access to data, but rather making effective use of the data for strategic and risk management decision-making. Some firms have made market research an active part of the strategic planning process to produce so-called market intelligence services that proactively scour the business environment for opportunities and competitive risks that can be converted into opportunities. These improve on and then institutionalize an ongoing process for drawing on different sources of information to bring them to bear on important decisions in the business. These market intelligence centers also help build expertise, and generally facilitate improved decision-making if necessary by asking some awkward questions. Such centers can also act as an advocate for external parties such as customers, alliance partners, and suppliers.

Further information: For further information on business intelligence, see the sections on organizational learning and relationship management. Kahaner's book, *Competitive Intelligence: How to Gather, Analyse, and Use Information to Move Your Business to the Top,* by Larry Kahaner, (February 1998), Touchstone Books explains business and market intelligence in a clear, no nonsense style. Another useful guide is provided by *Corporate Radar: Tracking the Forces that Are Shaping Your Business* by Karl Albrecht, 1st edition (October 1999), AMACOM. Albrecht proposes a business scanning model of eight dimensions— customers, competition, economics, technology, social factors, politics, law, and geophysics.

10.4 PROJECT RISK MANAGEMENT

Need for Project Risk Management

Project management is becoming more important within financial services firms as more activities become one-off and unrepeated, and as firms move toward individual empowerment and flatter organizations. A critical aspect of project management is the evaluation of the risks of the project, necessary whenever a firm is faced with new procedures or processes, management changes, staffing changes, new or unique programs, or changes in problem patterns. Unfortunately, project risk management is made especially difficult by its one-off nature. It involves unfamiliar tasks with unfamiliar risks, often with staff unfamiliar with each other, and an organizational structure with poorly defined project goals. All these combine to exacerbate the risks. Furthermore, identification and measurement can be more difficult for project risks than for ongoing operational risks. There are two reasons for this. First, the absence of historical data makes much detailed analysis not worthwhile. Second, the order of activities in the project makes a difference to the level of risks in the project. Such is rarely true of operational processes, for which we can assume a steady state, borne out of long experience with the process.

Cost and Schedule Risks

There are two critical risks within any project. First is *cost risk*, which results in uncertainty in project costs and revenues. Second is *schedule risk*, which threatens the timely completion of the project. Schedules are harder to predict than costs because, as well as the uncertainty in the component times, you also have to incorporate uncertainty about the dependencies between activities. The main difference between cost and schedule risks is that a schedule incorporates the structure of activities whereas a cost risks is just a list of costs to be summed. When labor is the main cost in a project, cost and schedule risks are usually very similar because cost and time are linked through the hourly rate. For many projects, it can be assumed that the plan is carried out by a team of fixed size and therefore the cost and the duration of the project will be proportional; if the project takes 5 percent longer, it will cost 5 percent more.

Project Risk Models

A number of risk management approaches can be used for general risk assessment of a project. The simplest are issue-based methods, basically checklists of things that can go wrong with the project. Somewhat more sophisticated are subjective scoring techniques based on interviews and questionnaires, which assign rankings depending on the likelihood and impact of the disruptive event. More complex are a number of quantitative techniques that estimate event likelihood and impact in terms of project delay and cost overruns. These techniques include the Critical Path Method (CPM), Probabilistic Evaluation and Review Techniques (PERT), Materials Requirements Planning (MRP), Monte Carlo simulation, and event-based simulation languages such as SLAM II. Although these techniques make a variety of assumptions about the relations between activities and the quality of the cost and time estimates, all of them use network analysis to plan and control a complex set of interacting activities. This may be deterministic, such as CPM and PERT—which focus on the critical path (shortest time) required to perform a set of activities or on the minimum cost of performing those activities. More sophisticated models, such as event-based simulation treat both project time and cost stochastically.

Stages of Project Risk Estimation

Typically, all of the different modeling techniques proceed through similar initial steps. First, identify project stakeholders and their risk priorities, for example, suppliers focus on money, but customers focus on quality, timeliness, and cost. From these, we can identify key success measures for the project. Starting with a baseline project plan—what is to be delivered, resource structure, activity plan (a GANTT or PERT chart)—project risk analysts should identify events and factors that place success at risk. Events' impacts on activity times and costs can be assessed in terms of subjective ratings or distributions; for example, for each activity one might produce a triangular distribution (lowest, median, highest) of the event's effect on planned work cost.

Financing Project Risks

Performance bonds and warranties provide some insurance for organizations as users and customer of other products. However, the limited duration of warranties and the potential for contributory negligence makes these only partially effective. Further, the premiums for negligence insurance tend to be high. Performance and Schedule Bonds are often used in large commercial undertakings to cover loss, from failure to complete contractual obligations. Fiduciary organizations can obtain financial bonds for personnel handing and disbursing funds. Another approach is the use of project financing techniques to isolate the potential loss from the project sponsor; this is a viable approach if the business can operate as an independent entity. See Chapter 14 for a more complete discussion of risk financing alternatives.

Further information: For further information on project risk management, refer to *Practical Risk Assessment for Project Management* by Stephen Grey, 1st edition (June 27, 1995) John Wiley & Sons and *Project & Program Risk Management: A Guide to Managing Project Risks and Opportunities* by R. Max Wideman (Editor), Rodney J. Dawson (May 1998), Project Management Institute Publications. For general information on project management with a special focus on information technology, refer to *Breakthrough Technology Project*

Management by Kathryn P. Rea, and Bennet P. Lientz (September 1998), Academic Press. For an entertaining but hugely insightful view of the realities of technology-based project management, refer to *The Mythical Man Month: Essays on Software Engineering* by Frederick P. Brooks, anniversary edition (July 1995), Addison-Wesley.

CHAPTER 11

LOSS PREVENTION

Loss prevention describes the activities that make an event less likely to occur. Most of these activities seek to redesign certain aspects of operations, making them less likely to have problems in future. Loss prevention has the effect of reducing the frequency of losses rather than affecting the severity of losses when they do occur. It is most appropriate for high-frequency events because of its large marginal effect on the risk.

FIGURE 11.1 Likelihood and Impact Revisited

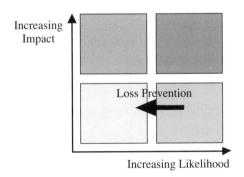

However, even in general, if loss prevention can be performed it is invariably more effective than loss reduction because it attacks the problem at the source rather than just address the symptoms of failure. A dollar of loss prevention is worth many dollars of crisis management. Prevention usually works through those underlying events (some call them incidents) that, although have a low or negligible impact, have a massive potential indirect impact by causing events that *do* have major associated losses.

Loss prevention changes the distribution of losses by affecting the distribution of loss-event frequency. For the most part, loss prevention changes the expected frequency directly (and therefore the expected losses) and only indirectly affects the variance (and therefore the unexpected losses). Fortunately, decreasing the mean level of the frequency also tends to decrease the variance of aggregate losses; hence, the unexpected loss tends to decrease as a side effect.

Figure 11.2 The Effects of Loss Prevention

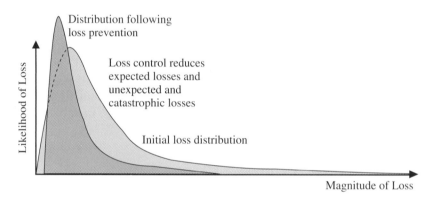

There are several management activities that fall (more or less) under the general rubric of loss prevention:

- Process reengineering
- Work and job restructuring
- Product and service redesign
- Functional automation
- Human factors engineering
- Fraud prevention and detection
- Enterprise resource planning
- Reliability-based maintenance

These are discussed in more detail in the next section.

11.1 PROCESS REENGINEERING

Basic Principles

Advocates of process reengineering argue that businesses are most efficiently organized around a few core business processes and the resources they utilize rather than any historically defined series of tasks. The firmwide application of the principles radically changes processes, resources, and management decision-making. Consider the case of securities processing where the move towards *straight-through processing* is really just a belated application of process reengineering techniques. Straight-through processing aims to automate every aspect of the process, from customer initiation, authentication and instructions, and EDI transfer (through SWIFT or the Internet for example), through to internal processing within a bank, and back to the customer. Ideally, manual authorization and review is reduced at every stage. The result is a reduction in cycle time, more accuracy, reduced sensitivity to volume-related losses, and most importantly, the opportunity to redeploy resources to higher margin, value-added services. It also means a reduction in operational risk, market risk, and credit risk. Operational risks are reduced because there is less re-input, more transparency, and less manual interventions. Market and credit risks are reduced because of the reduction in the length of settlement cycles.

More generally, processes are reengineered by simplifying them, typically by reviewing process flows for duplicate processes, any exceptions, or gaps handled manually. Simplification of processes can be effective because many operational risks are frequently the result of mismanaged complexity. For instance, one may simplify a process by removing manual interventions (say, of back-office processing using integrated electronic deal documentation), by integrating disparate systems, or by decreasing the complexity of transactions by using more standardized components (for example, fewer valuations of exotics on front-office spreadsheets).

Process-based reengineering has improved the efficiency of many business processes, particularly in the organizational interfaces between back-office operations and front-office marketing and sales. This is where many loss events tend to surface (usually because ownership of the loss is unclear). Simplification of processes also makes them more transparent by simplifying reporting lines and making process performance and its risks more visible to senior management.

Organizational changes build on top of the changes to operational processes. For example, one person might be held responsible for a particular process and the specific risks that affect the process; typically this will be the person who uses the output of the process. Decision-making in a reengineered organization is usually devolved to the point in the process where the work is performed, and any controls should be built in to the process rather than added on as an afterthought. Any information required for process decisions is captured once and at the source, and any subsequent processing of that information is ideally embedded in the business process that produces the information.

Resources are reengineered by ensuring that they are appropriate to the needs of the reengineered process. This may lead to changes in the quality/availability of the resource. For human resources, for example, reengineers typically aim to cut headcount while enriching the remaining jobs. This is done by removing the manual elements of processing and removing levels in the hierarchy to produce simpler and clearer reporting lines. Another good example of resource reengineering is work-flow and document-management systems that can help ensure that resources are available when and where they are needed. For instance, if a trader wants to see a draft confirmation, he can access it even though it may be under review by legal or credit staff. Immediate access to unstructured information can be an important tool to manage operational uncertainties. It can also improve compliance by making the process more transparent.

Process Mapping

In the course of a reengineering project, process engineers develop detailed process maps that develop management's understanding of which activities add value and which do not. These maps can also be used to show the location of risks found within the organization (Subsection 8.5). Process maps are a prelude to finding ways to eliminate non-value-added activities (such as most delays, physical movements, and inspection and appraisal activities). This is done by consolidating or rearranging process steps, rearranging the location of staff in the system to limit the amount of movement, changing work methods, changing the equipment used in the process, or redesigning forms and reports and documents for more efficient use. After these changes are implemented, process consultants may make recommendations to improve staff training, improve supervision, and more clearly identify the function of the process to all staff.

When Is Reengineering Appropriate?

From the perspective of the risk manager, reengineering is most appropriate in the following circumstances:

- If there are unacceptable catastrophic risks inherent in the existing process that must be prevented.

- If most loss events are the result of manual intervention at handover between subprocesses.

- If integrated support technologies (such as risk management databases) coupled with major organizational change are required to remove loss events.

The Risks of Reengineering

Unfortunately, there are many risks associated with reengineering projects. According to one widely quoted estimate (*The Economist*, 1994), 85 percent of reengineering projects fail. Companies may be putting themselves through an enormous amount of stressful change for no good reason. Massive process-change efforts often founder for a number of reasons. Perhaps the biggest risk factor for a reengineering project is the lack of adequate management buy-in to the results of the reengineering effort. Without ambitious and radical stretch targets, the strong support of senior management, and a realization of how the reengineering links with business strategy, reengineering projects are unlikely to be worth the cost and stress they entail. Fears of job losses may lead to business managers protecting their turf and can prevent successful completion of reengineering projects. Staff that remain may feel that their jobs—rather than being enriched—have just grown larger for the same level of pay, again resulting in a loss of staff cooperation. Another major barrier to effective reengineering of the back office are the myriad legacy systems, standards and protocols that defy immediate integration. Transfer risks as well as transfer costs need to be considered in any reengineering effort. This is because of the interdependencies between businesses—risks are passed from one business to another whenever a transaction is passed down a transaction pipeline. Automation, one of the main themes of reengineering, involves a number of risks, not least of which is the reliability of the system and its ability to handle out-of-the-ordinary events. Automation (in particular) and reengineering (in general) have a tendency to ignore contextual knowledge and thereby underrate the importance of some staff, particularly middle management whose role this is. Systems should be designed so that human operators can always take over and sort out problems themselves. Automation should always allow human monitoring of exceptions. Reengineering can actually increase risk if done purely for cost reduction because it often removes some of the organizational slack that helps predict, prevent, and manage risks. This is particularly the case if risk management functions such as inspection, appraisal, and analysis are viewed as superfluous and removed.

Further information: For further information on reengineering projects, see the sections on automation, organizational design, and work and job restructuring. Reengineering was first pioneered in the book, *Reengineering the Corporation: A Manifesto for Business Revolution* by Michael Hammer and James Champy (May 1994), Harperbusiness. Hammer has followed this with *Beyond Reengineering: How the Process-Centered Organization Is Changing Our Work and Our Lives* by Michael Hammer, 1st edition (August 1996), Harperbusiness. Another useful reengineering text is *Process Innovation: Reengineering Work Through Information Technology* by Thomas H. Davenport (October 1992), Harvard Business School Press.

11.2 WORK AND JOB RESTRUCTURING

Many potential operational losses can be prevented and mitigated through an intelligent restructuring of the work demands and allocating of staff to handle the work load. First, consider how we might restructure the work load:

Work Restructuring

In general, the provision of products and services can be performed in a number of ways, depending on the nature of the demand and the nature of the product itself. Products or services that are standardized items with continuous demand, high volumes, a standard range of transactions, and a small range of processing times can be performed by less-skilled clerical staff operating in an assembly-line environment. In assembly lines, different aspects of the assembly process are performed by different staff members. This only requires that the work task be divided into subtasks requiring similar amounts of time (otherwise bottlenecks are likely to occur). At the other extreme, products or services that are single unique items demand a process focus with lots of internal slack because of the large range of processing times. These job-shop structures typically require highly skilled clerical staff with extensive decision-making powers. A compromise between standardized assembly-line process and jobbing production is batch production, where groups of related or similar transactions are processed. Optimal batch sizes can be estimated, depending on the demand, set-up costs, and inventory costs.

Managing Workflow

Another important aspect of work restructuring, particularly in job and batch environments, is the sequence of work activities or workflow. Workflow in many offices can be dramatically improved. Layout planning can help develop physical office layouts that minimize materials handling and transportation within offices and also encourage (or sometimes discourage) interaction between staff working in different process areas. Another approach is the imposition of formal prioritization rules to help staff prioritize their work activities. For instance, activities can be prioritized by the scheduled start date—in effect performing operations as late as possible, but before the scheduled due date. Alternatively, activities can be scheduled by the earliest due date, that is, performing the job with the earliest due date first. Other simple strategies can be followed, such as "first come, first served," doing the most important job first, or doing the easiest job first. Any of these regimes can be followed, but it is important that operational managers make the scheduling explicit if they expect their staff to produce well-defined outcomes with little risk of operational delay. Another workflow approach is just-in-time (JIT) production, with transactions performed only when they are needed. By reducing the buffer provided by workflow, JIT methods decrease costs and throughput times. Unfortunately, JIT processes are particularly sensitive to any loss event that disrupts the process. For instance, transport failures to the site or failures in power or communications can have immediate impacts on the process and on the rest of the firm as well.

Job Restructuring

Job restructuring aims to match the demands of work to the capabilities of internal staff. Matching work complexity with staff competence is critical. A mismatch implies the worker is unlikely to perform the tasks adequately, or that there will be extensive opportunity costs of underutilized staff that may also lead to high staff turnover (Subsection 9.3). Since the very beginning of the assembly line, job simplification has been accepted as a fundamental way to increase throughput and decrease costs. This has often been fueled by time and motion studies, which have also been applied (mainly for manufacturing and clerical work) to estimate the time required for the basic tasks performed in a particular business function. However, in the past 30 years, a countertrend of job enrichment and enlargement has acknowledged the limitations of job simplification, in particular, its damaging effects on individual morale and the attendant human risks that result. Job enrichment means increasing the variety of tasks and their complexity. This can be done by changing the work directly or, more often, through organizational measures such as job rotation and self organization. Job enrichment, from a risk perspective, is effective if losses have been resulting from staff frustration and monotony. More difficult, but more effective in changing business environments, is job enlargement. Job enlargement seeks to increase the skills, interest, and initiative of the staff performing the tasks. The assumption is that job enlargement often leads to increased flexibility, which has its own benefits in terms of risk reduction. To some extent, job enlargement seeks to correct some of the difficulties involved in personnel selection where staff can be poorly matched to the necessary tasks. Obviously, job enlargement must be accompanied by the realization that it deserves greater remuneration; otherwise, staff may become disenchanted.

Separation of Duties

An important constraint to job restructuring is maintaining separation of duties. Initiation of a task and subsequent control of the task should be performed by different entities. When controlling any resource such as cash, people, or data, the motto should be "divide and conquer." For example, when a major deposit is made at a bank, the teller will go to the supervisor and have him or her check the transaction. When tellers empty ATMs at the end of the day, more than one staff member is always present. Nor is separation of duties restricted to cash. Data entry is always separated from data validation. Program testing is always separated from design and coding. Test systems are always separated from production systems.

Further information: For further information, refer to the sections on personnel selection (Subsection 9.3), reengineering (Subsection 11.1), and human factors engineering (Subsection 11.5). See also the book, *Methods, Standards & Work Design* by Benjamin Niebel and Andris Freivalds, McGraw-Hill, 1999, Boston. Taking more of a group perspective is *Work Redesign* by J. Richard Hackman and Greg R. Oldham (Preface), (January 1980) Addison-Wesley Publishing.

11.3 PRODUCT AND SERVICE REDESIGN

Just as process reengineering seeks to simplify and standardize internal processes and resources, the redesign of products and services can be used to prevent and mitigate event and factor losses. There are two basic extremes ranging from standardization to diversification of product and service strategies.

Standardization

The standardization of product and service lines decreases costs through consolidation and also decreases operational risks through economies of scale and learning. For example, in the securities processing industry, there is a steady convergence of the standards in the areas of trade initiation, confirmation and settlement advocated by bodies such as FIX, ISITC, and SWIFT. International efforts such as Global Straight Through Processing (GSTP) seek to speed up and standardize the cross-border flow of trade information between custodians, investment managers, clearing houses, brokers, and dealers. Standardization is typically part of a low-cost strategy of market penetration and would be appropriate for high-volume, transaction-oriented businesses such as retail or brokerage services. Standardization also makes sense if a predominant source of loss is service line personnel errors, and cost management is paramount because of low business margins. For example, derivatives processing has long been fraught with various errors and as a consequence several firms are developing a financial products mark-up language (FPML). FPML, is based on XML, the Internet standard for sharing data between applications, and provides a generic protocol to describe derivatives and their processing.

Standardization is also relevant after a merger or acquisition when a rationalization of the product and service line is needed to secure expected cost savings. Of course, standardization might get in the way of offering quality differentiated customer service. Standardization may also potentially lead to a decline in innovation, flexibility, employee morale, and, consequently, a decrease in customer service and an increase in staff turnover.

Differentiation

At the other extreme, differentiation of product and service lines diversifies many business risks because the firm's revenues are no longer tied to any single market or geographic area. It also allows firms to be more flexible in providing tailored offerings to particular market segments. In general, differentiated strategies lead to greater flexibility and lower operating exposures than cost leadership strategies. If there is uncertainty about possible future standards or protocols in a market, holding a diversified portfolio of product and service lines adds flexibility to the firm's business plans, thus decreasing business and technological risks. By contrast, more mature, price-sensitive products tend to more operating exposures because of their lower elasticity of demand. However, this have differentiated service-based approach will tend to increase some operational risks. For instance, operating in multiple markets may lead to foreign exchange exposures that can be handled using currency forwards and exchange-traded derivatives, or by local sourcing of services.

Mass Customization

Combining the best of both strategies is increasingly an option as firms attempt mass customization (Pine, 1993). This involves identification of the core building blocks of individual products and services, standardizing these, and then customizing product offerings by bringing these building blocks together in slightly different ways or by changing the promotional package surrounding the product or service. This typically involves careful segmentation of the markets to analyze the core standard products and services that constitute potential business or industry standards. Examples of mass customization abound in consumer banking services, in which basically similar functions are provided by global players operating in distinct local markets.

Further information: For further detail, see the sections on reengineering (Subsection 11.1), automation (Subsection 11.4), and work and job restructuring (Subsection 11.2). For insights on how to manage the broader portfolio of products and services, see *Service Breakthroughs: Changing the Rules of the Game* by James L. Heskett, W. Earl Sasser (Contributor), Christopher W. Hart (Contributor), (August 1990), Free Press. For an amusing discussion of the risks of poorly developed service strategies, see *At Your Service: Calamities, Catastrophes, and Other Curiosities of Customer Service* by Hal B. Becker Hal M. Becker and (1998), John Wiley & Sons.

11.4 FUNCTIONAL AUTOMATION

Automation is the use of machines to carry out functions traditionally regarded as only a capability of humans. The dramatically falling cost of computing power relative to the cost of staffing means that automated systems have become much more cost-effective compared with their traditional manual counterparts. Unlike machines, human operating staff are subject to vagaries of mood, skills, motivation, and attention, leading to variation in performance (unexpected losses). Automation has naturally been focused first, on manually intensive, low value-added activities (such as most back-office processing), however, increasingly it is being used for more complex activities. For example, a recent International Securities Dealers Association (ISDA) survey suggested automation has an important role in helping to manage the back-office operations of more complex securities such as OTC derivatives. Even in this area, automation can replace the total headcount by more than half. Automation, is particularly important where staff errors and staff turnover are high. Error rates following automation, typically fall by more than 30%. For example, many human errors can be reduced by using automated document-management systems. A bank trading 20 vanilla swaps every year with another bank should have a generic set of documents, eliminating the need to manually handcraft each one.

Automation and Context

Unfortunately, automation (much like reengineering) has its downside.

Automatic systems are insensitive to context, which may cast doubt on the reliability of the system as a whole and its ability to handle unusual or out-of-the-ordinary events that the systems designers did not consider. It is not uncommon for automated systems to swap unexpected losses for catastrophic losses. This *can* be avoided; exception reporting systems can be designed so that human operators can always take over and sort out problems themselves. Automated systems should also produce back-up hard copies of the essential information required to restart a process, if necessary, through paper or manual systems (even if at a much lower level of efficiency). Unfortunately, unless provided with adequate documentation and other support databases, operating staff are likely to forget how to handle these unusual events.

Automation and Slack

Automation, like reengineering, is often performed purely with cost savings in mind. This tends to focus on cutting headcount, particularly for those tasks that appear to be adding little value. At first glance, many risk management activities performed by middle management may fall into this category. It follows that automation can actually increase operating risk if done purely for cost reduction because it can remove some of the organizational slack that predicts, prevents, and manages risks. The resultant political costs of staff reallocation and retrenchment may also be heavy.

Further information: For further reference, see the sections on work and job restructuring, reengineering, and human factors engineering. Also see *In the Age of the Smart Machine: The Future of Work and Power* by Shoshana Zuboff, reprint edition (September 1989), Basic Books. Zuboff has investigated the implications of automation in office environments and argues that effective automation requires the development of tools to support (or *informate*) rather than replace human capabilities. Another useful guide to the broad range of software solutions in banks is provided by the annual *Automation in Banking—1999* by M. Arthur Gillis (June 10, 1999), Computer Based Solutions, Inc..

11.5 HUMAN FACTORS ENGINEERING

Many of the biggest operational risks result from staff members in positions of trust—able to commit the institution to very high-value transactions—making errors. The high leverage and considerable volume of high-value payments handled by these operations means that human factors are always going to be an important consideration in such activities. But risk managers should be wary of ascribing human error as the cause of major losses too quickly—it is often used as a way of avoid management responsibility and pushing the blame further down the hierarchy. Risk management solutions need to focus on underlying causes rather than the obvious smoking gun.

Types of Errors

Staff errors are usually either errors of commission or errors of omission. Errors of commission occur when a staff member performs a sequence of steps incorrectly or in the wrong order. These errors usually result from inadequate training, poor instruction, or limited support. Errors of omission—when some procedural step was omitted—and errors of commission usually occur because staff are confused or distracted. Errors of omission are particularly acute for ongoing routine tasks. A good example of an error of omission is found in clerical misfiling. Large US corporations lose a document approximately every 12 seconds. Three percent of all documents are incorrectly filed, and about 8 percent of paper documents are lost for good. Not surprisingly, US business managers spend about three hours per week searching for misfiled or misplaced documents (Levitt 1997). At least 20 organizations (out of 1,290 surveyed) said that they had lost information worth more than $1 million in 1994 (Panettieri, 1995).

A Systems View of Human Errors

Human factors analysis and engineering take a systems approach to understanding the factors that drive errors or loss events among operating staff. It typically assumes that most human errors occur because of the interaction between different system components. For instance, the factors determining human errors include equipment and tools, task design, environment, personnel selection, and training. Some errors are inevitable in a human system, but whether that error is translated into a loss event for the company depends on other characteristics of the work system. The philosophy of human factors engineering is that management should share the blame for staff members' errors because managers control the broader work system that allows these errors to occur. Understanding the work system is therefore the first step to improving it.

FIGURE 11.3 Causal and Contributory Factors for Loss Events

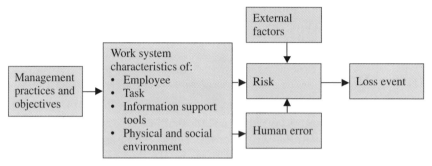

Consider in more detail some of the most important aspects of the work system that drive errors:

Employee-related Factors First, consider those attributes of operating staff that make them more likely to make errors. One of the most predictive factors for incidents is age. Younger people tend to have more incidents with incident rates peaking in the mid-20s. The reason for this is unclear; however, some suggest it is because as people get older they become more conservative and more risk averse. For many cognitive tasks, though, there is a decline in performance as employees become older. Another important characteristic that predicts error rates is work experience. A high percentage of errors (approximately 70 percent) occur within a person's first three years on the job and peak around the first three months. Another characteristic of error-prone staff is stress. Employee-related stresses include general life stresses (such as problems in one's personal life, labor-management relations, or health issues) and fatigue stresses (resulting from sleep loss or disrupted circadian rhythms—especially important for shift work and staff with jet lag). Those stresses that are idiosyncratic to specific individuals should be handled on a case-by-case basis, perhaps through counseling, training (Subsection 9.4), or mentorship programs. Alternatively, problem staff should be screened out by better personnel selection (Subsection 9.3). Those environmental and psychological stresses shared by many workers can be addressed using ergonomics techniques, by improving trust between management and staff, and by increasing participation through job enrichment, as well as increasing salary scales. These help improve morale, which in turn decrease the likelihood of human errors.

Task-Related Factors There also are some aspects of the task that make errors more likely. The psychological stresses faced by workers differ from the more objective work load stresses imposed by the task. If work load (the average amount of activity during a period) is too high or too low, errors tend to increase (interestingly, more errors occur during air-traffic controllers' low work load shifts rather than high work load shifts). Subsection 11.2 on work and job restructuring discussed many of these task-related risks. Within the work activity, the pattern of work–rest cycles can also make a major difference to staff errors. Introducing an obligatory break in the middle of the afternoon can easily pay for itself in terms of decreased reworking costs and fewer errors. Another effective way to limit work load-related stress (and thereby limit human errors) is the use of time allowances to compensate for the necessary rest and delays and interruptions in the normal daily work cycle. The structure of shift systems used to eliminate expensive overtime and continue processing transactions initiated in other time zones can make errors more likely. Shift patterns can cause errors resulting from the fatigue that comes from decreased sleep, affecting performance and attitude of the staff. Physiological factors such as circadian rhythms, ultradian rhythms, elapsed time since last sleep, duration of last sleep, and quality of sleep can increase stress levels and affect errors. Rotating shift systems, although typically more responsive to demand fluctuations and cheaper to operate, are less popular with workers than permanent shift cycles because they tend to cause sleep problems, which translate to increased human errors caused by the physiological problems of sleep deprivation and body temperature cycles.

Information Support Tools Information and control systems, displays, and reports can also make errors more likely. System designers should avoid absolute judgments about the single best way to reveal information to users. Reports should always be tailored to the decision at hand, but realize that anything out of the ordinary that might lead to unexpected losses should be flagged as an exception that requires more data, more analysis, and more management attention. Reporting systems should have an element of redundancy, particularly if they involve very different reporting structures. Similar but distinct data items are easily handled by computers, but can cause confusion in the minds of operating staff (AJB345 is very similar to AJB348 in code and yet may correspond to a completely different account or position). Displays and reports should not be too abstract; any critical variances should be easy to interpret in terms of the underlying stock or flows that they represent. The goal of such information support systems should be to minimize the operator's cost of accessing the critical information they need to make their decisions. This lowers the complexity of the task faced by staff operators and allows them to respond to the information more quickly and more accurately.

Environmental Factors These include environmental stresses—such as excessive/insufficient light, heat, humidity, or noise—and psychological stresses that result from the operator's perception of task difficulty, level of arousal, and motivation. Some of these environmental stresses can lead to hard-to-treat trauma; an obvious example is carpal tunnel syndrome that affects many operating staff tied to their keyboards.

Management Practices Poorly designed management practices can affect staff errors. For instance, poorly designed employee incentive programs (Subsection 14.7 on contractual risk transfer) can go a long way to increasing staff turnover, hurting staff performance and to a much lesser extent, increasing employee fraud. This said, financial rewards are probably most important not for the material needs that they satisfy but for their symbolic significance as measures of personal worth and status. Other management policies and procedures drawn up with little staff consultation can be frustrating and result in work-arounds that may lead to significant risks. Poor social norms about the importance of errors ("someone else will fix it"), low morale, and few incentives to avoid errors can dramatically increase expected and unexpected losses due to staff errors. Morale and motivation involve more than just monetary rewards. Other management levers, such as an individual's status in the organizational hierarchy, also make a difference as do intrinsic motivators such as meaningfulness of the work and the sense of personal accomplishment. Another key practice that affects error rates is the level of training (Subsection 9.4). Inadequate training prolongs the period in which staff are most likely to make major errors. Nor should it be assumed that the staff necessarily have a good understanding of the risks of errors, particularly their own impacts, which may be well downstream and unrealized in their business units. Better training and more transparent understanding of staff members' role in the broader business (say by putting process maps on an intranet) can help alleviate some of these problems.

Further information: The literature on human factors analysis breaks down into a number of different, but complementary, approaches such as function analysis, task analysis, environment analysis, and user analysis. Each focuses on a different driver of potential errors. For further information, see *An Introduction to Human Factors Engineering* by Christopher D. Wickens, Sallie E. Gordon, and Yili Liu (December 1997) Addison-Wesley Publishing. Also useful is *Methods, Standards & Work Design* by Benjamin Niebel and Andris Freivalds, McGraw-Hill, 1999, Boston.

11.6 FRAUD PREVENTION AND DETECTION

Types of Fraud

Fraud ranges from lying, and cheating to embezzlement and theft. Fraud can be internal—committed by insiders such as officers, directors, employees, and agents—or external—committed by outsiders such as counterparties, vendors, clients, contractors, and suppliers. Although the most costly frauds in financial institutions are external frauds, employee fraud is also a major concern. While it is the high-profile, white-collar crimes that make the headlines, the majority of internal frauds are performed by low-level corporate employees—looting that totals tens of billions of dollars each year. Common frauds committed by low-level employees include falsifying expense reports, embezzling funds, using corporate property for personal purposes, stealing corporate property, and accepting gratuities from vendors, contractors, and suppliers. Common fraud perpetrated by senior management entail misrepresenting financial statements, overstating assets, sales, and profit, or understating liabilities, expenses, and losses. Senior managers do this to deceive investors and lenders or to inflate profits and thereby gain higher salaries and bonuses.

Fraud Risk Factors

Risk factors that make fraud more likely are lax internal accounting controls and loose moral standards among the members of senior management. Another factor is the risk of collusion between employees and third parties, particularly for unmotivated employees working in devolved businesses. The absence of well-developed codes of conduct that tell staff what to do if they suspect a fraud is another factor. The absence of fidelity insurance and directors' and officers' liability insurance in many firms also contributes to the impact of fraud.

Fraud Prevention

Fraud prevention must begin with personnel selection and hiring (Subsection 9.3). Statistics suggest that many corporate workers will steal if they get the opportunity, while others will steal only if they think they can get away with it, and only a few will not steal under any circumstances. It follows that a large number of white-collar criminals are repeat offenders. Systematic vetting of prospective personnel can help catch these repeat offenders. Performing background checks, checking qualifications and dates, and looking for evidence of falsified identity or invented/exaggerated experiences is an essential part of corporate security. Consistent formal guidelines should be in place to help determine grounds for rejecting an applicant to avoid any allegations of discrimination by the company. If absolutely necessary, employees in high fraud risk positions can be bonded.

Two important organizational mechanisms for preventing internal frauds are personnel redundancy (Subsection 12.2) and separation of responsibilities (Subsection 11.2). For example, if only one person knows a critical function, then the firm is at risk if that person is away, chooses to leave the firm, or decides to behave in unauthorized ways. Cross-training, job rotation, and enforced vacations can be used to ensure personnel redundancy. Separation of duties separates the initiation of a task and the subsequent control of the task, for example, the classic breaks between trading, settlement and accounting, or between the receipt and disbursement of cash. Hand in hand with the need for separation of duties is the need for frequent reconciliation between the different parties. More frequent reconciliation stops small frauds before they have the chance to snowball into major losses.

Relationship management (Subsection 9.7) is another general means to prevent external fraudsters. Firms might periodically verify the vendors, clients, and counterparties through credit checks, visits to their premises, calling other customers, audit statements. For instance, fraud often occurs when invoices are paid to phony vendors or vendors who overcharge for supplies or services. Vendors or counterparties should only be paid from an approved list, maintained by a manager independent of accounts payable. Business partners should be encouraged to see external fraud as a shared problem demanding shared solutions, in the same way, for instance, that many smaller banks share information to prevent payroll check fraud. In some cases, firms should go one step further and try to outsource as much of the fraud-prone processing to some well-respected provider (Subsection 14.7). A good example of this is check disbursement, which can often be outsourced by daily transmissions of accounts payables files. Outsourcing can help dramatically reduce the risk of fraud, because of more stringent security measures at the external provider, and because providers are likely to reconcile accounts much more frequently.

Fraud Detection

There are several ways corporate fraud tends to be detected. Internal (and sometimes external) auditors and security investigators might follow up on accounting discrepancies or on any allegations of theft, corruption, or embezzlement. Many fraud are discovered purely by chance.

Fraud detection begins with the allocation of the necessary resources—security and control personnel to perform periodic reviews and any required investigations. But fraud detection cannot be seen purely as a staff function, nor can it be seen as too intrusive. For example, the widespread use of surveillance equipment can quickly send a signal that no one is to be trusted; motivation and morale are likely to suffer as a result. More effective as a mechanism to detect fraud is internal training. All internal staff should be trained to detect and recognize fraud, and be motivated to report any malfeasance. Formal codes of conducts can help, as can improving internal controls so they cannot be easily overridden by senior managers. Managers need to be aware of the many behavioral clues that suggest possible fraud. For example:

- Sometimes a staff member's reluctance to explain his or her job to someone else is a shield for unauthorized activities. Rotation of duties and cross-training can help catch these problems.

- Staff members who are never late or never take sick leave or holidays may be another symptom of potential wrongdoing. What would happen if these staffers were away? Are they worried a fraud might be revealed? For example, if a staff person is embezzling, he or she is obligated to prevent any potential alarms or warnings from reaching any superiors. Vacation time should be made compulsory for all staff.

- Changes in behavior may indicate possible wrongdoing, such as staff who were previously punctual consistently turning up late, or vice versa. Sudden increases in errors from a particular employee is another example. A sudden fall or rise in an individual's morale could, of course, be the result of personal factors, but may also suggest hidden problems at work. Is an employee living a very wealthy lifestyle, more than his or her job would suggest? Or is a particular employee looking especially strapped for cash? Any of these suggest possible problems.

- Sometimes a change in behavior is the result of a firing or an employee's decision to resign. During this period and potentially afterward, the firm is at risk from theft, errors, delayed damage (for example, logic bomb viruses), and unauthorized access. Well-designed policies on handling firings and resignations can eliminate many of these problems.

Many fraud also leave clues on internal computer systems. Specialized software packages can be used to look for evidence of fraud on back-up media such as tapes, zip drives, system caches, and mailboxes, TMP and BAK files, and slack space on computer disks; even deleted files can sometimes be resurrected by dedicated software tools.

For external fraud, particularly those that are retail-related, statistical and computational techniques such as logit regressions and neural networks can be used to estimate the likelihood of a fraudulent transaction and detect hot spots of criminal activity.

Further information: Other important mechanisms used for fraud prevention are discussed elsewhere in the book. These include organizational design (Subsection 9.6), diagnostic controls (Subsection 12.3), boundary systems (Subsection 12.4), computer security management (Subsection 12.6), physical security management (Subsection 12.7), and internal and external audit (Subsection 12.8). For further information on fraud auditing and detection, refer to the *Management Accountant's Guide to Fraud Discovery and Control* (Wiley/Institute of Management Accountants Professional Book Series) by Howard R. David and Patrick C. Coggins, (December 1991), John Wiley & Sons.

11.7 ENTERPRISE RESOURCE PLANNING

What Is ERP?

Enterprise resource planning (ERP) is a natural extension of the process view of the firm. ERP has evolved from traditional manufacturing inventory management techniques such as Economic Order Quantity (EOQ) and Material Requirements Planning (MRP), which focus on optimizing the management of materials and production. During the past 20 years, other resources of a manufacturing organization have begun to be integrated into the same systems. Combined with the development of the PC, client-server technology, and scaleable relational databases, these approaches have developed into ERP. ERP systems go beyond automation of single functions such as time-sheet entry, procurement, or budgeting to deliver fully integrated wall-to-wall support of a company's business processes. ERP systems attempt to integrate a firm's suppliers and customers with the processing and manufacturing environment of the organization and are made up of a number of separate modules representing the variety of functions that can be linked together. Examples of these modules include financial accounting, treasury, control, investment management, production planning, materials management, plant maintenance and service management, quality management, project management, sales and distribution, human resources management, and business intelligence. There are a large number of ERP vendors (for example, SAP, BaaN, PeopleSoft, QAD, RamcoSystems) offering a wide range of functional modules.

Most companies implementing ERP solutions have multiple operation and control locations. Hence, the online data transfer has to be conducted across different locations. To facilitate these transactions, the other important enabling technologies for ERP systems are workflow, workgroup, relational databases, client-server architectures, groupware, electronic data interchange (EDI), Internet, intranet, and data warehousing.

Reengineering and ERP

Reengineering is an essential precursor to any ERP implementation. If the business processes are not streamlined, any enterprise resource allocation will always be suboptimal. Like reengineering, ERP solutions streamline internal processes and ensure consistency of service across business lines. Like reengineering, ERP projects involve a great deal of project risk and need to be especially well-managed if they are to be effective. It follows that many of the issues discussed in Subsection 11.1 on reengineering are also relevant here; for instance, the need for strong management and business-wide support to allay potential turf battles.

ERP and Financial Services

ERP systems historically have focused on manufacturing, human resources (time and expenses), and billing. Today, most financial-services companies have moved toward ERP by implementing central accounting software. This consolidates information across the enterprise as the first step toward real-time business control and reporting. As a second step, many service industry companies are currently automating selected functions, for example, by implementing "point solutions" for the support of electronic time-sheet entry, expense reporting, or procurement. Such attempts, referred to as "functional automation" (Subsection 11.4) often demonstrate significant savings, but seldom offer competitive advantages. It is only when ERP goes outside the firm, by integrating and optimizing work processes with customers and suppliers, that ERP can help the company gain a competitive edge. ERP also has implications for operational risks, in particular project risks and risks resulting from overstandardization of business functions and services. On the other hand, the large user base of the commercial packages means that many of the potential problems associated with custom-tailored functional automation are likely to be lessened; for instance, system reliability is unlikely to be a major issue.

Further information: See automation, reengineering, and job and work redesign. Also see *Enterprise-Wide Software Solutions: Integration*

Strategies and Practices, by Sergio Lozinsky, Addison-Wesley, 1999, and *Enterprise Resource Planning (ERP): The Dynamics of Operations Management* by Avraham Shtub (March 1999), Kluwer Academic Publishers.

11.8 RELIABILITY-BASED MAINTENANCE

Maintenance activities aim to limit any disruptions to business function by ensuring the ongoing quality of key organizational resources. Although usually associated with hardware systems, similar reliability issues affect appraisal and inspection services in quality control environments, and training and professional development in human resource management. For financial institutions, these tasks range from maintaining distributed computer and communications networks to managing files, records, and databases; performing back-ups; and attending to more facilities-related tasks such as telecommunications, HVAC, lighting, and power supply. All of these systems are expected to break down or require attention and, therefore, require some maintenance.

Types of Maintenance

There are three basic types of maintenance. Typically the simplest, but most expensive, form of maintenance is firefighting or *reactive maintenance,* which occurs in response to a problem or a system failure. It tends to be expensive because it requires unexpected lead times (administrative, problem diagnosis, transportation, etc.) and requires unplanned resources be brought to bear on the problem. *Predictive maintenance* utilizes risk diagnostics to identify which part of the system is likely to have problems and should thus be repaired or replaced, thereby eliminating reactive maintenance. This is appropriate when the frequency of maintenance schedules can be based on the achievement of certain routinely measured conditions. Predictive maintenance techniques build on the causal and statistical models discussed in Subsection 7.4, which also depend on the availability of failure data or the existence of a prior causal model of the dependencies between events. *Preventive maintenance* is scheduled downtime during which a well-defined set of tasks such inspection, testing, repair, replacement, cleaning, or adjustment takes place. Traditional preventive maintenance is performed periodically with little regard to the likelihood of failure or to the importance of the subsystem to broader business continuity. For instance, similar levels of maintenance would be assigned to primary as well as any back-up units that may be available, taking no account of the redundancy in the system. However, risk or reliability-based maintenance schedules should be much less frequent for back-up systems. In practice, most preventive maintenance is time-based (although not necessarily periodic) and reflects the tendency for older subsystems to require more repairs and support. Scheduling time-based preventive maintenance focuses on performing maintenance for those systems with a known relationship between time (number of cycles, usage, number of batches, and age) and reliability. Typical relationships are described by Weibull distributions, often in the form of bathtub curves (see Subsection 7.3). Replacement/repair/repurchase decisions can then be optimized using techniques (such as *renewal theory*) that analyze the usually non-constant failure process and equate the marginal costs of continuing with the old resources with the marginal costs of replacement. Surprisingly, group replacement can often be cheaper than replacing individual elements only on failure.

Maintenance Planning

For complex hardware systems such as communication and computer networks involving thousands and sometimes millions of separate components that wear out over time, knowing *what type* of maintenance to perform and *when* to perform it can be critical. Faced with similar problems in the aircraft and nuclear power industries, engineers have developed reliability-centered maintenance techniques that select and design maintenance criteria for components based on the risk and cost criteria. Reliability maintenance typically involves developing a decision tree where different types of component failures determine different maintenance response actions. For example, we might have the following maintenance decision tree for a particular hardware system.

If component failure affects business continuity, then schedule task or design change (reactive maintenance).

Else If the failure is hidden from view but presents high risk of business disruption, then schedule inspections or operations check (predictive maintenance).

Else If any degradation in component performance is detectable by maintenance, then schedule period inspection or test.

Else If there is a known age versus reliability relationship, then schedule replacement (preventive maintenance).

Else No scheduled maintenance required.

Reliability-centered maintenance decreases operational risks of hardware components by providing a standardized justification for doing and not doing maintenance. The last is particularly important for highly reliable systems, for which the most likely reason for failure is poorly managed human intervention under the banner of preventive maintenance. So-called secondary maintenance failures are a major problem, but the use of well-trained staff (Subsection 9.4) and human factor engineering techniques (Subsection 11.5) can go some way in alleviating these issues.

Further information: For further reference, see the discussion (Subsection 7.3) on the use of bathtub models to model hardware systems with non-constant failure rates. For insight into managing the problems of secondary maintenance, see Subsection 11.5 on human factors engineering. For more detailed information, see *Risk-Based Management: A Reliability-Centered Approach* by Richard B. Jones, (February 1995), Gulf Publishing Co. Another useful guide is *Reliability Simplified: Going Beyond Quality to Keep Customers for Life* (The H. James Harrington Performance Improvement Series), by H. James Harrington, Leslie C. Anderson (June 1999), McGraw-Hill.

CHAPTER 12

LOSS CONTROL

Loss control curbs the tendency of relatively frequent and insignificant events to become more critical. Loss control does not prevent the underlying cause (usually another event), but it does prevent any critical implied events (which will have much greater impact) from occurring. It follows that loss control has the effect of decreasing the major loss event's frequency with only a limited effect on the event's impact (basically any costs associated with the less important events that gave rise to it). Loss control measures are generally less cost-effective than loss prevention for more likely operational events, but more effective for the higher impact events. Similarly, loss control is generally less cost effective than loss reduction for the high-impact events, but more so for the more likely events. As such, it provides a useful compromise between reducing the impact and reducing the likelihood.

FIGURE 12.1 Loss Control, Event Likelihood, and Impact

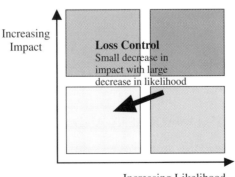

Increasing Impact

Loss Control
Small decrease in impact with large decrease in likelihood

Increasing Likelihood

The effect of loss control on the aggregate loss distribution is therefore similar to that of loss prevention.

FIGURE 12.2 Effects of Loss Control

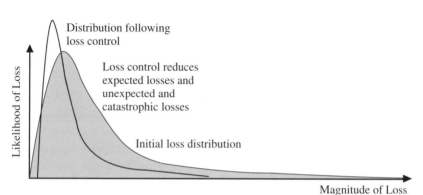

Loss control has its own costs, of course. When these are allocated to the expected losses associated with the event, loss control measures may actually increase expected losses beyond their initial level. Examples of loss control include:

- Inventory management and buffering
- Redundant systems
- Diagnostic controls
- Boundary systems (limits and sanctions)
- Compliance programs
- Computer security management
- Physical security management
- Internal and external audit
- Quality Control (Subsection 9.2)

12.1 INVENTORY MANAGEMENT AND BUFFERING

Inventory management and process buffers are really forms of organizational slack and generally have the effect of reducing unexpected losses at the expense of higher expected costs. Conversely, techniques such as reengineering, inventory management, JIT, and ERP try to eliminate as many of these buffers as possible to obtain the cost savings. Which approach is more appropriate depends on operational managers' perception of the trade-off between their processes' expected and unexpected losses.

Role of Buffers

All inventory stocks in a process act as a buffer between the outputs and the inputs of the process. Buffers act as shields that prevent uncertainty (caused by upstream loss events or risk factors) in one part of the system from being passed on to downstream parts of the system. This uncertainty may be either in the demand for the resource or in the supply of the resource. In either case, the uncertainty can lead to a high cost in terms of unfulfilled demand and potential business discontinuity. Even if fluctuations in demand/supply for products or services can be predicted, it is often too expensive to accommodate them by altering the processes directly. Buffers can obviate the need to quickly change process throughputs.

Types of Buffering

There are several different types of buffering.

FIGURE 12.3 Types of Buffering

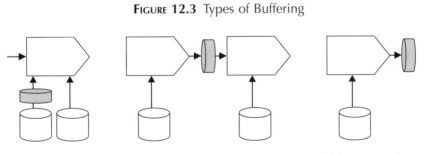

| Resource Buffering | Work-in-progress Buffering | Finished item Buffering |

Resource buffers, for instance, are appropriate when the supply or demand of a resource is uncertain and the resource can be inexpensively stored prior to use. One form of resource buffering is excess capacity used to handle unexpectedly high demand. The level of excess capacity is a trade-off between fixed set-up costs and the increased flexibility this slack offers. *Work-in-progress buffers* are appropriate in job-shop environments (Subsection 11.2) when it is difficult to predict the time needed for a particular subtask and underutilization of downstream resources would be very expensive. *Finished item buffers* are used when finishing and retooling costs of the process are high, or demand for the finished product is highly variable. Finished item buffers also protect the end-user or customer from fluctuations caused by internal events such as breakdowns, strikes, and staff shortages. Buffering can be expensive, though; inventory costs are tied to the cost of goods and the cost of handling or storage. To summarize, buffering makes sense when a combination of the following conditions is present:

- Processes have high start-up and retooling costs.

- There is a high cost associated with unfulfilled demand (for example, because of customer defection).

- Uncertain supply for a resource may lead to unfulfilled demand.

- Inventory costs for the resource are low.

Removing Buffers

Improved systems for prediction and control can obviate the need for such buffers. This is most clearly seen in the development of integrated ERP systems (Subsection 11.7), and JIT production. In addition, inventory control techniques can also be used to dynamically allocate resources to buffers. The trade-off between the expected losses associated with buffering and the unexpected losses associated with unfulfilled demand is at the heart of techniques such as the EOQ, MRP, and, ultimately, ERP. Simulation models such as those described in Subsection 8.2 can be used to optimize different buffering regimes.

Bullwhip Effects

Another caveat for the designer of organizational workflow is that buffers do not always decrease unexpected losses. A good example of this is the bullwhip effect in a simple linear process of independent companies or functions, each of which orders from upstream companies or functions. Because of innate conservatism, large batch processing, and forecast error, volatilities in downstream demand can cause even greater fluctuations in upstream supply. This leads to variations in downstream demand "cracking the whip" for upstream producers. The solution to this systemic effect is reduced batch sizing, better forecasting, lower inventories (fewer buffers), and generally more of a JIT process.

Further Information: See also the sections on work and job restructuring (Subsection 11.2) and ERP (Subsection 11.7). One of the best books on buffering and inventory management is *Best Practice in Inventory Management* by Tony Wild, 1st edition (March 16, 1998), John Wiley & Sons. It describes techniques such as Pareto analysis, JIT techniques, and MRP, and gives valuable advice about effective stock monitoring, forecasting, and setting stock levels. See also *Production and Operations Management: Manufacturing and Services* by Richard B. Chase, Nicholas J. Aquilano, and F. Robert Jacobs, 8th edition (February 1998), Richard D Irwin.

12.2 REDUNDANT SYSTEMS

When the tolerance for system-wide operational risk is much less than the combined reliability of the system's components (such as those for banking networks and stock exchanges), the simplest approach is to introduce system or functional redundancy. Redundancy is especially critical in financial services, where there is almost no leeway for systems failure. With increased competition and low transactions costs, a systems crash is more than just a temporary inconvenience, but can lead to a loss of reputation, and a rapid transfer of business away from the organization. Online brokers and other financial services are particularly sensitive to failure in the wake of huge increases in volumes of securities traded online. For example, websites are particularly vulnerable to crashes when investors flood brokers with orders at the opening of US stock markets, at 1330 GMT. To deal with this, trading systems have built in redundancy at every stage, from multiple communications links, different telecoms providers, to mirroring entire processing capabilities offsite.

In general, a redundant design describes a system in which there are two or more independent means for converting inputs into outputs. Redundant design alters the extent to which operational risks are correlated; for instance, by having *off-site* back-up trading rooms or by using different vendors' systems. The effect of redundant design, like other forms of organizational slack, is to reduce (for a price) the unexpected losses associated with the system—the failure of one subsystem would only partially damage the performance of the whole system because the other subsystems would remain unaffected.

Functional and System Redundancies

Redundancies can be accomplished by having multiple systems (system redundancy) or by providing the same system with different functional mechanisms (functional redundancy) to perform the task. System redundancies involve the use of redundant resources (such as multiple staff, multiple processors, channels, memory arrays, disk drives, or controllers) or processes (for example, front-office and back-office reconciliation or dual entry of deals). An example of a functional redundancy is the use of different telecoms providers, different pricing models.

Non-hardware Redundancies

Redundancy is not restricted to hardware resources. *Any* unique resource places the business at risk. Personnel redundancy means having more than one person who can accomplish a given task. If only one person knows how to perform a critical function, the firm is at risk if that person is away or decides to leave the firm (see Subsection 11.6 on fraud prevention). The benefits of redundancy also apply to the suppliers of business resources. By maintaining a broad portfolio of local and global suppliers for every market in which the firm operates, the effects of supplier failure or sudden increases in supplier prices are limited.

Estimating the Effect of Redundancies

To understand the cost-effectiveness of redundant systems requires a knowledge of how the structure of components affects the system's ability to function. In general, processes without redundancies can be viewed as a series of independent component processes, the failure of any one of which would lead to failure of the whole.

FIGURE 12.4 Series Components

In this case of series components, the likelihood of system failure is just one minus the probability of the system performing correctly. Assuming the individual components are independent of each other, the probability of correct performance is the product of all the probabilities of the subcomponents working correctly. As the number of components increases, the probability of all the components working correctly decreases, and with it falls the reliability of the system as a whole. Equivalently, the reliability of the combined system is the product of the component reliabilities:

$$R_s(t) = \Pi_i R_i(t)$$

(see Subsection 7.3 for a discussion on reliability). By analyzing the probabilities of failure over time (the failure rate), one can show that for a system containing independent components in a series, the failure rate (λ) is just the sum of the failure rates of the individual components:

$$\lambda_s(t) = \Sigma_i \lambda_i(t)$$

This means that constant failure rate components in a series produce constant failure rate systems.

In contrast, a system containing n redundancies is equivalent to a system of n parallel components, the failure of all of which is required before the system as a whole will fail.

FIGURE 12.5 Parallel Components

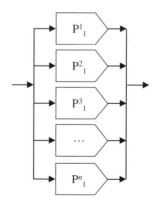

For a system containing n redundancies, the probability of system failure is the product of all the individual components' probabilities of failure. Equivalently, the system reliability is given by:

$$R_s(t) = 1 - \prod_i^n [1 - R_i(t)]$$

Unlike serial systems, constant failure rate components in parallel do not produce constant failure rate systems. From these simple models, we see that additional identical independent components dramatically reduce the likelihood of system failure and, therefore, any associated business discontinuities.

Limitations of Formal Models

By knowing the reliability or the failure rate of individual components, we can infer the probability of failure of the general systems comprising serial and parallel components. However, it is important to realize that the estimates of system reliability assume the different components are independent, i.e., that their losses are uncorrelated. If there are dependencies between components, caused by so-called sneak events or conditions that affect all the components, then we may be dramatically overestimating system reliability. In this case, we must use more powerful techniques such as Markov analysis or simulation to estimate the reliability of the system as a whole. For instance, in developing off-site back-up facilities, firms often assume that the alternative off-site location gives them continuity in the electrical power supply. But unless there are separate grids supplying power to the two sites, this might not be the case. Or in the case of regional blackouts, even redundant grids may experience problems.

Levels of Redundancy

The level at which redundancy occurs is also important. System redundancy can be obtained in two ways. The first is by having low-level components in parallel and then using these in series. Alternatively, we can have higher level systems in parallel. In general, low-level redundancies are more reliable than high-level ones because there are fewer ways for the system to fail.

FIGURE 12.6 Low-level Redundancies

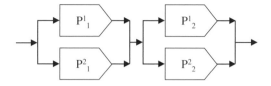

FIGURE 12.7 High-Level Redundancies

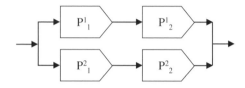

Redundant Design in Practice

Typically, redundant design is used to provide core business utilities such as communications (through alternative routes and carriers), computers (back-up networks), heating, ventilation and air conditioning (HVAC), and power (UPS systems) facilities on which a host of other business areas depend. Redundancies are appropriate when the components are cheap or when highly fault-tolerant systems are required. Redundancy by providing back-up resources is a standard approach to managing resource unavailability; however, the more unique the resources, the more expensive it will be and the less likely the back-ups will be available (particularly an issue with skilled staff members). Redundant secondary systems need not be functionally identical to the primary ones they back up, especially since these are less likely to have correlated failure modes, but they are probably more expensive because of the higher interfacing costs. The high cost of redundant systems can be limited by entering reciprocal agreements with similar businesses to use their facilities in the case of emergencies. The problem here is interfacing costs and the possible competitive implications concerning information security.

Another important issue is the timeliness with which any redundant or back-up systems kick in to provide functionality. Even a small delay in power supply can cause massive damage to computer systems such as servers and telecommunications equipment. In 1993, trading on the New York Mercantile Exchange halted for 25 minutes after a power surge disabled phone switches located in the World Trade Center. Related to this is the existence of any necessary support infrastructure for the back-up. This is the distinction between so-called hot and cold back-up sites to keep the process going. Hot sites come prequalified with all the data centers or office space facilities needed to ensure business continuity—electrical connectivity, communications access, configurable space, data, systems, supplies, provisions for transport, catering, lodging, and environmental conditioning. Cold sites come without any process-related equipment. Just like primary systems, cold sites or back-up systems that have not been integrated, maintained, and tested can be cost-effective provided the set-up time during a potential crisis is much less than the latest time by which the process must be functioning. If this is not the case, cold sites are often a waste of resources; worse still, they may encourage the delusion that the contingency is under control when it is not.

Further information: For further information on redundant design, see the sections on contingency planning, reliability-based maintenance, and quality management. The book, *Disaster Planning and Recovery: A Guide for Facility Professionals* by Alan M. Levitt (April 1997), John Wiley & Sons, discusses the importance of redundancies in facilities management. Also see *Reliability Simplified: Going Beyond Quality to Keep Customers for Life* (The H. James Harrington Performance Improvement Series), by H. James Harrington and Leslie C. Anderson (June 1999), McGraw-Hill.

12.3 DIAGNOSTIC CONTROLS

What Are Diagnostic Controls?

Diagnostic control systems are used to motivate, monitor, and reward achievement of specified goals. Diagnostic control systems are feedback systems that monitor key organizational outcomes and correct deviations from predefined standards of performance. Three features distinguish diagnostic control systems:

*   The ability to measure the outputs of a process.

*   The existence of predetermined standards against which actual results can be compared.

*   The ability to correct deviation from standards.

Diagnostic control systems can help allocate resources efficiently to specific problems. They can also motivate managers by providing them with clearly defined goals and help evaluate the same managers *ex post*. Examples of diagnostic control systems abound and include operational variances, profit plans and budgets, project monitoring systems, revenue monitoring systems, inventory control, traders' performance measurements and bonus payments, cost management using variances, cash management, asset–liability management for liquidity risks and interest-rate risks, sales performance measurements, supplier management, margin management, and portfolio trading.

Developing a Diagnostic Control

Developing a diagnostic control system requires identifying the business variables that are crucial and defining ongoing specific standards for them. This is followed by periodic measurement of these variables using operations profiles or control charts (Subsection 15.4) and comparison with the standards. Management incentives should be linked to achievement of these standards. Incentives and business efficiency can then be easily estimated in terms of the difference (variances) between measures and standards.

When Are Diagnostic Controls Appropriate?

Diagnostic controls are only appropriate when performance standards can be predefined. The use of diagnostic controls assumes there are a small number of important process outputs that can be measured without extensive error or time lag. This implies that variation in processes (their unexpected losses) results from a small number of controllable events or factors. Data to justify standards for good performance must also exist. Therefore, any loss events that give rise to variances must generally be either very frequent or measurable risk factors that vary continuously. Formal diagnostic control systems may be superior to human adaptive decision-making because of human biases, flawed reasoning, fatigue, and so on (Subsection 6.6).

Diagnostic controls are usually not so appropriate if the underlying loss event that drives the risk is associated with a staff resource such as HR or IT services. Time lag may also be an issue: if the process's response to input changes is slow or detection of deviations is slow, then changes in inputs may exacerbate through positive feedback rather than diminish fluctuations in outputs. An example of this is found in the use of insurance to smooth income; if the insurance policy pays out in a financial period different from the period of the underlying loss, the net effect of insurance might be to increase—rather than decrease—volatility. Systems and control theory models can be used in this context to understand the sensitivity of outputs to time lags and input fluctuations.

Further information: See Section 12.4 on boundary systems. For more detailed reference, see the research on systems theory and causal models which, offers some insight into the challenges of developing diagnostic control systems. Peter Senge (1990) and Karl Weick (1979) provide interesting overviews of these techniques, and the use of feedback and feed-forward systems to manage these risks. For a more specific view of control systems, look at *Levers of Control: How Managers Use Innovative Control Systems to Drive Strategic Renewal* by Robert Simons (November 1994), Harvard Business School Press. Also full of practical examples of diagnostic controls is *The Balanced Scorecard: Translating Strategy into Action* by Robert S. Kaplan and David P. Norton (September 1996), Harvard Business School Press.

12.4 BOUNDARY SYSTEMS (LIMITS AND SANCTIONS)

What Is a Boundary System?

Boundary systems comprise formally stated rules, limits, and proscriptions with defined sanctions and credible threats of punishment. The goal of boundary systems is to allow individual freedom within well-defined bounds. Boundary systems define risks to be avoided and set limits on opportunity-seeking behavior. Sanctions are imposed if those limits on behavior are transgressed.

Limits

If an activity is very risky, limits should be tied to the level of the risk and the firm's tolerance for the risk. Ideally, limits should be flexible enough to reflect prevailing context, rather than slavishly being drawn in tablets of stone. Limits must also be compatible with performance measurement if confusion is not to result. However, limits *must* be modified according the extent to which experience with the risk taker's performance dictates that he or she can control the risk and to the extent that the firm trusts that person not to take advantage of the situation for his or her own ends. An important aspect of determining limits is the ease and the cost of detecting limit violations. In turn, this depends on the frequency and type of monitoring or sampling (either random or periodic), which can be a major cost in itself.

Breaking Limits and Sanctions

Limits without sanction will quickly be revealed for the paper tiger they are. All limit violations must be handled consistently. Special cases *cannot* be made, after the fact, for any limit-breaker; otherwise, this will send conflicting messages to the entire organization. Furthermore sanctions must be transparent and immediate if they are to produce useful signals for modifying behavior.

Examples

Typical boundary systems include risk policies, codes of conduct, operational guidelines, and trading limits. The latter, for instance, usually involve dollar limits on total purchases of each type of financial instrument, on the total investment in any single issuer, and on the total purchases of any single issue. They may also involve limits on the levels of risk taken by specific trading areas or business units.

When Are Boundary Systems Appropriate?

Senior managers create boundary systems when they are operating in very uncertain business environments or if the level of trust between senior management and staff is low. This is typically the case when operating with new staff in new markets or when decision-making is distributed or decentralized. Boundary systems are particularly important when individuals have a great deal of leverage to commit the firm to major transactions that could cause a loss of reputation.

Issues

Boundary systems in many organizations incorporate arbitrary limits and sanctions. Even if the boundary system is well-designed, its rationale often gets forgotten and is not adapted to suit changing circumstances. Unfortunately, in most firms, limits tend to be developed and modified in an *ad hoc* fashion; a "safety first" attitude prevails, leading to a surplus of controls that limit process efficiency rather than enhance it. In some cases, the limit system may delude firms into a false sense of security because it ignores the changing nature of the risks. Limits may also disregard the context of specific situations, which leads to working according to rules rather than independent and responsible decision-making. Boundary systems can also be expensive. There may be extensive monitoring costs as well as the opportunity costs that result when these limits prevent the firm from getting into businesses that would have been allowed if the limits were not in place.

Further information: See also diagnostic control systems (Subsection 12.3), compliance (Subsection 12.5), and internal and external audit (Subsection 12.8). See also the discussions on developing a formal risk policy (Subsection 4.6) and on control charts (Subsection 15.4). For further reference on boundary systems and a comparison with diagnostic control systems, see *Levers of Control: How Managers Use Innovative Control Systems to Drive Strategic Renewal* by Robert Simons, (November 1994), Harvard Business School Press.

12.5 COMPLIANCE PROGRAMS

Nature of Compliance

Compliance programs share many of the same features of other boundary systems, except that the standards are external and the sanctions that result are legal and may be more significant because of the reputational effects involved. The goal of compliance programs is not to prevent undue risks per se, but rather to prevent criminal misconduct, the threat of regulatory and statutory penalties, and the possible loss of reputation. Examples of controllable events that often cause a failure of compliance, imposition of regulatory penalties, and potentially much larger reputation costs include fraud, unauthorized trading, and unfair business practices.

Changing Role of Compliance

Laws are becoming stricter and courts are beginning to convict companies for what they should have known and should have told their customers; increasingly, *caveat emptor* is being replaced by *caveat venditor*. For example, the number of product liability suits filed in the

United States increased 1,200 percent between 1974 and 1990. Large corporations—because of their deep pockets and their wariness of facing a long drawn-out legal battle—will be tempted to settle out of court. Despite the rise of directors' insurance, executives who ignore corporate ethics take the risk of both personal and corporate liability. Sentencing guidelines are beginning to base their fines on the extent to which companies have taken steps to prevent the misconduct. Risk management actions can thus be used as a defense against excessive fines. Sentencing guidelines base fines on some percentage of the loss suffered by customers (which ranges from 5 percent to 200 percent of the customer loss). The precise percentage depends, in part, on the existence of a strong compliance program, cooperation with authorities, acceptance of responsibility for the crime, adequate reporting of the crime, and the level of senior management involvement.

A good example of the need for a defensive and proactive stance to compliance occurred at Salomon Brothers in 1991, when four top executives failed to take appropriate action in response to unlawful activities on the government trading desk. Although company lawyers found no strict legal requirement that they disclose the improprieties, a delay in disclosing the information and a failure to reveal their prior knowledge prompted a crisis of confidence among employees, creditors, shareholders, and customers. The executives lost the moral authority to lead and subsequently resigned. Their lack of action compounded the trading desk's legal offenses. The estimated cost was around $1 billion in legal costs, increased funding costs, and lost business.

Elements of Effective Compliance Programs

Developing a compliance process involves several steps. First, businesses need to know the regulatory and legal restrictions for the areas in which they operate. This should be followed by well-defined standards of compliance that are overseen by high-level legal and operational staff. These standards should be designed and implemented with employee input; this will help avoid rebellion and damage to staff morale. Compliance should not purely focus on sanctions and wrongdoing. It is *essential* that compliance encourage and reward exemplary behavior (right-doing) if the image of compliance as internal policeman is to be avoided. Standards need to be communicated and staff need to be trained to identify and report any misconduct or violation.

Compliance managers can work with human resources to effectively communicate the company's standards and procedures through induction, ongoing training, or internal publications.

Monitoring for Effective Compliance

Audits and ongoing limit monitoring should be performed as a matter of course. Compliance also needs to enforce a system where employees can report criminal misconduct without fear of retribution. When an offense is detected, the firm should respond immediately but appropriately. A rapid and appropriate response is especially essential for major transgressions because of the huge potential reputational damage that could affect the business should news of the problem go public. Compliance standards must be consistently enforced through appropriate disciplinary measures. Following any compliance investigation, compliance officers should analyze what went wrong and take reasonable steps to prevent similar offenses in the future

Proactive Compliance

Compliance can be proactive in several ways. The concept of regulatory risk can provide a focus for much compliance activity through an analysis of regulatory priorities (based on their pronouncements and historical industry penalties). In combination with internal histories of compliance failures and audit assessment of potential loss events that would lead to such a failure, firms can develop systematic estimates of regulatory risks and thereby direct scarce audit and compliance resources more efficiently. Further, because of the increasing number of international institutions with regulatory responsibility, compliance must continuously scan the legal environment to detect any changes (see Subsection 10.3 on business and market intelligence). Compliance should also work with industry groups and public relations organizations to influence the rules and regulations that matter to them (see Subsection 9.7). However, compliance must acknowledge that, for the most part, its legal compliance programs rarely address the root causes of misconduct. They largely control—rather than prevent—these risks. Compliance managers must work with other functional areas to prevent these risks; most importantly, with human resources staff to develop hiring and promotion procedures (Subsection 9.3) that avoid delegating discretionary authority to those likely to act unlawfully.

Further information: See also the subsections on boundary systems (Subsection 12.4), fraud prevention and detection (Subsection 11.6), computer security management (Subsection 12.6), organizational design (Subsection 9.6), organizational learning (Subsection 10.2), and internal and external audit (Subsection 12.8). For further insights into the changing role of compliance in banking, refer to *The Handbook of Compliance: Making Ethics Work in Financial Services* by Andrew Newton (1998), Financial Times–Pitman Publishing. A more academic discussion is provided by *Banking Law and Regulation* by Jonathan R. MacEy and Geoffrey P. Miller (June 1997), Little Brown & Co. Law & Business. For a more technical discussion on compliance issues for brokers, dealers, and investors, see *Securities Law Compliance: A Guide for Brokers, Dealers, and Investors* by Allan H. Pessin (December 1989), Richard D. Irwin. To understand the changing climate of international securities laws, see *Risk and Regulation in Global Securities Markets* by Richard Dale (August 1996), John Wiley & Sons. A wide variety of compliance materials are available on the Web, including a number of online references of the rules relevant to compliance (for example, www.complinet.com—a subscription service for UK compliance professionals).

12.6 COMPUTER SECURITY MANAGEMENT

Computer security management tries to prevent a wide range of computer-related threats to internal and external networks, software, information, as well as the hardware and the support infrastructure. These threats range from disruptive computer viruses to unwanted access and white-collar fraud.

Limiting Unwanted Access

Physical access can be largely controlled by conventional physical security measures such as access cards, integrated alarms, and CCTV monitoring (see Subsection 12.7 on physical security management). But in an era of "Internetworking," the most damaging breaches in security are electronic. Systematic and sometimes automated hackers will seek to penetrate firms' networks from the outside and any security weaknesses will be ruthlessly broadcast and exploited. Although few companies will admit to break-ins from hackers, most *will* be subject to attacks, and the majority of these will go undetected.

The first line of defense is the widespread and effective use of *passwords*. Password access should be tied to particular system resources (data, networks) with varying levels of business sensitivity. Those without the need to access the resource do not need a password. Corporate security services should also enforce password-based resource protection by requiring staff to periodically change their passwords. They should warn against obvious passwords and remove any unprotected guest accounts or backdoors to systems. In particular, security should be on the alert for so-called *social engineering hacks*, which try to trick staff members into revealing their passwords. In an effort to hunt down hackers, *access tracking systems* can help data security administrators monitor access to corporate networks and sensitive corporate data. These can be used to flag any suspicious activity that may be occurring on their systems and networks in real time.

One commonly used method of preventing access to data or information in transit is *encryption* and *authentication*. Security software typically incorporates programs that encrypt and decrypt transmitted information in a way that is extremely difficult for anyone else to decode during transmission. A number of standards exist, such as SSL (*Secure Sockets Layer*) for transactions over the Internet. The Internet is not the only target for unwanted access; wireless communications and phone lines intended for data (such as remote-maintenance lines and field-office access lines) offer avenues of access to internal systems and require their own encryption procedures. Encryption and authentication technologies can also dramatically improve the security of wire transfer and Automated clearing house/electronic data interchange (ACH/EDI) transactions. Encryption also incurs a cost in terms of systems and decreases accessibility. It follows that the level of encryption used should depend on the value of the information and the security of the communications system.

Another common way to prevent unwanted access is the use of *network firewalls*, which protect a trusted computer network from an untrusted one. In many cases, a secure firewall serves as the only connection point between a corporate network and the Internet, allowing only authorized traffic (as defined by the local security policy). Of course, firewalls do not address insider attacks or insider abuse of authorized access. Given that some experts believe that insiders cause the bulk of all security problems, other access tracking and fraud prevention techniques must be used.

Limiting Disruption

Most large organizations have experienced virus infections. A virus is an independent program that reproduces itself. It may attach to other programs or it may create copies of itself (as in companion viruses). Viruses will usually damage or corrupt data, change data, or degrade the performance of a computer system by utilizing resources such as memory or disk space. Some 90 percent of organizations with more than 500 PCs experience at least one virus incident per month. The cost of incidents averages more than $8,000 and can run as high as $100,000, with surveys indicating that the problem is getting worse rather than better. Common viruses include Trojan viruses, worms, and logic bombs. A Trojan virus is a program that performs an unauthorized function and is hidden inside an authorized program. Worms reproduce by replicating themselves over and over, from system to system, and causing damage in the process. They are self-contained and use the networks to spread in much the same way that viruses use files to spread. Logic bombs are code that is triggered when a designated condition is met; for instance, deleting someone's hard drive on a specific date. The battle against viruses is ongoing. Virus scanners can detect some known viruses, but no virus scanner can detect all the viruses likely to be seen in future. Viruses are typically spread over the Internet and through e-mail (usually by downloading files or by opening attached documents), but many virus infections occur when people introduce infected floppy disks or systems directly into the network. Firewalls can help prevent malicious code coming from another network, and proper antivirus policies and procedures can reduce these risks. Also useful for mitigating the damage caused by viruses are systematic backup procedures, using back-up logs or diaries for all internal computer systems and databases.

Computer Fraud

Most computer security techniques focus on preventing attacks from outsiders, but an even bigger threat is from within. American businesses lose as much as $1 billion annually to just computer fraud (Anonymous, 1995). Losses of trade secrets, sales strategies, and price quotations occurred most frequently, with internal staff responsible for about two-thirds of the incidents (Anonymous, 1996). Given that the perpetrators may have completely authorized access to the system resources, it follows that only an organizational approach to managing fraud will be effective; fraud is more than a systems problem. See Subsection 11.6 on fraud prevention for more details.

Further information: See also the subsections on physical security management (Subsection 12.6) and fraud prevention (Subsection 11.6). Donn B. Parker's book, *Fighting Computer Crime*, John Wiley & Sons, provides a solid overview.

12.7 PHYSICAL SECURITY MANAGEMENT

Physical security means different things to different people. Burglary, vandalism, theft, pilferage, employee theft, shoplifting, data misuse, copyright infringement, industrial espionage, drug abuse, counterfeiting, fire, bugging, and emergency evacuation are just some examples of the potential threats. Physical security covers the protection of both tangible and intangible assets. The more specialized areas of computer security and fraud prevention use many of the same techniques, but warrant a separate discussion (Subsections 11.6 and 12.6). Physical security has traditionally meant asset protection through, for example, better bolts, specialized locks, bomb-proofing, and armor plating. But these days, it usually focuses on access control.

Access Control

Access control prevents unauthorized individuals from entering restricted physical spaces that may contain resources vulnerable to tampering or compromise, for example, the preprinted checks, or the signature plates used to sign large numbers of checks. Effective access control depends on matching the control to the extent of the threat and the vulnerability of the resources. Access control systems range from the systematic use of master keys for different locks to protect corporate assets, to swipe card access systems. Access control systems integrate firmwide sensors and alarms; for instance, area sensors protect detection zones, such as a wall surface or the exterior of a safe, and signal when an intruder causes sufficient change in the capacitance in the zone. Other automatic alarms may signal unauthorized entry through break-in (or other conditions requiring urgent attention, such as fire and temperature rise). Monitoring equipment, such as fixed or pan/tilt/zoom CCTV, can be used to monitor doors, corridors, and similar interior areas.

These access control systems are usually coordinated through a central remote terminal area for alarm monitoring, video signals, and camera controls. A centralized approach to physical security means that the control area must be especially secure since it is the linchpin to the entire building security. For example, emergency back-up power should be available. This approach is slowly changing, however, as security systems are becoming integrated and accessible on a computer network, thus making security monitoring and control available from any location at any time.

Further information: See also the discussions on contingency planning (Subsection 13.3), computer security management (Subsection 12.6), and fraud prevention (Subsection 11.6). For an excellent introduction to electronic access control, refer to *Security, ID Systems and Locks: The Book on Electronic Access Control* by Joel Konicek and Karen Little (August 1997), Butterworth-Heinemann. Another useful reference is *Effective Physical Security: Design, Equipment, and Operations* by Lawrence J. Fennelly (Editor), (April 1992), Butterworth-Heinemann. It discusses the elements of effective security program, such as environmental design, security surveys, locks, lighting, and CCTV.

12.8 INTERNAL AND EXTERNAL AUDIT

Role of Audit

Historically, fraud has been the major concern of internal and external audit. These days, internal and external audit—have gone beyond their traditional role of quantifying and confirming the existence of the assets and liabilities for which the firm is responsible (and accountable)—and are also focusing on other elements of shareholder value-added such as operational effectiveness and efficiency. Internal and external audit should be complementary; external audit provides an independent but high-level review of policies and procedures while internal audit validates in detail the ongoing operational effectiveness and efficiency targets and ensures the reliability of reporting. External auditors establish the existence of assets/liabilities, confirm the accuracy and completeness of records, check the valuation of assets and liabilities, check the quality of any risk assessments, and validate any presentation and disclosure materials. In many financial institutions, internal audit's role has also changed from checking compliance with guidelines (now a role largely taken by compliance and risk management staff) toward reviewing the integrity and consistency of firmwide operations and risk management. This typically involves a number of techniques, including due diligence reviews; analysis by process, transaction, and account; audit sampling; evaluation of physical controls; checking the segregation of duties; and evaluation of information processing reports.

Risk-Based Audits

The bottom-up approach of many audits has tended to make them organized idiosyncratically around available audit expertise and immediately pressing concerns rather than long-term risks. Faced with more complex businesses and tight resource constraints, auditors are increasingly adopting a risk-based audit strategy. This means that business processes and resources that auditors believe have high levels of unexpected and catastrophic risks should direct the efforts of internal and external audit. This is particularly so if these losses result from largely controllable risk factors such as staff turnover, level of training, age of technology systems, and level of manual processing. Risk categories may conform closely to accounts in the general ledger, enabling a risk breakdown by account to be used to direct audit procedures. The allocation of audit resources across different business lines can also be facilitated by ranking these risk factors across those of the other business lines (Chapter 8). This would then be followed by a number of substantive tests for high-risk businesses, analysis, and the completion and issuance of an audit opinion.

Issues

The major issue facing internal auditors is their limited independence, while external auditors have only limited time. Another major problem is the wide range of complex businesses and techniques that auditors need to be able to handle (ranging from accounting checklists to advanced mathematics, from IT security to organizational design and corporate governance). This makes it much harder to tackle line staff about the more complex operational exposures.

Further information: See other subsections on internal control (Subsection 1.6), diagnostic control systems (Subsection 12.3), boundary systems (Subsection 12.4), and compliance (Subsection 12.5). For the basic elements of the audit function, see *Principles of Auditing* by O. Ray Whittington and Kurt Pany, 2nd edition (June 1998), Richard D. Irwin. For a general guide to operational auditing with lots of useful checklists, refer to *The Operational Auditing Handbook: Auditing Business Processes* by Andrew Chambers, Graham Rand (Contributor), (August 1997), John Wiley & Sons. For auditors of computer systems, the book, *Information Systems Control and Audit,* by Ron Weber (November 1998), Prentice-Hall, is most helpful. It describes audit procedures to evaluate whether computer-based systems safeguard assets, maintain data integrity, achieve organizational objectives effectively, and consume resources efficiently. For a discussion of the increased importance of audit for risk management, see *Beyond COSO: International Control to Enhance Corporate Governance* by Steven J. Root (May 1998), John Wiley & Sons. This book also describes the various models of internal control and evaluates their strengths and weaknesses.

CHAPTER 13

LOSS REDUCTION AND CONTINGENCY MANAGEMENT

Loss reduction involves activities that mainly reduce the severity—but do not affect the frequency—of losses. Loss reduction changes the distribution of losses by affecting the distribution of the impact of loss events. The extent that loss reduction affects the standard deviation of the impacts of loss events also largely determines its effect on unexpected losses.

Loss reduction activities are usually appropriate for external events, the occurrence (and therefore, frequency) of which is difficult or even impossible for firms to manipulate. Loss reduction then takes two approaches. First, it decreases the impact of the event before the event occurs by the planning of one form or another, for example, loss isolation, disaster and contingency planning. Second, it reduces losses after the event, by effective crisis management.

FIGURE 13.1 Loss Reduction, Event Likelihood, and Impact

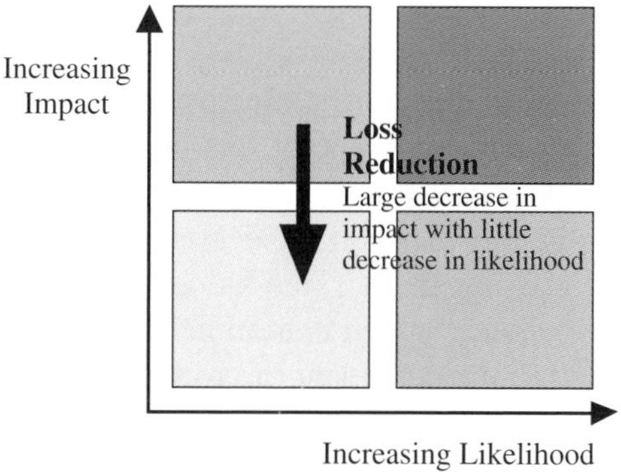

403

Examples of loss reduction and contingency management include:

- Legal risk reduction

- Loss isolation and asset protection

- Contingency planning

- Crisis management

13.1 LEGAL RISK REDUCTION

Besides preventing losses through effective compliance programs, legal safeguards work to reduce losses after the event through adequate legal defenses.

Types of Legal Risks

Legal risks abound. Firms face legal challenges from *any* of their many stakeholders. From customers come charges of negligence and product liability. From employees come unions, health and safety issues, wrongful dismissal, harassment, and discrimination. From competitors and suppliers come claims of anti-competitive practices and computer "downstream liability." From investors and creditors come malfeasance claims. From government come claims of regulatory non-compliance, criminal acts, and incorrect interpretation of legislation. From the broader community come charges of negligence and malfeasance. For example, the Securities and Exchange Commission (SEC) in the United States charged Merrill Lynch with negligence for failing to warn investors of the risks. The firm agreed to pay a $2 million penalty for its part in the 1994 bankruptcy of Orange County in California.

Legal Defenses

Obviously, the details of the various legal defenses vary by case and legislature and are beyond the scope of this book. But historically in the United States, for example, one important standard was *contributory negligence*—basically, this means if the defendant contributed to the loss, then the defendant was not liable. This has evolved to a standard based on *comparative negligence*, which determines the pro rata proportion of blame to be allocated to the defendant (up to some maximum percentage, usually 50 percent). In some cases, another legal defense is that the plaintiff voluntarily and knowingly assumed the risk, in which case the defendant is not liable. For strict liability cases (usually involving product liability, abnormally dangerous activities, or torts committed by employees in the scope of their employment), there is no need to prove intent or negligence because the liability is held to be inherent to the activity.

Reducing Legal Risks

Highly skilled defense counsel is of course essential in an era of defense costs averaging hundreds of thousands of dollars per case, with about a third of the claims resolved in favor of the claimant and close to half of those claims exceeding $1 million. But also important is more proactive involvement by legal staff. Legal risk can be significantly reduced by getting legal staff involved in operational activities that may have any legal dimension, typically those activities involving customers or other major stakeholders. For instance, all contract and marketing documentation for new businesses should require a legal review. This goes a long way in decreasing the risk of legal action. Of course, the interaction between operations, line staff, and legal support should be carefully managed to avoid resentment and damage to morale.

Having an ongoing compliance program is also essential to reduce the risk of legal proceedings from regulators. Many of the same aspects of effective compliance will help the development of a legal defense should the need arise. For example, having well-defined and explicitly written procedures and an audit trail for internal decision-making can be used to justify legal arguments about who knew what and when. Legal staff should be immediately involved when any potential legal problem is unearthed, since any delay by legal staff usually exacerbates legal offenses. The extent and effectiveness of other internal risk management efforts can also be important in making the defense case. Has the firm had a history of similar offenses? Does the firm respond appropriately when offenses are detected? Are standards consistently enforced through appropriate disciplinary measures? Does it take reasonable steps to prevent the occurrence of similar offenses in the future? The knowledge-management techniques discussed in Subsection 10.2 can go a long way to systematize these information flows to produce a legally effective audit trail.

Settling Suits

The decision to settle legal suits against the firm should reflect the long-terms costs and benefits of continuing the suit. This might not be consistent with the ethical or legal merits of the case. Reputation costs and their effects on customers, funding costs, and so on, can quickly outweigh the tactical benefits of winning a suit. On the other hand, large companies with deep pockets may feel the strategic need to not set a precedent of settling out of court.

Further information: See also Subsection 12.5 on compliance programs and how they can reduce the risk of regulatory penalties. See also the discussion on loss isolation and asset protection (Subsection 13.2). For some types of legal risks, insurance is available, for example, product liability insurance and officers' and directors' insurance (Subsection 14.4). For a general overview of the changing legal risks facing financial services, see *21st Century Money, Banking & Commerce* by Thomas P. Vartanian, Robert H. Ledig, and Lynn Bruneau (March 1, 1998), Fried, Frank, Harris, Shriver & Jacobson. It provides a comprehensive analysis of the operational and legal risks surrounding electronic financial products and services and electronic commerce. Obviously, more detailed references should be consulted for specific advice. For derivatives, for example, the book, *Over-The-Counter Derivatives Products: A Guide to Business and Legal Risk Management and Documentation,* by Robert M. McLaughlin (September 1998), McGraw-Hill, provides a good overview of how corporations should select, record, and control the derivatives they employ to hedge their operational and interest-rate risks.

13.2 LOSS ISOLATION AND ASSET PROTECTION

Barriers

From offshore bank accounts to project financing, a useful way to defend key target assets from external threats is by isolating the loss or by protecting the assets threatened by the loss. Through operational and, more often, legal and financial means, asset protection approaches seek to separate the threat in time/space from the target (loss isolation), isolate the threat or targets, strengthen the target (asset protection), or reduce the effect of the threats. This is easiest understood in terms of barriers that prevent a threat or risk from affecting its target. Multiple barriers often are needed because any single barrier may have holes.

Examples

The most important legal barrier is the limited liability of corporate shareholders, that is, shareholders cannot be held liable for claims against the company greater than the value of the corporation's assets. This has many implications. For instance, when faced with a business promising high returns but involving very high potential risks, firms typically create distinct corporations (derivatives trading and self-insurance companies, for instance) with special financing (for example, project financing) to carry out the activity. These forms of risk financing assume that the risk taking entity is capable of producing its own revenues to cover its costs. Provided that formal procedures are followed to identify it as a separate company empowered to act on its own initiative, this structure can be used as a legal protection from suits against the parent company.

Obviously, this also requires the firm be endowed with a reasonable amount of money to carry on its business and has the authority to act in its own best interests. Judicious use of subsidiaries can dramatically reduce the exposure of a parent company to large tort liability claims that would otherwise threaten the parent or other subsidiaries. Of course, this does not mean that in the event of a claim that exceeds the assets of the subsidiary, the parent will declare the subsidiary bankrupt and walk away from any claims—the reputation costs would be too high. An even more extreme form of asset protection is to place the assets offshore, away from a presumed legal or taxation threat. This might involve setting up offshore accounts, joint ventures, or incorporating in a foreign jurisdiction. Protective measures from potential legal threats can be implemented within the business. Chinese Walls within the organization may offer an easier alternative to divestment or spin-off, when communications only need to be restricted on a case-by-case basis (for instance, over different consulting projects, or between the corporate finance and treasury arms of an investment bank).

Developing Barriers

The development of asset protection and loss isolation cannot be done purely by operational staff because it requires close coordination of strategic planning, legal, and tax if the protection against risk is not to become a barrier to control or even a major liability. For example, placing assets offshore runs the legal risk of expropriation, the relationship between corporation and subsidiary might not be sufficiently arm's length. Moreover, barriers between risks and assets, if they are legally effective, may also tend to prevent control and communications from one part of the organization to another.

Further information: See the subsections on legal risk reduction (Subsection 13.1), insurance (Subsection 14.4), and self-insurance (Subsection 14.5).

13.3 CONTINGENCY PLANNING

What Is Contingency Planning?

A disaster is an out-of-course event whose consequences lead to the organization or business failing to function. A disaster is not a hurricane or a flood or a terrorist bombing. A disaster occurs when products cannot be produced or when services to customers—external or internal—cannot be provided. Contingency planning aims to prevent a business disaster from occurring when a very rare event strikes the organization and tries to provide for continuity of operations between the impact of the event and the return to normal functioning. It does this by first identifying the key business processes of an organization and the likely threats to those processes. From this information are built the plans and procedures that ensure these processes can continue whatever the circumstances.

Elements of Contingency Plans

Contingency planning involves a number of steps. The first is making efforts to avoid the crisis if at all possible. Many of the techniques discussed in the earlier chapters on loss prevention (Chapter 11) and especially loss control (Chapter 12) are relevant here. Second, it prepares to manage a potential crisis. This is the major focus of this section. The later discussion on crisis management (Subsection 13.4) considers the next steps—recognizing when there is a crisis happening, resolving the crisis, and trying to profit from the crisis.

Contingency planning involves a number of different activities:

1. Identifying critical contingencies

2. Describing and analyzing the evolution of contingencies

3. Developing repair and management procedures for the contingency

4. Establishing a crisis center

5. Testing and updating contingency plans

6. Performing ongoing monitoring of trigger events

7. Estimating loss settlement

8. Identifying responsibility for reputation management following the contingency

Identify Critical Contingencies Much of the material in Chapter 5 on risk identification is relevant here. The only difference is that contingency planning will focus on high-impact events that disrupt the business rather than the measurement of operational risks per se. It is often easiest to start with the different processes and resources and ask how critical each process/resource is to the business as a whole. For example, system reliability is especially critical for electronic trading. The speed with which financial markets operate means that there is almost no leeway for systems failure. With increased competition and low transactions costs, a systems crash is more than just a temporary inconvenience, but can lead to a loss of reputation, and a rapid transfer of business away from the organization. In marked contrast to trading, some financial reporting activities could be interrupted for as much as several weeks before becoming critical. Contingency planning is expensive and should focus only on these *critical* processes and resources and investigate the contingencies that would affect them. For less critical processes and resources, time is less an issue and crisis management responses are more likely to be sufficient.

Mostly, critical contingencies are uncontrollable events with major catastrophic impacts, with much of the impact the result of subsequent reputational losses. Typically, these events should be reasonably likely to occur in the next 40 years or, alternatively, should have occurred to more than one businesses in the industry during the previous year. Less frequent events should be managed when the crisis occurs. Obviously, the more likely the event and the greater the reduction of impact as a result of planning, the greater the level of detailed planning that should be performed. For example, the article "Fortune 1000 companies commit to Crisis Management," *Contingency Planning & Management,* May 1996, prepared a survey of the relative importance of different types of hazards for senior managers. They found the following risks most worrying to respondents (in this order): A stock price drop or loss of market share, employee whistle-blowing and scandals, hostile takeovers, mergers and acquisitions, downsizing, facility closure, union troubles, product tampering, copyright and patent infringement, trade secret leaks, counterfeiting, rumors, and media and press crises.

Describe and Analyze the Evolution of Contingencies This usually involves mapping out how specific contingencies would play out in terms of their short-term and long-term resource losses and how these losses would escalate over time (Subsection 8.4). Also included in the same analysis should be time scale within which time-sensitive processes or resources must be restored. This provides senior management with reliable data on which to base decisions on risk mitigation and continuity planning.

Diagrams such as Figure 13.2 would be produced.

FIGURE **13.2** Evolving Contingencies

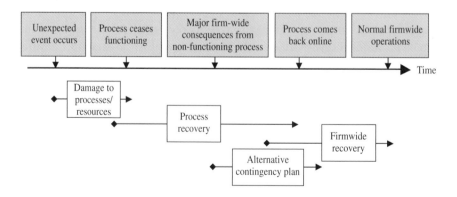

In some cases, this description would also show how any trigger events might cause or lead the contingency. Dependency models (particularly event trees, described in Subsection 7.4) can be used to capture these triggering relationships.

Develop Repair and Management Procedures for the Contingency This is a vast area reflecting the huge range of possible disasters that contingency plans may seek to address. Much of the rest of the book is relevant here (for example, strategic and business planning, redundancy, automation, and so on), but contingency planning does have its own unique role.

For instance, contingency planning should be distinguished from strategic or business planning in that the latter should focus on those trends and events with known causes that evolve over a long time. Examples of these strategic business events include a steady decline in stock price or market share loss, mergers and acquisitions, downsizing, and facility closures. Contingency planning for these stakeholder-induced business events really reflects a failure of internal strategic and business planning to judge ongoing developments among these stakeholders. Instead, contingency planning should focus on those events that are much harder to predict, and are not the result of ongoing trends or patterns on the part of key stakeholders, technologies, social changes, demographics, and so on. Take just a few examples: the markets can cause a loss in share value as a result of unfounded rumors, poor public relations, or external pressure groups. Disgruntled employees can blow the whistle on potentially damaging practices within the organization. There can be union troubles, perhaps as the result of downsizing or retrenchment. Customers can charge the firm with negligence. Competitors can launch hostile takeovers or charge the firm with infringing patents or copyrights. Governments and regulators can cause business events by introducing unexpectedly onerous regulations or taxes. For these business events, crisis management (Subsection 13.4), legal defenses (Subsection 13.1), and responsive leadership are most effective.

In contrast with these business events, most operational contingencies result from events that affect operations and thereby threaten business continuity. Although some operational contingencies are internal—the result of human and technological failures, unintended or deliberate—most are external, resulting from the failure of the infrastructure on which the business depends. Internal operational failures can be managed using clearly defined good practices, whether through policies statements, diagnostic control systems, audit, or quality checklists. The last, for example, can be used to identify vulnerabilities in the heating, ventilation, air-conditioning, elevators, fire detection, alarms, and computer systems (Levitt, 1997). Being far harder to control, external operational failures require well-developed contingency plans. Consider just a few examples:

People-centered Events: These may result from poor design, carelessness, theft, arson, mischief, vandalism, terrorist attacks, sabotage, kidnapping, bombing, and espionage. Events such as these may be caused by individuals connected with the organization, or from outside. For the former, those related to the organization, only screening at the initial interview is likely to be effective (Subsection 9.3). Often these acts are the result of extensive employee alienation stemming from a sense of powerlessness, meaningless, and isolation from others or, ultimately, themselves. For those individuals unconnected with the organization, such as those responsible for the bombings of the Federal Office Building in Oklahoma and in the World Trade Center in New York City, heightened security, protective barricades, access and parking restrictions, and greater surveillance techniques can be used to thwart malicious activities (Subsection 12.7). Computer simulation of the effects of disruptions to the most vulnerable parts of a business facility may also be useful for high-visibility facilities.

Infrastructure Problems: These include failures in construction, water, gas, mains breaks, power failures, HVAC problems, contamination, telecom outages, and road damage. These are often triggered when weather-related events put too much load on the surrounding infrastructure. Examples of such triggers include earthquakes, hurricanes, snow, tornadoes, typhoons, tidal waves, floods, lightening, rains, winds, and droughts. These should not be viewed as particularly rare events. For instance, a hurricane hits New York City about once every 10 years, an earthquake affects Tokyo approximately every century. Fortunately, early warning for tornadoes, thunderstorms, tidal waves, and earthquakes can be obtained from various national agencies, such as in the US, the Federal Emergency Management Agency (FEMA). It is inevitable that these weather-induced disasters will effect the weakest link, typically the supporting infrastructure, rather than specific operational systems. For instance, in 1993, a snow-laden roof in Clifton, New Jersey, collapsed and brought down 5,000 ATMs (Jones, 1993). As well as predicting weather-related triggers, construction risks such as this demand quality assurance techniques and proper supervision. Another common weather-related event is loss of electric power, one of the major uncontrollable events faced by a financial institution. Unfortunately, as the dependence on electric power increases, utilities have less control over the quality of the power provided to the user. This, combined with the increased power sensitivity of systems such as servers and telecommunications equipment, means an increasing number of power-related problems. Power-related events include outright failures, outages (blackouts), shortages, sags or voltage drops (brownouts), spikes or transients, surges, and electronic noise.

Every year, a typical US computer location undergoes 36 power spikes, 264 voltage sags, 128 voltage surges, and 15 power outages. Power anomalies account for 50 percent of data loss inside computer data centers (cited by Deltec Electronics Corporation, attributing information to the National Power Lab, the Power Electronics Applications Center, and the Contingency Planning Research Inc.). For instance, on September 19, 1991, the phone service in New York City was significantly disrupted (more than 5 million calls blocked) because of the failure of a back-up power source at a switching center (Andrews, 1991). In 1993, trading on the New York Mercantile Exchange halted for 25 minutes after a power surge disabled phone switches located in the World Trade Center. Sometimes the reason for power outages reaches into the bizarre. In 1987, a squirrel crept into the electrical transformer servicing the NASDAQ computer center in Connecticut and began to eat insulation off some cabling. The resulting short circuit caused a power outage and led to trading being suspended for several hours. Strangely, something similar happened to the same computer center in 1994.

To counter power problems, power conditioning systems can be installed to reduce the risk of data loss or damage to sensitive equipment. Furthermore, UPS (uninterruptible power supply) systems can be used to provide back-up power. Depending on the magnitude of the damage to business continuity, managers may wish to develop redundant systems in the form of hot or cold back-up site-processing if onsite facilities are inadequate. Off-site systems do need to be maintained and tested just like primary systems, although not necessarily with the same frequency. Back-up generators often fail to operate effectively because of poor maintenance and discontinued support.

The failure of other common utilities can cause major problems. These range from breaks in telecom lines, disconnected water mains, flooding, transport delays, denied office access, and fire to riots, insurrections, fuel shortages and work stoppages (say of a telecom provider or the post office).

For example, in 1990, an AT&T fiber optic cable was accidentally severed in Newark, New Jersey, halting ATM transactions at 23 banks, and forcing the New York Commodity Exchange and Mercantile Exchange to close; it also blocked 60 percent of the long-distance telephone traffic out of New York City (Crockett, 1990). The following year, a 41-year-old water pipe burst, disrupting two office buildings on Wall Street. The New York Exchange and American Stock Exchange were disrupted, as were a number of security firms, banks, and law firms (Levy, 1992). But the biggest utility-related business failure of all, the Chicago Flood, occurred on April 13, 1992. Construction workers damaged the lining of an unused tunnel system in Chicago, and 250 million gallons of water from the Chicago River flooded into abandoned railway tunnels then used for telephone and electrical cabling. The damage covered 100 blocks of Chicago's downtown Loop district and affected 250,000 workers in Chicago in 600 buildings and 400 data centers. Fifteen of the buildings were closed for at least a week and some for up to 3 weeks. Economic losses were estimated at $1.8 billion, and the cost of repairs, direct business losses, and clean-up totaled $337 million. As a result, 150 companies soon failed (Cronon, 1992).

For these utility failures, contingency planning is predominantly about environmental scanning (Subsection 10.3) and provision of back-ups for these services (see Subsection 12.2 on redundancies). The most critical systems will need to have built in redundancy at every stage, from multiple communications links, different telecom providers, to mirroring entire processing capabilities off-site. Insurance, legal remedies, reciprocal agreements with similar companies (allowing the other to use their site, resources or facilities during a disaster), service level agreements, and crisis management can also offer some relief.

Establish a Crisis Center This means selecting, in advance, key personnel to become members of a contingency crisis team to handle similar contingencies, and assigning specific individuals within the team responsibility for managing particular contingencies. The team members should be used to working with each other in stressful situations, and should reflect the major constituencies of the business. The crisis team should also comprise a staff member willing to play the role of devil's advocate to challenge any contingency planning assumptions. Inevitably, individuals are likely to find themselves in over their heads during a crisis, so it is essential that any required documentation and training be distributed to relevant staff members before (not after) the contingency event. The crisis team should be based in a crisis center from which disaster recovery is directed and tracked; the center also would serve as a reporting point for deliveries, services, press, and all external contacts.

Another prerequisite for a crisis center is the availability of critical business resources such as customer and vendor information, office equipment, and communications and dealing equipment. A common failure of business contingency plans is the lack of accessible and usable information critical for business functioning. Some businesses have developed Crisis Information Management Systems (CIMS) to coordinate information and data before, during, and after a crisis. Even if this is not necessary, effective records management should be in place to prevent data from being damaged by the event and make it accessible when needed by anyone. This typically requires the remote capture and storage of electronic data, using database techniques such as journaling, electronic vaulting, and database shadowing. Hard copy information about the current state of the business process should be produced periodically. In some cases, back-up manual "paper" systems should be in place at the crisis center to allow the process to continue functioning, albeit at a lower level of efficiency.

Test and Update Contingency Plans The plans should be independently validated and tested (if possible) before they are needed, and updated as changes in the business context warrant. Testing can be done through announced or unannounced execution of business continuity plans. As well as evaluating existing plans, testing can also highlight the need for additional plan development. In some cases, simulation models can be used, in some cases, particularly for large facilities management. Simulation is especially useful in helping facilities planners to estimate the impact of disasters (fire, power failures, communications failures, HVAC failures, flooding, explosions, and so on) in one part of the physical facility and evaluate its impact on staff and materials in other parts. Simulation is also heavily used for analyzing evacuation alternatives (given the characteristics of staff, time of day, detection systems, internal geometry, facilities for the disabled, PA systems, and so on) and developing effective contingency plans before they are needed.

Any changes to contingency plans should be summarized to all members of the crisis team. Crisis team members should verbally review each step of a plan to assess its effectiveness and identify enhancements, constraints, and deficiencies. Furthermore, contingency plans should be made accessible through redundant mechanisms (hard copy, off-site, and intranet) in a form that enables rapid implementation of the plan to all crisis team members.

Perform Ongoing Monitoring of Trigger Events   Rapid response to a crisis depends on rapid detection of the problem. Monitoring the functioning of processes is critical to preventing low-level events from occurring and escalating into more critical loss events. Business and market intelligence (Subsection 10.3) can be used to scan for potential trigger business events. Control systems, detectors, and alarm systems can alert managers to critical events occurring internally.

Estimate Loss Settlement   This is the reserve account (an extraordinary operating expense) available to the crisis team immediately after an event seriously affects the financial position of the organization. It is essentially a form of loss provision and should reflect the expected losses associated with the contingent event. As well as direct losses, the reserve account should cover any indirect losses. For instance, it should include the business costs of a backlog of work that develops when a system or process is unavailable for a long period, and which may take a considerable length of time to reduce.

Identify Responsibility for Reputation Management Following the Contingency   This final component of a contingency plan is discussed in more detail in the section on crisis management.

Evaluating Contingency Plans

Contingency plans should be evaluated according to three criteria. The first is *reliability*—the degree of protection provided by the plan against major unexpected events affecting the business process. The second dimension of plan quality is *availability*—the time it takes to return to normal business functioning. The last dimension is plan *maintainability*—the cost and adaptability of the plan to changes in resources and processes. For instance, as a result of a reliable and maintainable contingency plan, Fuji Capital Markets office was able to recover within two days of its office at the World Trade Center being bombed. Of the three dimensions of contingency plan quality, the maintainability of plans is probably most crucial.

The quality of a contingency plan is proportional to the time and effort staff have put into it. Contingency planning can be expensive because the events must be thought out and communicated in advance, but the effectiveness and overall quality of recovery will be higher; that is, lower risk of recovery failure. In some circumstances, such as a computer crash, poorly managed recovery can create even more damage when, for example, the wrong back-up files are copied, or a total rollback to earlier data is performed when only a partial one was necessary. Again, cost and benefit must be weighed, but the additional risks introduced by recovery procedures must also be considered.

Obtaining resources for contingency planning can be difficult. Although contingency planning is important, it is usually not urgent and, as a result, it is often pushed to the back burner. Managers will never be congratulated for a well thought-out contingency plan if the event does not occur. Contingency planning should result from systematic risk identification and measurement if it is not to be de-emphasized and *ad hoc*.

Further information: See the subsections on strategic and business planning (Subsection 10.1), and redundant design (Subsection 12.2), and crisis management (Subsection 13.4). There are also several useful books, such as *Contingency Planning & Management. The Encyclopedia of Disaster Recovery, Security & Risk Management* by Tari Schreider, (November 1, 1998), Crucible Publishing Works, provides one of the most general overviews of this area particularly useful for disaster recovery planners, risk managers, and security administrators. For more detail on facilities-related contingencies, *see Disaster Planning and Recovery: A Guide for Facility Professionals* by Alan M. Levitt (April 1997), John Wiley & Sons. For IT-related contingency planning, a useful guide is *Disaster Recovery Planning: For Computers and Communi-*

cation Resources by Jon William Toigo, 1st edition (December 21, 1995), John Wiley & Sons. Little has been written specifically for financial institutions, but in the case of dealing rooms, refer to *Contingency Planning for Dealing Rooms* by Roger Edmunds (December 1989).

13.4 CRISIS MANAGEMENT

Crisis management should be seen as a sequel to contingency planning rather than a replacement for it. Although crisis management is not a substitute for planning or other forms of risk management, there are situations—critical loss events are completely unpredictable and uncontrollable or very unlikely, or the costs of prediction, planning, mitigation, or prevention are just too high—when it is entirely appropriate.

Recognizing a Crisis

Crisis management involves recognizing there is a crisis happening, resolving the crisis, and, finally, trying to learn and profit from the crisis. The immediate reaction to a crisis is usually one of denial, followed by panic. A formal firmwide declaration that the firm is facing a major crisis is necessary to focus attention and other resources on resolving it. In such a case, quick decisive action from the firm's senior managers (usually the CEO) can make the difference between corporate survival and disaster. A crisis team and the necessary support resources should become operational immediately. These would include financial resources—such as releasing any financial provisions for the loss—and operational ones, such as the start of hot-site operations. Preparations for the crisis organization should have been largely in place before the crisis (see Subsection 13.3 on contingency planning), although in real situations there are likely to be last-minute changes to the crisis team to reflect availability and the nature of the contingency. Firewalls should put in place between the crisis team and rest of the operating business. It should be made clear throughout the firm that the firm will survive and crisis resolution is job number one. One member of the crisis team should be the point of reference for reputation management following a contingency. This is typically the CEO, but that individual should be comfortable and well-prepared in dealing with the media (through press conferences and "on-site" or ambush interviews). Consider the response of Warren Buffet following Salomon's crisis within its treasury trading operations in the 1990s. He took the following strategy for his initial press release: first he acknowledged that he did not know all the facts, but was working hard to get to the source of the problem as quickly as possible. He followed this by saying what he did know about the situation.

Typically, senior managers wait too long to declare the crisis, believing that various stakeholders (particularly the markets) will react very negatively. Event studies of markets' reactions to firm crises suggest that although there is an initial market price fall, it is usually only transient (unless the crisis is poorly managed). It is as if the crisis is important only insofar as it tells investors (and other stakeholders) something about the competence of senior management in handling it.

A hesitant response is exacerbated by the fact that different constituencies within the organization will advocate different approaches. The legal department says "say nothing"; public relations says "tell everything"; and engineering says "wait for more data." Evidence suggests that overdisclosure is probably safer than a concern over legal niceties. In a crisis, firms must establish their perspective on the truth and get it into the public domain as quickly as possible. Journalists will always find someone to comment. Other stakeholders will hear through the informal rumor mill anyway; rumors that are likely to exaggerate the problems and, worse still, be communicated to the press. Nor should communications focus only on the press, shareholders, and the general public; maintaining the trust of other stakeholders (such as creditors, employees, and suppliers) is also essential, and can only be done through open channels of communications about the crisis and how it is likely to affect them.

A good example of the importance of public relations management was seen recently following accusations by some Jewish groups against some Swiss banks, which claimed the banks had possession of gold and money taken from them by the Nazis during the Second World War. Pressure from Jewish groups forced the banks to back-pedal on their initial stance of claiming they were unable to trace any funds and demanding the presentation of legal documents (most of which had been lost) before any payment could be made. Such clear and emotive issues raise public passions and huge political pressures irrespective of the logic or ethics of the case.

Dealing With the Crisis

Crisis resolution and recovery involves a brutal triage, prioritizing crisis team efforts to the most critical and least resilient business processes and resources. One aspect of this is financial viability analysis to determine if a crisis-affected company needs to be restructured to achieve sufficient profits required to pay down debt within acceptable time frames dictated by the creditors. This might involve drawing on lines of credit or taking on additional short-term debt. Much of this analysis can jump-start the risk assessment performed as part of pre-crisis contingency planning, although some aspects will be crisis-specific. Resolution then requires recovery—the activities needed to repair, rectify, and restore the damage from the impact of the event and its consequences.

Making Lemons From Lemonade

Finally, the crisis team should be alert to the possibility of redemption. The challenge is to reframe the crisis as an opportunity, making lemonade from lemons. This is easiest when the disaster affects a number of players in the industry and offers a shake-up of the competitive playing field that the business can exploit. Customers, clients, or counterparties who are temporarily poorly served by other firms facing a crisis may be ripe for poaching. Even if the crisis is firm-specific, managers can at least extol the firm's response to the crisis as an example of the firm's superior risk management capabilities. Alternatively, the crisis may have revealed a previously underutilized resource that could be further exploited. These risk management capabilities might even be the basis for future marketing or service lines.

Further information: See also the sections on contingency planning and strategic and business planning. Also see *Crisis in Organizations: Managing and Communicating in the Heat of Chaos* by Laurence Barton (August 1992), South-Western Publishing. This is an excellent book, with lots of case studies describing what happens during a crisis, how to prepare and minimize damage, and how to recover. A more recent work that focuses on the role of negotiation in managing crises is *Managing Outside Pressure: Strategies for Preventing Corporate Disasters* by Matthias Winter and Ulrich Steger, (September 1998) John Wiley & Sons. For a thoughtful guide to rebounding after a crisis, see *Crisis & Renewal: Meeting the Challenge of Organizational Change* (The

Management of Innovation and Change Series) by David K. Hurst (September 1995), Harvard Business School Press. Also useful is *Only the Paranoid Survive: How to Exploit the Crisis Points That Challenge Every Company* by Andrew S. Grove, 1st edition (March 16, 1999) Bantam Books. A variety of organizations promote contingency planning and business continuity; for example, the Business Continuity Institute (BCI) aims to foster the standards of professionalism in the industry, while The International Emergency Management Society provides a forum for academics and practitioners to exchange ideas and experiences in emergency management.

CHAPTER 14

RISK FINANCING

The way a business is financed affects its ability to survive catastrophic losses. Catastrophic losses typically involve rogue trading, insider fraud, bad lending, poorly understood derivatives, new products, emerging markets, counterparty failures, natural disasters, or snowballing reputational losses. Although the frequency of catastrophic events is low, their impact is devastating.

FIGURE **14.1** Risk Financing and the Risk Matrix

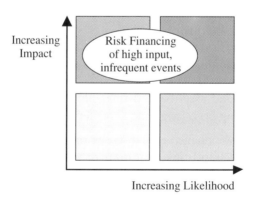

Risk financing involves either transferring the loss to some external party for a fixed premium or restructuring the organization to be more able to handle the risk. Consider the case of risk transfer to external parties first. One way of containing the impact of uncontrollable loss events is to transfer risks outside the firm to others who—because of economies of scale and scope (perhaps through the pooling and netting of risks), superior information, or better knowledge—are better able to manage the risks. Common mechanisms for transferring risk involve hedging, insurance, surety, contracting, securitization, or project financing. Alternatively, firms can decrease the likelihood of default directly by internal restructuring. This could involve providing more capital, decreasing debt levels, decreasing operating leverage, improving internal credit management, increasing the extent of corporate diversification, or developing a self-insurance program.

Bear in mind the famous *Modigliani-Miller proposition*, which suggests that assuming perfect markets, risk transfer or financial reorganization does not add value to shareholders. Risk transfer is therefore only done for a price. Inefficiencies such as tax savings, improved planning, and decreased bankruptcy costs may make this price worth paying. Further, managers should transfer risks if they believe some external party has a comparative advantage in managing these risks. For example, an investment bank is able to underwrite the risks with floating new securities issues better than other financial institutions because of its special expertise in judging market conditions. An insurance firm has a more diversified portfolio of exposures and so can help decrease unexpected losses.

There are several approaches to financing losses:

- Financial restructuring—debt is the cheapest form of external financing, and can allow firms to capture tax benefits, as well as important economies of scale and scope. Increased debt, however, means an increased risk of default. Techniques such as credit management and asset-backed financing help manage the trade-off by restructuring both long- and short-term liabilities.

- Asset–liability management—focuses on restructuring the portfolio of assets and liabilities to minimize sensitivity to liquidity and interest rate risks.

- Corporate diversification—acquisitions or investments in other firms or projects whose cash flows are not perfectly correlated with the firm's other cash flows can decrease the total risk of the firm's net revenues.

- Self-insurance—the firm retains the obligation to pay for part or all of the losses.

- Insurance—an external insurer promises to provide funds to cover specified losses in return for a premium from the purchaser at the inception of the contract.

- Hedging—uses financial derivatives to offset losses occurring from movements in interest rates, commodity prices, and forex rates.

- Contractual risk transfers—these transfer risks through contracts; for instance, by outsourcing or by using independent contractors.

14.1 FINANCIAL RESTRUCTURING

Long-term Financing

The degree of a business' financial leverage (its ratio of debt to equity) does not affect the firm's exposure *per se*, but does affect the firm's ability to survive any major losses. However, it also confers some important advantages over all-equity financing.

Benefits of Leverage   Debt can offer tax benefits over equity financing because interest income is taxed only once at the personal level, whereas equity income (dividends) is taxed both at the corporate and personal levels. Debt is also usually a cheaper means of raising capital than equity issues not only because underwriting fees tend to be less, but also because asymmetries in information between managers and investors make equity offerings less attractive. Another advantage of debt is that it disciplines managers and prevents them from taking things too easy, by increasing their bonuses, or engaging in empire building.

Disadvantages of Leverage   Corporations can be understood as having several distinct tranches of insurance against losses. The first tranche is provided by equity capital, and covers unexpected losses. The second tranche of the insurance, so-called disaster insurance is provided by debt holders. In the case of a bank, the final tranche of the insurance is provided by its depositors. It follows that catastrophic losses exceeding the level of equity will cause the firm to default. Higher levels of debt increase the likelihood of default by making the threshold that much more achievable. Having a high level of debt also makes it difficult to return to the debt markets or go to the banks for top-up financing.

FIGURE 14.2 Financial Leverage and the Likelihood of Default

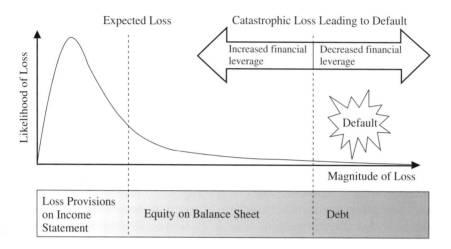

This means that the more highly leveraged firms will find risk management efforts more useful. Conversely, it also implies that risk management can let firms take advantage of the benefits of debt financing. Although the appropriate level of debt is an issue still open to much debate, it seems that debt financing tends to be most prevalent in firms that need a great deal of external financing, perhaps because these firms operate in industries with extensive economies of scale. Businesses with less-risky operational cash flows also tend to carry a larger debt load. For example, real estate companies can be highly leveraged because of the low variance in their operational cash flows (rents). High leverage is less common for risky businesses or when management wishes to maintain a high level of control over the business.

Short-term Financing

Short-term debt is used to finance short-term requirements, such as for financing inventory, or for short-term bridging loans. In no case should short-term debt be used for long-term financing. Short-term debt includes issues of commercial paper or issues of CDs, secured loans, and lines of credit from finance companies, banks, or insurance companies. Although short-term debt is likely to be much less risky than long-term debt (there is less opportunity for a major loss to cause a default), short-term debt does increase interest rate exposures and therefore subtracts from the available risk capital; hence, its use should be carefully monitored.

Credit Enhancement

As well as the level of the debt in the firm's capital structure, its form and structure also affects the risk profile of the business. Credit enhancement restructures the nature of the debt held by the business, in order to make it more marketable, cheaper to issue and service, and thereby less risky. The most important tools for credit enhancement are covenants. These are restrictions on management risk taking and aim to reduce the amount of loss in the event of default. Covenants, for example, might prevent large dividend increases or require that the credit standing stay above some threshold. Breaking a covenant forces immediate renegotiations with debt holders. Collateral and third-party guarantees are also important components of any structured credit enhancement program. These act much like insurance, except that in the event of default, the value of principal is less certain. Structured transactions combine the use of collateral, guarantees, and covenants in equity and debt issues to isolate the risk of the transaction from that of the borrower, and better market the securities to the requirements of the primary markets. Structured or hybrid securities can also be used to minimize conflicts between bond holders and equity holders. For example, *convertible* bonds contain equity options allowing bondholders to participate in the upside, *puttable bonds* give their holder the option to put the bond back to the issuer, while *rating-sensitive notes* make the coupon payments conditional on the firm's credit rating.

Asset-backed Financing

Another increasingly used method of restructuring the risks on the firm's balance sheet ties the financing to specific assets. With asset-backed financing techniques such as *securitization*, investors might purchase securities whose cash flows are payable directly from collections on mortgages, auto loans, credit cards, and other forms of receivables. Through the sale of risky but well-defined assets, securitization decreases balance sheet risks, thereby freeing expensive risk capital. It also diversifies funding sources. Of course, securitization would have limited value if it had a negative impact on profitability. The decision to securitize depends on the risk of the original assets, the market credit spreads across ratings classes, the potential savings in risk capital, the costs of insuring the flows to investors, and the direct costs of setting up and managing the securitization structure.

Leasing is most common means of asset-based financing. There are two basic forms of leases—operating and financial leases. An operating lease is an agreement for a lessor to hire an asset to a lessee for a series of payments. The lessor retains ownership and, therefore, much of the risk of asset loss or damage, but conveys to the lessee the right to use the asset. Operating leases are short-term and cancelable during the contract period at the option of the lessee. Short-term operating leases can be convenient and useful in reducing risk because any unexpected losses are maintained or insured by the lessor. There may also be some tax benefits to using operating leases. Leasing with an option to cancel is especially useful when dealing with equipment (such as IT) that will become obsolete quickly; in effect, the risk of obsolescence is passed from the lessee to the lessor. Unlike an operating lease, a financial lease transfers much of the risk and rewards of ownership to the lessee. Financial leases are longer term and extend over the life of the asset and can only be canceled if the lessor is reimbursed for any losses. Under most financial leases, the lessee promises to insure and maintain the asset. Financial leases are basically the equivalent of secured loans, since if the lessee fails to make the required payments, the lessor will come and repossess the asset. There are some differences in the treatment of leases and secured debt from a tax perspective and also in the case of bankruptcy.

Another increasingly used form of asset-backed financing is *project financing*. Large risky projects tend to be very large users of capital. Project financing allows creditors greater control over the project at the cost of creditors having limited recourse (if any) to the project sponsors. However, the complexity of the project financing may lead to high transaction costs. Project financing may reduce financing costs, allow for a reduction in long-term debt, and help control cash flows. Project financing can be arranged when a related set of assets can function as an independent economic unit. Project equity and debt are then issued, which are self-liquidating from the project revenues. Alternatively, projects can be financed through a variety of sources such as commercial loans, supplier credits, government credits and subsidies, import/export banks, private investors, prepaid output, international banks, public subscriptions, public bonds, and worker ownership. Project financing is repaid through a variety of terms such as fixed-term repayment and fixed interest, fixed-term capital repayment and variable interest, constant amount repayment for interest and capital, adjustable-term repayments and interest on outstanding capital balance at fixed or variable rates, and balloon payments.

Further information: See also Subsection 2.6 on catastrophic risk. For a discussion on the decision-making process behind the selection of a firm's capital structure, see the classic text (particularly Part 5) *Principles of Corporate Finance* (McGraw-Hill Series in Finance) by Richard A. Brealey and Stewart C. Myers (Contributor), (July 1996), McGraw-Hill College Division. A good discussion of credit enhancement and credit risk management is provided by *Managing Credit Risk: The Next Great Financial Challenge* (Wiley Frontiers in Finance) by John B. Caouette, Edward I. Altman, and Paul Narayanan (October 1998), John Wiley & Sons. For a discussion on project financing, see Subsection 10.4, and also *Project Financing: Asset-Based Financial Engineering* by John D. Finnerty (September 1996), John Wiley & Sons. Also useful is *Risk Management in Project Finance and Implementation* by Henri L. Beenhakker (October 30, 1997), Greenwood Publishing Group.

14.2 ASSET–LIABILITY MANAGEMENT

Asset–liability management (ALM) focuses on two particular types of risk that affect the long-term assets and liabilities on the firm's balance sheet—liquidity and interest rate risks. ALM aims to reduce variation from these risks given the firm's expectations of interest rates and its funding needs.

Liquidity Risks

Taking a bank as an example, the majority of its assets are its customers' long-term loans, while its liabilities are made up of short-term customer deposits. Liquidity gaps occur when there is a difference between the level of assets and liabilities required in a particular future time period. Liquidity risks result from those future periods in which liabilities exceed assets and from the uncertainty surrounding the obtaining of funding to cover these gaps. Liquidity risk management requires an understanding of the time profile of available funds, as well as the timing of investment needs and debt payments. The simplest approach to managing liquidity risks is *cash matching*, which involves continuously raising new funds to make the time profile of net assets and net liabilities identical. More sophisticated techniques such as *layering* can be used to pile on layers of new debt to maintain flexibility and be in line with managers' interest rate expectations.

Interest Rate Risks

These occur whenever there is a gap between assets and liabilities at some future date. If liabilities exceed assets, there is an excess of funds; this causes an interest rate risk because of our uncertainty of the prevailing interest rate at which to invest these funds. If assets exceed liabilities, there is a shortage of funds; as well as liquidity risk, there is also an interest rate risk that the bank will have to raise money at expensive rates. Interest rate gaps are defined as the differences between fixed-rate assets and fixed-rate liabilities for a given future period. It can be shown that the interest rate gap in a period is a measure of the sensitivity (or duration) of P&L to changes in interest rates for the same period. Like liquidity risks, controlling interest risks is then translated into a problem of controlling balance sheet interest rate gaps.

Limitations

Gap models for liquidity and interest rate risk management make a number of assumptions. First, they assume that all cash flows can be dated. But this is often not the case with, for example, demand deposits or loans with prepayment options. Second, they assume all cash flows can be mapped to particular time points. Although there are several ways to map intra-period flows, none is without its approximations. Third, interest rate gap models assume that all floating rate assets and liabilities can be treated equally as having no interest rate exposure. This is untrue because of the different floating rate indexes that can be used and the potential resetting of rates during the period. As an alternative to these simple ALM techniques, Monte Carlo simulation models of interest rate movement offer a much richer view of the sensitivity of assets and liabilities to such changes. These models typically involve developing a large number of consistent interest rate scenarios based on formal term structure models and evaluating the changing P&L in each scenario.

Further information: See also the subsections on financial restructuring (Subsection 14.1) and hedging using derivatives (Subsection 14.6). Another helpful introduction, particularly for ALM issues, is *Risk Management in Banking* by Joel Bessis (January 1998), John Wiley & Sons. More in-depth and ALM-specific is *Financial Risk Management in Banking: The Theory and Application of Asset and Liability Management* by Dennis G. Uyemura and Donald R. Van Deventer (Contributor), (November 1992), Probus Publishing.

14.3 CORPORATE DIVERSIFICATION

Firms can reduce their operational risks by diversification—acquiring or investing in other firms or projects whose cash flows are not perfectly correlated with the firm's other cash flows. This has the effect of decreasing the total risk of the firm's net revenues.

How Can Diversification Add Value?

Risk management is rarely the only reason for corporate diversification. There may be economies of scale and scope that drive corporate diversification. There may also be synergies whereby the value of the firm with the acquisition is greater than its value without. In general, when there are economies of scale and scope and synergy, there also tends to be positive correlations between the risks (thus lessening the effect of risk reduction).

There are two distinct forms of diversification—across unrelated businesses and across related businesses. Although the extent of risk reduction for unrelated businesses is greater than for related businesses, there is some evidence that diversification in related businesses (particularly horizontal integration) leads to higher performance than diversification in unrelated businesses.

Unrelated businesses For unrelated businesses, diversification usually involves the acquisition of companies in need of external capital or professional management. Controversially, diversification across different businesses assumes that managers have better knowledge than outside investors. Alternatively, it may be appropriate if there is sensitive information about the company's prospects that cannot be passed to outside investors.

FIGURE **14.3** Diversification Strategies and the Extent of Risk Reduction

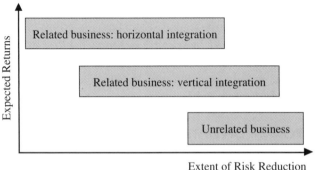

Related Businesses In general, banks, insurance companies, and securities companies have broadened their market coverage and business scope by expanding (mainly through acquisition) into related businesses such as commodity and metal brokering, credit cards, real estate, fund management, and many other finance-related services previously offered only by specialist companies. Risk reduction may be an important rationale for diversification, particularly for vertically integrated businesses. For instance, one firm may be a net borrower (say, a credit card company) and the other a net lender (say, a commercial bank); therefore, the combination reduces the short-term interest rate exposure. More commonly, the rationale for diversification across related businesses (either horizontally through competitors or vertically into customers and suppliers) is the belief that activities shared across the two businesses will lead to lower costs or potential synergies. For example, there are often economies of scale and scope in developing shared IT, communications, product, research, sales, and distribution. Alternatively, there may be revenue synergies across the businesses. Perhaps greater market power (particularly with horizontal integration) leads to greater returns. Perhaps economies of scale, greater learning, and more integrated services allow increased differentiation. For example, many diversifying financial service firms argue the need for one-stop shopping or a financial supermarket. There are many advantages to size, particularly in network-related companies (such as credit cards) where firms can spread the fixed costs over a larger market and more effectively deal with geographically diverse and mobile customers. Another commonly used justification for diversification is that management can transfer a brand, a core competence, or a reputation for a competence from one business to another.

Costs of Diversification

Despite the long list of potential rationales for diversification, for the most part, the expected benefits have not been seen. One reason for this is that business diversification is not cheap. M&A and start-up costs are considerable. There may be diseconomies of scope, particularly if firms branch into very different businesses. With diversification also comes complexity and additional operational risks that are potentially offsetting. For example, turnover of key personnel, incompatible systems platforms, regulatory antitrust concerns, culture clashes, and disgruntled clients are all likely in the aftermath of mergers and acquisitions. Another cost of diversification is the tendency for internal control to suffer and management skills to become diluted, thus increasing the risk of large losses (such as internal fraud).

When Is Diversification Appropriate?

The problem of corporate diversification is that it has major costs, and it may simply replicate the ability of shareholders to diversify on their own. For private companies, diversification is often appropriate because most of the owners' assets are likely to be invested in the business rather than in a diversified securities portfolio. For public companies, shareholders themselves are able to diversify their risks and are not willing to sanction the company doing this for them. From a purely risk perspective, corporate diversification is only appropriate when shareholders find it more difficult than companies to diversify away the risks. This is rarely the case, unless there are relatively unique situations (such as closed markets to which particular firms are granted special access); otherwise, investors can use the technique for themselves equally well.

When Is Diversification Not Appropriate?

Diversification, unfortunately, has tended to be performed for the wrong reasons. For example, some senior managers pursue diversification with an eye to building empires, increasing their own paychecks, and improving their own career prospects. Even when the logic for diversification is sound, diversification has had limited success to because of difficulties exploiting the benefits. Business integration, culture clashes, staff turnover, difficulties developing incentives to cooperate, and problems of control have all made it difficult to realize the potential benefits of diversification.

In reaction to the failure of many diversification strategies, numerous businesses have restructured extensively to refocus on their core business(es). Arm's-length joint partnerships and industry consortia offer less-troublesome diversification alternatives to mergers and acquisitions. This specialization strategy potentially reduces diversification and increases unexpected losses.

Further information: For a discussion of the logic behind diversification and its role in corporate strategy, see Subsection 10.1, and also the collection of articles, *Strategic Synergy* by Andrew Campbell (Editor) and Kathleen Sommers Luchs (Editor), 2nd edition (July 1998), International Thomson Business Publisher. Also helpful is the collection of articles on corporate growth strategies in *Harvard Business Review on Strategies for Growth* (Harvard Business Review Series) (September 1998), Harvard Business School Press. A more practical guide on the process of going through an merger or acquisition is *Mergers Acquisitions and Corporate Restructuring* by Patrick A. Gaughan (Preface), 2nd edition (August 20, 1999), John Wiley & Sons. In response to disappointing results of many firms' diversification strategies, many businesses are looking to refocus on their core businesses. A useful guide in this regard is the book, *Downscoping: How to Tame the Diversified Firm,* by Robert E. Hoskisson and Michael A. Hitt (Contributor), (September 1994), Oxford University Press.

14.4 INSURANCE

Insurance contracts transfer some (but not all) of the risk from the insured (the firm being insured) to the insurer. A typical insurance contract requires the insurer to provide funds to pay for specified losses in exchange for a premium from the purchaser at inception. Insurers then reduce their risk by diversification using a large pool of relatively uncorrelated exposures.

Effects of Insurance

Insurance has the effect of decreasing the standard deviation (unexpected losses) associated with the losses on individual claims. Unfortunately, it may actually *increase* the expected losses associated with the loss because of the insurance loading on the premium; that is, the administrative costs (for example, distribution costs, underwriting costs, and loss adjustment expenses) and the risk adjusted return to insurers.

FIGURE 14.4 Effect of Insurance on the Aggregate Loss Distribution

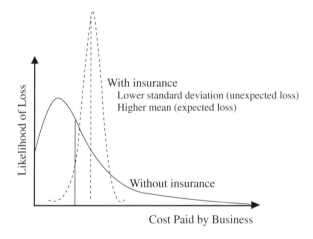

Insurance for Financial Services

The most common forms of insurance relevant to financial services operations include:

• Fidelity insurance

• Electronic computer crime insurance

• Professional indemnity

• Directors' and officers' insurance

• Legal expense insurance

• Stockbrokers indemnity

Fidelity Insurance   This in the form of bankers' bonds or commercial bonds covers against dishonest or fraudulent acts of employees, as well as various forms of on-premises losses, damage to offices, in-transit losses, forgery, counterfeit currency, and some forms of trading losses. While the bankers' blanket bond covers losses associated with employee fraud in a bank's automated systems, it does not usually cover fraud perpetrated by third parties using telecommunications links connected to the computer systems.

Electronic Computer Crime Insurance   This covers computer systems (internal or external service bureau), computer operations, data, viruses, electronic communications, electronic transmissions, electronic securities, and forged Electronic Funds Transfer transactions.

Professional Indemnity Insurance   This covers liabilities to third parties for claims arising out of employee negligence, typically in the course of providing professional services to clients. Professional indemnity policies may also cover the loss of client documents, as well as libel and slander.

Directors' and Officers' Insurance   D&O covers directors and officers for the expenses associated with legal actions arising from the performance of their official duties. The increase in recent years of company insolvency, both small and large, has meant that shareholders and creditors increasingly look for ways to recoup losses against directors. A directors' and officers' policy protects the individuals' personal assets in the event of an action brought against them. Protection is also offered in respect to amounts that the financial institution must reimburse the directors and officers. An alternative to D&O is legal expense insurance, which provides the funds needed to defend claims.

Stockbrokers' Indemnity Insurance   indemnifies the insured against losses sustained as a result of their day-to-day business activities as stockbrokers, in accordance with local regulations and applicable laws. Types of coverage include legal liability arising from transactions entered into pursuant to exchange rules; loss of securities and/or cash; cost of replacing lost securities; and direct losses sustained by the insured arising from fraud, dishonesty, or forgery by employees.

Other common forms of insurance for financial services include general liability, electronic data, safe deposit, excess burglary and robbery, professional liability, fiduciary liability, kidnap and extortion, buildings and contents, and workers' compensation. Protection can also be purchased for terrorism, business interruption, property damage, third-party liabilities, failure of completion, *force majeure,* and political risks.

The Structure of Insurance Policies

Even for a given loss event, insurance policies do not provide full coverage of risks. Deductibles and coinsurance limit the possibility of moral hazard and also reduce the costs of processing very frequent claims. Policy limits restrict the amount that an insurer will pay out for a loss—used when the insured has information about the losses that is very costly for the insurer to obtain. The following exposure diagram shows how the contract apportions the loss between the insurer and the insured.

FIGURE **14.5** The Range of Insurance Coverage

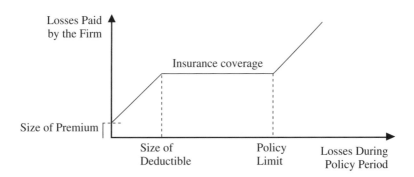

In general, the amount rebated off premiums for each dollar of deductible is greater than that added for each dollar increase in the limit. In other words, a high deductible sends a positive signal that the insured is unlikely to face the risk. Policy limits should be chosen based on the volumes of transactions or the size of assets at the firm. Another issue in the policy structure is the choice of individual or aggregate coverage. For instance, for many fidelity bonds, the limit is based on aggregate payout over a time period rather than on individual occurrences of the loss. The premiums for aggregate loss are usually lower than those for an individual occurrence policy. At issue is whether the loss is remotely likely and that more than one catastrophic event will occur in the same policy period. Another distinction is the use of claims made or loss sustained coverage policies. *Claims made* policies cover any loss discovered within the policy period, whether or not the event actually occurred within the period. *Loss sustained* policies only cover claims that occurred and were reported within the policy period. Not surprisingly, loss sustained policies tend to be cheaper.

When Is Insurance Appropriate?

Insurance is only appropriate for a subset of all possible loss events, those for which the following conditions hold:

- Losses (and therefore claims) in a given firm are largely independent of losses experienced in other firms. This is what allows insurance companies to diversify their risks by pooling. When losses are highly correlated across potential policy-holders, the effect of pooling will be limited and premiums will have a high loading, thus discouraging insurance. Examples of correlated losses are major earthquakes, hurricanes, war, and contagious diseases.

- The distribution of future losses should be predictable. This usually requires the existence of extensive historical data.

- There should be a large demand for the insurance (otherwise, a large pool of insureds is impossible).

- Loss events should be fairly homogenous; that is, have similar frequency and impacts. If this is not the case, insurance companies will be faced with adverse selection, with only the most risky cases insuring and the less risky cases self-insuring.

- Loss must be fortuitous, accidental, and not controllable. Otherwise, moral hazard is likely, whereby the purchase of insurance changes incentives to take reasonable risk management precautions. Traditionally, insurance firms will not insure those risks for which the insureds themselves potentially have better information.

- Individual losses cannot be catastrophic for the insurance company; the insurance carrier only has limited capital to cover the loss. In some countries, however, government guaranty funds may exist to partially cover excess losses.

Advantages of Insurance

Insurance companies have four comparative advantages in bearing risks. First and foremost, insurance companies can pool similar risks by holding a large diversified portfolio of policies, which means that they can dramatically reduce a firm's unexpected losses. Second, their experience in insuring similar risks means that they probably have good estimates of the likelihood and impacts of loss events. Third, the quality of their advisory services may help businesses reduce their risks through various loss prevention and control activities. Fourth, they have access to the wholesale reinsurance markets because of their large volume of transactions.

Disadvantages of Insurance

Of course, insurance firms do have their disadvantages:

Limited Coverage A major limitation of insurance is that many operational risks cannot be insured away. Conventional financial insurance policies cover only 10–30 percent of the available operational losses. Few insurance companies can provide sufficient coverage to handle all the needs of large financial institutions. Insurance firms usually provide offerings such as blanket bonds and professional indemnity, which rarely map precisely to the operational risk categories that banks are increasingly coming to use as described in Subsection 5.5. Worse still, many fraud-related crimes are not covered even by these policies. Furthermore, insurance only reimburses the firm with a preset amount of money to cover the insured loss. This may not be sufficient for events with very uncertain impacts.

Difficulties Covering Large Liabilities Some very large liabilities are difficult to place even among large insurance companies; for example, claims for asbestosis against members of Lloyds of London have already mounted to $5 billion. This problem is particularly acute for claims on correlated losses.

Delays in Settling Claims Sometimes insurance can even act against risk management objectives. For instance, firms that are seeking to limit fluctuations in income may be stymied if there is a sizable delay between the loss event and the settlement of the insurance claim.

High and Uncertain Premiums   There is some evidence that there is an underwriting cycle, related to the business cycle, in which fairly priced premiums are followed by excess premiums and then fair premiums again. Nonetheless, insurance premiums are traditionally expensive. The Surety Association of America has reported that for years less than 65 percent of premiums have been paid out in the form of cash settlements to banks. The administrative costs (just the legal fees can swallow millions) can be large, and will be reflected in the excess of the premium over the expected losses. For insureds, the premiums charged may be not be fair if the market is not efficient. Not surprisingly, high premiums and uncertainty in the premiums have encouraged the use of self-insurance, captive insurance companies, and even hybrid products (such as catastrophe derivatives) to manage risks.

Effective Insurance Management

This requires a systematic approach to risk assessment rather than the traditional *ad hoc* approaches to insurance of particular assets in which one type of risk is insured and another risk—perhaps more important to insure—is ignored. The rules of thumb outlined below can help guide insurance managers when looking at insurance to cover operational risks:

Define insurance requirements   The first step is to develop an insurance requirements document that details the risks concerned. Buying excess, inappropriate, or inadequate insurance coverage may expose directors and officers to personal liability for misuse of corporate funds.

Insurance does not solve operational problems   A business should never insure something it cannot afford to lose. Insurance does not provide recovery from disaster nor does it replace recovery plans. Insurance should be a safety net for some catastrophic losses. When possible, other approaches should be given priority—approaches such as loss control, prevention, and acceptance—because it is usually more cost effective to do so.

Focus on high-impact, low-likelihood events   Exposures with low severity are not likely to be insured because of the high fixed costs of underwriting and distributing policies. Exposures with high frequencies are not likely to be insured because of the high administrative costs.

Figure **14.6** The Use of External Insurance

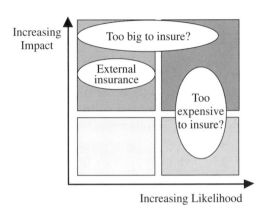

Increasing Impact

Increasing Likelihood

Insurance should only be purchased when the consequences of loss would have a major effect on profits, business continuity, reputation, or the long-term viability of the firm. The purchase of insurance should not be automatic unless it is required by regulation, as is the case for many US banks.

Learn from internal and external loss experiences Companies with relatively good controls and internal risk management should consider experience rating of premiums (*Bonus Malus* systems) or the highest possible deductible for their insurance. They must always be sensitive to the problems of adverse selection that insurance companies face. Adverse selection occurs when an insurance company cannot distinguish between good and bad risks. This tends to make buyers with high expected losses buy more coverage than those with low expected losses when charged with the same premium. The result is that the first group is cross-subsidized by the second, and members of the second group will tend to migrate elsewhere. Adverse selection forces insurers to identify as many factors as possible that may determine expected losses. Risk classification and experience ratings of insureds can be used to better capture the expected losses. Of course, such identification of risk factors is not costless and there are legal limits on the criteria by which insurers can base their premiums.

Find natural hedges   Systematic identification of exposures can lead to unexpected natural hedges within operations, which can cut insurance requirements. An example of such correlated process risk diversification is seen in the increasing tendency of global firms to put manufacturing, sales and marketing operations closer to their major markets, in essence acting as a natural hedge to sovereign currency risks. Recently, a California telecom company, for instance, thought it would lose heavily when a 1994 earthquake destroyed uninsured telephone masts along the San Andreas fault line, but it found these losses were outweighed by windfall revenues when worried families started telephoning relatives. Similarly, LVMH, a French luxury-goods firm, reckons that losses in its Japanese warehouse from the Kobe earthquake were more than paid for by the binge of brandy drinking that followed (*The Economist,* July 18, 1998, Issue 71).

Perform comparative analysis of policies   Comparative analysis usually involves evaluating the insolvency risk of the insurers and comparing contractual provisions, deductibles and limits, legal issues, and so on. These should be carefully documented and systematically followed because they may help show that management has acted prudently and with due care if challenged in court. Of particular importance is industry experience with the insurer. Insurance carriers have a vested interest to trip, stumble, hinder, and delay incoming claims. Low premiums may be a signal that insurance simply swaps an operational risk for a legal one.

Compare the expected annual cost with premiums offered   The difference should reflect the state of the insurance market and the administrative costs associated with the insurance provision. If premiums are much higher, perhaps because of the uniqueness of the risk or the possibility of moral hazard, the company might be well advised to self-insure or accept the risk. Another way firms attempt to cut premiums is through the use of purchasing groups. Several insurance buyers band together, typically on a national basis, to purchase their liability insurance coverage from an insurance company. Purchasing groups tend to have homogeneous members; that is, those engaged in similar businesses or activities that expose them to similar liabilities.

Compare insurance costs against the internal cost of capital After screening potential insurable losses, analyzing internal and external loss data, evaluating any offsetting natural hedges, and comparing the cost of insurance with the expected losses, insurance managers should evaluate the risk adjusted return on the use of insurance. Managers should retain the risk if the cost of the internal risk capital supporting the asset is less than the cost of insuring the asset.

New Trends

Faced with the wide variety of operational exposures and high possibility of legal risks in insurance contracts, one emerging trend is the use of insurance contracts based on losses across a variety of exposures. For example, US giant, Honeywell aggregates pure risks (asset, liability) and currency price risks in the same insurance contract. Contracts such as this are called various names such as *integrated, combined,* or *basket* policies. Whatever their name, their aim is to help firms manage their catastrophic losses, usually by bundling financial and operational risks into a single package. One of the first insurance companies to take this approach to operational risk underwriting is Swiss Re. Its Financial Institutions Operational Risk Insurance product provides coverage for a wide range of exposures and offers immediate liquidity following a disaster. However, the difficulty facing insurance firms, is many-fold. First, the scale and scope of potential operational losses is huge, which makes policy negotiation complex and time-consuming. To manage this and mitigate against moral hazard, insurance firms will typically set very high deductibles for their catastrophe insurance, often as much as $100 million.

Another innovative approach to risk financing is the use of structured debt financing that bundles insurance into debt contracts. These contracts have a structure such that the principal or interest on the debt is forgiven if some major loss event occurs. In 1997, the US Automobile Association raised capital by issuing bonds with the interest and principal contingent on the occurrence of a hurricane catastrophe in the gulf or eastern United States. In Japan, Tokio Marine issued bonds worth $100 million with interest and principal payments linked to the occurrence of an earthquake in Tokyo. In 1998, in the UK, a group of insurers offered an integrated package to British Aerospace that protected the company from credit losses. The boundary between insurance and debt and equity financing seems set to blur still further as many of the traditional insurance (and reinsurance) providers move into the securities markets and banks move into insurance provision. Threats for insurance providers do not only come from securities firms, but also from the insureds themselves. Alternative risk transfer techniques such as risk captives, rent-a-captives, or high self-insured retentions are ways of bundling risks so that the firm benefits from its own diversification across different classes of risks over a long time period (see Subsection 14.5 for more details).

Further information: Many good books provide an overview of insurance theory and practice. One is *Risk Management and Insurance* (Irwin/McGraw-Hill Series in Finance, Insurance, and Real Estate) by Scott E. Harrington and Gregory R. Niehaus (October 1998), Richard D. Irwin. Another useful book for insurance managers is *Risk Management* by Emmett J. Vaughan and Therese Vaughan 1st edition (August 19, 1996), John Wiley & Sons.

14.5 SELF-INSURANCE

Types

When a business self-insures, it retains the obligation to pay for part or all of the losses. There are several common approaches firms use to pay for self-insured losses:

- Using internal funds
- Establishing lines of credit
- Raising external funds
- Using a captive insurer

Internal Funds These include cash flows from ongoing business activities, working capital, or liquid assets to finance losses. Liquidity can be an effective form of risk management. Some firms, particularly some European and Japanese industrial corporations, have so much liquidity that most unexpected losses can be easily cushioned. The ease with which operating cash flows can cover business losses depends on their variability. Somewhat easier is the use of dedicated liquid assets (such as marketable securities) set aside to fund losses when they occur. Of course, it may take some time to build a pool of assets sufficient to cover losses. There is also the challenge of holding a sufficiently large balance of liquid assets to guarantee cash solvency, but not so much as to cripple shareholder returns.

Lines of Credit   These are usually prior arrangements with a bank to borrow up to some predetermined amount at a specified interest rate during a particular time period. If losses were to occur, the firm would draw on these lines of credit as needed. The problem with this is the high premium that banks will charge to guarantee that the funds will be available when needed.

External Funds   The firm can attempt to arrange a bank loan or issue debt following a loss. This is unlikely to be used, however, because it is expensive and time-consuming. Further, in the wake of a business crisis, high transaction costs and severe market underpricing will make external funds (traded debt and, particularly, equity) especially expensive. Interestingly, some insurance companies have issued contingent equity, whereby investors pre-commit to purchasing new stock at agreed-upon prices if a major loss occurs. In particular, these are being used for earthquake and hurricane insurance, for which the losses are highly correlated. Similarly, insurance companies have also issued catastrophe bonds, the interest and principal payments of which can be delayed in the occurrence of a major catastrophe.

Captive Insurance   One increasingly popular way to self-insure is through captive insurance, which involves making payments to a wholly owned subsidiary—known as a captive insurer—which then pays losses. Captive insurers often have insurance transactions with other firms. These are usually established in offshore locations such as Bermuda or the Cayman Islands because of their light regulatory requirements and low taxes. Sometimes captive insurance companies can be rented (so-called rent-a-captives). The main reason for forming a captive insurance company is the different tax treatment for insurance compared with retention. Insurers receive lower tax rates because they can deduct the discounted value of incurred losses during the year, unlike non-insurers, who can only deduct losses that were actually paid during the year. This distinction allows insurers to deduct losses earlier than non-insurance companies, which increases the present value of the deductions. Captive insurers may be a vehicle to allow firms more direct access to the reinsurance markets, which have fewer regulatory constraints because of their wholesale nature. Sometimes captive insurance companies have multiple parents, enabling pooling of the risks across the group members—usually within a specific industry. In that case, they are usually known as *risk retention groups.* As risk retention groups (RRGs) are owned by their members, their key advantage is the extra control members obtain over their liability programs. This control often translates into lower rates, broader coverage, faster payouts, more effective loss control/risk management programs, access to reinsurance markets, and stability of coverage, notwithstanding insurance market cycles. To be effective, a risk retention group will tend to have homogeneous members who are engaged in similar businesses or activities that expose them to similar liabilities.

When Is Self-insurance Appropriate?

The use of self-insurance or, more generally, alternative risk transfer strategies largely reflects the limitations of traditional insurance coverage, such as the lack of insurance coverage for many operational risks, high and volatile premiums, moral hazard, and adverse selection. Traditionally, self-insurance is most used for relatively routine risks that cannot be easily removed through risk prevention, control, and mitigation. These routine losses are relatively predictable and, therefore, there is little point in paying premiums to an insurance company and receiving a fairly constant proportion in claims. Conventional insurance and reinsurance should be used for large potential losses that can cause financial distress.

FIGURE **14.7** The Use of Self-insurance

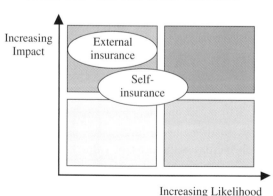

One way to understand the trade-off between conventional insurance and self-insurance is to ask, "Who has the comparative advantage in handling the risk?" Equivalently, firms should retain the risk if the cost of the risk capital supporting the asset is less than the cost of insuring the asset. If the risk is relatively unique to the firm, *no* insurance company will be able to pool its risks and thereby limit its exposure; hence, it will have to charge high premiums to cover the risk.

FIGURE **14.8** External and Self-insurance

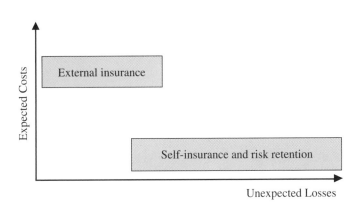

Some firms, such as BP, have challenged this conventional wisdom. BP argued that it makes sense to let local managers insure against relatively routine risks because insurance companies have an advantage in assessing and pricing risks and the markets are relatively efficient. However, BP decided that it would not insure externally against losses above some high threshold. For these larger, more specialized risks, BP felt that insurance companies knew less than it did. Also, the very largest risks (more than $500 million) were impossible to insure anyway. In other words, for large, low-probability risks, the stock market is a more efficient risk absorber than the insurance industry.

More important than the precise philosophy of firm's risk retention is the need for a systematic approach to risk assessment. This should replace the *ad hoc* approaches to insurance of particular assets in which one type of risk is insured and another risk—perhaps more important to insure—is ignored.

Further information: See the subsections on insurance (Sub-section 14.4), hedging (Subsection 14.6), and organizational design (Subsection 9.6). For more detail about the benefits and disadvantages of self-insurance, see *Risk Management and Insurance* (Irwin/McGraw-Hill Series in Finance, Insurance, and Real Estate) by Scott E. Harrington and Gregory R. Niehaus (October 1998) Richard D. Irwin. Also see the following websites: Risk Retention Reporter—provides information on risk retention and purchasing groups for affinity group liability in the alternative risk transfer marketplace: http://www.rrr.com/. A number of reinsurance providers target the alternative risk transfer insurance market, for example, Artis Group Reinsurance: http://www.artisgroup.com/; General & Cologne RE: http://www.genre.com/grn.nsf/doc/grnhome/; Discover Re Managers, Inc.: http://Discover-Re.com/.

14.6 HEDGING USING DERIVATIVES

What Is Hedging?

Hedging involves the purchase of financial contracts such as derivatives (particularly swaps, forwards, and options) to fully or partially offset or hedge the risk of moves in various market factors. Market risks can result from holding financial or non-financial assets whose marked-to-market values co-vary with market risk factors.

For example, businesses' foreign trade and investments in different countries require financing in different currencies exposing them to currency risks; increases in exchange rate volatility has led to the use of FX derivatives such as swaps, forwards, and futures to hedge these risks. Financial institutions use interest rate swaps, futures, and options to hedge their exposures to changes in various interest rates, for instance, by swapping floating rate exposures into fixed ones. Producers' and consumers' commodity risks for electricity, agriculture, metals, oil, and gas risks can be hedged through futures and swaps. Similarly, equity risks can be hedged through equity futures and options, covering possible threats posed by competitors, suppliers, and customers. They may also form part of an effective performance incentives scheme for employees. Nor are market risks the only type of risk that can be hedged using derivatives. Increasingly, credit risks too can be offset through the use of credit swaps and third-party guarantees. So too, some forms of operational risk; for example, catastrophe options have been issued at the Chicago Board of Trade, with pay-offs dependent on estimates of insured losses from catastrophes in particular geographic areas during a particular time period.

Types of Financial Exposure

There are three basic types of exposure. *Operating exposures* are changes in the long-term competitive position of the firm as a result of fluctuations in financial risk factors such as foreign currencies, equity prices, interest rates, or credit spreads. Operating exposures affect economic profits and losses through the demand and the margin rather than through the price. Operating exposures depend on a variety of factors, for instance, the length of time it takes to adjust the production to the demand, the extent to which production is outside the control of the firm, the firm's competitive position and therefore its ability to pass price changes to customers.

Sometimes firms may try to manage other forms of exposure, such as transaction or translation exposures. *Transaction exposures* threaten the results of specific transactions subject to market risk factors (usually shifts in exchange rates). These risks are either passed to customers, in the form of higher prices or to suppliers by coupling advance sales with advance purchases. Alternatively, these risks can be easily hedged using financial instruments such as forwards, futures, and options. *Translation exposures* change the values of assets and liabilities held in foreign currencies. They are not economic exposures and are purely the result of financial reporting requirements; therefore, translation exposures are rarely hedged.

Estimating Exposures

Operating exposures tend to be estimated in a top-down fashion by looking at how firmwide revenues and expenses are affected by different risk factors. Transaction exposures, by contrast, are estimated in a bottom-up fashion by looking at the risks of specific transactions or marketable assets, the desirability of passing these risks to other parties, and aggregating the risks across the business as a whole. See Chapter 3 for a review of the benefits and disadvantages of top-down versus bottom-up models of risk.

Estimating Operating Exposures: Operating exposures are typically estimated in one of three ways. The first is through a statistical analysis of historical revenues and expenses, typically using linear regression models. By assuming that these relations will continue to hold in the future, the firm can estimate its exposures (these are the regression coefficients or betas). The second approach to estimating operating exposures argues that all the firm's exposures can be mapped to a small number of distinct risk buckets whose risk characteristics are known. This is the approach adopted by asset–liability managers for interest rate and liquidity risk. The third approach to estimating operating exposures uses Monte Carlo simulation to model demand, prices, and costs, as well as competitor responses. Although difficult to implement, simulation models allow a wider range of alternative assumptions to be explored and are not restricted to historical patterns. In practice, it is very difficult to hedge most operating exposures with financial instruments. This is because the precise nature of the exposure is hard to define—the timing and the extent of risks are unclear. For instance, operating exposures need to consider not only the effect of price moves on the firm, but they must also predict the impact of price moves on the firm's customers, competitors, regulators, and other stakeholders. Combining these interactions is extremely complex, although qualitative techniques such as scenario analysis and stress testing can provide helpful simplification.

Estimating Transaction Exposures: Many financial services have large portfolios of marketable assets such as loans, securities, and derivatives on (and sometimes off) their balance sheets. Measures of the sensitivity (often called delta) of the value of individual assets to shifts in financial risk factors can be summed to produce the net sensitivity of the entire portfolio to risk factors. Given these sensitivities and estimates of the covariance between different risk factors (a major issue in the tightly coupled financial markets), we can even estimate the portfolio's Value at Risk.

Building Risk Profiles: Whether through modeling operating exposures or by aggregating transactional exposures, firms can develop a perspective on their exposures to particular market risks. For example, most retail banks and S&Ls typically have long maturity assets (such as 30-year mortgages) funded by short-term deposits, which means that they have a net negative interest rate sensitivity (or duration). The operating risk profile for an S&L might then be estimated to look like the following:

FIGURE **14.9** Risk Exposure Profile for a Retail Bank

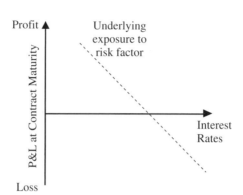

Hedging Vehicles

Market risk (and increasingly, credit risk) is usually offset through financial derivatives either traded on exchanges or over the counter. The value of derivative instruments such as forwards, futures, swaps, and options changes with fluctuations in the value of various underlying assets. Numerical and analytical models for derivative pricing can then be adapted to produce estimates of the derivative's sensitivity to changes in various underlying pricing factors. The most commonly used hedging vehicles include exchange-traded futures and options, as well as over-the-counter forwards, swaps, options, and a variety of hybrid securities made up of combinations of these simpler instruments:

Forwards and Futures Futures contracts are agreements to buy or sell some underlying asset at some future delivery date at a predefined contract price. Traded on organized futures exchanges, they can be used to hedge against changes in commodity prices, interest rates, and exchange rates. A forward contract is like a futures contract except that it is traded in the over-the-counter market. Unlike futures contracts, forward contracts are not settled daily and no funds are exchanged until the contract is settled at maturity. Forwards and futures can be priced in terms of an equivalent position in the spot (the underlying) funded by selling a bond with maturity equal to the delivery date.

FIGURE 14.10 P&L Diagram for Futures/Forward Position at Maturity

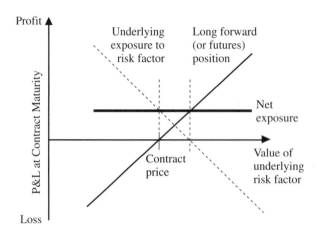

Swaps Swaps obligate two counterparties to exchange cash flows at specific times and are used to hedge existing liabilities and reduce the costs of bond issues. The most common are *interest rate swaps,* in which counterparties swap either a floating interest rate loan for a fixed one or a different floating rate loan. *Currency swaps* exchange fixed-rate cash flows in one currency for floating rate cash flows in another.

Options An option is an agreement giving the holder the right to buy or sell a particular asset during a limited time period at a specific exercise price. These include options on stock indexes, stock index futures, T-bonds, T-bond futures, and foreign currencies among others. Unlike forward contracts, which have no value at initiation, options offer rights (without obligation) to the buyer; this implies that the buyer must pay an up-front cost—the premium of the option. There are two basic types of options: call and puts. *Call options* give the buyer of the call the right to buy the underlying asset at some specific price before some specific date (this is known as an *American option*; *European options* allow purchase or sale only on some specific date). Call options are appropriate if the buyer is trying to hedge some negative exposure (in option terminology this is a negative delta) or expects some increase in the level of the risk factor (the underlying asset). *Put options* give the buyer the right to sell the underlying asset at some specific price before some specific date. Put options are appropriate if the buyer is trying to hedge some positive exposure (positive delta) or expects some decrease in the level of the underlying risk factor. The combination of negative exposure and long call position leads to zero exposure at maturity (no unexpected losses). Similarly, the combination of a positive exposure and a short put position also leads to a zero exposure.

FIGURE **14.11** Negative Exposure and a Long Call

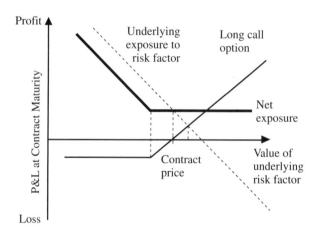

Hybrids The basic building blocks of futures, options, and swaps can be put together in hybrid combinations to tailor specific contingent cash flows. For example, *swap options* (or *swaptions*) give the buyer the right to enter into a swap agreement in the future (usually at some specific date). Similarly, *swap futures* are futures agreements for which the underlying is an interest rate swap. *Caps, floors,* and *collars* are more examples of how swap and option contracts can be combined into useful hybrid combinations. For example, caps are a series of call options on interest rates; when combined with a floating rate swap, they let firms take advantage of falling interest rates and yet offset any major interest rate rises. Similarly, floors are a series of put options on interest rates, and collars are a combination of floors and caps.

FIGURE **14.12** Positive Exposure and a Long Put

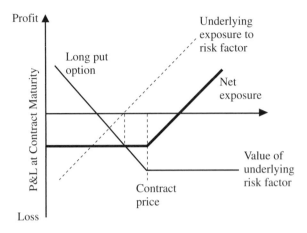

The choice of derivative used to hedge an exposure is not trivial

It depends on a variety of factors. For instance:

Desire for Upside   Option positions offer some participation in the upside should a risk factor move in the company's advantage, whereas forwards and futures lock in a particular price. Of course, this comes at the cost of the up-front premium.

OTC versus Exchange-traded Instruments   In general, over-the-counter instruments such as forwards and swaps are simpler and require less monitoring than exchange-based futures and options. However, the downside is the absence of a liquid secondary market and the importance of managing the credit risks associated with OTC counterparties. If the hedges are part of an active risk management process performed by skilled managers, exchange-traded instruments are more appropriate; otherwise, customized OTC positions typically provide better if more expensive hedges.

Minimize Basis Risks   Hedging requires the existence of closely co-varying marketable assets to use as hedges. The *basis* is the difference between the behavior of the underlying exposure and the hedging vehicle—it is the risk of an imperfect hedge. The effectiveness of a hedge depends on the extent to which the hedge decreases the variance of the hedger's profit. Basis risks result from a poor estimate of the exposure (particularly for operating exposures), or from differences between the derivative's underlying and the firm's basic exposure, or from differences in the maturity of the instrument and the completion of the underlying exposure. For instance, when using forwards to hedge an FX transactional exposure, risk managers should choose a delivery month that is as close as possible to, but later than, the end of the life of the hedge. When there is no futures contract on the asset being hedged, managers should choose the contract whose futures price is most highly correlated with the asset price.

Non-linear Effects There may also be non-linear relationships between asset values that cannot be easily captured in simple linear (constant delta) models. Non-linear relationships are often the result of embedded options. For example, many bank loan contracts (such as mortgages) have an implicit option in that they provide customers with the opportunity to prepay their loan before maturity. If interest rates fall, the value of these options will increase dramatically. To capture non-linear effects, risk models need to incorporate additional risk sensitivities such as the gamma of the position (the sensitivity of delta to changes in the underlying rates or prices).

When Is Hedging Using Derivatives Appropriate?

A more fundamental question that risk managers should consider is under what circumstances financial hedging is appropriate for hedging operational exposures.

• Financial hedging assumes that a firm's operational risk factors are related to market variables in some way, typically through prices or demand volumes.

• Hedging also requires reasonably accurate estimates of the risk exposure. This is less an issue for liquid financial instruments or illiquid instruments for which we establish liquid proxies, but is problematic for many operating exposures. In practice, it is very difficult to hedge most operating exposures with financial instruments. This is because the precise nature of the exposure is hard to define; that is, the timing and the extent of risks are unclear.

- Hedging requires the existence of hedging vehicles with limited basis risk. Derivatives are most common for price-related risk factors because any losses from price moves often have offsetting gains to other parties. For example, an increase in the JPY/USD exchange rate harms the US buyer of Japanese goods but benefits the US seller of American goods to Japan. Most non-price risk factors (for instance, fire damage) do not involve offsetting gains to other firms, and so cannot be hedged.

It is instructive to compare derivatives with insurance. Derivative contracts are used to hedge risks that arise from unexpected changes in market risk factors, whereas insurance contracts are typically used to hedge risks from losses specific to the insured. It follows that specific insurance contracts are of interest only to one firm, whereas derivatives can be traded on a liquid secondary market. Another implication of the contractual structure of derivatives is that basis risk is much more of an issue than it is for insurance. Despite these differences, many of the services provided by traditional insurance can now be performed using options, floors, and caps. For example, there are weather heating degree day index futures, catastrophe options for earthquakes and hurricanes, or Year 2000 options for the millennium bug.

Further information: See the subsections on insurance (Subsection 14.4) and Value at Risk (Box 1.14). See also *Risk Management and Analysis: Measuring and Modeling Financial Risk* (Wiley Series in Financial Engineering) by Carol Alexander (Editor), John C. Hull, Volume 1 (March 1999), John Wiley & Sons. This book provides a methodical analysis of financial risks and the instruments used for hedging. Another useful book on financial risk measurement is *Beyond Value at Risk: The New Science of Risk Management* (Wiley Series in Financial Engineering) by Kevin Dowd (April 1998), John Wiley & Sons. For more details on the derivatives used to hedge exposures, including analytical and computational approaches for valuation and sensitivity analysis, see *Derivatives: The Theory and Practice of Financial Engineering* (Wiley Frontiers in Finance Series) by Paul Wilmott (November 1998), John Wiley & Sons.

14.7 CONTRACTUAL RISK TRANSFER

Contractual risk transfer uses the legal contracts that define relations between stakeholders to shift risks from the business to another party. This other party may be an employee, a customer, a counterparty, a supplier, or even the general public.

Employment Contracts

Employees are essentially a form of debt holder. In return for a prior claim (lower downside risk) on the assets of the firm, they relinquish participation in the upside. An employee of a firm renders services in return for remuneration. An employment contract lets employers control the action of employees—both what they are supposed to do and the manner in which these tasks are performed. In return for this control, employers face additional risks. Employers are vicariously liable for the actions of employees while they are acting in the course of their employment. Of course, various forms of fidelity insurance can be used to transfer some of these employee risks. Employees may post bonds in the case of high risk positions. Another risk reduction mechanism implicit in employment contracts is the form of payment. Payment by time, payment by unit of work (piece rates), payment by results, and bonuses all provide different ways of structuring the remuneration component of the employment contract. Payment by time makes the remuneration a fixed cost, thus increasing the firm's operating leverage and its unexpected losses. Piece rates and payment by results make remuneration a variable cost, thus decreasing the operating leverage and the firm's unexpected losses. The results may be tied to individual results or to office, division, or firmwide results, as in the case of stock options. In general, however, motivation is most likely to be improved if performance measures are directly under the control of the individual employee. This obviously becomes difficult at more senior levels of management; for example, when executives held responsible for corporate performance hold stock call options or warrants whose value increases with increases in the stock price.

Independent Contractors

As with the piece-rate employee, any form of external contracting converts fixed costs to variable costs, which decreases operating leverage—a major risk factor for net income. Unlike an employment relation, employers cannot control the manner in which an independent contractor performs the work, leading to the potential for unexpected operational losses. Nor is the employer vicariously liable for the actions of an independent contractor. Firms that hire independent contractors routinely enter into contracts known as "hold harmless and indemnity agreements" that require the contractor to protect the business from losing money due to lawsuits that may arise if people are injured by the contractor (lower unexpected legal losses). Knowing this, of course, the contractor is likely to charge a premium for his or her services.

Outsourcing/Factoring

Outsourcing is the passing of operational risks associated with performing a task inside the firm to an outside vendor. Outsourcing of routine services such as custodial services, property management, computer servicing, and HR, has been extended to include many technology based staff areas. The most striking example of this to date, was JP Morgan's decision in 1996 to outsource much of its technology infrastructure in several key centers, everything from data centers to voice services, from payroll to trade processing, to the Pinnacle Alliance, an industry consortium consisting of JP Morgan, CSC, Andersen Consulting, AT&T Solutions and Bell Atlantic Network Integration. Application service providers (ASP) such as Cygnifi are beginning to allow banks to outsource even high-end analytical services in investment and corporate banking.

At first glance, outsourcing moves resources from the balance sheet to the income statement, swapping one set of internal costs for external ones. But it also swaps operational risks. In particular, it replaces them with relationship, legal, and default risks of the vendor; possible security risks; loss of innovation; and organization integration problems. A recent survey by Dun & Bradstreet, suggested that between 20 percent and 25 percent of all outsourcing relationships failed within two years and half failed within five years. Furthermore, factoring or outsourcing is rarely appropriate for areas involving a firm's core competence because it essentially commoditizes the services and products produced.

On the other hand, outsourcing has a host of potential benefits. Outsourcing may improve business focus by releasing management and capital resources. It may give access to best-in-class capabilities, thus reducing operating costs. Outsourcing is therefore most appropriate for out-of-control or poorly performing operations with high volumes involving a mature technology and non-proprietary capabilities.

Service Contracts

A variety of mechanisms—such as pricing, warranties, and service-level agreements—can be used to share the risk of unexpected losses between buyer and seller. Of course, there is no inherently best allocation of risk between the two sides of the transaction. From the seller's perspective, risk reduction must be balanced with the need to add value and further differentiate its products and services. From the buyer's perspective, cost reduction (an expected loss) needs to be balanced with the need to limit unexpected losses.

Pricing For contracts involving services that are incurred over a protracted period, the costs of service provision may fluctuate dramatically, thus leading to unexpected transaction losses. This can be mitigated by the pricing structure. The choice of pricing contract has a large effect on assignment of risks between buyer and seller of products and services. For example, a fixed-price contract assigns all the risk to the seller, whereas a cost plus contract shifts the risk to the buyer. Somewhere between these two extremes, service providers can have renegotiation clauses, or use index or quality-based pricing to partially offload the risk to the buyer. The choice of currency and the precise timing of the cash flows also shifts the risks from buyer to seller, depending on whether payments are a lump sum on completion, by installments, or progress payments made as the work is carried out.

Terms of Sale Another aspect of risk management between suppliers and users are the terms of sale. When customers or suppliers are in low risk businesses, sellers will generally demand less-strict terms of credit. Sellers' choice of different commercial credit instruments such as promissory notes, commercial drafts, trade acceptances, and letters of credit shift the risk of non-payment of bills from the seller to the buyer and other third parties. Credit managers will offer different terms of sale to different classes of buyers. Credit checks, bond ratings, credit scoring, and financial ratios can all be used to predict the likelihood of non-payment. Even if payment is not forthcoming, *collection agencies*, third-party *receivables factoring,* and even *credit insurance* can be used to limit the unexpected losses caused by non-payment.

Warranties and Service Agreements   Warranties commit the service provider to specific quality levels. These can be viewed as service providers' selling put options on the value of the service or product. In this way, warranties transfer the risk of unexpected losses facing the business user to the service provider. Much like warranties, *service level agreements* are written contracts between service providers and business users defining the level of service acceptable to both parties. Particularly common in the provision of IT and telecom services, they typically define levels of service availability, quality, reliability, performance, recoverability, pricing, billing, and auditing. Businesses service providers and users should tailor their SLAs according to the most critical aspects of the service; this will differ according to the type of service required. For example, SLAs for an insurance company's mission-critical applications (say, a phone center) will emphasize pricing and very high levels of reliability. SLAs for high-visibility applications (such as payroll) may emphasize recovery and auditing. SLAs may even be dynamic, changing pricing in response to changing loads; for example, some telecom providers will do this.

From the perspective of the service provider, service level agreements have a number of advantages. They help differentiate the service, facilitate communication between the provider and the business user, and also demonstrate the provider's commitment to proactive management. Of course, guaranteeing these levels of service may be expensive in terms of staff, hardware, and software; the firm may require high levels of redundancy to cope with widely varying loads and user demands.

From the business user's perspective, SLAs reduce unexpected operational losses by providing an objective basis for gauging service effectiveness, assuming that staff is assigned to monitor the compliance of the SLA. Of course, they also tend to lock customers in, and may prevent them from shopping for lower rates.

Accreditation, Guaranty, and Suretyship

Another form of contractual risk transfer focuses on removing uncertainty about the risks rather than managing the underlying risk (recall that uncertainty is subjective and dependent on the observer, whereas risk is objective and dependent on the situation—see Subsection 2.3 for a discussion). *Accreditation* reduces uncertainty by confirming performance to a well-defined standard. This is done for a fee with few subsequent legal obligations on the part of the accrediting agency. For example, quality assurance firms offer ISO 9000 certification services, ratings agencies offer credit ratings. *Guaranty* and *surety* services reduce uncertainty by precisely ascertaining the exposure of an individual case. Unlike accrediting agencies, guaranty and surety services charge a premium/service charge to cover the residual likelihood of default. For example, a title guaranty company might investigate a real estate title, assure itself that there is no uncertainty about the title, and then guarantee the validity of the title. Insurers offer surety bonds—written agreements that provide for compensation if a principal fails to perform certain acts as promised. Credit assurance and guarantee companies can provide credit risk protection, in the same way an investment bank assumes the risks by underwriting the issue to guarantee a given offer price.

Further information: A legal contract is only one component of a business relation. For a discussion of relationship management, refer to Subsection 9.7. Contractual risk transfer hinges on the vagaries of contract law, which varies by legal jurisdiction. For information about US contract law and its implications, see the famous *Basic Contract Law* (American Casebook Series), by Lon L. Fuller and Melvin Aron Eisenberg, 6th edition (June 1996), The West Group. For further information on outsourcing refer to Ernst & Young and J.P. Morgan's Internal Audit department, which offers a series of guidelines on their Vendor Risk Management Program. The Federal Bank of New York in October of 1999 produced a useful report on "Outsourcing Financial Service Activities: Industry Practices to mitigate risks." There are also a number of outsourcing supplier websites with extensive case histories, such as www.eds.com, www.ibm.com and www.csc.com.

Operational Risk Management in Practice

The practical implementation of systematic operational risk management on a firmwide basis is a major challenge. To mitigate against project risk and leverage the firm's risk management efforts, it is imperative that the results of any risk analysis and risk management interventions be systematically monitored and reported. Chapter 15 develops tools for risk reporting while Chapter 16 considers the downstream use of operational risk measures for capital allocation.

CHAPTER 15

MONITORING AND REPORTING OPERATIONAL RISKS

15.1 LEARNING AND RESPONSE LOOPS

One of the major themes of this book is that effective management response to risks should follow a systematic assessment of the firmwide risks. It should not simply be a knee-jerk response to specific loss events; otherwise, management will fall in to the trap of reactive firefighting. Nor should managers be insensitive to the possibility that the risks may have changed and therefore their assessments may be in need of update. As described in Sections II and III, the different steps of risk identification, assessment, analysis, and developing effective management interventions, is an ongoing process of response to changes in the operational exposures. Simultaneously, risk managers should learn to recognize any structural changes that could make their existing models and loss data less relevant or even obsolete. The entire risk control system comprises these two interlocking and dynamic processes of response and learning (Figure 15.1). These two dynamic processes of operational response and learning must be explicitly structured and monitored using a series of reports discussed later in this subsection.

FIGURE 15.1 Risk Management Learning and Response

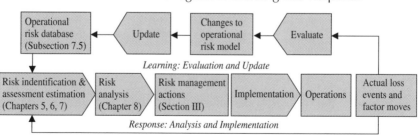

Risk Reporting

Understanding the status of the entire risk control system at different times requires a systematic reporting structure. Gerald Corrigan, the former president of the Federal Reserve Bank of New York, described risk management as "getting the right information to the right people at the right time." Given the importance of both response and learning loops, effective risk reports must capture the state of both, either periodically or in response to specific exceptions. Reports should target critical aspects of the sense/response loops and should be structured accordingly. The generic structure shown in Figure 15.2 is typical.

FIGURE 15.2 Risk Management Reports

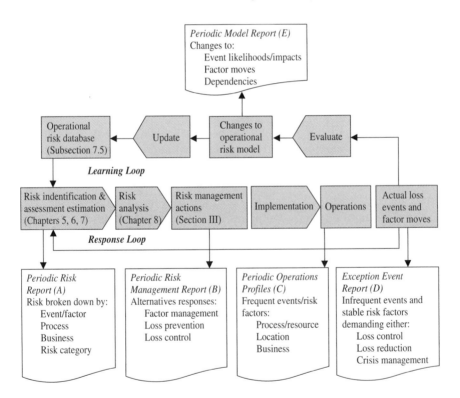

For example, the following periodic reports might be found in a typical operations group:

TABLE 15.1 Critical Risk Management Reports

Report	Frequency	Addresses following issues	Ref. (Subsection)	Contents
Risk report (A)	Depends on volatility	What major exposures do we have? How can we prioritize them? Where do they come from? Any common themes?	15.5	Describes the projected risks in a given time period broken down by event, process/resource, geographic location, risk category, controller, source.
Risk management action report (B)	Weekly	What can we do about particular risks? How effective is it likely to be? How effective are any current risk initiatives?	15.6	Develops action item agenda for follow-up meetings with line managers. This should be combined with an action status report describing the progress of action items.
Operations profiles (C)	Daily	Is there a major change in some risk factor that could put operations at risk?	15.4	Monitors key performance indicators such as level of internal risk factors and the number and description of exceptions.
Event report (D)	Exception	What happened? How did it happen? What did we do about it? What can we learn?	15.3	Describes recent loss events, causes, impacts, and adequacy of firm's responses.
Model report (E)	Monthly	Is the model accurate? Useful? Does the model need to be changed?	15.8	Shows ongoing model performance relative to real event occurences.
Summary reports	Periodic	How effective is our approach to risk management?	15.7	For example, executive report: describes monthly provisions, impact, frequencies update, and write-offs. Also quarterly overview risk reports to audit committee, control committee.

These reports should be accessible online, rather than in paper form, and will need to be archived to provide internal learning and proof of due diligence. We will discuss each of these different reporting elements, but first it is helpful to discuss more general issues that make a reporting structure effective.

Further information: For further information about control and reporting structures for risk management, particularly market risk management, see *Risk Management For Financial Institutions: Advances in Measurement and Control* by Risk Books.

15.2 GUIDELINES FOR EFFECTIVE REPORTING

One of the challenges of operations management is coordinating, preparing, and interpreting the plethora of management reports that describe the process. Firms are starting to develop more formal guidelines for their reports. Without a systematic approach to reporting, any risk management system is doomed to irrelevance. There are some basic principles of effective operational reporting that are especially important for operational risk management. Reports need to be clear, in context, complete, consistent, user-focused, timely, and actionable with limited redundancy.

Clarity

Good reports are efficiently organized to provide clear answers for the issues under analysis. Many reports fail to do this by just supplying numerical tables, thus leaving the reader to do the vital last step of inferring the answer to the question from the data given. Complex reports based on statistical or analytical models are difficult for most general managers to quickly comprehend without the necessary training; as a result, they may be reluctant to trust the implications of the model and the message of the report. Making the model as transparent as possible is the key to management credibility. Reports should identify the questions/ issues that the audience of the report is seeking to answer and not overload the user with extraneous detail. For similar reasons, precision is less important than accuracy and in any case should never be overdone. For instance, uncertainty in variables and management responses makes it impossible to justify, in most cases, more than one or two decimal places of precision. The use of graphical displays, particularly for aggregate risk reports, can get the message across much more effectively than numeric tables. Of course, any report should at the same time avoid distorting the data. For this reason, drill-down facilities should always be available so that users can, if required, have access to the underlying data and make their own judgments.

Need for Context

It has been estimated that 20 to 30 percent of risk management executives' time is spent "understanding context or explaining it to others." For instance, a report that claims a firm's credit rating is "AA" must be interpreted in terms of the rating agency that produced it and the risk rating of the sovereign nation under which jurisdiction it falls. Risk data should not be shown out of context. Context can be simple comparisons with other time periods, firms, locations, or processes, or it can be defined by the various assumptions made by managers about the internal and external environment. Risk reports are invariably tools to support comparison of different data elements; for example, the risk across different processes or offices, or a model's predictions versus the actual outcomes. It follows that the reports should be designed to encourage the reader to link different related pieces of data.

Another important aspect of providing a context are the assumptions required to interpret the data. Actuarial loss models or models of VaR are meaningless without some understanding of the assumptions made by that particular model. All reports based on a model must outline the assumptions made by the model and state explicitly where the assumptions fail to hold. This said, because assumptions are not usually the primary focus of the report, they should not intrude into the foreground of the report and should be accessible only when needed. Also useful for setting context are simple schematic diagrams of the key variables in the model and how they are integrated to produce an aggregate risk estimate.

Completeness

Reports should be complete and capture all material loss events and risk factors that affect the processes and resources of the organization. No material exposures that are relevant to the audience of the report should be omitted.

Consistency

Risk reports should consistently measure risks using standard criteria and be applied in the same way across different business areas. There is a strong possibility of reporting error if different models are used to calculate risk numbers in different areas of the firm and then aggregated. For instance, one model with a 10-day holding period and another with a 1-day holding period cannot be readily aggregated without additional assumptions (about the evolution of asset values over time). Any assumed correlations also need to be made explicit. One way to ensure consistency is to develop a standardized and transparent process for producing risk reports, rather than leaving them to the vagaries of individual preparation and usage.

User-focused

Reports should only contain information focused on those aspects of risk that are relevant to the readers of the report. For instance, the level of aggregation described in the risk reports should be appropriate to the audience of the report. Conversely, the circulation of the reports should reflect their contents. Without a user focus, information overload is likely to make the reports irrelevant or, worse yet, disruptive because of their utilization of scarce management time and attention.

Timeliness

The frequency of periodic reports should be chosen to reflect the variance of the underlying risk exposures and the lead times for managers' remedial actions. Operational risk reports can be *exception-based* or *periodic.*

Exception Reports   Exception reports describe critical loss events or major risk factor moves, their causes, potential impacts, and how these events might be mitigated or prevented in the future. Exception reports, as the name implies, should only be used for infrequent events with high potential impact. Summaries of exception reports should be entered into the organization's internal loss log for subsequent updating of risk estimates. Exception reports should also be filed for future reference— they can be usefully incorporated into stress tests and scenario analyses and may also be used to benchmark risk management initiatives. The readership of the exception report should depend on the nature of the event and what can be done to predict, prevent, and mitigate it in future. Exception reports should not be simply focused on handling the particular event; they can also be used at the start of analysis to determine, for example, if unexpectedly high losses are the result of an ongoing trend, bad luck, or problems in the model. Exception reports, particularly those for factor moves, may also update a *watch list*. The watch list focuses on events and risk factors as they become more likely than before. This is particularly easy to do if the causal structure of events and risk factors has been well-mapped. Some operational risk models (for example, Bayesian Belief Networks) can estimate events' new conditional probabilities and use that to direct more resources to preventing the event (such as additional reporting, more staff allocated, and increased audit and monitoring).

Periodic reports Unlike exception reports, which focus on specific events and risk factor moves, periodic reports capture systematic changes in the state of the organization's process and resources. Explicit to every periodic report is the time dimension—how the state has evolved since the previous report, which is taken as a benchmark. For example, control charts can be used to show how some attribute (such as event frequency or impact) has evolved over a time period; patterns in these time series can then reveal previously hidden structural changes that need to be managed. Periodic reports can then lead to exception reports, such as when actual losses exceed some limit as defined in the periodic report.

Actionable

Reported risk should be actionable—people can do something about it. Reports should suggest changes rather than merely describe the existing state of the system. Reports should avoid the temptation to produce a list of causes that no one can actually change. If changes are proposed, the expected costs and impacts of the changes should also be evaluated.

Lack of Redundancy

Reports should be non-redundant; that is, information contained in one report should not be needlessly replicated in other reports.

Further information: For further information on the art of developing clear reports and graphics, see the seminal book, *The Visual Display of Quantitative Information,* by Edward R. Tufte (February 1992), Graphics Press. Also useful is *Information Graphics: A Comprehensive Illustrated Reference: Visual Tools for Analyzing, Managing, and Communicating* by Robert L. Harris (November 1997), Management Graphics.

15.3 EVENT REPORTS

Event or *incident reports* are short, usually unstructured reports produced by a staff manager close to some recent and unexpected event with a significant negative impact. Event reports try to direct loss control and loss reduction activities, and improve the organization's understanding about the causes of the event and how they might have been prevented or better controlled. Event reports may range from a terse memo demanding immediate action to an in-depth case study to facilitate strategic and organizational learning. Obviously, exception reports should not slow down the process of controlling or reducing the loss. All exception reports try to answer some of the following questions as quickly as possible:

- What really happened?
- Why did it happen?
- What needs to be done immediately to reduce or control the loss?

More detailed (and time-consuming) event reports will also address:

- What was the (direct and indirect) damage or consequence?
- What was different or unusual about this event?
- What additional controls might have prevented this?
- Did any event or action occur that might have made it better or worse?
- Did staff do what they were supposed to do?
- Did staff know what they were supposed to do?
- Has this happened before?
- What was done before to fix it, if anything?
- Who reported this?
- What are the organizational or policy implications of the event?

Well-designed event reports can focus management attention on problems and their immediate solutions. They can only be used to facilitate organizational learning about the risks (see Subsections 6.4 and 6.5 on historical event data) if they are integrated into internal loss logs, from which new frequency and impact distributions are then produced. However, event reports do have their limitations. An overemphasis on rapid crisis management response (Subsection 13.4) through e-mails or online event reports may only encourage a reactive approach to risk management.

15.4 OPERATIONS PROFILES

Content and Preparation

Operations profiles describe both indicators of key risks (KRIs) and of process performance (key performance indicators—KPIs, sometimes called pulse points). KRIs can either be attributes of the events (such as their frequency or impact), or of risk factors, whereas KPIs target resources, or process throughput. Operations profiles capture some important and potentially volatile aspect of the state of the system—the elements that an experienced senior manager might check on during daily rounds. For operational risk management, for instance, KRIs usually correspond to the level of aggregate losses or the number (frequency) of losses in the previous day or week. Operations profiles are most relevant as measures of volatile risk factors or frequent loss events. For instance, if power outages are infrequent, occurring on average only every few years, there is little point in producing weekly reports. The operations profile should also include contextual information to help managers understand why a particular variable may have changed. Information about change events (such as new staff, new systems, new transactions, and so on) and risk factors (such as the level of overtime or the volumes of transactions) can aid interpretation.

Ideally, operations profiles should be generated automatically by on-line transaction systems. Some (but not necessarily all) of the risk information for operations profiles should come from the internal loss log and the change event log (Subsection 6.4).

Control Charts

Operations profiles are usually structured in the form of a statistical control chart, which identifies specific variables of importance to an operational manager.

Control charts are a technique borrowed from statistical quality control. Although most prevalent in manufacturing, they are becoming increasingly used in the financial services. Control charts describe the variation over time intrinsic to a sampled variable, and test if the distribution of this variable has changed in terms of level, range, or form (see Figure 15.3 for an example). The variable chosen is usually some aspect of the quality or performance of the process or product under analysis. Examples of such variables might be the number of particular loss events over time (such as trading errors), the number of transactions, excesses over limits, the number of unreconciled items over time, or the levels of important risk factors (such as the level of volumes or outstanding positions). Any significant change in the measured variable indicates that the process is no longer "in statistical control." Depending on the distributions ascribed to the variables under study, limits reflecting management control bounds can also be defined and appropriate management responses prescribed.

FIGURE 15.3 Basic Control Chart

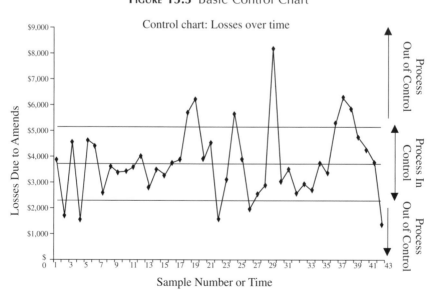

Control charts have three basic parameters: the *sample size,* the *frequency of sampling,* and the *width of the control limits.* These are all related; as frequency increases, sample size decreases and control limits become wider. Managing the trade-off between these three parameters lies at the heart of developing effective control charts:

Sample Size   Does every transaction or process component need to be surveyed? If the unexpected loss associated with individual transactions is relatively low, then exhaustive sampling of every transaction may not be appropriate. If the unexpected loss associated with individual transactions is high (although the expected loss may be small), then the control chart should cover all the transactions produced by the process; that is, an exhaustive sample. Unfortunately, exhaustive sampling can be expensive. One compromise between random sampling and exhaustive sampling uses *dollar-based sampling,* which is based on the dollar size of a potential loss—typically the size of the transaction. In this way, critical transactions are much more likely to be sampled rather than low-value vanilla transactions. When dealing with very infrequent events, event frequencies (such as the number of failures in a time period) may be less useful than the times between events (times between failures). In the case of infrequent samples of infrequent events, control limits usually require very asymmetric distributions (such as exponential for constant failure processes), and this tends to make interpretation and explanation of control limits difficult.

Frequency of Sampling   Control charts typically take samples based on readily comparable work periods such as shifts, trading days and work weeks. If we use chronological time as the baseline for our analysis, sample sizes may also need to vary to compensate for changing volumes (for example), which in turn means that the control limits will fluctuate over time (see Figure 15.4 for an example).

FIGURE **15.4** Control Chart With Dynamic Limits

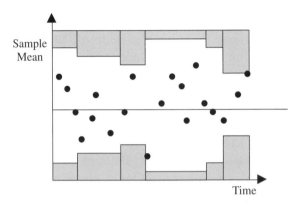

Control Limits: If we assume that the underlying variable is normally distributed, then the sample mean will also be distributed normally and the limits become multiples of the standard deviation (typically $\mu \pm 3\sigma$). If the underlying variable is not normal, the mean is still approximately normally distributed for a sufficiently large sample because of the *Central Limit Theorem*. The Central Limit Theorem also suggests that the individual observations will have a variance that equals the sample variance times the sample size.

FIGURE **15.5** Limits in a Control Chart

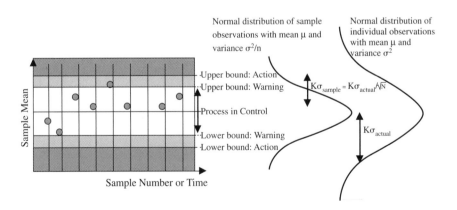

Limits can be simple—prompting warnings or actions if the last sample statistic is beyond some bound—or more sophisticated triggers—perhaps if either of the two most recent observations are beyond $\mu \pm 2\sigma$ levels or if there are more than three consecutive increases in the variable. Control charts can be used for sample ranges $(x_{max} - x_{min})$ as well as sample means. The distribution of the range of samples taken from a normal distribution has its own well-defined distribution, the details of which can be found in a good text on statistical process control. Range charts used in conjunction with mean charts identify whether the variables' mean is stable while the variance has shifted or whether the mean has shifted while the variance has remained constant.

Qualitative Control Charts Control charts can be used for qualitative attributes as well as quantitative ones. Quality engineers often look at a range of quality measures and incorporate them into a single measure of acceptability much as process engineers often talk about process "fails" such as the number of payments made in error or distributed late. For example, a sample of 500 invoices might be randomly selected and checked to see if they have been prepared correctly. Using binomial distributions to estimate control limits, the number of fails can be tracked on a control chart as easily as any continuous normally distributed variable. The fraction of the sample failing is the ratio of the number of failed transactions in the population relative to the total number of transactions. Binomial distributions are often used to model the distribution of such fractions. Suppose a process has a probability p of a particular transaction failing and that successive transactions are independent of one another. Then the number of failed transactions (F) in a sample of n is given by the binomial distribution with parameters n and p.

$$p(F = x) = \binom{n}{x} p^x (1 - p)^{n-x} \text{ where } x = 0, 1, 2, \ldots n$$

The mean of the random variable F is np and its variance is $np(1-p)$. From the sample, we can estimate the mean as the number of fails in the sample relative to the sample size (F/n). The standard deviation of this sample mean is given by:

$$\sqrt{\frac{p(1 - p)}{n}}$$

Knowing the standard deviation, we can easily construct the control limits, perhaps $\mu \pm 3\sigma$:

$$p \pm 3\sqrt{\frac{p(1 - p)}{n}}$$

Using Control Charts   Control charts are concerned with controlling a process that produces an output. The process is studied by sampling its output and then making statistical judgments on what is happening to the process. Control charts are used to plot the performance of the process. If the process starts to go wrong, it can be stopped before many errors are made. An experienced eye looking at the control chart can often determine the source of potential problems. For example:

TABLE 15.2 Diagnosing Control Charts

	Chart type	Diagnosis
	Large number of runs—sequences of increasing (or decreasing) points	Observations are not independent. Look for changes in staff, tools, or processes coincident with runs
	Cyclic patterns	Problem with the process such as seasonal effects, fatigue, work load build-up, or staff rotation
	Mixture is shown when points have a tendency to flip between the control limits with few points near the center line	This can result from overcontrol or from mixing results from very different sources with different distributions

TABLE **15.2** Cont'd

	Chart type	Diagnosis
	A shift in process level	May occur as a result of new staff, new systems, new processes
	Clustering around the mean	The control limits are incorrectly estimated or estimated using historical data that are no longer relevant
	Trend	Learning or the presence of supervision or fatigue

The goal, of course, is to use control charts to improve the process. More detailed analysis of historical charts, coupled with root cause analysis, FMEA, fault tree analysis, and other causal modeling techniques (see Subsection 7.4) can later be used to discover the reasons for the process breakdown and ways to control it in the future. Additionally, statistical experiments on the effect of interventions can be performed by noting the timing of any process control interventions on the control chart and producing a time-based record of intervention and their impacts. For further information, see Subsection 6.4 on loss logs, and Subsection 7.4 describing the use of statistical experiments.

Limitations and Costs When using control charts or any other form of inspection or quality control procedure, it is critical to remember that inspection as a means to detect the quality of a process is always going to be expensive. Prevention is almost always a more cost-effective solution for reducing errors to such low levels that no inspection or sampling is needed. The costs of control charts lie in sampling and in management interpretation of the reports. In both cases it makes sense to develop control charts for high risk processes and resources or those upstream processes and resources that cause risk elsewhere in the system. This assumes that the results of the control chart are passed quickly to the managers and staff involved in the process.

Control charts can be expensive and time-consuming; if found to be unhelpful, they should be quickly removed. Control charts have traditionally focused on statistical aspects of the failure process (such as the mean and standard deviation), and have historically ignored the costs of sampling and analysis, and the indirect costs of failure (such as other events caused and reputational costs.)

Control charts typically focus on the last plotted point and disregard information contained in the entire sequence of points. This can be remedied by using a cumulative sum chart or exponentially moving average charts that aggregate shifts in the levels so that they can be seen more clearly. This is really an application of *time series analysis* and usually suggests that observations are not, as assumed in most control charts, independent of one another. ARIMA models can be used to test this, basically regressing the level of failures in the current sample against the number of failures in prior samples. Control models such as this are, in essence, assuming a Poisson distribution for the failure rate; that is, constant probability of failure over unit time. As discussed in the section on reliability engineering, non-constant failure rates—such as Weibull failure rates or combinations of different failure processes— are also possible.

Further information: For further information on operational profiling and control charts, see Subsection 9.2 on quality management and, for a technical discussion on sampling and probability, control charts, designed experiments, and other statistical process control tools, see *Introduction to Statistical Quality Control* by Douglas C. Montgomery, 3rd edition (August 1996), John Wiley & Sons. Also useful is *Implementing Six Sigma* by Forrest W. Breyfogle III (1999), John Wiley & Sons. For further details of attribute sampling, see *British Standard Specification BS6001*, *Inspection*, and *Statistical Process Control*.

15.5 RISK REPORTS

Unlike event reports (which describe specific historical incidents) and operations profiles (which describe the current performance of a process), risk reports are forward-looking, and focus on the potential for future losses due to operational events and risk factors. Their goal is to proactively identify risk "hot spots." These may be events, processes, offices, and even businesses that contribute a great deal to expected, unexpected, or catastrophic losses.

Event Risk Reports

Event risk reports detail the potential for loss from different events. The information for event risk reports comes directly from loss event tables (see Subsection 7.5). The following table shows a simple event risk report describing events, their likelihood, impacts and risks, and the processes and resources affected. Information about the potential for unexpected and catastrophic losses can also be helpful (particularly for ranking exposures). Also useful is information about the risk factors or other events that make these events more frequent or more severe. Event risk reports facilitate management responses in two ways. First, they prioritize the most critical events by ranking them according to the extent of their risks. Second, event risk reports can direct managers' attention to the most appropriate responses to prevent or control loss events. Both aspects of event risk reports encourage and facilitate a firmwide and systematic response for dealing with the most critical events.

As well as quantitative data, operational risk reports should contain more qualitative information, also available in the operational risk database. For instance, reports might answer questions such as: What has been done about the same risk in the past? What should be done about the risk now? How does the risk decompose into different categories? Which back-office areas are responsible for dealing with the most critical risks? Making the answers to these questions explicit and readily available is imperative for developing a core competence in back office operations.

TABLE **15.3** Example Event Risk Report

Event ID	Loss event description	Prob. (pa)	Impact ($)	Expected loss ($)	Processes and resources affected
E107	Y2K software bugs	100% (in 2000)	30,000,000	30,000,000	Sales process, retail banking processes, trading process, brokerage process
E102	Legal suit against the firm by client	10%	30,000,000	3,000,000	Financial resources, reputational resource
E104	Senior trader leaves	20%	5,000,000	1,000,000	Trading process
E112	Power outage in New York trading room	5%	5,000,000	250,000	All New York-based processes such as confirmation process, settlement process
E114	Electronic fraud by outside parties (hackers)	2%	10,000,000	200,000	Commercial banking operations
E123	Confirmation not received within one day	4%	1,000,000	40,000	Confirmation process, settlement process

Process/Resource/Business Risk Reports

Naturally enough, managers care most about those processes, resources, and businesses for which they are responsible. Process/resource/business risk reports aggregate risks according to the loss events' impacts on particular processes, resources, or businesses. The information for process/resource/business risk reports comes from qualitative assessment or from risk aggregation using the simulation techniques described earlier (see Subsection 8.1). This requires mapping events to processes/ resources/businesses, as well as knowledge of the statistical and causal dependencies between events and risk factors. When adding risks over interdependent processes, resources, business, or categories, it is *essential* that the total risk incorporate any statistical or causal

TABLE 15.4 Example Process Risk Report

Process or resource	Unconfirmed_Deal	Misplaced_Deal	Inacc_Confirm	Late_Confirm	Pwr_Fail	Unauth_Deal	Reg_Err	Doc_Err	Comms_Fail	Cntpy_Wdrl	Expected process value	Unexpected loss by process	Catastrophic loss by process (99%)
Description — Expected loss	$371,766	$108,992			$67,037	$13,109	$417,631	$2,188,827	-$637,694	$14,036,345			
Description — Unexpected loss	$229,898	$58,862			$346,222	$6,463	$215,819	$1,637,085	$700,067	$5,440,821			
Confirmations	100%	100%	100%	100%	20%	100%	50%	100%	34%	20%	$939,979	$2,687,913	$18,647,790
Physical receipts/deliveries					20%				33%	40%	$1,982,111	$2,227,412	$8,539,851
Free deliveries					20%		20%				$1,957,397	$69,406	$1,701,408
Fail to receives/delivers					20%				33%	40%	$3,788,231	$2,180,694	$10,433,858
Cash receipts/payments					20%		30%				$3,237,578	$354,747	$1,384,383
	100%	100%	100%	100%	100%	100%	100%	100%	100%	100%	$1,515,346	$6,668,534	$32,492,258

dependencies between the losses. Monte Carlo simulation allows these dependencies to be readily incorporated. Alternatively, analytic techniques can be used, but these require major simplifying assumptions (such as independence, normality, or perfect positive or negative correlation).

For example, the process risk report shown in Table 15.4 describes how particularly critical loss events affect the expected and unexpected losses of different processes.

Sometimes, graphical maps of process risks highlighting high risk areas (see Figure 8.10 for an example) are more effective than tabular displays of numbers.

Process/resource/business risk reports target high risk processes and resources for loss reduction (particularly through contingency planning) and risk financing. They also reveal how different subprocesses and resources contribute to the possible loss and, therefore, provide a guide to selecting processes and resources for further analysis. They can also help in internal risk transfer pricing between different upstream and downstream business areas.

Other Risk Reports

Risks of similar loss events can be assigned to any user-defined set of categories. Hierarchical categories of different types of risk, such as the one shown in Table 5.8, are particularly useful. These summarize exposures in high-level categories (for instance, business event risks) that let users to drill down into lower-level risks (such as business event/ disaster/war risks). As described in Subsection 8.1, loss events are assigned to specific risk categories (at any level of the hierarchy), and thereafter any simulated cash flows associated with the loss events or risk factors are also allocated to the risk category. Based on the cash flows allocated to the category, we can estimate the expected loss, and unexpected and catastrophic losses (99 percent) as in Table 15.5.

Given different ways to categorize risks, say by process, business, location, or risk type, we can cross-tabulate results. For instance, Wilson (1996) advocates cross-tabulating risks across different risk categories and then comparing them across processes or business areas to produce a report such as in Table 15.6:

TABLE 15.5 Example Risk Category Report

Risk category	Expected loss	Unexpected loss	Catastrophic loss
Operational.Business Event.Credit Rating Shift	$62,022	$36,694	$188,234
Operational.Business Event.Disaster.Market Collapse	$62,022	$36,694	$188,234
Operational.Business Event.Disaster.Natural Disaster	$62,022	$36,694	$188,234
Operational.Business Event.Disaster.War	$62,022	$36,694	$188,234
Operational.Business Event.Legal	$62,022	$36,694	$188,234
Operational.Business Event.Regulatory.Capital Requirement Breach	$62,022	$36,694	$188,234
Operational.Business Event.Regulatory.Regulatory Changes	$62,022	$36,694	$188,234
Operational.Business Event.Reputation	$14,326,566	$4,574,109	$30,483,781
Operational.Business Event.Taxation	$62,022	$36,694	$188,234
Operational.Operations.Technology.Contingency Planning	$23,158	$10,045	$57,066
Operational.Operations.Technology.IT Systems Outage	$23,158	$10,045	$57,066
Operational.Operations.Technology.Power Outage	$51,139	$67,088	$578,733
Operational.Operations.Technology.Mark-to-Market Error	$23,158	$10,045	$57,066
Operational.Operations.Technology.Model	$23,158	$10,045	$57,066
Operational.Operations.Technology.Programming Error	$23,158	$10,045	$57,066
Operational.Operations.Technology.Telecommunications Failure	$565,739	$386,786	$2,515,039
Operational.Operations.Transaction.Booking Error	$2,076	$1,145	$8,086
Operational.Operations.Transaction.Commodity Delivery	$2,076	$1,145	$8,086
Operational.Operations.Transaction.Execution Error	$2,886,509	$1,865,595	$11,811,607
Operational.Operations.Transaction.Product Complexity	$2,076	$1,145	$8,086
Operational.Operations.Transaction.Settlement Error	$425,227	$263,910	$1,283,876
Operational.Operations.Transaction.Counterparty Error	$283,693	$204,764	$1,222,073
Operational.Operations.Transaction.Confirmation Error	$2,076	$1,145	$8,086

TABLE 15.6 Example Risk Category Report

| Trading process | Human resource risks | | | Technology risks | | | Facilities risks | Relation-ship risks | Process |
	Staff turnover	Human error	Fraud	Hardware	Software	Commun-ications			
Settlement	$150,000	$400,000	$200,000	$300,000	$400,000	$500,000	$400,000	$600,000	41%
Clearing	$340,000	$30,000	$220,000	$240,000	$300,000	$500,000	$100,000	$400,000	24%
Trading	$450,000	$40,000	$400,000	$300,000	$500,000	$500,000	$200,000	$300,000	35%
Total	$583,609	$403,113	$498,397	$487,442	$707,107	$866,025	$458,258	$781,025	100%
% of total risk	11%	5%	8%	8%	16%	25%	7%	20%	100%

Cross-tabulating risks across different types of risk and different geographic sources of the risk is also useful, as in Table 15.7:

TABLE 15.7 Example Aggregate Risk Report

| Risk category | Subrisk | C/U/I | Business unit/Process | | | Total | % of total |
			New York	London	Tokyo		
Human resource risks	Staff turnover	I	$150,000	$340,000	$450,000	$583,609	11%
	Human error	I	$400,000	$30,000	$40,000	$403,113	5%
	Fraud	I	$200,000	$220,000	$400,000	$498,397	8%
Technology risks	Hardware	C	$300,000	$240,000	$300,000	$487,442	8%
	Software	C	$400,000	$300,000	$500,000	$707,107	16%
	Communications	I	$500,000	$500,000	$500,000	$866,025	25%
Facilities risks		I	$400,000	$100,000	$200,000	$458,258	7%
Relationship risks		I	$600,000	$400,000	$300,000	$781,025	20%
Total risk by unit			$1,114,675	$855,862	$1,041,201	$1,749,028	100%
			41%	24%	36%	100%	

15.6 RISK ACTION REPORTS

Risk action reports have three objectives. First, they must help managers identify appropriate actions to manage a specific risk exposure, basically asking what can be done about particular risks. Second, they must help evaluate different potential risk management activities. Finally, risk action reports should help evaluate and monitor the effectiveness of any current risk initiatives.

Identification of Actions

Section III described a variety of risk management activities (risk avoidance, factor management, loss prediction, loss prevention, loss control, loss reduction, and risk financing) and discussed the general benefits and disadvantages associated with each. Subsection 8.3 described heuristics for managers to identify specific actions within these categories. Of course, these are only heuristics for guidance; there must be brainstorming meetings with line managers to fully develop a list of action items on a risk action report.

Evaluation of Potential Actions

Subsection 8.1 explained how proposed risk management activities are evaluated in terms of their NPV. Briefly, this involves estimating the effect of risk management actions on aggregate losses associated with specific events or risk factors. Furthermore, the effects of controls can be used to re-estimate the risk profile of loss events, risk factors, processes, and resources with the new controls in place. This lets us see how the intervention of risk management affects business areas' or processes' expected value added, unexpected losses, and catastrophic losses.

TABLE **15.8** Example Action Report

Action	Target risks	Loss prevention, control, or reduction	Extent risk	PV of risk reduction	PV of action cost	NPV
Implement price data integration tool	Model risk Price verification risk	P P	−10% −10%	$1,000,000 $3,000,000	$710,000 $290,000	$3,000,000
Build analyst incentive system	HR risk Fraud risk	P R	−5% −1%	$7,000,000 $5,000,000	$4,500,000 $7,000,000	$500,000
Conduct model release program	Model risk	P	−2%	$2,000,000	$2,500,000	−$500,000
Develop liquidity risk management program	Liquidity risk	P	−20%	$1,000,000	$1,000,000	$0

Projects should be analyzed on a case-by-case basis. The decision to invest in a risk management project then boils down to one of selecting the highest NPV project. After the highest NPV project has been selected, the analysis should be redone, assuming the first project has already been implemented. Decreasing marginal benefits of risk management mean that risk management actions should be considered singly and not as a portfolio. For major investments, sensitivity analyses, typically describing how the investment's NPV varies with different levels of risk factors, are often helpful. Similarly, the effect of incorporating different assumptions about risk management effects can also be usefully included into the report.

Evaluation of Ongoing Actions

Action reports should not only be directed toward capital budgeting, they should also be integrated with more frequent status reports describing the ongoing progress of various action items. Ongoing status reports are essential for monitoring the implementation of risk reduction activities. Risk management status reports should answer a number questions about each ongoing risk management activity: Are these activities being carried out? Are adequate resources being allocated to these activities? Are they reducing the risks? Are they under budget? What is their risk adjusted return? Economic or regulatory risk capital measures can be used to provide a common risk adjusted performance benchmark. Metrics such as EVA™, RAROC, and RORAC suggest whether activities are adding or detracting from shareholder value. Chapter 16 discusses how these measures of ongoing risk management activities can be produced and how they should be interpreted.

15.7 RISK SUMMARY REPORTS

Summary reports seek to provide reassurance to senior management regarding the effectiveness of internal risk management. These can be executive reports describing monthly provisions, impacts, frequencies, and write-offs. There may also be quarterly overview risk reports aimed at audit and control committees and the board of directors. Inevitably, these reports will have elements of the other reports already discussed. For instance, from operational profiles they may obtain high-level performance measures; from event reports, information about any major problems during the last period; from action reports, the status of major capital investments; from risk reports, perhaps the five most critical exposures facing the business. These can be coherently structured to summarize information by hiding the detail, but do make the details accessible on demand. Hierarchies of information such as those found in "balanced scorecard"-based reporting systems can be useful to structure these reports.

Further information: For further information see *The Balanced Scorecard: Translating Strategy into Action* by Robert S. Kaplan and David P. Norton, (September 1996), Harvard Business School Press. Graphical summaries such as the process risk map (see Figure 8.10 for an example) can also be helpful.

15.8 EVALUATING AND UPDATING THE RISK MODEL

Risk managers must periodically evaluate the quality of the risk model embodied in the operational risk database (see Subsection 7.5) on which they base much of their analysis. Performance evaluation of the model, often called back-testing, analyzes any discrepancies between realized losses obtained from the general ledger and the model's historical estimates of operational risks. This is essential for three reasons: first, it helps evaluate the reliability and accuracy of the risk model. Second, it helps ascertain whether some important structural change to the system has taken place in the interim. Finally, back-testing can focus attention on important risk trends that may cause bigger problems or suggest business opportunities down the line.

Performing the Back-test

Any back-test of a risk model is performed by selecting a given percentile (say, 75th for the risk measure) and comparing the number of actual P&L exceptions during this period against the theoretical (just 25 percent of occasions). The model quality is then evaluated in terms of the magnitude of any discrepancy. Back-testing should be performed using real loss data outside the sample of losses from which the model was developed. Risk models should be back-tested periodically and also following any major loss event or factor move. An annual qualitative high-level review of the model should be conducted to see if there are any new operational risk areas to manage (for example, new business units, new processes, or new events), and also to determine if any

490 ■ Measuring and Managing Operational Risks in Financial Institutions

currently monitored and managed areas are no longer risky (or are being disposed of, reorganized, redesigned, and so on). It is also important that the role of *back-testing* the model be separated from *developing* the model. Model developers (usually from risk management) have too much invested in justifying the effectiveness of a given model to be unbiased observers. Typically this would mean that external and internal audits would be responsible for checking the quality of the risk estimates, as well as the quality of financial records.

If a back-test reveals a large discrepancy between model and actual losses, it is certainly strong evidence that the model needs changing. It is not conclusive, however. There are several steps a risk manager should follow before deciding to update a risk model:

1. Check that there is no substantive reason for a change in the risk, such as a process change, product change or staff changes. The change log should be the first source of information for any such changes.

2. Find the extent to which historical data exist for the losses. The greater the historical evidence behind the losses, the less likely it is that the new losses carry new information about the underlying distribution. It follows that new processes are more likely to produce unexpected losses.

3. If there are substantive reasons for changes in the level of risk, it may be only a temporary factor, in which case there may be little point in updating the model.

4. Find out the reliability of the new loss data. If the data sources are unreliable or delayed, again there may be no point in changing the model.

5. Realize that the losses could simply be random and not require any changes in the underlying model. This is especially likely for catastrophic and, to a lesser extent, unexpected losses, because the likelihood of major discrepancies between the theoretical risks and the actual losses increases as the percentile chosen for the risk increases. This means while expected losses can be reliably estimated, unexpected—and even more so, catastrophic—losses have a large standard error associated with them. It follows that strong evidence is required to justify changes in the model since

TABLE **15.9** Procedure for Updating the Risk Model

Implications	Evidence	Causes
Incremental change to model; for instance, changes in frequency and impact distributions.	1. Given the model distributions, there is a very low probability of obtaining the observed losses. 2. Only isolated individual events and risk factors are affected.	Relatively minor changes have occurred to invalidate the estimates of loss frequency and impact.
Structural change to model, such as new events, new businesses, new risk factors, and new dependencies.	1. Substantive business changes. 2. Given the model distributions, there is a very low probability of obtaining the observed losses. 3. More than one risk factor or event is anomalous. More so if the events or risk factors are causally related or affect the same process or resource.	Underlying structure of events, factors, resources, and processes has changed.
Model does not need changing and effect is random or temporary; e.g., temporary promotion.	1. Substantive changes have not occurred to invalidate the estimates of loss frequency and impact. 2. Large body of historical evidence exists to back up the model. 3. Large error associated with loss statistic.	Random noise. Temporary change has occurred that is not reflected in the model (and will cease to have an effect shortly).
Check the online transactions for data error; e.g., additional zeros accidentally typed.	1. Substantive changes have not occurred to invalidate the estimates of loss frequency and impact. 2. Losses are orders of magnitude different from experience.	Data are in error, caused by inexperienced data-entry staff or perhaps data transmission problems.

back-testing can never guarantee that the correct conclusion is drawn from the limited out-of-sample data set available for the back-test.

Updating the Model

In general, a conservative rather than a reactionary approach is best when dealing with model updates. Unnecessary changes caused by overreaction often cause more problems than they solve because they make the model more complex and more likely to be in error. Nonetheless, the model will sometimes need to be updated; for instance, if there has been a substantive change in the business or if the previous model has performed poorly. If there is a major radical structural change, the historical data are unlikely to be helpful and may need to be discarded completely. If the change is cumulative and evolutionary, more recent loss information should be integrated with historical risk estimates. In this case, simple scaling or more sophisticated Bayesian techniques can be used to integrate ongoing loss data with existing distributional assumptions about event frequencies and impacts. Analysts should avoid the temptation to overemphasize more recent loss information. Although more recent losses may be more representative of the current state of operations, they also tend to understate the likelihood of catastrophic failures that, because of their rarity, are not represented in the more recent database.

CHAPTER 16

RISK-BASED CAPITAL

Subsection 8.1 discussed the use of simulation models to estimate the present value of various operational risk management interventions. This chapter turns to the problem of evaluating the risks and performance of existing business activities. These might be different operational activities, different transactions, or even different business lines. Any evaluation must be based on both the expected income and any unexpected losses that the activity might impose on the firm. There are several ways to adjust business returns for risk; all involve evaluating the projects' expected returns by either subtracting or dividing by a penalty to reflect the project's risk. There are two forms of risk penalty. The first uses *loss provisions* to cover *expected* losses. The second is *risk capital*, a cushion provided by equity holders against *unexpected* losses.

16.1 ESTIMATING LOSS PROVISIONS

Need for Provisions

Management should set aside formal provisions for its major expected losses. Not doing so is tantamount to assuming that none of these losses (whether counterparty defaults, credit write-offs, systems failures, or instances of consumer fraud) will occur. This overstates revenues and can represent a breach of fiduciary responsibility.

Defining Reserve Accounts

Ideally, operational risk management needs to work with the accounting department to develop a section of the general ledger to track specific loss events. The goal is to use the accounts to track economic losses as they are incurred. The loss accounts then feed into formal loss provisions that have been set aside to cover expected losses in particular areas. To do this consistently with accepted accounting principles demands a number of additional accounting entries. The precise set of general ledger loss accounts used depends on the nature of the firm's losses. Individual loss events are probably too specific for most companies' loss reserve accounts. Having too detailed a set of accounts makes it more likely that there will be unexpected losses. Furthermore, additional reserve accounts mean more entry corrections will be required to adjust the books at the end of the year.

Determining Provision Levels

Ideally, the levels of provisions and reserves should be based on the *expected* levels of losses, given the levels of other risk factors or loss events that affect those losses. Simply measuring dollar loss can be misleading if the business is growing or contracting or changing in some fundamental sense. To take a simple example, if the losses are driven by a single major risk factor (such as revenues), rather than use absolute loss levels, *relative losses* (such as the ratio of losses to revenues) can be used. Of course, this ignores the losses' correlation with other losses or the possibility of other risk factors.

TABLE 16.1 Estimating Loss Provisions

Quarter	Process loss ($ million)	Process revenue ($ million)	Loss/revenue (%)
1999 Qtr 2	2.0	30	7
1999 Qtr 3	2.3	23	10
1999 Qtr 4	1.1	28	4
2000 Qtr 1	5.4	32	17
2000 Qtr 2	3.2	35	9
Expected loss		Mean	9
Unexpected loss		Standard deviation	5

In this case, the provision for losses would be 9 percent of projected revenues. If the loss to revenue ratio has been stable with no time trends, then the expected loss provision should be adequate to cover losses during a sufficiently long period. For a shorter time period, risk capital will need to be allocated to cover unexpected losses.

In practice, provisions are set according to accounting and fiscal conventions, particularly for credit loss-based provisions. Moreover, provisions are often recorded late, after risks have already turned into highly likely or certain losses. This means that these provisions are no longer economic measures of expected losses, but instead are merely convenient place-holders for actual losses, understating balance sheet liabilities in the process.

16.2 ECONOMIC CAPITAL ALLOCATION

Need for Risk Capital

One of the most critical resources in any business is its capital. Capital can be narrowly defined as equity plus reserves, or more broadly to also include some types of long-term subordinated debt. Typically, in most non-financial businesses, capital levels are determined by firms' trading off the benefits of cheap debt with their increased risks (Subsection 14.1). In many financial services (for example, commercial banks), minimum capital levels are required by regulators, as discussed in Subsection 1.6. Although regulatory risk capital requirements are risk based, they fail to capture many of the subtleties of a real financial service business. In particular, requirements focus on credit and market risks, and despite efforts to introduce risk-based capital for operational, reputational, and liquidity risks, no formal proposals have been made at the time of press. Instead, these risks are "covered" by the use of an arbitrary multiple of the credit and market risk exposures. Given that one of most important functions of capital is to cover unexpected losses that threaten the firm (catastrophic losses), many firms are beginning to estimate their aggregate capital requirements on the basis of objective estimates of their business risks. Once the aggregate capital level has been calculated, it can be allocated to different parts of the business in proportion to their respective risks. This helps ensure that capital is treated as a scarce resource, and its use is in line with the maximization of business returns.

Capital at Risk

The economic risk capital is the capital required to cover the risk of potential losses. A firm's *Capital at Risk* (CaR) is the capital required to cushion against unexpected capital losses up to some level of insolvency risk. It does not include expected losses because these should already be captured in loss provisions. The economic CaR is basically the VaR of net losses with a threshold determined by the desired insolvency probability. Equivalently, over a single reporting period, CaR is the EaR divided by the risk-free rate. See Subsection 1.6 for a discussion of VaR and EaR.

FIGURE 16.1 Capital Risk

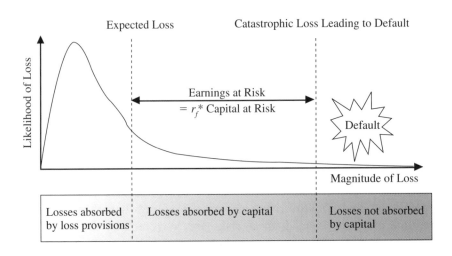

Risk capital is a scarce resource and therefore the cost of risk capital needs to be included in all business performance measures. Economic capital allocation is management's attempt to answer whether a particular investment adds to or detracts from shareholder value.

For non-financial firms, the problem is straightforward (at least in theory); the returns derive directly from the expected cash flows, the capital required is the up-front funding (usually the up-front cost), and the cost of capital can be estimated from the market price of the firm's stock. Investors invest in a project if the expected return exceeds the weighted cost of capital (made up of a weighted average of the cost of equity and the cost of debt). Projects whose expected returns exceed this hurdle rate add value to shareholders. This assumes that new projects have similar risks to existing projects in the firm's portfolio, but in practice this is not very likely—after all, new projects are invariably more risky than existing ones. There are other complexities in financial firms that need to be considered:

• Many firms engage in activities that do not require up-front funding; for example, forward agreements or swaps. Nonetheless, these activities are risky and therefore deserve some capital allocation. This requires managers to make a distinction between levels of funding and capital allocation for risk management purposes (see next section).

• Positions also must be considered in terms of their portfolio effects. A project is not a black box. Correlation effects may make one investment an effective hedge, while another with similar expected returns could actually increase portfolio risks. The appropriate risk measure for a new project is therefore its marginal risk contribution, rather than its stand-alone risk (see next section).

Funding versus Allocated Capital

Capital allocation should not be confused with the levels of actual funding that different businesses require. In many financial businesses, these may be quite distinct. Managers must distinguish between the capital physically invested in assets and the way capital is allocated to those assets. Although no funds are actually transferred to the different business units, economic capital allocation provides a measure of the amount of risk capital required to cover the risks contributed to the firm by the business area.

The process by which businesses can allocate their capital involves two steps: first, determining the total capital available for allocation and, second, allocating this capital to the different businesses that make up the firm as a whole. In the next section we will discuss how risk capital can be combined with estimates of future business returns to produce risk adjusted performance measures, but for now consider each of these steps in more detail.

Determine the Available or Required Capital for Allocation

This may simply be the regulatory capital or the current levels of capital. Neither is optimal for financial firms, which ideally should calculate the required economic risk capital in one of the following ways:

1. Based on a target credit rating and an associated level of insolvency risk.

2. Based on the actual risks of current operations.

The first approach to calculating economic capital requires estimating the CaR based on a target credit rating for the firm—a particular level of insolvency risk that management and shareholders feel comfortable with. Given a desired credit rating, an approximate acceptable default frequency can be derived, as in Table 16.2.

TABLE **16.2** Credit Ratings and the Likelihood of Default

Approximate Moody's ratings (note that actual default rates will vary)	Yearly default likelihood (%)	Multiple of yearly earnings volatility (assumes normally distributed losses)
	16	1
B	10	1.28
	4.95	1.65
Ba	2.5	1.96
	1	2.33
	0.51	2.57
	0.35	2.7
Baa	0.19	2.9
	0.14	3.0
A	0.07	3.2
Aa	0.03	3.4
Aaa	0.02	3.6
	0.01	3.8

Source: Adapted from Moody's Reports

Furthermore, if we make the Herculean assumption that losses are normally distributed, then the multiple of loss standard deviations can be used as a proxy for the desired capital level, that is,

$$CaR = Multiple \times \frac{\sigma_{earnings}}{risk\text{-}free\ rate}$$

Alternatively, if the complete distribution of annual losses has been modeled, analysts can estimate the capital level required to support an earnings at risk for a given default likelihood, that is,

$$CaR = \frac{EaR_{99th\ percentile}}{risk\text{-}free\ rate}$$

The second approach to estimating aggregate risk capital evaluates the risks of existing operations and infers the required level of capital needed to support those risks. Capital usage depends on the stand-alone capital at risk associated with a business unit. Aggregating capital at the firm level should incorporate the correlations between different business units' losses.

This can be done two ways—using a bottom-up asset volatility approach or a top-down earnings volatility approach (see Chapter 3). The asset-based approach has been the focus of much of this book, and has the advantages of accuracy and of having an operational focus. The earnings-based approach looks at the volatility of the loss and earnings streams in the past. The earnings approach has the benefits of simplicity and of being relatively inexpensive to perform. Its disadvantages are that it is backward-looking and unhelpful in telling us what to do about the risks. In practice, many organizations will use both approaches to estimate their capital at risk using earnings volatility for initial estimates of the required risk capital and asset-based approaches for detailed capital allocation.

Allocate Risk Capital to Individual Business Lines

Individual business areas need to be charged the cost of the firm's risk-based capital according to the extent to which the business area contributes to the catastrophic risk. Hence, risk-based capital allocations are the head office's transfer prices for the risk-based capital that the firm must carry. Allocated capital should be based on a complete assessment of the risks of particular business areas. These assessments should include not only market and credit risks, but also operational risks that affect the variance of revenues through their impact on the variance of costs and correlation with revenues and costs. Assessments of different business areas' risks may be qualitative, for example, perhaps based on audit grades or industry practice, or quantitative, based on operating leverage, or business scale. Alternatively, capital can be allocated according to more objective estimates of the risk associated with the business areas, either using the top-down or bottom-up models described in Chapter 3.

If objective risk estimates are used, firmwide risk capital can be allocated to business units in several different ways, depending on the circumstances, for instance:

- Using business units' *Stand-alone risks* for performance measurement.

- Using business units' *Diversified risks* for capital allocation.

- Using business units' *Marginal risks* for business entry and exit analysis.

Stand-alone Risk Contribution   The stand-alone risk of a business is its intrinsic risk when considered separately from the rest of the firm. Capital can be allocated on the basis of the sub-unit's stand-alone risks, but because of portfolio effects this overestimates the total capital requirements. Portfolio effects and correlated losses mean that the risk capital of the firm as a whole will be less than the sum of the risk capital levels for the different business areas. Capital allocation based on stand-alone risk is most appropriate for performance measurement, because it reflects those risks directly under the control of managers within that particular business line and cannot be affected by other business lines' activities. Stand-alone risks at a particular level of a business are easily calculated using asset-based Monte Carlo simulation techniques. These approaches are described in Subsection 8.1, but briefly aim to aggregate the cash flows associated with the loss events and factors that affect a business area. The catastrophic losses of the particular business line are then a measure of the business line's stand-alone risk. These techniques incorporate both statistical dependencies (such as rank correlations) and causal dependencies (such as fault trees) between different losses that can affect a business area. Alternatively, instead of using stand-alone risks, capital allocation for performance measurement can be based on the concept of controllable risks (Subsection 2.7).

Diversified Risk Contribution   The risk contribution of a business is always defined in terms of a firm's broader portfolio of businesses. It is the product of the stand-alone risks of the business and the correlation of the business P&L with the total. It is the fraction of the total firm risk that can be allocated back to the specific business line. Unlike the stand-alone calculation, the diversified risk contributions of the individual businesses sum to produce the total stand-alone risk of the entire firm. Diversified risk contributions can be calculated using the historical earnings at risk of the different business units or using Monte Carlo simulation. The latter approach requires two steps. First, the simulation approach projects loss events and factor moves over the next time period based on any internal correlations previously defined. Second, the correlations between different business areas' simulated losses are calculated. These correlations are then used to adjust the simulated stand-alone risks to produce diversified risk contributions. Diversified risk contributions are most appropriate from the firmwide perspective of capital allocation with existing businesses. They are not appropriate for performance measurement because the actions outside a particular business line could affect the correlation and, therefore, the level of allocated risk capital, which in turn may affect the performance measurement for that business.

Marginal Risk Contribution   For a particular business line, the marginal contribution is defined as the difference between the risk of the firm with the business and the risk of the firm without the business. Unlike allocation based on stand-alone risks, or on diversified risks, marginal risk contributions sum to be greater than the stand-alone risks of the entire firm. Marginal risk contributions are helpful when evaluating entry or exit decisions or when evaluating new transactions, but arguably should not be used for performance measurement or resource allocation within existing business lines. Marginal risk contributions can be estimated using simulation techniques by performing a what-if calculation; consider the stand-alone risk of the business with the business, and then subtract the stand-alone risk without the business.

To summarize the different forms of risk capital allocation, consider the following simple example. It shows a bank with three business lines—retail banking, private banking, and trade finance. The retail banking business has a stand-alone risk of $20 million, just like the trade finance area, but is much more correlated with the entire firm's risks. Consequently, the diversified capital for retail banking is significantly higher.

TABLE 16.3 Diversification and Risk Capital

	Stand-alone CaR	Correlation Factor	Diversified CaR	Marginal CaR
Retail banking	20	0.5	10	7
Private banking	15	0.4	6	5
Trade finance	20	0.3	6	4
Sum	55		22	16
Entire firm	22	1	22	NA

Capital charges should also be made for one-off projects. In general, financial services typically allocate about 70 percent for credit risk and the remainder for operational and market risks. Future trends seem to be pointing toward approximately equal levels of capital allocated to operational risk, market risk, and credit risk.

Estimating the Cost of Capital The cost of capital for a particular business area is the cost of funds required to finance the business. It is also the minimum required return. It should be set as the return required by the market given the risk of the business. Estimates of the cost of capital can be developed by comparison with similar companies within the same industry or using market pricing models such as *Capital Asset Pricing Model* (CAPM) or *Arbitrage Pricing Theory* (APT) models. According to one commonly used model, CAPM, the business risk is defined by the beta of the business—the covariance of returns against those of a market portfolio. More precisely, CAPM states that the cost of capital is given by $R_i = R_f + \beta_i(R_m - R_f)$, where R_f is the risk-free rate, and R_m is the expected return on the market. CAPM betas (β_i) vary by business areas; for instance, typical beta levels for different banking areas would be as in Table 16.4.

TABLE **16.4** Typical Betas of Different Financial Service Lines

Type of business	Typical beta level
Retail banks	1.1
Investment banks	1.2
Trading	1.2
Global investment banks	1.5
Universal banks	1.0
Institutional asset managers	1.2
Asset managers	1.3

More detailed estimates of betas for different businesses can be obtained from various commercial sources. These betas assume all equity financing. The presence of debt increases the leverage of the business and thereby increases the risk. It has the approximate effect of increasing the beta by a factor of:

$$\frac{\text{Debt} + \text{Equity}}{\text{Equity}}$$

The risk premium $(R_m - R_f)$ is typically around 6% with a risk-free rate of around 6 percent, which would imply that a retail bank with a beta of 1.1 would have a cost of capital of 12.6 percent. This is after tax; before-tax return targets would therefore need to be:

$$\frac{\text{After-tax cost of capital}}{(1 - \text{marginal tax rate})}$$

say

$$\frac{12.6}{(1 - 0.3)} = 21\%$$

Keep in mind that these reflect minimum levels of returns. Ambitious banks will set a before-tax hurdle rate of 25 percent or more.

Further information: For further details on estimating the cost of capital, see any good text on corporate finance such as *Principles of Corporate Finance* (McGraw-Hill Series in Finance) by Richard A. Brealey and Stewart C. Myers (Contributor), 5th edition (July 1996) McGraw-Hill College Division.

16.3 RISK-BASED PERFORMANCE EVALUATION

Risk-based Performance Metrics

The primary goal of every publicly listed financial institution is to increase shareholder wealth. This means the firm's managers must do two things: invest only in new projects that are expected to create value and retain only those projects that create value on a continuing basis. The first is easy through the concept of NPV. The second is hard—this is the role of risk-based performance measures. Although NPV is the theoretically correct measure of long-term value added, it is not as helpful as a measure of ongoing performance because it is based exclusively on estimated future cash flows that may extend long into the future. Unfortunately, traditional measures of performance such as Return on Assets (RoA) and Return on Capital (RoC) largely ignore the risk of the investment and are often inconsistent with the NPV criterion. Performance must have a risk component; otherwise, it becomes almost impossible to effectively compare different business activities. Risk adjusted performance metrics have been developed; metrics such as EVA™, SVA, RAROC, and RORAC provide an alphabet soup of performance measures, each capturing different aspects of shareholder value. All of these measures can be used either ex post to evaluate historical performance (say, for managers' bonuses) or ex ante to project future performance to decide whether to discontinue a particular business line. *Ex ante* measures estimate expected net income flows and future economic risks embedded in these cash flows. *Ex post* measures calculate historical net income and either adjust for actual volatility of those cash flows during the period or adjust for the historical estimate of the risks associated with those cash flows.

Both *ex ante* and *ex post* measures adjust net earnings cash flows by penalizing them with the economic risks embedded in these cash flows. Expected and unexpected losses are treated somewhat differently. Expected losses are subtracted directly from net income through loss provisions. Unexpected and catastrophic losses are assumed to have a significance to shareholders only through the higher level of risk capital required by the firm. In this case, the penalty chosen is just the cost of scarce risk capital allocated to a particular business area (there may, of course, be other constrained resources that need to be considered, such as management attention, systems, staff, and liquidity). The expected net earnings (incorporating any expected losses) are then penalized by either dividing by (as in RORAC) or subtracting the cost of capital required (as in EVA™).

RAROC and RORAC

For many financial firms, risk adjusted performance measures such as RAROC, and RORAC are popular. Precise definitions vary depending on whether risk penalties affect expected earnings before or after division by the required capital levels. For example, a common definition of the RORAC divides the project's expected net earnings by the risk capital required to support those earnings:

i.e.,
$$\frac{\text{Expected earnings} - \text{Expected losses}}{\text{Allocated Capital at Risk}}$$

Earnings should include expectations of cash flows from transaction revenues, fees, sales costs, funding costs, and direct costs. They should also be estimated net of any allocated costs such as overhead and depreciation expenses. If this ratio is greater than a hurdle rate (see above discussion on estimating the cost of capital), then the project is initiated. The operational risk component affects both the numerator and the denominator of the RAROC ratio. It affects the numerator through the expected losses (assuming these are not already covered in provisions). It affects the denominator through the catastrophic losses, which determine the required level of risk capital. The allocated capital at risk is either the undiversified capital (if used for comparing performance across business lines) or the diversified allocated capital (if used for capital allocation).

FIGURE 16.2 Calculating Risk adjusted Performance Measures

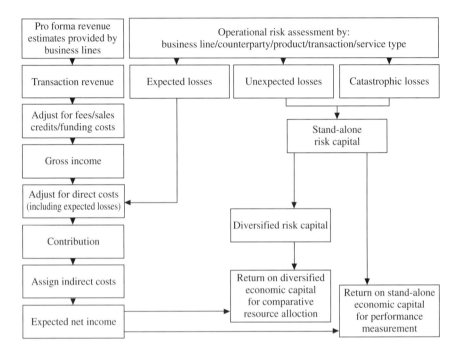

Adopting a risk-based performance measure is equivalent to evaluating activities on the basis of their effect on risk-based capital. For instance, if we assume the cost of capital is 25 percent, then all ongoing activities should have expected income greater than 25 percent of the capital at risk allocated to that activity. Activities that add shareholder value would then be those with an expected income sufficient to cover their risk capital requirements. Note that some activities (risk management activities, in particular) may hedge existing exposures and therefore have negative capital requirements; nonetheless, the expected income (or expected costs) should exceed (be less than) the total cost of allocated risk capital.

FIGURE **16.3** Risk Reward Profiles for Ongoing Activities
(assumes a 25% discount rate)

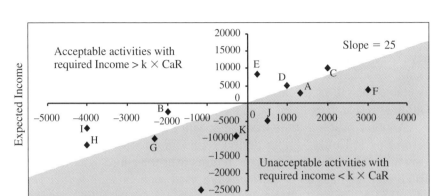

Allocated Capital at Risk

RAROC can be misleading if used for low risk businesses or positions (for which little risk capital is required). For instance, to obtain an infinite RAROC one need only hold a zero VaR portfolio such as overnight treasuries. RAROC-like measures also tend to encourage business contraction rather than expansion. For instance, it is always possible to increase the RAROC measure simply by ditching less-profitable projects.

Further information: See *Managing Bank Capital: Capital Allocation and Performance Measurement* by Chris Matten, 1st edition (August 6, 1996) John Wiley & Sons.

Economic Value Added Another approach to ongoing performance measurement uses the concept of *residual income,* commonly known by the *economic value added* (trademarked by Stern Stewart as EVA™). The economic value added of an activity is the expected earnings minus the cost of the risk capital required to produce those earnings:

EVA™ = Expected operating earnings − Hurdle rate × Capital at risk

An intervention with a positive EVA™ suggests that shareholder value was created over the period. Unlike RAROC-like measures, maximizing EVA™ in a period does not tend to lead to business contraction, nor is it biased toward overly safe positions.

Although EVA™ has been used in non-financial corporations to better align compensation with shareholder objectives, it is more problematic for financial firms because of limited flexibility that banks have over resetting their capital levels. For instance, there is some debate about what capital should be included—the regulatory capital, the available capital, or the diversified/undiversified economic risk capital? Different researchers in this area have different views.

Another problem with economic value added is its focus on the current period only; single-period return metrics do not incorporate growth or the sustainability of the returns over the entire asset life cycle. To correct for this, other measures are used such as *shareholder value added* (SVA) are used. SVA, sometimes called the *market value added*, is the present value of the stream of expected economic values added over future time periods. It can be shown that projects with a positive SVA have positive net present values. Estimating economic value added during a single period is difficult, and is still harder for multiple future periods. Calculating SVA requires estimates of any additional capital requirements in the future, as well as estimates of the changing costs of that risk capital. The process of calculating SVA and EVA™ is a multi-period extension of the process of calculating RAROC or RORAC in a single period, as shown in Figure 16.4.

Further information: see the book that started the move among corporations toward economic value added, *The Quest for Value: The EVA™ Management Guide* by G. Bennett Stewart III, and Joel M. Stern (Preface), (January 15, 1991), Harperbusiness.

FIGURE **16.4** Calculating EVA™ and SVA

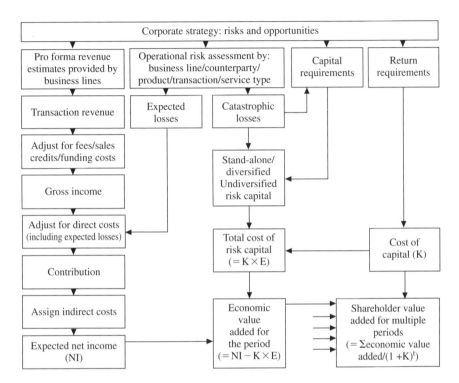

Once a shareholder value added has been produced, adding the book value of the firm's equity produces an estimate of the theoretical market value of the business as a whole.

Sharpe Ratio

Some financial firms, sidestep the issue of capital allocation and base performance measurement directly on the risk associated with the transaction, activity, or business line. One such measure is the *Sharpe ratio* of a particular business or investment. The simple Sharpe ratio of any investment is just:

$$\frac{E[R - R_b]}{\sigma_{R - R_b}}$$

the expected difference between the investment's annualized expected return (R) and some benchmark rate (R_b) divided by the standard deviation of this difference in returns (s). The benchmark rate should reflect the cost of funds required to finance the risky operational investment. Choosing between different investments then becomes a question of which investment has the higher Sharpe ratio. The simple Sharpe ratio assumes that the individual investments do not contribute to the risk of the broader portfolio of assets of the firm: that is the investment's returns are uncorrelated with the rest of the portfolio. (Note that this is equivalent to using stand-alone risk as the basis for risk-based capital allocations.) This is not the case for most operational investments—say, for investments such as major control interventions that may decrease portfolio risk, thus making them good investments even though they may have a low Sharpe ratio. This problem can be easily handled using the *generalized Sharpe ratio.* Instead of comparing the ratios of individual investments, it considers the investment's effect on the Sharpe ratio of the firm's entire portfolio of assets. The investment should proceed if the Sharpe ratio of the entire portfolio of assets *with* the investment is greater than the Sharpe ratio of the portfolio of assets *without* the investment:

$$\text{if } S^{old} < S^{new} \text{ where } S^{old} = \frac{E[R^{old} - R_b]}{\sigma_{R^{old} - R_b}} \text{ and } S^{new} = \frac{E[R^{new} - R_b]}{\sigma_{R^{new} - R_b}}$$

If we make the unrealistic assumption that returns are normally distributed, then catastrophic risks become a multiple of the standard deviation and the Sharpe ratio simplifies to a RORAC-based measure.

Further information: For further discussion on applications of Sharpe ratios to performance measurement, see the comprehensive *Beyond Value at Risk: The New Science of Risk Management* (Wiley Series in Financial Engineering) by Kevin Dowd, (February 1998) John Wiley & Sons.

USING RISK-BASED PERFORMANCE MEASURES

Risk-based performance measures have several major applications:

• To improve resource allocation.

• To help align managers' incentives with those of shareholders.

- To produce economic transfer prices for internal and external customers.

Improved Resource Allocation

Resource allocation should aim to increase shareholder value by allocating scarce resources to opportunities with high (diversified) risk adjusted returns. Capital is probably the most important resource in any financial institution. Instead of assuming capital to be a free resource, risk-based performance measures such as RAROC and EVA™ charge back the economic costs of capital to the business area. Moreover, risk-based capital measures that cover operational risks, as well as credit and market risks, discourage front-line activities (such as sales, trading, and marketing) from taking risks without regard for their effects on back-office operations. Although both RAROC and SVA analyses can be applied at various levels of the organization, the higher the level of the organization, the more likely the analyses will capture the effects of any natural hedges or synergies and thus accurately estimate the levels of diversified capital required.

Management Incentives

Risk-based performance measures can help make managers behave more like owners by realigning their incentive system, for instance, by having management bonus pools tied to RAROC or to a share of EVA™. Risk-based incentives require a focus on the controllable or stand-alone risks under the control of the managers concerned. Diversified capital measures are not suitable as management incentives because the results for one business can be affected by other businesses.

Transfer Pricing

All units of a company share common resources such as overhead, liquidity, debt, and capital. Transfer prices are internal prices used to transfer resources from one business area to another. They represent the internal valuation of the true economic cost of the resources being used. Without transfer pricing, there would be no basis for evaluating margins on different business nor any ability to charge customers economic prices. Economic transfer prices also provide an economic basis for estimating internal operating margins, target earnings, and risk adjusted pricing. Transfer prices should include all financial costs; including allocated overheads, expected losses, the cost of allocated capital, the cost of allocated debt, and the cost of liquidity.

Risk-based Pricing

Risk-based pricing for external customers builds on internal economic transfer pricing by incorporating the risk into the pricing of particular services and transactions. Risk-based pricing essentially requires the customer to pay for the risk (usually in terms of the associated risk capital) that the firm is carrying (see Subsection 14.7 on Contractual Risk Transfer). Risk-based capital costs, expected losses, the cost of debt, as well as operating costs associated with the transaction or service should be charged to customers whenever the competitive environment makes it feasible. Transactions should be priced to add value to shareholders, hence producing a positive economic value added:

$$\text{Expected revenues} - \text{Expected operating costs} - \text{Cost of debt} - \text{Allocated capital} \times \left(\text{Hurdle rate} - \text{Cost of debt}\right) > 0$$

This is equivalent to setting operating margins on top of internal economic transfer prices. Margins should also incorporate any commercial incentives consistent with business policies to develop a specific business area.

$$\text{Customer price} = \text{Economic transfer price} + \text{Commercial incentives} + \text{Margin}$$

External competition is obviously a major constraint on pricing. The financial markets determining the economic transfer prices may not be in synchrony with competitive prices. Nonetheless, banks that are price takers may not be able to price these risks, but they can at least decide whether the business as a whole is appropriate. Risk-based pricing also allows for pricing differentiation across customers of varying risks. If no such risk-based pricing is used, there is the danger that moral hazard and adverse selection will occur as the bank overcharges its low risk customers and undercharges its high risk ones, with the result that low risk customers will migrate, leaving only the high risk ones.

Further information: For the use of risk-based capital measures in determining internal and external transfer prices, see the very useful book, *Risk Management in Banking,* by Joel Bessis, (January 1998) John Wiley & Sons.

Appendices

APPENDIX A

GLOSSARY

This glossary contains definitions of many of the major types of risks that affect financial service organizations. Hierarchies of risk categories such as this one are useful because they suggest common approaches to organizing, predicting, preventing, controlling, reducing, and financing the risk. Of course, these risk categories are not necessarily mutually exclusive, and readers should adapt the meanings to suit their specific business context. Loss events can often belong to multiple categories; for instance, a major market move (market risk) can lead to a credit default (credit risk) and subsequent disruption of the business (business continuity risk), and subsequent legal suits (legal risk). Other categorizations, based on geography or on business units can also be helpful in diagnosing potential exposures (Subsection 5.5).

Many of these risk definitions are illustrated with a number of real-world examples as well as some guidelines as to the management techniques used to predict, prevent, control, and reduce these risks. When possible, cross-references (denoted by this alternate typeface*) have been included; these refer to other parts of the book (especially Section III) that expand these concepts still further. Finally, a number of additional external resources (ranging from books and articles to associations and websites) have been provided about the risk and how it may be better managed.*

ACCOUNTING RISK occurs when the firm engages in accounting practices for products or services in a manner that fails to comply with accepted market principles (such as those defined by GAAP—Generally

Accepted Accounting Principles or [US] FASB standards). Accounting risks may result in regulatory sanctions, shareholder litigation, and impaired reputation.

Accounting risks may be the result of accidents or happenstance; for instance, when different valuation models, miscommunication, or misunderstandings lead to discrepancies in the accounting treatments in the front and back office ledger. This is especially likely across different regional offices or departments. Alternatively, accounting risks may be the result of deliberate employee fraud (see Fraud Risk).

Another source of Accounting risk is uncertainty about the acceptable accounting standards. A good example of this is seen in the uncertainty in the US regarding the financial reporting of unrealized hedges. Changes in reporting standards and conflicts between different standards setting authorities (for example, FASB and SEC) also contribute to Accounting risks.

Risk Management: Effective management responses to prevent and control accounting risk include:

- Reliance on effective internal and external audit. Also helpful is the use of risk based audits and audit sampling techniques to efficiently sample high risk areas of operations (Subsection 12.8).

- Diagnostic controls—in particular, periodic and independent reconciliation between the front office, back office, and accounting systems. This should be followed by measurement and analysis of any unreconciled or unexplained aged debits and credits. Timely explanation of differences with comparison at reasonable intervals. Appropriate action should be taken with respect to any differences (Subsection 12.3).

- Fraud prevention and detection to detect white-collar fraud. In particular, refer to the discussion about the need for separation of duties (Subsection 11.6).

- Clearly defined authorizations and limits (see boundary systems); for example, transactions or access to assets that are executed strictly in accordance with management authorization (Subsection 12.4).

- Compliance management and organizational learning regarding the clearly defined internal accounting standards for transactions consistent with GAAP or regulatory criteria. Everyone should be familiar with how accounting principles affect their specific tasks (Subsection 10.2 and Subsection 12.5).

• Improved Internal Control and Corporate Governance—aligning managerial incentives with those of shareholders. See *Beyond COSO: International Control to Enhance Corporate Governance* by Steven J. Root (May 1998), John Wiley & Sons. This book also describes the various models of internal control and evaluates their strengths and weaknesses.

Further information: For further information on accounting standards, refer to the following websites: The International Accounting Standards Committee (IASC), <www.iasc.org.uk>. The IASC is an independent private-sector body working to achieve uniformity in the accounting principles that are used by businesses and other organizations for financial reporting around the world. The American Institute of Certified Public Accountants (AICPA) <www.aicpa.org> provides a gateway for users to access other useful accounting-related websites. The American Accounting Association (AAA) <www.aaa-edu.org> promotes worldwide excellence in accounting education, research, and practice. Pro2Net <accounting.pro2net.com> is another useful on-line tool for accounting-related news and research.

See also **Fraud Risk, Control Risk.**

AUDIT RISK. See **Accounting Risk**.

BUSINESS RISK includes risks, particular to the industry, that arise from the specific nature and characteristics of the products and services offered. Business risks tend to result from the actions of particular business units rather than the broader corporation as a whole. Business risks are a subset of Strategic Risks described later in the glossary. The following risks typically fall under the category of business risks:

Business Continuity Risk: The risk an organization faces when external events affect key functions for a sufficient period of time, resulting in total or partial interruption to normal business operations or services.

New Product Risk: The risk of introducing a new product that the firm does not have the systems or expertise to properly manage. Errors tend to be higher in the early stages of developing a new product. Ironically, some of the worst losses occur when a new product is spectacularly more popular than anticipated, resulting in potentially huge reputational losses and opportunity costs. For example, in the late 1990s, Tesco, the first UK supermarket to offer a savings account, was taken by surprise by the very high initial demand. Processing volumes were expected to be 2,000 a day, but turned out to be 15,000. The result was extensive delays and customer frustration while the scale of operations was increased to meet the demand.

New Market Risk: The risk of entering a new market without prior experience, knowledge, or expertise. Most operational risks losses tend to result from a major change in the business, because existing controls and procedures do not advance in lockstep. This is exacerbated of course in emerging markets.

Demand Risk: Uncertainty surrounding the future demand for a product due to the interaction of various unanticipated and uncontrollable factors; for example, unforeseen changes in regulation and changes in consumers' tastes. An important aspect of demand risk is the extent of risk of business cannibalization, whereby the marketing of one business/market/product area merely transfers profits (or passes risks) from another business area.

Risk Management: The following activities facilitate the management of business risks.

- Reduced levels of business activity and business exit: firms need to know when to cut their losses in a new market or product that has high fixed costs or is very risky (Subsection 9.1).

- Project risk management techniques can be used to measure and mitigate against schedule and cost risks associated with major business projects (Subsection 10.4).

- Business and market intelligence: data-gathering, analysis, and management actions based on that analysis can go far to limit demand, new product, and new market risks (Subsection 10.3).

- Organizational learning about best internal and external best practices helps firms limit the risks of developing new business services and new markets. For instance, intranet-based Process maps, and Plain English guides to internal products and services can help both staff and customers understand the product, how to value it and how to process it (Subsection 10.2).

- Strategic and business planning: at the business level, these techniques can be used to identify the different management approaches appropriate for businesses facing very different risks and opportunities at different stages of their life cycle (Subsection 10.1).

- Business development processes in the form of self administered checklists to identify business problems before new products and markets are developed. These may be used for new business or product appraisals and would involve staff from a number of functional areas including compliance, legal, and internal audit groups (Subsection 3.2).

- New product development should consider the effect of new products on the existing product portfolio (that is, business correlations) if product and service cannibalization is to be avoided.

- Contractual risk transfer and risk based pricing can be used to help businesses limit the effect of demand shocks on the firm's bottom line. Both decrease operating leverage by either decreasing fixed costs or by transferring the risk related capital costs to the customer (Subsection 14.7 and Subsection 16.3).

Further information: A useful book on the business risks associated with product and market development is *The Perpetual Enterprise Machine: Seven Keys to Corporate Renewal Through Successful Product and Process Development* by H. Kent Bowen (Editor), (September 1994), Oxford University Press; *Innovation and the General Manager* by Clayton M. Christensen (January 1999), McGraw-Hill College Division provides various case studies addressing the risks involved in managing business innovation.

See also **Strategic Risk, Competitor Risk, Business Continuity Risk.**

BUSINESS CONTINUITY RISK is the risk an organization faces when a disaster occurs that affects key functions for a sufficient period of time, resulting in total or partial interruption to normal business operations or services. Possible costs of business interruption include an impaired reputation and a consequent loss of business confidence, lost customers, damage to research and intellectual property, lower share value, delay in the launching of new products and services, as well as potential liability suits stemming from the inability to meet contractual agreements. A 1999 survey conducted by the UK Institute of Management together with the Business Continuity Institute, found that the five business continuity issues managers fear most are: (1) an IT failure, (2) fire, (3) damage to their company's image, (4) negative publicity, and (5) a loss of skilled personnel. Interestingly, the same survey revealed that despite these fears, very few businesses had plans to cover many of these issues.

Exchanges and brokerage services, because of their market-driven nature, are particularly sensitive to even the briefest business disruptions. In 1990, an AT&T fiber optic cable was accidentally severed in Newark, New Jersey, halting ATM transactions at 23 banks and forcing the New York Commodity Exchange and Mercantile Exchange to close; it also blocked 60 percent of the long-distance telephone traffic out of New York City (Crockett, 1990). On-line brokers are also particularly sensitive to failure in the wake of huge increases in volumes of securities traded on-line; for instance, NASDAQ's SelectNet network went down in the autumn of 1999, twice first for 10 minutes and then for less than one minute, with the effect that trades were rerouted and damaging the system's reputation for reliability. Business continuity risks are not unique to trading organizations, nor are they just the result of IT-related failures. In 1990, a power substation fire resulted in an outage to New York City, causing business disruptions to 4,150 customers, including more than 300 brokerages, financial institutions, and international banks (Levitt, 1997). Similarly, the great Chicago flood in 1992, which affected a large portion of Chicago's central business district, was estimated to have affected more than 250,000 employees in a three-week period.

Risk Management: Several proactive activities can help the secure business continuity in the wake of disaster.

- Contingency planning: proactive identification of potential threats to business continuity using scenario analysis followed up with a well-maintained response plan to deal with the threats (Subsection 13.3).

- Crisis management: senior managers must know how to effectively respond to disasters even if no contingency plan is available. Triage and public relations techniques are critical aspects of the crisis manager's toolkit (Subsection 13.4).

- Redundant systems: the speed with which financial markets operate means that there is almost no leeway for business interruption. Many firms respond to this by building in redundancy at every stage, from cross-training of key staff and multiple communications links to different telecom providers and even mirroring entire processing capabilities off-site (Subsection 12.2).

- Insurance coverage for losses due to business interruption (Subsection 14.4).

- Availability of emergency reserves through self-insurance techniques such as lines of credit and liquid asset reserves (Subsection 14.5).

- Contractual risk transfer techniques such as service level agreements and outsourcing can help decrease the likelihood of business continuity failures, by passing the risks to external parties better able to handle them (Subsection 14.7).

Further information: The Business Continuity Institute <www.business-continuity.com> provides a center for the collection and dissemination of information and knowledge about the subject of business continuity management. See its news site for more up-to-date information. Also useful are the resources provided by the Disaster Recovery Institute <www.dr.org>, which include training courses, certification and a journal (*Disaster Recovery Journal*). Also useful as a jargon-free introduction to the topic is *The Definitive Handbook of Business Continuity Management* by Andrew Hiles and Peter Barnes (June 23, 1999), John Wiley & Sons. For more detail on facilities-related contingencies, see the excellent guide to *Disaster Planning and Recovery: A Guide for Facility Professionals* by Alan M. Levitt, (April 1997), John Wiley & Sons. For a real-life account of a major banking crisis, the failure of Park Bank of Florida, read *Crash Landing: Surviving a Business Crisis* by Richard O. Jacobs, (June 1991) Glenbridge Pub Ltd.

See also **Business Risk.**

COMPETITOR RISK arises as a result of the actions of competitors. Competitor risk differs from business risk, which results from poorly executed or thought-out internal actions. Both competitor risks and business risks come under strategic risks facing the organization as a whole. For example, the following loss events would fall under this risk category:

Cherry Picking: for example, the entrance of a low-cost competitor targeting existing profitable markets resulting in a major fall in revenue.

More Efficient Operations: the faster adoption of new technology or new businesses may give a competitor a major advantage—not simply a cost advantage, but also improved reputation in terms of service reliability, sophistication, and flexibility.

New Product or Service: a new product or service introduced by a competitor may pose severe competition, leading to a loss of market share, a loss of reputation, and a decreased share value. A good example of competitor risks driven by new products and services, has been provided by the rise of web-based commerce. Established players have scrambled to counter the threat posed by smaller entrants with much lower distribution and marketing costs. For instance, the launching of Merrill Lynch's on-line trading platform was widely seen as a defensive response to prevent a loss in market share to lower priced alternatives like Schwab or E*Trade.

General Fall in Market Share: a steady decline in the firm's market share of a product or service. This is especially relevant for volume-based businesses such as brokerages and retail banking. Such was faced by CoreStates Financial. Since the takeover of CoreStates Financial in April 1998 and Money Store, First Union lost nearly 20 percent of the customers it obtained from the acquisition. Drastic cost-cutting measures and leadership changes have yet to secure the hoped-for turnaround. Similar issues face businesses driven by networks or reputation effects such as M&A or investment banking advisory services, where one-off crises can easily snowball into prolonged declines.

Risk Management: There are several countermeasures to competitor risk.

• To some extent, competitor actions can be forestalled through effective strategic and business planning. This may be through the development of new innovative services, new technology, strategic product placement, joint ventures, or one of host of other strategic moves (Subsection 10.1).

- Business and market intelligence: identification of customer wants and opinions regarding different product and service offerings can tell the firm much about the extent of customer loyalty. Scanning of the evolving product and service markets can help the firm spot potential threats and allow the business to rapidly respond; for example, through reverse engineering, alliances and legal trademark protection (Subsection 10.3).

- Contingency planning: potential competitor or market moves and effective responses can be played out in the form of "what if" scenarios. These force managers to ask difficult questions about how the firm actually adds value to its customers and the extent to which this value added is sustainable in a competitive environment (Subsection 13.3).

- Crisis management: when a worst-case competitive scenario becomes reality, effective and rapid response makes the difference between survival and a rapid decline (Subsection 13.4).

Further information: Obviously, managing competitor risks begins with gathering business intelligence about the competitors, but also important are more general business and economic resources, many of which are available on-line; for example, <www.ft.com>, <www.cnnfn.com>, <www.bloomberg.com>, and <www.economist.com>. Scenario analysis can be especially effective in playing out alternative competitive moves and countermoves. For more information, refer to the compendium of articles in *Learning from the Future: Competitive Foresight Scenarios* by Liam Fahey (Editor) and Robert M. Randall (Contributor), (October 1997), John Wiley & Sons. Another useful book by Liam Fahey is *Competitors: Outwitting, Outmaneuvering, and Outperforming*, 1st edition (October 16, 1998), John Wiley & Sons.

See **Business Risk, Business Continuity Risk, Strategic Risk.**

COMPLIANCE RISK. See **Regulatory Risk**.

CONTROL RISK is broader than accounting risk and includes the risks of failure of internal information systems, boundary systems, and diagnostic control systems through negligent operation, poor design, or deliberate fraud. Some examples of control risk particularly relevant to financial service firms include:

Position Reporting Risk: When the back office cannot provide an accurate position at the end of the day or within the day. May also result from failures to reconcile.

Valuation Risk: this exists if the back office cannot perform an independent valuation (either mark-to-market or back office models) of the front office portfolio. Also exists if there is a discrepancy between front office and back office valuations.

Reconciliation Risk: caused by an inability to reconcile between front and back office or between back office and general ledger (accounting breaks) or other accounts (*nostro* breaks). These may result from delay (for example, late booking of transactions, late confirmations, late settlements), from errors (for example, booking errors, counterparty errors), or from deliberate fraud.

Limit Risk: the risk of limits and the related sanctions being incorrectly set and the risk of staff accidentally or intentionally exceeding these limits; for example, traders with trading limits.

Management Information Risk: the danger of inaccurate information being passed on to senior management.

A classic example of a control failure embodying most of these different types of control risk occurred prior to the collapse of Barings Bank. Singapore-based trader Nick Leeson managed to persuade his managers that he could generate risk free profits by arbitraging the same Nikkei 225 contract on different exchanges in Japan and Singapore. He was believed to have generated £10 million in 1993, increasing to £28 million in 1984 as a result of this arbitrage (representing 20 percent of the profit of the entire group). Later, investigations showed that Leeson never made any money trading on behalf of Barings, but instead had hid his extensive losses in an internal suspense account. This account was hidden from management because of Leeson's position as head of trading, as well as the head of the back office.

Risk Management: there are several important guidelines to preventing, diagnosing, and limiting control risks.

- Separation of duties—independence between transaction initiation and transaction processing and control is essential. Well-defined work and job restructuring can help enforce separation of duties around critical resources (Subsection 11.2).

- Effective diagnostic controls with independent and daily reporting of any breakdowns in control. Diagnostic controls are especially useful when performance standards can be predefined against which actual results may be compared (Subsection 12.3).

- Boundary systems set limits on opportunity-seeking behavior through credible sanctions and punishment. This is appropriate when the firm is operating in a volatile environment or if there is a low level of trust between senior management and staff. Limits should be established for each risk and each limit excess should be thoroughly investigated and, if necessary, disciplined. This also ensures that the risk management and control function maintains credibility. Compliance programs, another form of boundary system, seek to confirm regulatory and statutory compliance (Subsection 12.4 and 12.5).

- Training of internal staff to recognize failures of control and detect the symptoms of internal and external fraud. In general, professional back office staff needs to have skills similar to those in the front office that they are trying to investigate and support (Subsection 9.4).

- Personnel selection to guard against employee risk factors that make control failures (especially internal fraud) more likely (Subsection 9.3).

- Internal and external audit should be given sufficient resources and independence. In particular, audit staff should investigate positive earning surprises with as much attention as negative ones. Real or imagined, unexpected profits may be the result of unexpectedly good or bad luck, incorrect reporting, or fraud; in any case, it is imperative to unearth the cause (Subsection 12.8).

- Fraud prevention and detection—Staff needs to be able to detect and recognize fraud, and be motivated to report any wrongdoing (Subsection 11.6).

- Functional automation—so-called straight-through processing can decrease the likelihood of human error leading to control failures. For example, automatic reconciliation of P&L between the front and back office can reduce the risk of reconciliation failures (Subsection 11.4).

Further information: For further information on different types of control systems and how they can limit control risks, see *Levers of Control: How Managers Use Innovative Control Systems to Drive Strategic Renewal* by Robert Simons (November 1994), Harvard Business School Press.

See **Accounting Risk, Human Resource Risk, Legal Risk, Regulatory Risk.**

COUNTRY RISK (aka political risk). This is the political risk surrounding firm's investments, project, loans, or assets held in a foreign country. Country risk can be attributed to the following:

Economic Mismanagement Risk: This stems from the likelihood that the government of a foreign country mismanages the economy by carrying out inappropriate policies (either through corruption or ineptitude), resulting in increased country risk.

Expropriation Risk: Expropriation arises from the possibility that a foreign government may take over a significant portion of the assets of the firm with little or no compensation. This is less of an issue for financial assets that are readily transferable. However, for commercial banks that have extensive fixed assets in the country or use fixed assets as collateral, expropriation loss may be a concern; for instance, because of the enforced nationalization of one of the bank's major creditors.

War, Civil Unrest, Revolution: These all cause uncertainty and potentially threaten the value of cash flows in a foreign country.

Repatriation Risk: when assets held abroad cannot be easily repatriated. This may be because of government restrictions on repatriation of foreign direct investments, devaluation, or because of the imposition of currency controls. For example, on August 17, 1998, Russia devalued its ruble and defaulted on some of its debt. Until then, a highly leveraged leading hedge fund, Long Term Capital Management (LTCM), ignored the major country risks and relied on historical correlations to trade on slight mispricings between bond prices in different currencies. Until

August 1998, this strategy yielded very high returns for LTCM investors. With Russian devaluation and the unenforceablility of contracts in Russian markets came a flight from risky markets and securities, making a mockery of historical patterns and losing around $2 billion less than one month after the crisis. Country risks also tend to have systemic effects. The Russian crisis came on the heels of a broader regional downturn in Southeast Asia. In 1997 came political crises in Malaysia, leading to the imposition of currency control in that country. The same downturn led to massive industrial unrest in South Korea as *chaebol* conglomerates were forced to restructure.

Risk Management: Country risk, being largely strategic in nature, demands investments in improved planning and financing to manage the risks.

- Risk avoidance—deciding when to reduce operations and wind up direct investments in particular countries (Chapter 9).

- Corporate diversification—diversification of foreign investment loans and assets among different countries can help reduce the unexpected losses associated with political loss events (Subsection 14.3).

- Financial restructuring—typically this involves financing the foreign investment through borrowing in the same country, creating a liability that offsets the foreign asset. It may also act as a bargaining lever to offset governmental powers (Subsection 14.1).

- Insurance—buying insurance against the components of the political risk attached to the investment. Historically, most insurance policies had specific exclusion clauses for political risks caused by war, strikes, riots, and civil commotion. These days, in countries like the United States and Canada, specialized government agencies like the Overseas Private Investment Corporation (US) or the Export Development Corporation (Canada) do offer insurance against political risks, usually for firms issuing securities hamstrung by low sovereign credit ratings in their countries of origin. Private insurers too are increasingly offering coverage against the effects of political risk on specific investments (Subsection 14.4).

- Contractual risk transfer through guarantees—political risk can be partially managed using investment guarantees such as those provided by MIGA (Multilateral Investment Guarantee Agency—a division of the World Bank). This is essentially used as credit enhancement to protect firms against political risk, in particular the risks of devaluation or of imposition of capital controls (Subsection 14.7).

- Loss isolation and asset protection—maintaining direct control of critical operations in the foreign project. This allows the firm to prevent operation of the project by others in the event of expropriation (Subsection 13.2).

- Relationship management—many foreign investments can be developed as joint ventures with equity partners in the foreign country. This makes local parties bear their share of the risks, and discourages too xenophobic an attitude from foreign governments. Alternatively, investors can limit the horizon of the investment by planning divestment and ultimate control to the locals (Subsection 9.7).

- Financial hedging—long put and short forwards positions on foreign equity indexes can be used to partially offset major downturns in the foreign markets (Subsection 14.6).

Further information: Several books describe useful techniques to protect financial investments from country and political risks. One such is *Managing International Political Risk: New Tools, Strategies and Techniques for Investors and Financial Institutions* by Theodore H. Moran (Editor), (August 1998), Blackwell Publishing. More of a compendium of the risks facing different countries is the *Handbook of Country and Political Risk Analysis* by Llewellyn D. Howell (Editor), 2nd edition (May 1998), PRS Group. Several consulting firms provide useful websites for those interested in identifying country risks. For instance, International Legal & Political Risk Consultancy <www.ilprc.com/>; the Political and Economic Risk Co. <www.asiarisk.com>; the Control Risks Group <www.crg.com/solutions.htm>; and Global Risk Assessments <www.grai.com/>.
See **Business Continuity Risk, Legal Risk.**

CREDIT RISK Probably the most important risk facing commercial banks, credit risk is the risk of loss due to exposure to the default of a counterparty (typically a borrower of funds). It is also used more generally to describe the risk of loss due to a change in a counterparty's ability to perform its contractual obligations to the lender. (It is to be noted that the counterparty may also be the firm itself). It comprises a number of subrisks:

Default Risk: The risk of loss due to counterparty, customer, supplier, or client default.

Credit Downgrade: The risk that an issuer's debt securities' ratings will be lowered because of its deteriorating financial condition. A ratings agency downgrade may be the result of changes in available capital, in industry perceptions or changes in regulatory agenda. Credit risk is also tied to market conditions. For example, a major market downturn might cause several of the firm's larger credits to be downgraded, say from aA to Ba. Although no default has occurred, credit spreads may have widened, the market value of the loan portfolio will have fallen, and risk capital requirements are likely to have increased.

Collateral Risk: This is the risk that the back office either fails to recognize a counterparty's failure to post collateral, or fails to demand an appropriate level of collateral given the credit risk. Either case may result in wasted collateral or incorrect margin calls or translate to loss if a counterparty defaults.

Settlement Risk: Following the failure of a counterparty (part of credit risk), this is the risk that settlements have not recognized this failure and possibly continue to make payments. It also denotes the risk of counterparty default in the period between delivery and settlement of funds.

Risk Management: Credit risk management is its own well-defined discipline and has developed its own rules of good practice, including:

- Expected losses from bad debt should always be used to determine and update any necessary loss provisions (Subsection 16.1).

- Contractual risk transfer—several administrative aspects of the contract can control or reduce credit exposures, such as (Subsection 14.7):

  (a) *Bilateral or multilateral netting* arrangements allowing counterparties to be responsible for the net payments between parties rather than the individual gross contracts between them.

    (b) Periodic settlement *between counterparties at periodic points within the contact.*

    (c) Inclusion of *credit triggers*, whereby the contract changes should the credit rating fall to some level.

- Financial restructuring—restructuring the financial terms of the contract can also help mitigate credit exposures (Subsection 14.1).

    (a) Credit can also be actively enhanced through management of *margin* and any collateral whereby the counterparty makes assets available to be surrendered in the event of default or downgrade. Increasingly, collateral management systems are being used to manage calls for collateral as the value of traded positions rises and falls and helps avoid disputes with counterparties over collateral postings. Disputes are surprisingly frequent, with many banks logging tens of disputes a month with their counterparties. This typically requires the careful management of the documentation flows associated with collateral agreements. Also important is the reconciliation of the collateral data with the transactional data held elsewhere in the firm.

    b) *Credit enhancement* through *guarantees:* by obtaining guarantees from third parties, non-payment only occurs if counterparty and guarantor both default (which is presumably much less likely).

- Diagnostic control systems—in particular, systematic and consistently applied credit scoring and credit management policies and procedures can be used to evaluate new credits and monitor and respond rapidly to changes in credit quality (Subsection 12.3).

- Boundary systems—periodic exposure reports describing position limits on counterparties or business sectors, and also any internal and external credit risk assessments (Subsection 12.4).

- Loss prediction of credit losses—there are two basic approaches. First, credit models of the value of loan portfolios based on historical credit spread volatilities, for instance, JP Morgan's CreditMetrics™ <www.riskmetrics.com/cm/index.cgi>. Alternatively, actuarial models can be used based on default frequencies and losses given default within a given credit rating; for instance, the CREDITRISK+ model developed by Credit Suisse Financial Products (CSFP) (Chapter 10).

- Hedging using derivatives—credit derivatives are bilateral financial contracts that isolate specific aspects of credit risk from an underlying instrument and transfer that risk between two parties (Subsection 14.6).

Further information: A large number of excellent resources on credit risk management are available. One of the best is *Managing Credit Risk: The Next Great Financial Challenge* (Wiley Frontiers in Finance) by John B. Caouette, Edward I. Altman and Paul Narayanan (October 1998), John Wiley & Sons. Also useful is *Credit Risk Measurement: New Approaches to Value at Risk and Other Paradigms* by Anthony Saunders, 1st edition (June 18, 1999), John Wiley & Sons. Credit risk issues are regularly discussed in the trade press such as *American Banker* <www.americanbanker.com> and *Risk Magazine* <www.riskpublications. com>. Consulting firms such as Fair Isaac <www.fairisaac.com> and Kamakura Corporation <www.kamakuraco.com> offer a range of credit risk related services, ranging from operational credit systems to complex analytical models of default frequency and recovery.

See **Country Risk, Customer Risk.**

CUSTOMER RISK Although having customers is a necessary part of being in business, they (especially new customers) are themselves the source of some financial services' most intractable risks, such as:

Credit Risk: The most important customer-related risk faced by banks is credit risk—the risk that a borrower of funds is unable or unwilling to fulfill contractual obligations to the lender, typically because of the default of the borrower. Credit risk is discussed in more detail elsewhere in the glossary.

Association Risk: The risk of taking on unsuitable business partners; for example, undesirable clients, drug dealers, or money launderers. This may lead to legal and litigation risks, as well as a loss of reputation.

Counterparty Authorization Risks: Does the trader on the other side of the deal have the authority to transact the deal? For example, some expensive losses for investment banks have resulted from *ultra vires* activities—transactions that were not part of the client's charter. A classic example occurred in the UK when the Hammersmith and Fulham council avoided $175 million in losses by claiming it was not legally permitted to engage in swap contracts and therefore the contract was null and void. Losses had to be written off not only by the counterparties directly involved in the swaps, but also by many other banks because of the large number of similar contracts with local authorities in place at the time

Suitability Risk: The risk that the institution sells the client the "wrong" product, which the client later claims to be inappropriate for its needs or level of expertise. For example, in 1994, US-based Gibson Greetings lost about $20 million, which grew from a $3 million loss, because it is claimed that Bankers Trust deliberately understated the loss, believing the loss might turn around. It did not, and Gibson did not understand the derivatives that it purchased from Bankers Trust. Banker's Trust was censured for deceptive practices and heavily fined. Similarly, in 1998, Merrill Lynch agreed to pay a $2 million penalty for its part in the 1994 bankruptcy of Orange County, California. Merrill Lynch had been accused of negligence for failing to warn investors of the risks.

Risk Management: Customers should be seen as partners in the overall business enterprise; thus it follows that many of the techniques for managing supplier or employee risks are relevant to managing customer risks. For example:

- Relationship management—background checks should be performed on new clients and counterparties, as well as periodic checks on current clients and counterparties. Customer risks (both credit and association risks) are especially prevalent for new clients and counterparties that the firm has not had prior dealings with (Subsection 9.7).

- Credit management—the use of external credit checks and systematic credit-scoring procedures should be in place and consistently followed (Subsection 14.6).

- Fraud prevention and detection—within the firm and at the counterparty/client, the authority to commit the institution to transactions needs to be well-defined and clearly communicated. The firm should maintain updated lists of authorized staff at each of its counterparties. At the same time, management should recognize that the legal notion of "apparent authority" may bind the organization to transactions to which unauthorized individuals have committed (Subsection 11.6).

- Training—internal trading and sales staff should be equipped with the necessary skills or experience and satisfy all relevant licensing requirements. This is especially important if the firm is to manage the risk of unsuitable clients (Subsection 9.4).

- Legal defenses—develop formal and documented suitability checks and procedures to examine the clients' needs and sophistication fit with the type and scale of the product sold. Remember the adage, "If a client loses a little money, he calls his banker; if he loses a lot, he calls his lawyer." Legal staff must review all sales and marketing literature and spot-check sales staff to ensure they are providing adequate disclosure to clients (Subsection 13.1).

- Organizational learning—firms should produce plain English guides to their products and services to help sales staff and customers understand the product, as well as explain the rights and responsibilities of the counterparties. One firm uses laminated place mats at every trader's workstation to show these requirements. Each transaction should have documented indemnity agreements with a specific statement of the risk of the transaction (Subsection 10.2).

- Boundary systems—stratified client signatory requirements so that transactions with high risks need more senior signers (Subsection 12.4).

- Use of collateral and collateral management systems.

- Risk based pricing to pass the cost of carrying the risk back to the customer (Subsection 16.3).

Further information: Most of the material on customer risks is specific to credit risk, which is, strictly speaking, a subset of customer risk. Nonetheless, much of the material on customer service management is relevant. Three concepts in particular are especially important. First, the importance of the lifetime value of the customer or client; knowing the expense of getting new customers should focus attention on managing suitability risks. Second, the importance of reputation in attracting and keeping customers; this amplifies the need to avoid association risk.

Third, service management techniques emphasize not only the need to find ways to add more value to customers, but also to identify which customers and clients to avoid. For a most insightful view of service management see *Service Breakthroughs: Changing the Rules of the Game* by James L. Heskett, W. Earl Sasser (Contributor) and Christopher W. Hart (Contributor), (August 1990), Free Press.

See **Strategic Risk, Credit Risk, Legal Risk.**

FIDUCIARY RISK. A fiduciary is a person or institution in a position of trust to one or more parties. An example might be a custodian of securities or money. Fiduciary risk arises from the potential loss that the fiduciary becomes legally liable to pay because of a claim made against the fiduciary for any alleged violation of its responsibilities, obligations, or duties as fiduciaries. Typically, fiduciary responsibility is gauged according to the standard of a "prudent person" or a "prudent expert" handling his or her own funds. The level of fiduciary risk varies by jurisdiction and by the type of banking organization. Insurance companies are expected to adhere to a higher standard of prudence than might an investment bank because of the latter's need to generate higher returns.

Fiduciary breaches of most common concern involve employees (typically senior managers and members of the board of directors) committing actions (usually fraud or theft) against the interests of shareholders or other employees. Shareholder suits have become more of an issue as senior officers' incentives have increased and shareholders have become more active and are no longer willing to rubber-stamp senior managers' business decisions. Employee litigation typically focuses on pension plan management, unfair dismissal, employee harassment, and unsafe practices.

Risk Management: Fiduciary risk management centers on loss reduction through insurance or prevention through relationship management and better alignment of the incentives of the different stakeholders.

- Risk based performance measurement and shareholder value management—organizing management around those activities that add shareholder value either in a single period (risk based performance measurement and resource allocation) or in the longer term (shareholder value management) (Subsection 16.3).

- Relationship management—keeping various stakeholders informed about the firm's actions can prevent a situation deteriorating to the stage of seeking legal remedies (Subsection 9.7).

- Fraud prevention and detection—limiting the opportunities for major breaches of employees' fiduciary responsibilities (Subsection 11.6).

- Insurance, in particular, the use of (Subsection 14.4):

  (a) Directors and Officers' insurance—fiduciary liability coverage—this protects the personal assets of a plan fiduciary against allegations of breach of fiduciary duties. Alternatively, given the small number of successful cases against directors, firms might consider legal expenses insurance as an alternative.

  (b) Fidelity insurance—this provides coverage against the dishonest or fraudulent acts of employees.

Further information: A useful guide to directors' responsibilities is provided by *The Business Judgment Rule: Fiduciary Duties of Corporate Directors* by Dennis J. Block, Nancy E. Barton and Stephen A. Radin, 5th edition (December 1998), Aspen Publishing. This discusses the role of the business judgment rule and directors' fiduciary duties of care, loyalty, and disclosure. It also discusses the use of directors' and officers' liability insurance. It argues that avoiding shareholder litigation is easiest done by actively focusing on shareholder value management at every stage of the business. Another excellent guide is *Creating Shareholder Value: A Guide for Managers and Investors* by Alfred Rappaport, revised edition (December 1997), Free Press. It provides tools and techniques on shareholder value applications to business planning, performance evaluation, executive compensation, and M&A. Employee pension plans are another source of fiduciary risks; for further details see *Pension Fund Excellence: Creating Value for Stakeholders* by Keith P. Ambachtsheer and D. Don Ezra, (1998) John Wiley & Sons. Also useful from a control and compliance perspective is *Trust Risk Management: Assessing and Controlling Fiduciary Risk* by Kenneth J. Namjestnik (1992) Bankers Publishing Company, which seeks to cover major fiduciary risk issues. At the end of each chapter, a useful compliance checklist is provided.

See **Legal Risk.**

FRAUD RISK ranges from lying, and cheating to embezzlement and theft. Fraud can be internal—committed by insiders such as officers, directors, employees, and agents—or external, committed by outsiders such as counterparties, vendors, clients, contractors, and suppliers. Although the most costly frauds in financial institutions are external frauds, employee fraud is also a major concern. While it is the high-profile, white-collar crimes that make the headlines, the majority of internal frauds are performed by low-level corporate employees—looting that totals tens of billions of dollars each year. Common frauds committed by low-level employees include falsifying expense reports; embezzling funds; using corporate property for personal purposes; stealing corporate property; and accepting gratuities from vendors, contractors, and suppliers. Common frauds perpetrated by senior management entail misrepresenting financial statements; overstating assets, sales, and profit; or understating liabilities, expenses, and losses. Senior managers do this to deceive investors and lenders or to inflate profits and thereby gain higher salaries and bonuses.

Risk Management: Fraud prevention and detection techniques (Subsection 11.6) such as personnel selection and internal and external audit are obviously highly relevant. Also refer to the earlier discussion on computer security management (Subsection 12.6) and physical security management (Subsection 12.7).
See **Human Resource Risk**.

FUNDING RISK is the potential for unanticipated costs or losses due to a mismatch between asset yields and liability funding costs. The risk may be due to different maturities of assets and liabilities, changes in credit quality, or a variety of other causes. In addition to these basis-type risks, funding risk can take the form of a liability to meet cash or collateral requirements, forcing premature liquidation of a position.

Risk Management: Asset-liability management techniques such as *immunization* and *layering* are used to address liquidity gaps between long-term loans and short-term customer deposits (Subsection 14.2).
See **Liquidity Risk**, **Market Risk** (especially Interest Rate Risk).

HERSTAT RISK. See **Settlement Risk**.

HUMAN RESOURCE RISK arises from variations in the quality and availability of the firm's internal personnel and includes:

Human Error: An unintentional mistake made by an employee. Staff errors are usually errors of commission or errors of omission. For example, a data-entry clerk who makes a mistake while keying in data within the settlement office, which results in the wrong account being transacted. Human errors increase dramatically with problem complexity, and when duties are performed under stress. A dramatic example of a staff error occurred recently, when a customer walked into a retail bank's branch office, and asked for 5 million lire to be transferred from a US dollar account in the UK to his account in Italy. Despite various checks, the bank clerk transferred US$5 million to the account (Rachlin, 1998).

Incompetence: Staff inadequately vetted on hiring or insufficiently trained, leading to inadequate job performance.

Malice: An aggrieved employee seeking revenge on the firm by damaging firm assets, especially computer-based information assets.

Key Personnel Loss and Staff Unavailability: An unexpected removal or loss of key personnel from a position of responsibility without an immediate substitute. This affected Arthur Andersen & Company following a plane crash that killed several high-level partners, and resulted in several million dollars worth of damage to the business from the loss of key personnel. Soon after, a policy was created whereby groups of executives were not to travel on the same aircraft, and a tracking system was created to monitor executive travel.

Fraud: When dishonest employees assume positions of responsibility in the some aspect of front or back office operations. Typically, there are two forms. First, fraud in which individuals manipulate outside individuals and firms to gain an advantage on behalf of themselves and/ or the firm. Second, when individuals manipulate internal control systems to produce spurious profits, usually to obtain large bonuses. Consider a recent example. On December 10, 1999, the New York superintendent of banks closed Golden City Commercial Bank of Flushing, New York. Both the bank's chairwoman and the majority shareholder were charged with multiple counts of fraud involving the granting of loans in exchange for monetary compensation. The New York State Banking Department stated that Golden City caused a "complete loss of confidence" by defying the state agency's orders, breaking banking laws, and operating in an unsafe manner.

Information Risk: All internal computer systems should have back-up procedures. Back-up logs or diaries can be helpful.

Risk Management: Much of management is ultimately the problem of managing human resource risks. However, the following aspects are especially important:

- Personnel selection—poor performance, staff turnover, and employee fraud management should begin with selection criteria for hiring and promotion to ensure adequate fit between the employee's profile and the needs of the position (Subsection 9.3).

- Human factors engineering analyzes the entire system of human, task, and technology in order to understand the factors that create errors or loss events among operating staff (Subsection 11.5).

- Fraud prevention and detection—the risk of fraud often depends on two factors: the existence of weaknesses in the systems of the firm and on the motivation for the crime. Not surprisingly, the motivation for fraud is seriously affected by the likelihood and magnitude of any potential penalties. A major driver of fraud is the distance from the firm's central operations or controls. It is not accidental that many of the major frauds have occurred far from the firm's main focus of operations (for example, Barings, Daiwa, and Drexel) because that is where the firm's controls tend to be at their weakest. This is especially the case when new products or markets demand cross-functional flexibility, overstepping the usual mandate for segregation of duties (Subsection 11.6).

- Training—most applicable to issues involving a lack of internal staff competence. A 1997 survey of operational risk management practices in UK banks by Coopers & Lybrand and the British Bankers Association found that only 16 percent of banks tied their risk evaluation of different business areas to training in those areas. This is probably a mistake. According to the *Consultative Paper on Training and Competence* issued by the Financial Services Authority

(November 1999), insurance companies and stockbrokers with fund management arms will be forced to spend more than £10m training back office staff to ensure they are competent to run crucial administration systems (Subsection 9.4).

- Computer security management techniques such as firewalls, encryption, and authentication can track, prevent, and detect many computer-related breaches by internal staff (Subsection 12.6).

Further information: A general guide to HR management is provided by *Strategic Human Resource Management: Corporate Rhetoric and Human Reality* by Lynda Gratton et al. (May 1999), Oxford University Press. This book examines how internal and external variables impinge on the ability of management to conduct effective human resource policy. It also looks at how corporate strategies affect everyday managerial and individual behavior. A useful introduction to human factors engineering is the book, *An Introduction to Human Factors Engineering* by Christopher D. Wickens, Sallie E. Gordon and Yili Liu (December 1997), Addison-Wesley Publishing Company. For further information on competency and behavioral-based recruitment, see *Competency-Based Recruitment and Selection* by Robert Wood and Tim Wood (1998), John Wiley & Sons. To understand fraud prevention and detection issues, refer to *Fraud Auditing and Forensic Accounting: New Tools and Techniques* by G. Jack Bologna and Robert J. Lindquist (1995), John Wiley & Sons.
See **Fiduciary Risk, Control Risk, Fraud Risk.**

LEGAL RISK Legal risk has two basic forms. The first aspect of legal risk comes from uncertainty about the source of the threat. For instance, legal suits can arise from any one of the various stakeholders connected with the firm's activities:

- Employees—for wrongful dismissal, harassment, and discrimination.
- Customers—for negligence and product liability.
- From competitors and suppliers—charges of anti-competitive practices, trademark, and patent infringement.
- Investors and creditors—malfeasance claims.
- Governments and regulators—non-compliance, criminal charges, and incorrect interpretation of legislation. See the discussion on regulatory risk.

In general, addressing these different sources of legal risk through, for example, adequate control systems, well-designed contracts, and skilled personnel is always more effective than reducing legal risks after the fact.

The second aspect of legal risk concerns uncertainty regarding legislation, its interpretation, and the judicial process. Two elements of this are particularly important to financial service firms, as follows:

Geographical/Cross-border Risk: Banks may face different legal and regulatory requirements when they deal with customers across national borders. For new forms of retail electronic banking (such as Internet banking) and electronic money, there may be uncertainties about legal requirements in some countries. In addition, there may be jurisdictional ambiguities with respect to the responsibilities of different national authorities. Such considerations may expose banks to legal risk associated with non-compliance with different national laws and regulations, including consumer protection laws, record-keeping and reporting requirements, privacy rules, and money laundering laws.

Documentation Risk: Risk that products and deals are not properly covered through well-designed agreements (for example, an ISDA document) that are properly executed and supported by timely confirmations. The result of documentation risk might be difficulties enforcing transactions in the event of a dispute.

Risk Management: Relationship management (Subsection 9.7) and business and market intelligence techniques (Subsection 10.3) are the primary mechanisms to deal with the legal threats, while quality legal defenses, standardization, and documentation offer some respite from the vagaries of the judicial process.

- Loss isolation and asset protection—legal separation of entities should be carefully managed. Creditors are increasingly able to go back into the layers of organizational structure to reach the key asset holders (Subsection 13.2).

- Legal risk reduction—a legal review of all product and service documentation and marketing and sales practices. The legal department should maintain a report of the status of transaction contracts and agreements used, as well as any supporting materials; for example, for supporting confirmations (Subsection 13.1).

- Standardization and documentation of procedures and practices, especially those involving litigious stakeholders. For example, trading desks need to ensure the use of International Swaps and Derivatives Association (ISDA) swap agreements and International Foreign Exchange Master Agreements (IFEMA) to avoid documentation error. This should be standardized among counterparties to ensure consistency of netting credit triggers and legal jurisdiction. Legal staff should develop and maintain a documentation database of standard contract types and confirm its usage throughout the organization.

- Business and market intelligence—the legal benefits of a proactive external business intelligence function are manifold. For instance, banks that choose to provide services to customers in different national markets will need to understand different national legal requirements, and develop an appreciation for national differences in customer expectations and knowledge of products and services. A bank may also face difficulties in enforcing the fulfillment of a foreign service provider's obligations. More proactively, business intelligence can also be used as a preamble to managing the firm's reputation, staving off potential threats from non-governmental organizations and the media (Subsection 10.3).

- Relationship management and credit management—senior management should ensure that existing systems for credit extension and liquidity management take into account potential difficulties arising from legal exposures (Subsection 9.7).

- Organizational learning—firms may wish to develop a litigation database that shows—within the industry—the reasons for and the frequency of occurrences and losses associated with particular classes of litigation by clients, counterparties, suppliers, and regulatory penalties. This could be incorporated into the main external loss database. Legal categories should include the source of the litigation problem; for example, sales error (Subsection 10.2).

Further information: A good overview of many of the legal risks surrounding financial services in the future is provided by *21st Century Money, Banking and Commerce* by Thomas P. Vartanian, Robert H. Ledig, and Lynn Bruneau (March 1, 1998), Fried, Frank, Harris, Shriver & Jacobson. Also useful as a general guide to managers of legal risks is *Managers and the Legal Environment: Strategies for the 21st Century* by Constance E. Bagley and Ernest W. King, (April 1999) Southwestern Publishing Company. Obviously, more detailed legal references should be consulted for specific advice.

See **Business Continuity Risk, Customer Risk, Accounting Risk, Regulatory Risk, Reputational Risk, Supplier Risk, Settlement Risk.**

LIQUIDITY RISK. The markets for many assets and liabilities, e.g., real estate, small capitalization stocks, many debt markets, are inactively traded, and therefore subject to liquidity risk. This is the risk that transactions cannot be executed at any price. It is especially prevalent during periods of massive market volatility, and is a major additional complexity for models of market risk, which usually assume continuous price movements.

See **Market Risk, Funding Risk.**

MARKET RISK is the risk of adverse fluctuations of the marked-to-market value of a financial portfolio (either on or off the balance sheet) during the period required to liquidate the portfolio. Market risk factors include:

Interest Rate Risk of both on-balance sheet positions (for example, loan portfolios) and off-balance sheet risks (for example, options, swap positions). Furthermore, when interest rates fluctuate, so too do most financial institutions' earnings and expenses. Within interest rate risks are many subrisks, such as *repricing risks,* which reflect uncertainty in the repricing of floating rate assets and liabilities; *yield curve risk,* concerning the uncertainty in the slope and shape of the yield curve; and *credit spread risk,* reflecting uncertainty about the yields for non-sovereign credits.

Equity Risk associated with specific companies or portfolio indexes.

Foreign Exchange Risk resulting from changes in the relative prices of different currencies. See also settlement risks and counterparty credit risks.

Commodity Risk resulting from variance in the prices of electricity, metals, oil, gas, and agricultural commodities.

Market rate movements ranging from minimal to extreme may subject a financial institution to (1) significant losses resulting in capital adequacy problems and/or regulatory intervention; (2) loss of market capitalization; and (3) an inability to raise necessary levels of capital. The consequences can be severe, resulting in regulatory sanctions including receivership.

The availability of market data has encouraged the development of complex models for market risk assessment, particularly for traders with a short-term investment horizon. Unfortunately, the quality of data and the restrictions imposed by some of the model assumptions (for example, liquid markets, normal return distributions) severely limit the quality of the risk estimates, a point dramatically illustrated with the downfall of the high-profile quantitative hedge fund LTCM in 1998.

Risk Management: Much of the daily management of market risk is the management of position and market data. A sound system of records should keep track of all transactions on a trade-date basis and provide access to all supporting information. Positions should, when possible, be marked to market. There should be separation of duties between trade initiation and trade recording and control. Systematic processes and procedures should be in place to obtain, clean, and analyze the data, as well as back-test any analytical conclusions. Other important themes underlying effective market risk management include:

*   Hedging using derivatives—reducing interest rate, commodity, foreign exchange, and equity risks by purchasing financial contracts such as swaps, forwards, and options that reduce the transaction's exposure to short-term market fluctuations. Hedging swaps the underlying risk exposure for *basis risks* (the risk of a mismatch between the underlying exposure and the hedging vehicle) (Subsection 14.6).

*   Asset-liability management techniques that focus on long-term interest rate, and funding risks associated with medium- and long-term assets and liabilities on the firm's balance sheet (Subsection 14.2).

*   The use of regulatory capital and economic capital to cover market risk exposures (Chapter 16).

*   Boundary systems to develop a series of limits and sanctions regarding internal trading. These limits can be used constrain the

extent of positions, concentration of risks, extent of loss (for example, stop loss provisions), and counterparty exposures (Subsection 12.4).

• Diagnostic control systems (Subsection 12.3) using measures such as Value at Risk (see Subsection 1.6), scenario analysis (Subsection 3.1), and stress testing (Subsection 3.2).

Further information: Myriad resources exist on market risk and financial risk management. For a good overview, refer to *Risk Management and Analysis: Measuring and Modeling Financial Risk* (Wiley Series in Financial Engineering) by Carol Alexander (editor) and John C. Hull, Volume 1 (March 1999), John Wiley & Sons. Also useful is *Beyond Value at Risk: The New Science of Risk Management* by Kevin Dowd (1998), John Wiley & Sons. *Risk Magazine* <www.riskpublications.com> provides excellent articles on cutting-edge issues in derivatives and market risk management. Also helpful is a search engine the magazine provides, available at <www.financewise.com/risk> To understand the regulators' perspective to market risks, see The Bank for International Settlements at <www.bis.org>; it also publishes consultative papers on frameworks for various risk (credit, market, operational, and so on) management techniques.
See **Credit Risk, Liquidity Risk.**

OPERATIONS RISK is the risk of failures within various internal operations processes. These failures can occur at any stage of the value-adding process through mistakes in marketing, sales, transaction booking and back office operations. For example:

Product Marketing Risk: The danger that the marketing and sales departments do not fully understand a product. This may lead to misleading the consumer, which may result in lawsuits against the firm (see **Legal Risk**).

Sales Risk: The risk that inappropriate sales techniques have been used to increase sales volumes. Over-zealous sales representatives (for example, loan officers or relationship officers) may be tempted to stretch the truth regarding the customer's overall financial condition to sell enough loans to meet sales targets. Thus, volume is overemphasized over profitable, measured growth. May also include the risk of churning accounts to increase brokerage fees.

Booking Risk: Trades might not be correctly captured due to data errors/ processing in the deal capture or because of staff errors—written errors on the deal ticket, illegible handwriting, or errors copying the deal ticket. Common booking errors include entering a buy order instead of a sell order or vice versa, crediting a transaction to the wrong fund, or even recording a purchase of the wrong class of an issuer's securities. Booking risks can lead to unreconciled positions, incorrect P&L, counterparty withdrawal, or incorrect hedging.

Organizational Structure Risk: The risk that the firm might not have an independent reporting structure on the position, valuation, and control of products. May be part of **Accounting Risk**.

Risk Management: Process redesign and the application of quality management techniques to all the resources utilized by operations processes should be a management priority for the prevention of operations risks. Specifically:

- Process re-engineering—redesigning the entire process avoids uncontrollable risks being passed downstream; for example, from deal processing to other operational areas such as confirmations and settlement. Consequently, well-designed deal processing should be central to any risk management initiative in the back office (Subsection 11.1).

- Automation—limiting human interventions at every stage of the process reduces the likelihood for many common errors; for example, by incorporating trading restrictions into an automated compliance system that rejects improper transactions or produces exception reports of suspect transactions (Subsection 11.4).

- Human factors engineering—given that human intervention is necessary, what are the aspects of personnel, task, and technology that improve throughput, and conversely, tend to make errors more likely (Subsection 11.5).

- Organizational design—for instance, through having a clearly defined reporting structure and a separation of staff duties in the front and back offices (Subsection 9.6).

- Training—to enable staff to recognize the symptoms of potential losses; for example, some of the indicators of internal fraud or money laundering (Subsection 9.4).

- Organizational learning—user-friendly, concise summaries of important procedures and restrictions should be made accessible to the staff that need them. Similarly, the knowledge gained by individual staff members about handling unusual situations, new products, new regulations, new models, and new markets should be made available and searchable by the rest of the organization (Subsection 10.2).

- Work and job restructuring—organizing work flow by reorganizing the sequence of tasks or the allocation of resources to task can dramatically affect the risks of operations. The same is true of product and service redesign of the product and service outputs to streamline and standardize the operations processes that deliver them (Subsection 11.2).

- Risk based performance measurement and risk based incentives in the front office—Implementing an incentive compensation plan that fails to incorporate operations risk of the products they sell will only pass the risks on to the middle and back office (Subsection 16.3).

- Diagnostic control systems that link the front office to the back. For example, dealer trade input should be followed by a daily position sign-off by traders and daily explanation of any reconciliations (Subsection 12.3).

Further information: For good review of risks in securities operations and how to combat them, refer to *Securities Operations: A Guide to Operations and Information Systems in the Securities Industry* by Michael T. Reddy, 2nd edition (March 1995), Prentice Hall Press. Also useful is *Bank & Brokerage Back Office Procedures and Settlements* by Mervyn J. King (January 12, 1999), Glenlake Publishing Company, which describes legal, operation, management, and financial risks associated with back office and settlement. From insurance companies' perspective, refer to *Insurance Operations* by Bernard L. Webb, Connor M. Harrison, and James J. Markham, 2nd edition (May 1997), Ferguson Publishing Company.

See **Human Resource Risk, Control Risk, Business Risk,**

Business Continuity Risk, Strategic Risk.

PHYSICAL ASSET RISK includes all forms of physical damage to assets such as offices, trading rooms, computers, and communication lines. The causes of damage can be internal (for example, office theft) or external (for example, natural disasters such as flood, fire, earthquakes, and hurricanes) or manmade disasters such as war and civil unrest. The causes may also be intentional; for example, arson, or unintended, for example, faulty wiring. Examples of physical asset risks abound, from the threats related to infrastructure (for example, the 1992 Chicago Flood), to those related to people (such as the bombing of the World Trade Center in New York), and other external events (such as the destruction by fire of the Credit Lyonnais trading room in Paris in 1996).

Risk Management: Several activities can help prevent, control, and finance physical asset risks:

- Facilities planning staff can develop contingency planning programs for alternative sites and suppliers to ensure that asset loss does not affect business operation. They can also ensure that there should be redundancy in critical assets (redundant systems) such as back-up trading sites, computing facilities, communications lines, and other support resources (Subsection 13.3).

- Contractual risk transfer techniques such as leasing can be used to pass the risk of asset loss to an outside party (Subsection 14.7).

- Self-insurance (Subsection 14.5) and external insurance (Subsection 14.4) can be used to fund some of the financial losses associated with the asset damage or loss. For instance, firms can obtain Act of God Bonds from insurance companies—bonds whose principal, interest, or both are linked to the company's losses from disasters. Losses exceeding a designated size would change interest payments, delay principal repayments, or otherwise change the debtor/creditor relationship. Catastrophe derivatives fulfill a similar role.

- For external intended threats, physical security management can be used to prevent access to sensitive assets (Subsection 12.7).

- Computer security management techniques can prevent and mitigate damage to a firm's hardware and software resources (Subsection 12.6).

Further information: Facilities management references have a host of materials on the management of physical assets. There are two streams of thought. First, managing asset risk through contingency planning. See, for example, *Disaster Planning and Recovery: A Guide for Facility Professionals* by Alan M. Levitt (April 1997), John Wiley & Sons. Alternatively, facilities planners can focus on effective design and redundancy to take a more preventative view of asset risks. A good guide to this approach is *Facilities Planning and Design for Financial Institutions: A Strategic Management Guide* (A Bankline Publication) by Paul Seibert, ringbound edition (November 1995), Irwin Professional Publishing.

See **Business Continuity Risk, Human Resource Risk, Supplier Risk.**

POLITICAL RISK See Subsection 10.4 on **Country Risk**.

PROJECT RISK See discussion on project risk management in Subsection 10.4.

REGULATORY RISK is a subset of legal risks that arise from the non-compliance of regulations. The most important aspect of regulatory risks relates to inadequate disclosure of operations, as follows:

Disclosure Risk: Regulatory penalties arising from inadequate disclosure to regulators. For example, Shinji Yamada, a former head of Credit Suisse Financial Products (Tokyo), a subsidiary of Credit Suisse Group, was alleged to have obstructed an inspection of his branch by the Japanese Financial Supervisory Agency. CSFP staff were also accused of destroying documents. CSFP has been indicted for the "systematic evasion and obstruction of inspections" and of selling products that "deeply undermined the soundness of Japanese financial markets." On November 30, 1999, CSFP's Tokyo branch became the first bank to have its local banking license withdrawn by Japanese regulators.

Firms should take a expansive view of their disclosure responsibilities. For example, in 1991, four top executives from Salomon Brothers failed to take appropriate action in response to unlawful activities on the government trading desk. Although, company lawyers found no legal requirement that they disclose the improprieties, a delay in disclosing and a failure to reveal their prior knowledge prompted a crisis of confidence among employees, creditors, shareholders, and customers.

The executives lost their moral authority to lead and resigned. Their lack of action compounded the trading desk's legal offenses, resulting in $1 billion in legal costs, increased funding costs, and lost business.

Compliance Breach: Firms' non-compliance with existing regulations, especially those regarding marketing practices to retail customers. For example, in 1997, the UK-based Royal Victoria Friendly Society failed to ensure sound systems and practices in its life insurance operations. In 1997, visits from the UK regulator resulted in fines of £0.9 million for serious and widespread compliance failings. The company was ordered to carry out a full review of certain types of business and to provide compensation to customers.

Other components of regulatory risk include:

Capital Requirement Breach: Failure to have adequate capital reserves to cover risks in market, credit, and operating portfolio.

Regulatory Change Risk: Regulatory change may not lead to losses directly, but may lead to regulatory errors, accounting errors, compliance failures, or client litigation if not complied with.

Tax Risk: Not taking tax considerations into account with specific products; for example, complex derivatives. Tax risks may also include the operational risk of not maintaining the data required for tax authorities (a form of non-disclosure), which may result in their removing any tax advantages for particular products.

Risk Management: Many of the general issues surrounding **legal risks** also pertain to regulatory risk management. However, because of the ongoing nature of relationships with regulators and the large reputational costs of non-compliance, some issues should be further emphasized:

- Compliance programs—formal compliance programs should be developed. Compliance programs, along with other more general boundary systems (such as risk policies, codes of conduct, operational guidelines, and trading limits), provide clear rules, limits, and proscriptions with defined and credible threats of punishment. These programs should also reflect the reality that compliance resources are limited and that some mistakes are more important than others. Another rule of thumb for compliance officers is that consistent compliance with simpler procedures will usually achieve greater risk reduction than inconsistent compliance with more comprehensive procedures (Subsection 12.5).

- Internal and external audit should review and monitor bank policies and procedures for compliance and take corrective action for instances of non-compliance (Subsection 12.8).

- Business and market intelligence staff should monitor regulatory pronouncements for any potential impact on the firm and its clients (Subsection 10.3).

- Careful relationship management with regulatory officials. One way to do this is to invest in flexible data-sorting systems to provide compliance reports to regulatory bodies when demanded on short notice, especially when a crisis breaks out (Subsection 9.7).

Further information: The first source of regulatory information is the regulators themselves. Some of the more important bodies that can provide further regulatory information are: the US Securities and Exchange Commission <http://www.sec.gov>, the UK Financial Services Authority <www.sib.co.uk>, and the Bank for International Settlements (BIS) <www.bis.org>. A useful guide to the role of compliance in banking is *The Handbook of Compliance: Making Ethics Work in Financial Services* by Andrew Newton (1998), Financial Times/Pitman Publishing.

See **Legal Risk.**

REPUTATIONAL RISK are those risks that threaten to tarnish a firm's reputation and include:

Contractual Disagreement Risk: Specific disagreements with the detailed terms of a particular contract.

Dissatisfaction Risk: General disenchantment with the terms of a particular contract; for example, the manner in which Banker's Trust's marketing practices were criticized following legal suits by Gibson Greetings and Proctor & Gamble.

Media Attack: Unfounded attack by media or industrial or political group with its own agenda, undermining the firm's reputation. Often a media attack follows a major loss in another part of the same industry.

Risk Management: Many of the other operational risks presented in this glossary, if inappropriately handled, have the potential to lead to reputational risks. Nonetheless, reputations can be managed using a combination of the following techniques:

- Crisis management—the ability to respond quickly and honestly to events. When effectively done, it can even lead to positive results. For example, despite a serious security flaw with its Internet share-dealing service in November 1998, Halifax's swift action to publicly apologize to its 10,000 customers saw it losing only two accounts. Halifax attributes this to its honesty and speed in communicating the problem, as well as assuring its customers that the flaw had not led to anyone losing any money. The bank was forced to switch off its on-line brokering system after a few customers gained access to other accounts. Although a few customers were affected, the entire system had to be taken offline (Subsection 13.4).

- Effective relationship management with the media via a strong corporate affairs team (Subsection 9.7).

- Survey clients to determine level of satisfaction.

- Contingency planning—developing responses to reputation crises before they occur (Subsection 13.3).

Further information: Reputation management is a relatively new discipline. For an overview, refer to *Waltzing with the Raptors: A Practical Roadmap to Protecting Your Company's Reputation* by Glen Peters (1999), John Wiley & Sons. This book introduces the concept of reputation assurance—a framework for measuring a company's reputation and social accountability. Read also *Reputation Risk Management* by Peter Sheldon Green (1992), Financial Times/Pitman Publishing.

See **Business Risk, Business Continuity Risk, Legal Risk.**

SETTLEMENT RISK results from the potential for inaccurate, delayed, or non-payment of funds from one counterparty to another. Settlement risks result from the fact that asset transfer is rarely instantaneous and often not final and, therefore, financial organizations engaged as counterparties or as intermediaries face a credit risk. Settlement risks have a number of subcategories including:

Counterparty Default: Given that the counterparty has failed (part of credit risk), this is the risk that internal staff have not recognized this failure and continue to make payments. In other words, this is the risk that a bank might pay the funds it owes on a transaction, but not receive the funds due from its counterparty. Settlement risk is especially critical in the foreign exchange markets for two reasons. First, offsetting payments are typically in different currencies, which can preclude payment netting. Second, time zone differences can cause delays between the timing of one payment and the reciprocal payment in another currency.

Late Settlement: A failure to make timely deliveries and settlements, hence incurring late penalties and reputational costs. Late settlement is partly driven by onerous margin or collateral requirements. Late settlement may lead to liquidity risks caused by the inability of buyers to respond to adverse changes in the markets. The availability of securities lending and borrowing mechanisms can limit the extent of late settlement risks.

Forex Settlement Risk: Cross-border settlement is typically accompanied with foreign exchange transactions, which are themselves subject to settlement risk. The extent of this risk depends on the quality of global/local custodians and dealers involved, and is typically managed by intraday forex limits. An important industry initiative in this area is *Continuous Link Settlement* (CLS), which aims to eliminate settlement risk for certain forex transactions.

Delivery Risk: This arises when the buyer of a security or other asset pays but does not receive delivery.

Custody Risk: Non-residents are not usually direct participants in local depositories, and so must settle transactions through local custodians or brokers. Custody risk is the danger of asset loss because a local broker or custodian becomes insolvent or actively seeks to defraud investors. The only risk management approach for custody risks is due dilligence regarding all intermediaries with which the bank deals.

Collateral Risk: This is the risk that the back office either fails to recognize a counterparty's failure to post collateral, or fails to demand an appropriate level of collateral given the credit risk. Either case may result in wasted collateral or incorrect margin calls, or may translate to a loss if a counterparty defaults.

Legal Risks: There are many different settlement-related aspects of legal risk–for example, there is the danger that a foreign government will introduce exchange controls, onerous taxation, or other forms of regulatory barriers. Legal risks also comprise the uncertainty regarding the choice of law used to determine ownership rights and finality of securities transfers. Clear and adequate documentation is the first barrier to legal risks.

Systemic Risk: Although not unique to forex, systemic risks are particularly associated with large-dollar international payments systems. These worldwide networks operate 24 hours a day, offering payments, clearing, and settlement systems that handle trillions of dollars each day. Given the estimated $1.25 trillion of foreign exchange trades arranged daily, the resulting large exposures raise significant concerns for individual banks and the international financial system as a whole. Systemic risk is the possibility of a major disruption in the foreign exchange settlement process due to a major settlement failure causing a chain reaction of other failures throughout the banking system. Concerns about systemic risks first crystallized following the failure of the German Herstatt Bank. On June 26, 1974, that bank had already taken in all its foreign currency receipts in Europe, but had not made any of its US dollar payments when German banking regulators closed the bank down at the end of the German business day. The failure of the bank left $620 million of unsettled forex trades, for which counterparties had paid their leg but had not received the other currency.

Risk Management: Most of the efforts to reduce settlement risk are multilateral, requiring the intervention of agencies such as the Bank for International Settlement (formed after the Herstatt incident), rather than unilateral in scope. For instance, reducing the time between trade date and settlement date reduces the likelihood of a settlement loss. It is expected that the international target of T+1, or even settlement on the trade date, should significantly reduce counterparty default-related losses. In many exchanges, investor protection funds or trade guarantee funds are also used to reduce the risks of counterparty default, but the maximum payout is limited and so it effectively protects only the smaller investors. Also important in reducing settlement risks multilaterally is the use of netting procedures. Unfortunately, getting international agreement to change settlement practices followed by different governments is far from easy.

Measures that banks can adopt unilaterally to manage their settlement risk exposures include:

- Expected losses from settlement-related losses should always be used to determine and update any necessary loss provisions (Subsection 16.1).

- Automation—the risk of principal loss can be eliminated if there is true delivery versus payment (known as DVP) in the market. DVP requires electronic links between securities transfer and payment systems, with both allowing simultaneous and irrevocable exchange of value (Subsection 11.4).

- Financial restructuring—restructuring the financial terms of the contract can also help mitigate credit exposures (Subsection 14.1).

  (a) Credit can also be actively enhanced through management of *margin* and any *collateral* whereby the counterparty makes assets available to be surrendered in the event of default or downgrade. Increasingly, collateral management systems are being used to manage calls for collateral as the value of traded positions rises and falls and helps avoid disputes with counterparties over collateral postings. Disputes are surprisingly frequent, with many banks logging tens of disputes a month with their counterparties. This typically requires the careful management of the documentation flows associated with collateral agreements. Also important is the reconciliation of the collateral data with the transactional data held elsewhere in the firm.

  (b) *Credit enhancement* through *guarantees:* by obtaining guarantees from third parties, non-payment only occurs if counterparty and guarantor both default (which is presumably much less likely).

(c) *Bilateral netting* arrangements allowing counterparties to be responsible for the net payments between parties rather than the individual gross contracts between them. Similarly *netting by novation* allows old contracts to be replaced by a new contract sometimes with a new counterparty.

(d) *Periodic settlement* between counterparties at periodic points within the contact.

- Diagnostic control systems—in particular, systematic and consistently applied credit scoring and credit management policies and procedures can be used to evaluate new credits and monitor and respond rapidly to changes in credit quality (Subsection 12.3).

- Boundary systems—periodic exposure reports describing position limits on counterparties or business sectors and also any internal and external credit risk assessments (Subsection 12.4).

- Hedging using derivatives—credit derivatives are bilateral financial contracts that isolate specific aspects of credit risk from an underlying instrument and transfer that risk between two parties (Subsection 14.6).

- Loss prediction—the detailed settlement risk exposures depend on the characteristics of the transfer, the participants, controls, and the structure of networks used. For instance, by measuring forex settlement exposure properly and using tools that frequently (once or twice a day) update current and future global exposures as they execute new trades and as trades move through the settlement process. This would treat forex settlement activities on par with other operations that create credit exposures (such as loans or deposits) (Chapter 10).

- Risk avoidance—reducing excessive forex settlement exposures with particular counterparties (Chapter 9).

- Process redesign and re-engineering—for example, by adopting better operational policies regarding settlements, such as eliminating overtly restrictive payment cancellation deadlines and shortening the time it takes to identify the final and failed receipt of bought currencies. Continuous link settlement is a good example (Subsection 11.1).

Further information: Regulators, fearful of systemic risk, have developed most of the resources on settlement risk; most notable is the Bank for International Settlements <www.bis.org>. For instance, reports such as *Clearance and Settlement Systems in the World's Securities Markets* (1989); *Settlement Risk in Foreign Exchange Transactions*, Committee on Payment and Settlement Systems of the central banks of the Group of Ten Countries, Bank for International Settlements, Basle March 1996. For a technical overview, refer to *Bank Operating Credit Risk: Assessing and Controlling Credit Risk in Bank Operating Services* by Paul F. Mayland.

See **Customer Risk, Credit Risk.**

STRATEGIC RISK is the risk of implementing an unsuccessful or ineffective strategy that fails to secure required returns. Many strategic risks derive from the threats posed by different stakeholders in the broader enterprise, all of whom have potentially conflicting agendas and motivations. It follows that strategic risk includes:

Regulatory Risk: Legal risks that arise from non-compliance with regulations.

Customer Risk: Such as credit risks, association risks, client suitability risks.

Supplier Risk: Major failures of critical outside contractors to deliver quality services.

Competitor Risk: Innovations by competitor firms that change the nature of the entire business. A good example of this was provided by JP Morgan with the introduction of its RiskMetrics™ datasets in 1994, which changed the nature of market risk management services.

Strategic risks also include major changes in the business environment. For example:

Mergers and Acquisitions: The trend that is likely to follow after the mega-bank mergers of the 1990s are mergers that extend across geographical boundaries, as well as across industries, involving a combination of banks, insurance companies, and retail brokers.

Technology Changes: The rise of the e-commerce and the worldwide web has dramatically changed the economics of distribution and marketing, with the effect of changing whole industries. Similarly, massive technological changes are promised by innovations such as genetic engineering and broadband personal communications.

Social Changes and Demographics: The savings rate is the major determinant of the funds flowing into the financial sector for subsequent investment. The savings rate is closely tied to demographic changes, such as the rise of an aging population coming to retirement.

Risk Management: Strategic risk management is an outgrowth of corporate strategy and involves:

- Strategic and business planning—developing and communicating a coherent but flexible strategic direction throughout the firm. Employees at all levels should understand the direction the firm is working toward so they can strive toward the same results (Subsection 10.1).

- Scenario analysis (Subsection 3.1) and contingency planning (Subsection 13.3)—can be used to identify those events with the potential to shift the nature of the business.

- Market and business intelligence—knowing the broad trends within the marketplace (Subsection 10.3).

- Organizational learning—leveraging individual insights for the benefit of the business as a whole (Subsection 10.2).

- Hedging using derivatives of long-term economic risks faced by the firm (Subsection 14.6).

Further information: Refer to *Managing in the Turbulent World Economy: Corporate Performance and Risk Exposure* by Lars Oxelheim and Clas Wihlborg (Contributor), (August 1997), John Wiley & Sons. Also of interest is *Risk, Strategy, and Management* (Strategic Management Policy and Planning, Vol. 5) by Richard A. Bettis and Howard Thomas (Editor), (September 1990), JAI Press.

See **Customer Risk, Regulatory Risk, Supplier Risk, Competitor Risk, Business Risk, Technology Risk.**

SUPPLIER RISK is faced by financial services firms because of failures of outside parties to provide contractually agreed-upon services. With increased outsourcing of many less-critical operational functions (for example, IT, billing, custody), these risks have become more important. For instance:

Utility Failure: Failures in power, water, and heating, ventilation and air-conditioning (HVAC) services can cause massive disruption to business operations.

Custody Risk: The failure of a custodian or depository institution to safely keep securities or other assets on behalf of its clients.

Service Provider Failure: Degradation or outright failure of the service provided by a critical supplier. For example, a computer malfunction at EDS' New Jersey computer center resulted in 3,000 ATMs across the East Coast going down.

Supplier Default: See the discussion on credit risk.

Risk Management: Many of same interventions described under credit risk are also relevant here for example, hedging using derivatives (Subsection 14.6) and diagnostic control systems (Subsection 12.3). Some other risk management interventions uniquely appropriate for supplier risk include:

- Contingency planning (Subsection 13.3) and scenario analysis (Subsection 3.1)—these can be used to brainstorm management responses before supplier failure.

- Contractual risk transfer—performance-based contracts and service level agreements can be used to tie service provider costs to performance (Subsection 14.7).

- Relationship management—due diligence in the initial selection of providers can identify the risks before they occur. It is also wise to secure agreement before problems emerge as to who takes the risks of service provider downtime (Subsection 9.7).

- Credit risk measurement of would-be suppliers can be used to estimate the likelihood of financial distress at potential suppliers. Similarly, credit enhancement measures such as collateral, credit triggers, and so on, can be used to reduce losses due to supplier default.

- Using redundant systems, either by having multiple suppliers or by have multiple delivery mechanisms for the services provided by the supplier (Subsection 12.2).

Further information: Strategic supplier management, particularly in manufacturing environments, is very much concerned with the trade-off between cost and risk, usually in terms of playing one supplier off against another, and developing a relationship with suppliers. For instance, refer to *Balanced Sourcing: Cooperation and Competition in Supplier Relationships* by Timothy M. Laseter (October 1998), Jossey-Bass Publishers.

See **Business Continuity Risk, Credit Risk.**

TECHNOLOGY RISK is the potential for failures associated with computer and communications hardware, software, and data. Some important aspects of technology risk include:

Data Risk: Corruption of critical data. Particularly acute for static data concerning customers, instruments and transaction data. Errors here may be passed on to settlements and may contribute to settlement errors, late deliveries, and so on.

Model Risk: Valuation and risk models that are either incorrectly implemented or that make use of questionable assumptions, or assumptions that no longer hold in a particular context. For example, in 1998, Royal Bank of Canada compensated 5,200 customers for errors in mortgage prepayments dating from 1993. Some staff had inadvertently used the wrong calculation method after product conditions had been changed. This required C$2.5 million in compensation, costs of an independent audit firm, and internal resource costs.

Software Risk: The likelihood of design and programming errors. For example, the customers of St. George Bank in Australia found their cash cards "gobbled up" by ATMs during one weekend when newly installed software failed. The bank had to face high costs of customer dissatisfaction and rectification.

Systems Outage: For example, failure of a major computer system, that disrupts trading and support systems and leads to loss.

Telecommunication Risk: The possibility of a major telecommunications failure.

Information Risk: Leaking or loss of critical customer information that embarrasses the firm and leads to the possibility of litigation loss through the breaking of privacy laws.

Computer Security Breach: Unauthorized persons gaining access to firm's offices or systems. This also includes virus damage. For example, in 1994, a group of Russian hackers made $10 million of illegal transfers out of Citibank. All but $400,000 was ultimately recovered, but there was a greater loss to the business—20 of its top customers all moved their business to other banks, claiming the need for more stringent security.

Risk Management:

- Quality management techniques (Subsection 9.2) have been applied to software development and testing. For example, source code control, regression testing, structured programming and object-oriented development. Similarly, systematic and frequent system testing should take place across a range of transaction types simulating a range of volume and market scenarios. Regression testing should be routinely performed to compare results from the new systems with those produced by the previous legacy systems.

- Physical security management—providing physical access controls to secured areas (Subsection 12.7).

- Computer security management—including controls around access to external computer systems: firewalls, passwords and authorization procedures, encryption, and dial-back systems (Subsection 12.6).

- Contingency planning—computer disaster recovery procedures with hot/cold back-up sites (Subsection 13.3).

- Standardization and code reuse—flexible function models should be made available as a firmwide application, also accessible by clients in a client-server environment. Such applications would use a common data depository to avoid data movement and decrease data-handling errors.

- Training—staff should keep pace and be up to date with technological change (Subsection 9.4).

- Organizational learning—system assumptions should be documented explicitly, including the calculation methods, internal logic and data checks, and the individuals responsible (Subsection 10.2).

- Contractual risk transfer—use of external consultants for expert opinions on complex issues (Subsection 14.7).

Further information: An excellent guide to computer and software risks is *Assessment and Control of Software Risks* (Yourdon Press Computing) by T. Capers Jones (February 1994), Prentice Hall. This handbook summarizes the major problems of building and maintaining software and technology projects, and outlines some management prevention and control responses. Also useful for technical project management is *Technical Risk Management* by Jack V. Michaels, (September 1995), Prentice Hall.

See **Project Risk, Business Continuity Risk.**

TRANSACTIONS RISK. See **Operations Risk**.

APPENDIX B

OPERATIONAL RISK MANAGEMENT SOFTWARE AND SERVICES

Algorithmics Inc.

Algorithmics' advanced operational risk management tools integrate top-down capital allocation and bottom-up operational control. Algorithmics provide four types of risk models—a set of questionnaire-based assessment models to get an external view of operations; processing models to measure transaction losses; reliability models for business continuity; and assurance models for control audit. There is support for risk aggregation, scenario modeling, and simulation. Their *WatchDog* tool uses explicit causal models based on Baysian Belief networks for failure prediction.

The website address is: <www.algorithmics.com>

Arthur Andersen Consulting

The Callisto OR toolset developed by the financial service arm of Arthur Andersen implements a bottom-up continuous improvement methodology aimed more toward operational control than operational risk quantification. The core of the toolset is risk profiling through superior Key Performance Indicators (KPIs). The toolset allows linking these to specific risks, controls, processes, and objectives. There is also built-in support for operational risk project management and performance measurement. Related services include fraud investigation and business process risk assessment.

The website address is: <www.arthurandersen.com> and their operational risk address is oprisk@uk.arthurandersen.com

Cap Gemini

Cap Gemini does not have a software offering as such, but provides operational risk management consulting. Its methodology consists of establishing risk governance, risk assessment through mathematical forecasting models, and qualitative or quantitative risk management including data warehousing for risk databases.

The website address is: <www.capgemini.co.uk/risk/index.htm>

Ernst & Young Consulting

Ernst and Young and JP Morgan have launched Horizon, a web-based tool for operational risk assessment. It has three components—a self-assessment engine that contains templates that identify and define major business processes, activities, risks, control procedures, and management responses; a performance analyzer; and a reporting module.

The website address is: <www.HorizonCSA.com>

Decisioneering Inc.

Its web-enabled Crystal Ball, Monte Carlo simulation software can be used to build turnkey or end-user operational risk simulation software. It has the advantage of a large installed base in financial service firms and consulting firms.

The website address is: <www.decisioneering.com>

IBM Risk Management Consulting

IBM has been considering implementing causal modeling tools using Bayesian approaches. The standard parametric approach toward building operational loss distributions is also supported. It has strength in providing a superior IT architecture and middleware technology to make different systems talk to each other leads to claims of shorter implementation time.

The website address is: <www.ibm.com>

Infinity

Infinity has developed a set of middle-ware workflow tools called *Panorama* incorporating enterprise-wide risks including Market, Credit and Operational Risk. Rather than risk measurement *per se*, their intent has been to develop an extensible and robust operational solution that makes extensive use of the Internet as a delivery mechanism.

The website address is: <www.infinity.com/prod/panorama/index.htm>

MicroBank

MicroBank Software offers an interesting collection of tools to support automated exception reporting within operational processes. Its exception management system (STEP) builds on top of straight through processing to improve operational efficiency and identify problems quickly. Microbank also offers report mining and report management tools.

The website address is: <www.microbank.com>

Netrisk

Netrisk's RiskOps 1.0 was one of the first operational risk management systems in market. It is now fully web-based. This system provides the ability to model frequencies, severity, and capital-at risk profiles using multiple methodologies. Results from different scenarios can also be combined. The core of the RiskOps system is a database of industry losses. Netrisk is also heavily involved in Multinational Operational Risk Exchange (MORE), a non-profit data exchange initiative sponsored by the Global Association of Risk Professionals (GARP). See the following websites for more details.

RiskOps: <www.netrisk.com/riskops.htm>
MORE: <www.morexchange.org>
GARP: <www.garp.org>

Operational Risk Inc.

An offshoot of Banker's Trust, this firm offers two operational risk products. CORE (Compilation of Operational Risk Events) Loss Database™ lists the loss experience of other firms in relevant business lines (that is, an "external" database), and supports actuarial analysis for operational risk capital calculations. The CORE historical database consists of more than 200 industry losses. It uses hundreds of different categorizations of losses to enable managers to tailor their risk estimates. Its web-based ORCA (Operational Risk Control and Analysis) tool is divided into three components: a risk profiling tool, a reporting tool that aggregates risk by different views, and a risk capital allocation tool that supports external actuarial and statistical modeling.

The website address is: <www.operationalrisk.com>

Palisade Corp.

@Risk for Microsoft Excel is one the world's most used general-purpose simulation tools. Palisade also offers visual process simulation tools and system dynamics tools that can be used for end-user operational risk models.

The website address is: <www.palisade.com>

PricewaterhouseCoopers (PwC)

PwC has produced several highly influential industry surveys on operational risk. It has also developed the OpVaR industry database that lists more than 5,000 loss events in excess of $1 million each. PwC also offers services include business continuity planning, operational risk management, measurement and reporting, financial process review, services contractor compliance, and IT value management.

The website address is: <www.pwcglobal.com>

RiskMatters

RISKMATTERS offers the Minda™ series of products, designed as benchmarking and training tools for operational risk management.

The website address is: <www.riskmatters.com.au>

Relex Software

Relex Software specializes in software analysis tools, training courses, and seminars in all aspects of reliability engineering. Relex offer a range of software packages that include: Reliability Prediction (including MIL-HDBK-217, Bellcore, Mechanical, NPRD), Failure Modes & Effects Analyses (FMEA/FMECA), Maintainability, Reliability Block Diagram (RBD), and Life Cycle Cost tools.

The website address is: <www.faulttree.com>

Symix Systems

This company has recently taken over Pritsker Corp., a well-known developer of discrete event simulation tools. Its advanced planning and scheduling systems division offers AWESIM, a visual and animated general purpose simulation engine that can be used to build models of financial operations and discover bottlenecks and sources of inefficiencies.

The website address is: <www.pritsker.com>

BIBLIOGRAPHY

Abromovitz, Hedy and Les Abromovitz. *Insuring Quality: How to Improve Quality, Compliance, Customer Service, and Ethics in the Insurance Industry.* CRC Press, 1997.

Albrecht, Karl. *Corporate Radar: Tracking the Forces that Are Shaping Your Business.* AMACOM, 1999.

Alexander, C., (editor). *Risk Management and Analysis: Measuring and Modelling Financial Risk.* New York: John Wiley & Sons, 1998.

Allison, G. T. *The Essence of Decision.* Boston: Little, Brown & Co., 1971.

Ambachtsheer, Keith P. and D. Don Ezra. *Pension Fund Excellence: Creating Value for Stakeholders.* : John Wiley & Sons, 1998.

An Internal Model-based Approach to Market Risk Capital Requirements. Basle, Switzerland: Basle Committee on Banking Supervision, 1995a.

Andrews, E. "AT&T Admits Failure to Notice Alarms." *New York Times,* 1991.

Annual Cost of Risk Survey. New York: Risk and Insurance Management Society.

Ansell, J. I. and M. J. Phillips. *Practical Methods for Reliability Data Analysis.* Oxford: Oxford University Press, 1994.

Ardis, P. M. and M. J. Comer. *Risk Management: Computers, Fraud and Insurance.* Maidenhead, UK: McGraw-Hill, 1987.

Avery and Belton. *Economic Review.* Federal Reserve Bank of Cleveland, Q4, 1987.

Bagley, Constance E. and Ernest W. King. *Managers and the Legal Environment: Strategies for the 21st Century.* Southwestern Publishing.

Barton, Laurence. *Crisis in Organizations: Managing and Communicating in the Heat of Chaos.* Southwestern Publishing, 1992.

Becker, Hal B. and Hal M. Becker. *At Your Service: Calamities, Catastrophes, and Other Curiosities of Customer Service.* John Wiley & Sons, 1998.

Beenhakker, Henri L. *Risk Management in Project Finance and Implementation.* Greenwood Publishing Group, 1997.

Bessis, J. *Risk Management in Banking.* Chichester: John Wiley & Sons, 1998.

Bettis, Richard A. and Howard Thomas (editor). *Risk, Strategy, and Management* (Strategic Management Policy and Planning, Vol. 5). JAI Press, 1990.

Bickerstaffe, G., (editor). *The Complete Finance Companion: The Latest in Financial Principles and Practice from the World's Best Finance Schools.* London: Pitman, 1998.

Block, Dennis J., Nancy E. Barton, and Stephen A. Radin. *The Business Judgment Rule: Fiduciary Duties of Corporate Directors,* 5th edition. Aspen Publishing, 1998.

Bologna, G. Jack and Robert J. Lindquist. *Fraud Auditing and Forensic Accounting: New Tools and Techniques.* John Wiley & Sons, 1995.

Bowen, H. Kent (editor). *The Perpetual Enterprise Machine: Seven Keys to Corporate Renewal Through Successful Product and Process Development.* Oxford University Press, 1994.

Box, George E. P. and Gwilym M. Jenkins. *Time Series Analysis: Forecasting and Control.* Holden-Day, Inc., 1976.

Brealey, R. and S. Myers. *Principles of Corporate Finance.* New York: McGraw-Hill, 1981.

Breyfogle, Forrest W. III. *Implementing Six Sigma.* John Wiley & Sons, 1999.

British Standard Specification BS6001, Inspection and Statistical Process Control. British Standards Institute.

Brooks, Frederick P. *The Mythical Man Month: Essays on Software Engineering,* anniversary edition. Addison-Wesley Publishing, 1995.

Cameron, Kim S. and Robert E. Quinn. *Diagnosing and Changing Organizational Culture: Based on the Competing Values Framework* (Addison-Wesley Series on Organization Development). Addison-Wesley Publishing, 1998.

Campbell, Andrew (editor) and Kathleen Sommers Luchs (editor). *Strategic Synergy,* 2nd edition. International Thomson Business Publisher, 1998.

Chambers, A. and G. Rand. *Operational Auditing Handbook: Auditing Business Processes.* New York: John Wiley & Sons, 1997.

Chase, Richard B., Nicholas J. Aquilano, and F. Robert Jacobs. *Production and Operations Management: Manufacturing and Services,* 8th edition. Richard D. Irwin, 1998.

Christensen, Clayton M. *Innovation and the General Manager.* McGraw-Hill College Division, 1999.

Clearance and Settlement Systems in the World's Securities Markets, Group of Thirty, 1989.

Collis, David J. and Cynthia A. Montgomery. *Corporate Strategy: A Resource-Based Approach.* Richard D Irwin, 1997.

Crane, D. (editor). *The Global Financial System: A Functional Perspective.* Boston: Harvard Business School Press, 1995.

Crockett, B. "NY Rocked by Big AT&T. Fiber Outage." *Network World,* December 31, 1990.

Cronon, W. "Mud, Memory and the Loop." *New York Times,* 1992.

Crosby, Philip B. *Quality Is Still Free: Making Quality Certain In Uncertain Times.* McGraw-Hill, 1995.

Cruz, M., R. Coleman, et al. "Modeling and Measuring Operational Risk." *Journal of Risk* 1(1): 63–72, 1998.

Currency. Banking Circular 235. Washington DC, Office of the Comptroller of the Currency, 1989.

Daft, Richard L. *Organization Theory and Design,* 6th edition. Southwestern Publishing, 1997.

Dale, Richard. *Risk and Regulation in Global Securities Markets.* John Wiley & Sons, 1996.

Davenport, Thomas H. *Process Innovation: Reengineering Work Through Information Technology.* Harvard Business School Press, 1992.

David, Howard R. and Patrick C. Coggins. *Management Accountant's Guide to Fraud Discovery and Control* (Wiley/Institute of Management Accountants Professional Book Series). John Wiley & Sons, 1991.

Derivatives and the Internal Auditor. London: Risk Publications and PricewaterhouseCoopers, 1998.

Derivatives: Practices and Principles, Group of Thirty, 1993.

Dowd, K. *Beyond Value At Risk: The New Science of Risk Management.* Chichester: John Wiley & Sons, 1998.

Ebeling, C. E. A*n Introduction to Reliability and Maintainability Engineering.* New York: McGraw-Hill, 1997.

Edmunds, Roger. *Contingency Planning for Dealing Rooms.* 1989.

Embrechts, P., C. Kluppelberg, et al. *Modelling External Events for Insurance and Finance.* Berlin: Springer Verlag, 1997.

Evans, J. R. and D. L. Olson. *Introduction to Simulation and Risk Analysis.* Upper Saddle River, NJ: Prentice Hall, 1998.

Fahey, Liam (editor) and Robert M. Randall (contributor). *Learning from the Future: Competitive Foresight Scenarios.* John Wiley & Sons, 1997.

Fahey, Liam. *Competitors: Outwitting, Outmaneuvering, and Outperforming.* John Wiley & Sons, 1998.

Fennelly, Lawrence J. (editor). *Effective Physical Security: Design, Equipment, and Operations.* Butterworth-Heinemann, 1992.

Finnerty, J. D. "An Overview of Corporate Securities Innovation." *Journal of Applied Corporate Finance*, 4: 23–39, 1992.

Finnerty, John D. *Project Financing: Asset-Based Financial Engineering.* John Wiley & Sons, 1996.

Fisher, Roger, William Ury, and Bruce Patton (editor). *Getting to Yes: Negotiating Agreement Without Giving In,* 2nd edition. Penguin USA, 1991.

"Fortune 1000 Companies Commit to Crisis Management." *Contingency Planning & Management,* May 1996.

Froot, K. A., D. S. Scharfstein, et al. "Risk Management: Coordinating Corporate Investment and Financing Policies." *Journal of Finance:* 1629–1658, December 1993.

Fuller, Lon L. and Melvin Aron Eisenberg. *Basic Contract Law* (American Casebook Series), 6th edition. The West Group, 1996.

Garvin, David A. *Managing Quality: The Strategic and Competitive Edge.* Free Press, 1988.

Gaughan, Patrick A. (preface). *Mergers Acquisitions and Corporate Restructuring,* 2nd edition. John Wiley & Sons, 1999.

Gillis, M. Arthur. *Automation in Banking—1999.* Computer Based Solutions, Inc., 1999.

Gratton, Lynda et. al. *Strategic Human Resource Management: Corporate Rhetoric and Human Reality.* Oxford University Press, 1999.

Green, Peter Sheldon. *Reputation Risk Management.* Financial Times/ Pitman Publishing, 1992.

Grey, Stephen. *Practical Risk Assessment for Project Management.* John Wiley & Sons, 1995.

Grove, Andrew S. *Only the Paranoid Survive: How to Exploit the Crisis Points That Challenge Every Company.* Bantam Books, 1999.

Guldimann, T. "Beyond the Year 2000." *Risk:* 17–19, 1996.

Guldimann, T. *RiskMetrics Technical Document.* Morgan Guaranty Trust Company, 1995.

Hackman, J. R. and G. R. Oldham. *Work Redesign.* Reading, MA: Addison-Wesley, 1980.

Hammer, Michael and James Champy. *Reengineering the Corporation: A Manifesto for Business Revolution.* Harperbusiness, 1994.

Hammer, Michael. *Beyond Reengineering: How the Process-Centered Organization Is Changing Our Work and Our Lives.* Harperbusiness, 1996.

Hardy, Charles O. *Risk & Risk-Bearing.* Risk Books, 1999.

Harrington, H. James and Leslie C. Anderson. *Reliability Simplified: Going Beyond Quality to Keep Customers for Life* (The H. James Harrington Performance Improvement Series). McGraw-Hill, 1999.

Harrington, S. E. and G. R. Niehaus. *Risk Management and Insurance.* Boston: Irwin McGraw-Hill, 1999

Harris, Robert L. *Information Graphics: A Comprehensive Illustrated Reference: Visual Tools for Analyzing, Managing, and Communicating.* Management Graphics, 1997.

Harvard Business Review on Strategies for Growth (Harvard Business Review Series). Harvard Business School Press, 1998.

Henley, E. J. and H. Kumamoto. *Probabilistic Risk Assessment— Reliability Engineering Design and Analysis.* New York: IEEE Press, 1991.

Heskett, James L., W. Earl Sasser (contributor), Christopher W. Hart (contributor). *Service Breakthroughs: Changing the Rules of the Game.* Free Press, 1990.

Higgins, Jackson. "How Vulnerable Is Your Network?" *Communications Week*, 1996.

Hiles, Andrew and Peter Barnes. *The Definitive Handbook of Business Continuity Management.* John Wiley & Sons, 1999.

Hirschman, Albert O. *Exit Voice and Loyalty: Responses to Decline in Firms, Organizations, and States.* Harvard University Press, 1972.

Hoffman, D. and M. Johnson. "Operating Procedures." *Risk,* September 1996.

Hoffman, D. G. "New Trends in Operational Risk Measurement and Management." *Operational Risk and Financial Institutions.* London:

Risk Publications in association with Arthur Andersen., 1998: 30–42.

Hoskisson, Robert E. and Michael A. Hitt (contributor). *Downscoping: How to Tame the Diversified Firm.* Oxford University Press, 1994.

Howell, Llewellyn D. (editor). *Handbook of Country and Political Risk Analysis,* 2nd edition. PRS Group, 1998.

Hoyland, Arnljot and Marvin Rausand. *System Reliability Theory: Models and Statistical Methods,* (Wiley Series in Probability and Mathematical Theory). John Wiley & Sons, 1994.

Hurst, David K. *Crisis & Renewal: Meeting the Challenge of Organizational Change* (The Management of Innovation and Change Series). Harvard Business School Press, 1995.

Iman, R. L. and W. J. Conover. "A distribution-free approach to inducing rank order correlation among input variables." *Communications of Statistics,* 11(3): 311–334, 1982.

Internal Control-Integrated Framework. Jersey City, NJ: Committee of Sponsoring Organizations of the Treadway Commission, 1992.

Jacobs, Richard O. *Crash Landing: Surviving a Business Crisis.* Glenbridge Publishing, 1991.

Jensen, F.V. *An Introduction to Bayesian Networks.* Springer Verlag, 1996.

Jones, C. *Assessment and Control of Software Risks.* Englewood Cliffs, NJ: Prentice-Hall, 1994.

Jones, K. "Teller Machines Are a Casualty of the Blizzard." *New York Times,* 1993.

Jones, R. B. *Risk-Based Management: A Reliability-Centered Approach—Practical, Cost-Effective Methods for Managing and Reducing Risk.* Houston: Gulf, 1995.

Jorion, P. *Value at Risk: The New Benchmark for Controlling Market Risk.* Chicago: Irwin/McGraw-Hill, 1997.

Juran, J. M. *Quality Control Handbook.* New York: McGraw-Hill, 1999.

Juran, Joseph M. (editor) and A. Blanton Godfrey (editor). *Juran's Quality Handbook,* 5th edition. McGraw-Hill Textbook, 1999.

Kahaner, Larry. *Competitive Intelligence: How to Gather, Analyse, and Use Information to Move Your Business to the Top.* Touchstone Books, 1998.

Kaplan, R. S. and D. P. Norton. *Balanced Scorecard: Translating Strategy Into Action.* Boston: Harvard Business School Press, 1996.

Kaplan, Robert S. and Robin Cooper. *Cost & Effect: Using Integrated Cost Systems to Drive Profitability and Performance.* Harvard

Business School Press, 1997.

Kendal, M. G. *Rank Correlation Methods.* London: Edward Arnold, 1990.

King, Mervyn J. *Bank & Brokerage Back Office Procedures and Settlements.* Glenlake Publishing, 1999.

Klein, R. A. and J. Lederman (editors). *Derivitives Risk and Responsibility.* Chicago: Irwin Publishing, 1996.

Klugman, S. A., H. H. Panjer, et al. *Loss Models: From Data to Decisions.* New York: John Wiley & Sons, 1998.

Konicek, Joel and Karen Little. *Security, ID Systems and Locks: The Book on Electronic Access Control.* Butterworth-Heinemann, 1997.

Krogh, George Von (editor), Johan Roos (editor), and Dirk Kleine (editor). *Knowing in Firms: Understanding, Managing and Measuring Knowledge.* Sage Publications, 1999.

Kudla, Ronald J. *Voluntary Corporate Liquidations.* Quorum Books, 1988.

Kupiec, P. and J. O'Brien. "Recent Developments in Bank Capital Regulation." *Regulation of Market Risks,* Federal Reserve, 1995.

Laseter, Timothy M. *Balanced Sourcing: Cooperation and Competition in Supplier Relationships.* Jossey-Bass Publishers, 1998.

Laycock, M. "Analysis of Mishandling Losses and Processing Errors." *Operational Risk and Financial Institutions,* London: Risk Publications in association with Arthur Andersen: 131–145, 1998.

Levitt, A. M. *Disaster Planning and Recovery: A Guide for Facility Professionals.* New York: John Wiley & Sons, 1997.

Levy, C. "Burst Pipe Disrupts Wall Street." *New York Times,* 1992

Littlejohn, G. "Risk Management in Financial Institutions in Europe." *Financial Times,* 1995.

Lozinsky, Sergio. *Enterprise-Wide Software Solutions: Integration Strategies and Practices.* Addison-Wesley, 1999.

Mabberley, Julie. *Activity-Based Costing in Financial Institutions: How to Support Value-Based Management and Manage Your Resources Effectively,* 2nd edition. Financial Times–Prentice-Hall Publishing, 1999.

MacEy, Jonathan R. and Geoffrey P. Miller. *Banking Law and Regulation.* Little Brown & Co. Law & Business, 1997.

Makridakis, S. and S. Wheelwright (editors). *The Handbook of Forecasting.* New York: John Wiley, 1987.

Makridakis, S., S. C. Wheelwright, et al. *Forecasting: Methods and*

Applications. New York: John Wiley & Sons, 1998.

Marshall, C. L., L. Prusak, et al. "Financial Risk and the Need for Superior Knowledge Management." *California Management Review,* Spring 1996.

Matten, C. *Managing Bank Capital.* New York: John Wiley & Sons, 1996.

Mayland, P. F. *Bank Operating Credit Risk.* Chicago: Bankers Publishing, 1993.

McLaughlin, Robert M. *Over-The-Counter Derivatives Products: A Guide to Business and Legal Risk Management and Documentation.* McGraw-Hill, 1998.

McNeil, A. J. *Calculating Quantile Risk Measures for Financial Return Series Using Extreme Value Theory.* Zurich: ETH Zentrum, 1998.

Meeker, W. Q. and L. A. Escobar. *Statistical Methods for Reliability Data.* New York: John Wiley & Sons, 1998.

Micheals, Jack V. *Technical Risk Management.* Prentice Hall, 1995.

Miller, M. H. "Financial Innovation: Achievements and Prospects." *Japan and the World Economy,* 4 (2), 1992.

Montgomery, D. C. *Introduction to Statistical Quality Control.* New York: John Wiley & Sons, 1997.

Moran, Theodore H (editor). *Managing International Political Risk: New Tools, Strategies and Techniques for Investors and Financial Institutions.* Blackwell Publishing, 1998.

Musgrave, James and Michael Anniss (contributor). *Relationship Dynamics: Theory and Analysis.* Free Press, 1996.

Nader, J. S. *Risk: The Definitive Guide for Banking, Financial Services and Business Professionals.* Dublin: Intuition Publishing, 1998.

Namjestnik, Kenneth J. *Trust Risk Management: Assessing and Controlling Fiduciary Risk.* Bankers Publishing, 1992.

Neter, John, William Wasserman, and Michael H. Kutner. *Applied Linear Regression Models,* second edition. Richard D. Irwin, 1989.

Newton, Andrew. *The Handbook of Compliance: Making Ethics Work in Financial Services.* Financial Times/Pitman Publishing, 1998.

Niebel, Benjamin and Andris Freivalds. *Methods, Standards & Work Design.* Boston: McGraw-Hill, 1999.

Operational Risk and Financial Institutions. London: Risk Publications in association with Arthur Andersen, 1998.

Operational Risk Management—The Next Frontier. Pricewaterhouse Coopers, 1999.

Operational Risk Newsletter. Risk Publications, Jan. 2000.

"Outsourcing Financial Service Activities: Industry Practices to Mitigate Risks." Federal Bank of New York, October 1999.

Oxelheim, Lars and Clas Wihlborg (contributor). *Managing in the Turbulent World Economy: Corporate Performance and Risk Exposure.* John Wiley & Sons, 1997.

Panettieri, J. "Security." *Informationweek*, 1995.

Parker, Donn B. *Fighting Computer Crime: A New Framework for Protecting Information.* John Wiley & Sons, 1998.

Penrose, Edith T. *Theory of the Growth of the Firm,* 3rd edition. Oxford University Press, 1995.

Perrow, Charles. *Complex Organizations: A Critical Essay,* 3rd edition. McGraw-Hill College Division, 1986.

Perrow, Charles. *Normal Accidents: Living With High-Risk Technologies.* Basic Books, 1984.

Pessin, A. H. *Securities Law Compliance: A Guide for Brokers, Dealers and Investors.* Homewood, IL: Dow Jones-Irwin, 1990.

Peters, Glen. *Waltzing With the Raptors: a Practical Roadmap to Protecting Your Company's Reputation.* John Wiley & Sons, 1999.

Pindyck, R. S. and D. L. Rubinfeld. *Econometric Models & Economic Forecasts.* New York: McGraw-Hill, 1991.

Pine, B. J. *Mass Customization: The New Frontier in Business Competition.* Boston: Harvard Business School Press, 1993.

Planned Suplement to the Capital Accord to Incorporate Market Risks. Basle, Switzerland: Basle Committee on Banking Supervision, 1995b.

Porter, M. *Competitive Advantage.* New York: The Free Press, 1985.

Porter, M. *Competitive Strategy.* New York: Free Press, 1980.

Prusak, Laurence (introduction). *Knowledge in Organizations (Resources for the Knowledge-Based Economy).* Butterworth-Heinemann (Trade), 1997.

Rappaport, Alfred. *Creating Shareholder Value: A Guide for Managers and Investors,* revised edition. Free Press, 1997.

Rea, Kathryn P. and Bennet P Lientz. *Breakthrough Technology Project Management.* Academic Press, 1998.

Reddy, M. *Securities Operations.* New York: New York Institute of Finance, 1995.

"Re-engineering reviewed." *The Economist* (July 2, 1994).

Report of the Board of Banking Supervision: Inquiry Into the

Circumstances of the Collapse of Barings. Board of Banking Supervision, Bank of England, 1995.

"A Review of Financial Market Events." Bank for International Settlements, August 1998.

Risk Management for Financial Institutions. London: Risk Publications, 1997.

Risk Management Guidelines (Vol. 16) for OTC Derivatives. Basle Committee, 1994.

"Risk management moves in-house." London: The Economist Newspaper, Ltd., 1998.

Robinson, Dana Gaines and James C. Robinson (contributor). *Training for Impact: How to Link Training to Business Needs and Measure the Results* (The Jossey-Bass Management Series). Jossey-Bass Publishers, 1989.

Rolski, Thomas, et al. *Stochastic Processes for Insurance and Finance* (Wiley Series in Probability and Statistics). Chichester: John Wiley & Sons, 1999.

Root, S. *Beyond COSO: Internal Control to Enhance Corporate Governance.* New York: John Wiley & Sons, 1998.

Sanford, C. S. "Financial Markets in 2020." Federal Reserve Bank of Kansas City Economic Symposium, Jackson Hole, WY, 1993.

Saunders, Anthony. *Credit Risk Measurement: New Approaches to Value at Risk and Other Paradigms.* John Wiley & Sons, 1999.

Schein, Edgar H. *Organizational Culture and Leadership* (Jossey-Bass Business & Management Series), 2nd edition. Jossey-Bass Publishers, 1997.

Schreider, Tari. *Contingency Planning & Management. The Encyclopedia of Disaster Recovery, Security & Risk Management.* Crucible Publishing Works, 1998.

Schwartz, Peter. *The Art of the Long View: Planning for the Future in an Uncertain World.* Doubleday, 1996.

Seibert, Paul. *Facilities Planning and Design for Financial Institutions: A Strategic Management Guide (A Bankline Publication)*, ringbound edition. Irwin Professional Publishing, 1995.

Senge, P. M. *The Fifth Discipline: The Art & Practice of the Learning Organization.* Ney York: Doubleday Currency, 1990.

Settlement Risk in Foreign Exchange Transactions. Bank for International Settlements, 1996.

Shtub, Avraham. *Enterprise Resource Planning (ERP): The Dynamics of Operations Management.* Kluwer Academic Publishers, 1999.

Simons, R. *Levers of Control.* Boston: Harvard Business School Press, 1995.

Smith, C. W., C. W. Smithson, et al. *Managing Financial Risk.* New York: Harper and Row, 1990.

"Squirrel causes crash at NASDAQ." *Informationweek,* 1994.

Stewart, G. B. *The Quest for Value: The EVA Management Guide.* Harper Business, 1991.

"Strategic Financial Risk Management." *The Economist,* 1995.

Sullivan, K. "Disaster-recovery Planning: Pricey But Worth It." *PC Week,* 1993.

"Supervision." *Operational Risk Management.* Basle: Basle Committee on Banking Supervision, 1998.

Toigo, Jon William. *Disaster Recovery Planning: For Computers and Communication Resources.* John Wiley & Sons, 1995.

Townsend, Patrick L. and Joan E. Gebhardt (contributor). *Commit to Quality.* John Wiley & Sons, 1990.

Trading Activities Manual. Board of Governors of the Federal Reserve System.

Tufte, Edward R. *The Visual Display of Quantitative Information.* Graphics Press, 1992.

Uyemura, Dennis G. and Donald R. Van Deventer (contributor). *Financial Risk Management in Banking: The Theory and Application of Asset and Liability Management.* Probus Publishing, 1992.

Van der Heijden, Kees. *Scenarios: The Art of Strategic Conversation.* John Wiley & Sons, 1996.

Vartanian, Thomas P., Robert H. Ledig, and Lynn Bruneau. *21st Century Money, Banking & Commerce.* Fried, Frank, Harris, Shriver & Jacobson, 1998.

Vaughan, D. "Trickle-Down Effect: Policy Decisions, Risky Work, and the Challenger Tragedy." *California Management Review,* July 1, 1997.

Vaughan, Emmett J. and Therese Vaughan. *Risk Management.* John Wiley & Sons, 1996.

Vose, D. *Quantitative Risk Analysis: A Guide to Monte Carlo Simulation Modelling.* Chichester: John Wiley & Sons, 1996.

Webb, Bernard L., Connor M. Harrison, and James J. Markham. *Insurance Operations,* 2nd edition. Ferguson Publishing, 1997.

Weber, Ron. *Information Systems Control and Audit.* Prentice-Hall, 1998.

Weick, K. *The Social Psychology of Organizing.* Addison-Wesley, 1979.

Whittington, O. Ray and Kurt Pany. *Principles of Auditing,* 2nd edition. Richard D. Irwin, 1998.

Wickens, C. D., S. E. Gordon, et al. *An Introduction to Human Factors Engineering.* New York: Longman, 1998.

Wideman, R. Max (editor) and Rodney J. Dawson. *Project & Program Risk Management: A Guide to Managing Project Risks and Opportunities.* Project Management Institute Publications, 1998.

Wild, Tony. *Best Practice in Inventory Management.* John Wiley & Sons, 1998.

Wilmott, Paul. *Derivatives: The Theory and Practice of Financial Engineering* (Wiley Frontiers in Finance Series). John Wiley & Sons, 1998.

Wilson, D. "VaR in Operation." *Risk,* Number 8, 1995.

Wilson, P. F., L. D. Dell, et al. *Root Cause Analysis.* Milwaukee: ASQC Quality Press, 1993.

Winter, Matthias and Ulrich Steger. *Managing Outside Pressure: Strategies for Preventing Corporate Disasters.* John Wiley & Sons Ltd., 1998.

Wonnacott, Thomas H. and Ronald J. Wonnacott. *Introductory Statistics,* third edition. New York: John Wiley and Sons, 1977.

Wood, Robert, Tim Wood, and Tim Payne. *Competency-Based Recruitment and Selection* (The Wiley Series in Strategic Human Resource Management). John Wiley & Sons, 1998.

Zuboff, S. *In the Age of the Smart Machine.* New York: Basic Books, Inc, 1988.

INDEX

M